OUR FUTURE IN NATURE: TREES, SPIRITUALITY AND ECOLOGY

Well-Being and Peace

EDMUND BARROW

BALBOA
PRESS
A DIVISION OF HAY HOUSE

Copyright © 2019 Edmund Barrow.

All rights reserved. No part of this book may be used or reproduced by any means, graphic, electronic, or mechanical, including photocopying, recording, taping or by any information storage retrieval system without the written permission of the author except in the case of brief quotations embodied in critical articles and reviews.

This book is a work of non-fiction. Unless otherwise noted, the author and the publisher make no explicit guarantees as to the accuracy of the information contained in this book and in some cases, names of people and places have been altered to protect their privacy.

The version of the Bible I use is "The New American Bible" sponsored by the Bishops' Committee of the Confraternity of Christian Doctrine, and published by Thomas Nelson Publishing, New York, 1971. I have quoted from the bible in many places in the book – especially the first 4 chapters

The Version of the Qur-ān I use is: The Holy Qur-ān, English translation of the meanings and commentary. Printing rights reserved for the Custodian of the Two Holy Mosques King Fahd Complex for the printing of the Holy Qur-ān, Al-Madinah Al-Munawarah.

Balboa Press books may be ordered through booksellers or by contacting:

Balboa Press
A Division of Hay House
1663 Liberty Drive
Bloomington, IN 47403
www.balboapress.com
1 (877) 407-4847

Because of the dynamic nature of the Internet, any web addresses or links contained in this book may have changed since publication and may no longer be valid. The views expressed in this work are solely those of the author and do not necessarily reflect the views of the publisher, and the publisher hereby disclaims any responsibility for them.

The author of this book does not dispense medical advice or prescribe the use of any technique as a form of treatment for physical, emotional, or medical problems without the advice of a physician, either directly or indirectly. The intent of the author is only to offer information of a general nature to help you in your quest for emotional and spiritual well-being. In the event you use any of the information in this book for yourself, which is your constitutional right, the author and the publisher assume no responsibility for your actions.

Brief Description of the Photographs used

Position of photograph in book	Brief Description of Photograph	Name of Photographer
Front and back cover	Baobab trees, Tarangire, Tanzania	Edmund Barrow
Page before chapter 1	Fortingall Yew tree, Perthshire, Scotland	Edmund Barrow
Page 42	Ancient Olive Trees in the Garden of Gethsemane at the foot of the Mount of Olives in Jerusalem	Edmund Barrow
Page 62	Tree adorned with prayers and pieces of cloth in Ireland	Edmund Barrow
Page 92	Bhimashankar Sanctuary and Sacred Grove, Maharashtra, India	Ashish Kothari
Page 136	Monastic forest, Ethiopia	Edmund Barrow
Page 176	Banyan (Fig) tree, Hawaii	Edmund Barrow
Page 216	Prayers to Fairies at Fairy Bridge, Isle of Man	Edmund Barrow
Page 258	Kalubai Sacred Grove, Maharashtra, India	Oikos, Pune, India

Print information available on the last page.

ISBN: 978-1-9822-2663-3 (sc)
ISBN: 978-1-9822-2664-0 (hc)
ISBN: 978-1-9822-2665-7 (e)

Library of Congress Control Number: 2019904840

Balboa Press rev. date: 05/14/2019

Contents

Foreword ix
Preface xi
Acknowledgments xiii

Chapter 1　Sacred Trees and Groves Transcend Race, Color, and Creed 1
　　　　　Background—We Depend on Nature 1
　　　　　　Dependency on Nature, but Have We Forsaken Nature? 1
　　　　　　How We Understand Sacred Nature and Ecology 4
　　　　　　Sacred Nature in the Context of Spirituality and Religion 6
　　　　　　Our Environmental Crisis—The Mess We Have Created 9
　　　　　　Reviving the Sanctity of Nature 11
　　　　　Spiritual and Scientific Views of Nature—Tensions 13
　　　　　Nature Is Much More than Consumerist Values and
　　　　　Materialism 17
　　　　　Spiritual and Cultural Values of Nature—Those
　　　　　Vital Intangible Values 22
　　　　　Sacred Groves in the Context of Much Larger Sacred
　　　　　Landscapes 29
　　　　　This Book—Sacred Trees, Sacred Groves, and Spirituality 33

Chapter 2　Religious and Spiritual Origins in a Time of Natural
　　　　　Resource Dependence and Abundance 43
　　　　　Our Origins Are in Nature 43
　　　　　Trees—A Key Ingredient for Life, Culture,
　　　　　Spirituality, and Religion 46
　　　　　The World Tree, Tree of Life, and Tree of Knowledge 53

What Can We Learn from Our Ancestors about
Conservation and Religion? 58

Chapter 3 Sacred Trees—Diverse in Every Culture and Country 63
Sacred Trees—Celebrating Diversity 63
Spirits Reside in and around Trees for All Sorts of Reasons 67
The Universally Revered Fig Tree 72
Trees Adorned.. 75
Trees Ordained 78
Trees as Part of Birth, Marriage, and Death......................... 79
Trees—Sacred Because of Tradition..................................... 81
Monastic and Temple Trees 84
Other Reasons for Trees Being Sacred.................................. 85
What Can We Learn from This Diversity, and What
Can We Do? 90

Chapter 4 Sacred Groves—Places of Mindfulness for Religion,
Spirituality, and Conservation 93
Sacred Groves Underestimated and Undervalued
across the Globe... 93
Home of the Spirits, Mother Earth, and Ancestors 98
Sacred Groves of Ghana 98
*Social Values of the Nyangkpe Sacred Groves of
Cameroon*..101
Sacred Groves in East Africa..101
Sacred Controls on Trees and Woodlands in Zimbabwe 103
Sacred Groves of Nepal... 104
Conserving Biodiversity through Sacred Groves in India.... 106
The Holy Hill Forests of the Dai in South West China 108
*Sacred Groves as Part of Community Forests in
Thailand* 110
Sacred Groves of St. Francis of Assisi in Italy 112
Sacred Groves—The Kayas on the Coast of Kenya............112
Other Examples of Sacred Groves..................................... 115
Sacred Groves around Wells and Springs 118
Sacred Groves Providing Goods and Services—India 118

   Monastic (Church, Temple, and Monastery) Groves 120
   What Lessons Are We Learning, and What Practical
   Action Can We Take? 129

Chapter 5 Conserved Areas—Whose and for What Purpose in
   the Context of Sacred Trees and Sacred Groves? 137
   Role of Conserved Areas for Sacred Trees and Sacred
   Groves—Takeover or Synergy? 137
   Species Diversity—Important Conservation Benefits
   from Sacred Groves 143
   Community Conservation—The Framework to
   Support Sacred Groves 145
   Whose Protected Areas—Intent or Tenure? 149
   Indigenous and Community-Conserved Areas
   (ICCAs)—Recognizing Sacred Groves 155
   Fitting Sacred and Spiritual Values in Place 158
   Getting Governance Right—The Importance of
   Local Institutions 160
   Secure Rights and Responsibilities Are Vital for
   Sustainability 165
   Having Power at the Right Level Is Key 168
   Some Key Principles for Sacred Trees and Sacred Groves 171
   Conservation and Spirituality/Religion Must Work
   in Partnership 173

Chapter 6 Religion, Spirituality, and Conservation in the
   Stewardship of Sacred Trees and Sacred Groves 177
   Stewardship—The Key for Management 177
   Stewardship—The Basis for Connecting and
   Reconnecting 181
   Religious and Spiritual Perspectives on Stewardship 188
   Conservation Perspectives on Stewardship 194
   Importance of Stewardship for Religion and Spirituality 201
   Importance of Stewardship for Conservation and
   Land Use 207

Chapter 7 Sacred Groves and Nature—Key for Education,
            Health, and Peace 217
           Importance of Learning from Nature 217
           Nature Deficit Disorder—When We Do Not Get
           Enough of a Good Thing 224
           Education for Awareness about and Reconnecting
           with Nature 230
           Trees and Woods Are Good for Our Health 240
           Sacred Trees and Sacred Groves—Places for Peace-
           Building 245
           Nature Offers Us Ways to Enhance Education and
           Our Health and Be a Means for Peace 254

Chapter 8 Increased Practical Engagement for Religion,
           Spirituality, and Conservation in Nature for a
           Sustainable Future 259
           We Simply Have to Learn from Nature and Our Past 259
           Sacred Trees and Groves Are Older than Formal
           Religions and Formal Conservation 266
           Religions and Spiritual Groups Have Responsibilities
           for Conservation 269
           Conservation Has to Better Integrate and Respect
           Sacred Trees and Groves 270
           Stewardship Is the Glue for Joint Action and Partnerships 273
           Sacred Trees and Sacred Groves Are Key for
           Education, Health, and Peace 275
           We Can All Do Something and Be the Change We
           Want as Sacred Nature Really Does Matter 277

Sources of Information and References by Chapter 283

Foreword

Our Future in Nature: Trees, Spirituality, and Ecology by Edmund Barrow is an important contribution to the quest for rebuilding humanity's damaged relationship with nature. Humanity has waged war on the earth, especially over the last few centuries with a combination of capitalism, patriarchy, statism, and racism. This forms the basis of the destructive project called *development*. Biodiversity loss, pollution, climate crises, and other manifestations of the madness of unlimited economic growth are upon us now, not in the future. Perhaps this is indicative of our stupidity that mocks our self-identity as an intelligent animal. But we have not yet declared a state of emergency. Nor have we taken the measures necessary to reduce our ecological impacts. These drastic measures will not come through further militarization in the name of security. Rather they will come from ordinary people rising to dethrone those who hold economic and political power over the rest of us and bring back real common sense.

At a time like this, we need to reconceptualize our relationship with the earth we inhabit. For millennia, indigenous and local communities showed us how to live lightly by respecting the nature they live amidst. Not that there is complete harmony between them and other species, but compared to *Homo industrialis* and *Homo urbanis*, they have shown greater wisdom. This was not because they did not have the technologies to be more exploitative. One of the fundamental elements of living was—and in many parts of the world continues to be—a worldview that held nature as sacred, as worthy of the same respect that one demanded for oneself as humans.

The project of modernist, rational development alienated us from such worldviews. We think we can subdue nature, make it do our bidding. To some extent, we succeeded, but at an enormous cost to other species and ourselves. The growing evidence of the impacts of such attitudes on the lives and livelihoods of billions of people—and on our psychological health—is alarming. It is clear that modern Western responses of setting up fortress-like protected areas that often violate fundamental human rights is not the answer. They are often islands amid devastated landscapes and seascapes.

A reconnection with the rest of nature is necessary. In this way we will see ourselves as part of nature, not apart from it. For this, we need to better understand what our age-old relationships were and to locate where the historical and current wisdom lies. This will enable us to make those reconnections. In this sense, the material that this book presents is a critical contribution. This provides a glimpse of both the practical possibilities and the conceptual frameworks of a wiser stewardship of the earth. Conservation needs to be community-centered, including through fully recognizing Indigenous and Community Conserved Areas (ICCAs). Such a framework stresses that our relationship with the rest of nature cannot be material (though that is also crucial) but spiritual and ethical. But we need to be cautious against the misuse of mainstream religions to bulldoze over local traditions that were (are) built on practical wisdom. This is a book of hope and inspiration. This is very important in an atmosphere of growing gloom and foreboding.

Bringing back the sacredness of trees and groves is not the only course correction we need. Saving ourselves and the Earth from another mass extinction will need a fundamental reshaping of political, economic, and social relationships and structures. But what Edmund says is one core component of what we need to do. I hope his message is read widely and incorporated into citizens' actions and policy-making at various levels. We owe this much to the earth that has given birth to us and to the other species we inhabit it with.

One of my fondest memories of the author is a visit to sacred groves near the city I live in, Pune, in India, many years back. I'm delighted to honor that memory with this foreword!

—Ashish Kothari (Kalpavriksh, India)

Preface

On this Earth, nature is the most beautiful and fascinating blessing of all. No other planet has what this Earth has. This Earth is given to man by God on a tray of gold, the dawn. The birds awake and sing. The light of the sun very gently spreads throughout the sky, issuing soft colours to the atmosphere. The sun rises very slowly with the brightest smile ever. It gives warmth. What a blessing! It makes everything grow. What a blessing! It is an inspiration. The sun is so bright, so revealing, yet it holds the secret of the universe. What a blessing!

—Gurumayi Chidvilasananda, 1990

The genesis of this book has been a fascinating voyage of discovery, and I have learned about the sacredness of nature and rediscovered my childhood links to trees. It started when I was working in Turkana (northwest Kenya) on a district natural resource management program from 1984 to 1989, which was more than thirty years ago. Turkana is dry. Rainfall is low, and temperatures are high.

During that time I visited the Holy Land, where there is similar vegetation (especially trees). These trees were important for the three Abrahamic religions of Islam, Christianity, and Judaism in their formative years. My interest piqued, I purchased several publications relating to trees, plants, and their religious significance. Back in Turkana, I wrote a draft sermon on the importance of trees in the Bible, which I gave to the Catholic bishop of Turkana to perhaps use in one of his Sunday sermons!

This sparked my interest in sacred trees and sacred groves in formal religious, indigenous, and local belief systems. Through the literature and from personal experience, I found that sacred trees and sacred groves are part of every religious and spiritual belief across the globe. Wherever there is a tree in the world, there is a sacred tree and usually a sacred grove. I was also pleasantly surprised as to the large literature base relating to sacred nature, and I was encouraged by the many people who shared articles, websites, and experiences.

As I have been with many sacred trees and sacred groves, I can only feel a sense of humbleness and humility. For example, I stood in the presence of the Fortingall Yew (Perthshire, Scotland), which is between four to six thousand years old, and tried to understand how this sentinel survived and what lessons it could share. Or as Ashish said in the foreword, we visited several Indian sacred groves north of Pune. I have treasured these and other experiences with sacred trees and sacred groves. They taught me a lot about presence, mindfulness, and silence. Nature is not an inanimate collection of pieces. Nature is a coherent, living whole. With that in mind, I try to walk amongst and be with trees and groves. They do not have to be ancient or sacred, though they can be.

This forms the basis of what you are reading. The book highlights how important sacred trees and sacred groves are for us now; how this can be a positive force for good in conservations, lifestyles, and livelihoods; and how this helps us connect with nature. It helped me see how we can use sacred trees and groves to foster peace in our time together with greater awareness about our fragile planet. I provide many practical ways by which you can engage with sacred trees and groves—as individuals or communities—and how the different formal religions and indigenous spiritual groups can all more strongly engage with sacred nature. In this way we can bridge the gap between religion and spirituality on the one hand and conservation and land usage on the other. Sacred trees and sacred groves are one means of connecting these seeming different groups.

I hope you will enjoy this book irrespective of your race, nationality, or creed, whether you are a conservation expert, an indigenous spiritual leader, a religious leader, or a teacher. It does not matter who you are. We can all learn something from sacred trees and sacred groves. I have, and I hope you will too.

Acknowledgments

I am grateful to the many people who have taken an interest in this subject, provided valuable comments and corrections, and also read and made comments on previous versions and chapters of this book. These people include the late Bishop Mahon (Lodwar Diocese, Kenya) for the early inspiration those many years ago (late 1980s) as well as Bishop Peter Barret, Manisha Gutman, Larry Hamilton, and Sally Jean-Renaud. All provided helpful comments and support for various chapters and early content, and I am very grateful to them.

I am particularly grateful to Liza Zogib (director, DiversEarth), Robert Fisher (University of Sydney), Nigel Crawhall (chief of section, Small Islands and Indigenous Knowledge, Natural Sciences Sector, UNESCO) for reviewing a final draft of this book, and Ashish Kothari (Kalpavriksh, India) for writing the foreword. Their constructive and interesting comment helped me improve and sharpen the text. However, any mistakes and errors are mine!

I have tried to minimize the use of acronyms to make the book easier to follow. In the end, I have used three—ICCA (Indigenous and Community Conserved Area); IUCN (International Union for Conservation of Nature), and SNS (Sacred Natural Site).

A short note on footnotes and references: a). I have used foot notes to refer to www sites that I have accessed. The footnote is referenced in the text as for example tree [a], or conservation, [b] and the full details of the footnote appear at the bottom of the page; b). The references and sources of information that I have used are referred to in the text as superscript bracketed numbers, for example [23]. This is done by chapter. This number refers to the number of the full citation in the sources of information section at the end of the book. All the references are then listed alphabetically by chapter.

I am particularly grateful to Rosie, my wife, and our two sons, Barney and Richard, for their perseverance and patience during the development and writing of this book. Without their support, I doubt that this would have got to the finishing line. Thank you, thank you.

Sacred Trees and Groves Transcend Race, Color, and Creed

CHAPTER 1

A thing is right when it tends to preserve the integrity, stability and beauty of the biotic community. It is wrong when it tends otherwise.

—Aldo Leopold

To see a world in a grain of sand and heaven in a wildflower, hold infinity in the palm of your hand and eternity in an hour.

—William Blake

Background—We Depend on Nature

Dependency on Nature, but Have We Forsaken Nature?

We depend on nature for the air we breathe, the water we drink, and the services nature provides. Nature allows us to go within, be silent, and reconnect. Who has not felt the silence, stillness, and peace when walking in a woodland, beside a river, or by the sea or observing a plant to connect with our inner spirituality? I was lucky enough to grow up on a farm in Ireland with hedgerows and trees, together with its own small forest (or so I thought at least). We farmed with nature. My father imbued in us a deep sense of respect for the soil and trees. I often walked along those hedgerows and, in the forest, exploring and being present. Then I was not aware that being silent and present was what nature taught. At six years old, I insisted on planting, though at the wrong time of year, more than three hundred chestnut trees. All the trees grew and are now more than sixty years old. I hope this book will give you similar ideas and inspire you. In this way, we will continue to have and respect trees now and in future so that we can still be with and learn from trees, ecology, and spirituality.

This book shows how nature sustains us and how important sacred trees and groves are for nurturing sustainable communities. I focus on sacred trees, sacred groves, and spirituality to show the key roles nature plays and how sacred trees and groves transcend race, color, and creed. The book explores the links between conservation and land use and religious and spiritual perspectives. I draw on examples from across the globe and from different religious and spiritual backgrounds. I hope this book will provide ideas and approaches for religious and spiritual leaders in their practical work at local, national, and global levels and for conservation and land use groups in integrating how important religion and spirituality are for conservation and nature. Pope Francis called for an ecological conversion. I hope this book will help you undergo such a conversion through a better understanding of the role of trees in our lives. For those working in conservation, I share important conservation insights of how conservation and spirituality can work together to be the change we want and what this means for people from all walks of life for meaningful change on the ground.

Our dependency on nature highlights why this book is important for different groups—those concerned with religion and spirituality; those concerned with conservation and land use; and others concerned with education, health, and peace. The examples, which are not exhaustive, of sacred trees and groves offer us ways to understand how important nature is, how we can connect with nature, and what sorts of actions each of us can take. As David Suzuki summarized, "Nature surrounds us, from Parks and backyards to streets and alleyways. Next time you go out for a walk, tread gently and remember that we are both inhabitants and stewards of nature in our neighborhoods."[a] As we rediscover our sense of

---

[a] Accessed November 17, 2019. https://www.brainyquote.com/quotes/david_suzuki_471840.

presence within our planetary community, we realize we cannot bargain with Mother Earth. [10]

It is important to internalize moral teachings and wisdom about the environment and our duties as individuals. We will then understand and respect why people live close to nature. This will help us defend nature-based cultures and be proud of our relationships with the land.[99] Many people don't get these connections because we have compartmentalized sectors of life so rigidly.[3] In this sense, I invite you to rediscover or discover through practical engagement your own heritage regarding nature and benefit from its healing powers. Use the examples and ideas from this book to engage more—to plant trees, be present and mindful with trees, and let your relationship with them be one means for prayers and thought.

If we lose touch with nature, we lose touch with our humanity.[57] Being spiritual helps us safeguard our sense of the sacred and value belonging. [107] Yet in our materially driven world, the separations among religion, spirituality, and the environment widen. But as Eckhart Tolle says, "We have what rocks, plants and animals still know. We have forgotten to be—to be still, to be ourselves, *to be where life is: Here and Now.*" [122] Since ancient times, trees have been symbols of wisdom, power, fertility, spirituality, life, and stillness. [15] Pope Francis reemphasizes what St. Francis said all those years ago, namely that our common home, Mother Earth, is like a sister with whom we share our lives, who sustains and governs us. [96] Mahatma Gandhi reminded us, "What we are doing to the forests of the world is but a mirror reflection of what we are doing to ourselves and to one another."[b]

Many people don't think about nature. We assume the vital role ecosystems and their services play. Our relationship to the earth is one of dependence. [36] We need to think and act in different ways if we are to solve contemporary environmental challenges. The dominance of economics will not solve the deeper challenges humanity now faces. We have to recognize the central importance of nature and ecosystems in our lives. Ecosystems are not

---

[b] Accessed October 3, 2018. https://quotefancy.com/quote/856337/Mahatma-Gandhi-What-we-are-doing-to-the-forests-of-the-world-is-but-a-mirror-reflection.

just a physical set of attributes (species, soils, location, connections, etc.). They are shaped and influenced by the cultures of people. Within we are spiritual, [127] though we may not realize this or understand its implications.

How We Understand Sacred Nature and Ecology

Sacred natural sites (SNSs) exist everywhere. You may think they only occur in remote places, preserved by ancient customs and indigenous peoples. Not so. Sacred lands have been part of Europe's heritage for millennia. [73] Sacred trees and groves can be found in cities and densely populated areas. Yet modern society downplays their relevance, and many sites have been destroyed. [6]

Julian Evans puts it like this: "God smiled when he made trees. They were perfect; he looked and could find no fault. Yet they appear so ungainly if it was not that we are so used to them—rooted to the ground but seeming to stretch with abandon in all directions. They are top heavy like a child's toy tree but endure storms and floods. Some trees living today were alive from before Abraham: others are so tall that they would over-top every Egyptian pyramid bar two." [31] Trees are at the heart of life, and our human ancestry began in trees. Without trees, humankind would not exist as we are, both because of our dependence on trees and for the spiritual fulfillment they give us. Perhaps this is why we are so attracted to trees. [124]

SNSs are places where humankind and nature can meet in spiritual terms. [129] Through nature, people may have complex relationships that are tangible, intangible, cultural, and spiritual. Spiritual in this context refers to how we revere or are in awe of something that could be a deity or some religious ceremony or usage, or it could be part of nature. Then SNSs "are those spaces imbedded in everyday life that can elevate visitors into a deeper, healthier and more peaceful relationship with themselves, their neighbors and the built world. ... Nature is often a key element of sacred spaces, for air, water, sun, and plants to satisfy our basic needs and connect to the deeper processes of life."c

---

c Accessed July 8, 2018. http://naturesacred.org/.

To understand the role of sacred trees and groves, we need to understand them ecologically. Ecology refers to a deep sense of home. It is the study of the relationships between living organisms and their environment. [96] Ecology is the study of the structure and function of nature and how humankind is a part of nature. [88] It is the science of relationships between organisms and their environments that emphasizes that everything is connected to everything else. [41, 109] The words ecology and economy have similar origins. *Oikos* (eco) means our home, the entire planet, home of all species. *Logos* refers to knowledge. So ecology refers to the fact we are all related. *Nomos* (in economy) is about managing our home, our planet.[d] Economy refers to more than gross domestic product. It implies having right livelihood coming from the heart. The emphasis on the dynamics of relationships in natural processes is key. [115] Human ecology helps us understand the role we play as members of nature and how the interconnectedness of the planet requires us to take care of the earth. [115]

The economy is a wholly owned subsidiary of ecology.[59] But economics operates as if it were the other way around. Governments, industries, and businesses, apart from some enlightened exceptions such as Bhutan, believe the economy comes first and its success is self-perpetuating despite fundamental flaws. David Attenborough says, "Anyone who believes exponential growth can go on forever in a finite world is either a madman or an economist." [4] Yet if there is no earthly well-being, there can be no human well-being and no good economy. As Schumacher said, "Nature is our true capital." [59] But traditional science and economics still dominate. We need a new worldview that embraces science and culture and integrates scientific reasoning with intuitive knowledge. [45]

Edward Wilson defines nature as "that part of the original environment and life forms that remains after human impact. Nature is all on planet Earth that has no need of us and can stand alone." [135] As Krishnmurti says, "Nature is the solitary tree in the field, the meadows and the grove. ... Nature is part of our life. We grow out of the seed, the Earth, and we are all part of that." [57] We know enough about ecosystems to know how little

---

[d] Satish Kumar, "Education with Hands, Hearts and Heads," TED Talk, accessed November 5, 2018. https://www.youtube.com/watch?v=VAz0bOtfVfE.

we know. This is why humankind exploits nature for short-term profit. Industrial agriculture and forestry fall into this trap. Many forests are degraded after high-value trees are extracted. [14]

Ecology is not the same as environment, which places humans at the center of "that which surrounds" [61] and divides humankind and the rest of the world. It is a false duality between organisms and their surroundings. The term environment is a more anthropocentric term. But ecology is about relations between biodiversity, the natural world, and humans within it, and it is ecocentric. Satish Kumar adds, "Together with Ecology and Economy we need a third 'E': Ethics. Our 'oikos', our planet home has to be built on the firm foundation of ethical and spiritual values. Without such a foundation our home will be unstable and unsustainable." [61] Buddhism understands the universe has an underlying ethical structure as well as physical and energy ones and that the law of nature is the overriding ethical principle.

Environmental philosophers separate values into categories—anthropocentric (human welfare and concerns), biocentric (which assigns moral standing to special characteristics and the ability to meet certain ends) and ecocentric (values derived from a concern of the ecology of communities and their relationships). The religious traditions of the Middle East (Islam, Judaism, and Christianity) view nature more in anthropocentric terms. Eastern religions (Buddhism, Hinduism, and Taoism) and the spirituality of most indigenous and traditional peoples relate to nature more in ecocentric terms. [46]

Sacred Nature in the Context of Spirituality and Religion

Pope Francis's powerful Encyclical on climate change and inequality emphasizes the sacredness of nature together with our duty as stewards. There are two key messages in the encyclical, which is a call to action (see box 1ᵉ). First, it affirms our interconnectedness, mutual responsibility to each other and to our common earth. Second, it denounces aspects of modern life that led to our current predicament. [90] Yet these two themes

---

ᵉ Accessed August 8, 2018. https://en.wikipedia.org/wiki/Encyclical. [96]

are one. They show our present failure to steward creation because the dominant worldview is materialist and based on economic growth.

> **Box 1: The Importance of Pope Francis's Encyclical on Climate Change for Us All**
>
> *Encyclical* means a circulating letter. For the Catholic church, a papal encyclical is a specific category of papal letter about Catholic doctrine, sent by the pope. A papal encyclical is for important issues and is second in importance only to an apostolic constitution. Encyclicals show high papal priority for an issue at a given time. The pope's encyclical on climate change is an instruction to the 1.285 billion Catholics on earth. But from reading the encyclical, we know it is much more. It speaks to humanity, irrespective of race, color, and creed. It calls upon us to steward Mother Earth, who sustains and governs us.

The major religions and spiritual traditions grew when people were close to nature and trees. Their writings attest to this. For example, consider the Bhagavad-Gita (Hinduism), Bible[f] (Christianity), Tanakh (Hebrew), and the Qur-ān[g] (Islam), and the Eastern faiths and the traditions of spiritual groups across the world. Humankind is a trustee of the world's ecosystems. This calls on religions to conserve the Earth. [29] "I will create a viceregent on Earth" (see Qur-ān 2:30 and other similar references, including 6:165, 35:39). Nature assumed a spiritual and religious importance. Yet our modern world has drifted away from religion, spirituality, and nature. Many of those who purport to be religious and spiritual have little real connection with nature. [76]

When the major religions evolved, nature was organic and living. A distinct picture of the intimate relationship between humankind and nature evolved. [25] Jains recognize the entire natural world is alive. We must treat all life as sacred and treat it with reverence. [66] In a similar way, Yanomami shamans of South America protect nature by defending the

---

[f] I use the New American Bible version, which is sponsored by the Bishops' Committee of the Confraternity of Christian Doctrine and published by Thomas Nelson Publishing, New York, 1971.
[g] I use the Holy Qur-ān, English translation of the meanings and commentary. Printing rights reserved for the Custodian of the Two Holy Mosques King Fahd Complex for the printing of the Holy Qur-ān, Al-Madinah Al-Munawarah.

forests, trees, hills, mountains, rivers, fish, wildlife, spirits, and human inhabitants. [103]

Spirituality is not the same as religion or a particular theology or belief. Spirituality concerns relationships, empathy, compassion, and wisdom. Sometimes we confuse the words spirituality and religion. Religion comes from the Latin *religio*, which means to bind the strengths of certain beliefs. Thus, religion binds us, while the root meaning of spirit relates to breath, air, and what is inside us.

Some people are uncomfortable with the term religion. Religion implies a set of doctrines and beliefs and provides a framework to build our worldviews. Religion comprises three basic aspects [20] —theology (intellectual understanding of spiritual experiences), morals (or ethics as in the rules of conduct based on the sense of belonging), and ritual (celebration of belonging by the religious communities). Krishnamurti says religion "is a series of beliefs, of dogmas, of rituals, of superstitions, of worship of idols, of charms and gurus that will lead you to what you want as an ultimate goal." [h] Religion, for Krishnamurti, "is the sense of comprehension of the totality of existence, in which there is no division between you and me."[i]

Spirituality comes from the Latin *spiritus*, which means breath or the breath of life. [20] This is the feeling of transcendence and drives religious worldviews in terms of mystical, religious, or spiritual experience. Without a framework, it is hard to focus spirituality. [125] The spirit moves, inspires, touches our hearts, and refreshes us. [58] Spirituality refers to experiencing my connection with what I understand exists. What we think is real shapes us. [1] Buddhist spirituality combines wisdom and compassion [67] and likens spirituality to mindfulness, which is rooted in us. [20] Compassion is more than tolerance and patience. It embraces empathy for the suffering of all (including the earth) together with the capacity to forgive.

---

[h] Accessed January 4, 2019. http://www.katinkahesselink.net/kr/religion.html.
[i] Accessed January 4, 2019. https://www.jkrishnamurti.org/content/religion-matter-belief.

Yet spirituality is an ambiguous, inclusive term that defies easy definition. [108] Spirituality refers to the fact we are alive and that we are more than our personalities. It is about our ground (or sense of place) in the world more than our place in the world (what we do, where we live). This ground includes love (promise of belonging), death (awareness of being), self (path of becoming), and soul (sense of beyondness). Spirituality plays a greater role in the public realm as one way to balance economics and growth. Most people have a sense of the spiritual. Spiritual experience has various core attributes—aliveness and intensity; belonging and connectedness; sense of caring and compassion for others; feeling of depth and calm; and ease, lightness, peace, and harmony. [108]

Our Environmental Crisis—The Mess We Have Created

The disconnect between nature and religion happened because (a) we promoted a nature-culture divide based on the mistaken rationale that humankind and their cultures are not connected to nature and (b) conservation science is now the main means for decision making and management, which is generally treated as being superior to social and cultural disciplines. [93] This dominance of science started with Newton and Descartes. Yet we only have one Earth, but we have many worldviews—whether from different faiths or spiritual traditions, from how we use nature, or from the idea that nature is imbued with spirit. Different worldviews determine how people perceive and interact with nature. We cannot understand ecosystems and conserve them without recognizing the cultures that shape them. [30] But we tend to frame our spirituality in terms of formal religions. [107] This is changing, and with this comes an increasing respect for and understanding of our spirituality.

The environmental crisis is not just ecological. It is a crisis for humanity and a moral challenge that calls us to examine how we use and share the goods of the earth, what we pass onto future generations, and how we live in harmony with God's creation. [56] We lose more than thirteen million hectares of forests per annum, [33] including sacred groves. For example, some sacred Kayas in Kenya (chapter 4) were destroyed to pave the way for tourist hotels. When this happens, we lose some of our biological and cultural heritage. [43]

The missing element is our relationship with nature, and here we have much to learn from the first nations and indigenous peoples. [102]

The mismanagement and destruction of biodiversity around the world is mindless. Edward Wilson points this out as it "lowers the quality of the planet's natural resources, destabilizes the physical environment and speeds up the spread of infectious diseases and invasive species." [136] We are now more aware of the spiritual importance of nature as modern life takes its toll on nature and sacred nature [138] and on us. We can transcend our differences and come together to reconnect with nature. Conserving nature is a spiritual imperative. This helps us reconnect with nature and realize what we have forgotten or ignored. [117] This loss of connection with nature relates to our wish for control, which is the root cause of so much destruction of the world's ecosystems. [119]

The problem lies inside our hearts. [40] For example, the National Parks in the United States set aside areas for protection rather than altering how people think about how they use nature in a more integrated and spiritual sense. [56] In a similar way, our forest practices and responses to trees reflect our

> **Box 2: The Vedic Hymn to the Goddess of the Forest**
>
> Aranyani is the goddess of the forest honored by song in the Indian Rig Veda (Hymn 146, Book 10). She animates and protects the forest and provides food. This beautiful image symbolizes the age-old connection between man and nature that is expressed in a multitude of cultural and religious forms. "Goddess of wild and forest who seemest to vanish from the sight. How is it thou seekest not the village? Art thou not afraid? What time the grasshopper replies and swells the shrill cicada's voice, seeming to sound with tinkling bells, the Lady of the Wood exults. And yonder, cattle seem to graze, what seems a dwelling-place appears: Or else at eve the Lady of the Forest seems to free the wains. For here one is calling to his cow, another there hath felled a tree: At eve the dweller in the wood fancies that somebody hath screamed. The Goddess never slays, unless some murderous enemy approach. Man eats of savory fruit and then takes, even as he wills, his rest. Now have I praised the Forest Queen, sweet-scented, redolent of balm, The Mother of all sylvan things, who tills not but hath stores of food" (http://aranyani.nl/en/about-aranyani).

dominant social values—consumptive rather than spiritual. Yet many of us view trees and forests in ways that may differ from those of the professional forester. However, it is not an issue of us (with a focus on the intangible values) and them (traditional foresters with a focus on growing trees and processing timber). A forest takes on sacred qualities and is a source of natural products. [16] In the Eastern tradition, the forest is a world of wisdom, peace, spirituality, and nonviolence (see box 2).

Western approaches to conservation now recognize the value of relationships with local and indigenous ecological and environmental knowledge. This was an important outcome of the Fifth World Parks Congress (Durban, South Africa, 2003). But there is less regard for the conservation potential of SNSs. Community-conserved areas, including SNS,[j] can complement conservation. [111] The Earth is not a set of disconnected animate and inanimate bits for humankind's use. [44] Earth is connected and integrated. But we have to give and act as responsible stewards. At present our relationship with nature is dysfunctional because of the skewed way we use and abuse nature. His Royal Highness the Prince of Wales said, "I believe that if we are to achieve sustainable development, we will first have to rediscover a sense of the sacred in our dealings with the natural world and with each other" (Reith Lecture, 2000) [89]

Reviving the Sanctity of Nature

We are all related and connected, and we share all we have, whether or not we appreciate it. Earth's health is humankind's health. [65] All life is important, and we all depend on those less visible parts of nature that sustain the larger life-forms—sacred trees and groves, plants, animals, soil, and us. We are inseparable and linked to the web of life. Pope Francis's encyclical is enlightening as it comes in the wake of previous papal statements on environment and faith. Pope John Paul II said the ecological crisis is a moral issue. But Pope Francis's encyclical is the first social encyclical of the Catholic church to address care for the environment and environmental justice in a direct, specific, and powerful manner. [97] Pope Francis writes,

---

[j] These are defined by IUCN as "areas of land or water having special spiritual significance to peoples and communities." [131] See http://sacrednaturalsites.org.

[96] "Our common home is falling into serious disrepair ... This is evident in large-scale natural disasters as well as social and even financial crises, for the world's problems cannot be analyzed or explained in isolation ... It cannot be emphasized enough how everything is interconnected." These are remarkable words from a remarkable leader.

Trees evolved over the last 370 million years and are more resilient than any animal. Some live for thousands of years. There are sixty thousand known tree species. Nature's living fossil tree, the Maidenhair tree *(Ginkgo biloba)*, is 270 million years old. [2] By studying trees, we can learn about survival, defense, sustainability, conservation, spirituality, and the creative possibilities of nature. [47] The tree that celebrates the benevolence of the soil becomes benevolent, offering its fruit to whoever is in need. The tree gives wood to fashion a chair and oxygen to maintain life. [64] In this way, sacred groves and sacred trees epitomize the interdependence between nature and society, and they are an example of the linkages between biodiversity and spirituality and of the interactions between social and natural sciences. Sacred groves are very relevant for the twenty-first century because they still survive and thrive. Given their scale and scope across the globe, they are one means to counter deforestation.

To revive the sacredness of nature requires us to revive our experiences of sanctity. Lao-Tzu wrote 2,500 years ago of the value of returning to the simplicity, stillness, and beauty of nature to achieve inner peace and harmony. [126] Many have written how nature can renew the spirit and put one in touch with oneself. To connect with nature restores a sense of relatedness to the spirit, to ourselves, and to one another. [46] Religious, spiritual, and conservation organizations are starting to acknowledge how important the environment is in people's spiritual and cultural well-being. The Assisi Declaration (1986[k]) called on world religions to conserve the environment. So too, the Convention on Biological Diversity called for enhanced conservation and community participation.

---

[k] Accessed May 5, 2015. www.arcworld.org/downloads/THE%20ASSISI%20DECLARATIONS.pdf.

Our Future in Nature: Trees, Spirituality and Ecology

If we no longer love nature's services and only want to use (and abuse) nature, we lose touch with life and that sense of tenderness and responsiveness to beautiful things. [57] We ought to renew our sensitivity to Mother Earth to understand what a true relationship is. "Only when the last tree has been cut down. Only when the last river has been poisoned. Only when the last fish has been caught. Only then will you find that money cannot be eaten" (Cree Prophecy[l]). Thomas Berry adds, "There is no such thing as human community without the Earth and the soil and the air and the water and all the living forms. Without these, humans do not exist. There is, therefore, no separate human community. Humans are woven into this larger community. The larger community is the sacred community. The Earth is a very special sacred community." [13]

Spiritual and Scientific Views of Nature—Tensions

People have become separated from nature in their quest for material well-being. This is exacerbated by population, land use and urbanization pressures hitherto not seen. This separation started with the move from hunter-gatherer societies to agriculture. Then the separation grew with the great early civilizations (e.g., in the Indus Valley or the Romans). Urbanization and industrialization made the separation worse with fewer people tilling the land. The separation was hastened with increasing urbanization and the industrial revolution in Europe. Now 55 percent of the world's population is urban (2014), up from 34 percent in 1960 and growing at 1.8 percent per annum.[m] The growing disconnection from nature is a threat to humankind. It is a moral challenge, and it calls us to examine how we share the goods of the earth, what we pass onto future generations, and how we live in harmony with nature. [56] John O'Donoghue notes, "We no longer walk the Earth with wonder. Instead of being guests of the Earth, we are now crowded passengers on the runaway train of progress and productivity … We desperately need to retrieve

---

[l] Accessed June 9, 2017. Cree Prophecy: https://www.quotes.net/authors/Cree%20Indian%20Prophecy.
[m] Accessed September 7 2014. http://www.who.int/gho/urban_health/situation_trends/urban_population_growth_text/en/.

our capacity for reverence." [87] These spiritual views of nature are being replaced by science, which only rarely has a spiritual presence. [78] Society treats nature as if it is comprised of separate parts. Humankind clears forests for crops, converts ancient trees to timber, overfishes and pollutes lakes and seas—all to satisfy our greed.

When we see ourselves as external to nature and free to manipulate and control her constituent parts, imagining somehow that the Earth can take care of itself, we harm both the planet and ourselves. This arrogant illusion ignores the degree to which we depend on nature. Nature has become so simplified that it is no longer the Mother Earth who animated the world for our ancestors. [51] Having become disconnected, we lost our sense of awe and reverence for the natural world. [6] Humankind lost its sense of the sacred and our sacred duty of stewardship. However, stewardship still implies a sense of separation and being above nature. Yet we are part of nature. We are nature. In some of our actions, we behave as masters of nature and others as bystanders. If we could rediscover our sense of being a part of nature, we would be less likely to see the world as a gigantic production system. [51]

The dominance and growth of science further divided things into separate entities and often ignored the interconnections. As a result, we became separate from nature in our quest for material well-being and from our cultural and spiritual ties with nature.[n] Economist Herman Daly pointed out, "The fatal flaw of the free market ideology is that sustainable growth is an oxymoron. Eventually growth runs up against sensitive ecosystems and the finite Earth. We are sacrificing the environment for economic growth, which is very dangerous in a very definitely finite world. As economic growth feeds on nature and communities, this shifts the unpaid costs back on them as well." [104] It looks as though we have created a global system that is (or could be) an ecological absurdity. This results from the choices we have made about how we have conducted public affairs and how we evaluate success. [91] Yet there are many spiritual scientists and spiritualists who are well grounded in science. Consider Aldo Leopold, Albert Einstein,

---

[n] Intangible values refer to values that enrich the intellectual, psychological, emotional, spiritual, cultural, and/or creative aspects of human existence and well-being.

David Suzuki, Edward Wilson, and Rachel Carson, all of whom made a huge impact on the importance of systems approaches to and a greater understanding of nature. It is clear not all science is reductionist, and many of these great scientists, including quantum physicists, think in integrated and more holistic ways. But the reality is environmental sustainability still has a back seat compared to the social and economic pillars of sustainable development, even though economics depends on ecology.

Humankind has intervened in nature since the beginnings of time. In ancient days, usage was sustainable and low. There pressures were nomadic and involved hunting and gathering. Since the industrial revolution and increased urbanization, this has changed. Now we seem to accept the impossibility of unlimited growth in a finite world. This may be attractive to economists and national finance ministries, but there is not an infinite supply of the earth's goods and resources. [96] Three very risky assumptions underpin such unlimited growth. First, everything is here for humankind. Second, "Problems cannot be solved with the same mindset that created them."° And third, technology supported by science, profit, and consumerism is the basis for progress and prosperity. [90]

Our ancestors saw nature in organic terms as a living entity. From about the 1600s, reductionist and scientific views of nature grew. Knowledge was science, while beliefs were not. Thus, beliefs were not true knowledge. Thinkers such as Galileo, Bacon, and Descartes viewed the world as a gigantic clockwork made of inert matter. This view was successful for the scientific exploration of nature to exploit for human gain. But these successes meant the loss of a sense of the sacred, which contributed to materialist perspectives and our alienation from nature. [25] Science prioritized quantitative thinking over qualitative approaches. Spiritual intuition and feelings of empathy for nature had little place in the new sciences. Yet Fritjof Capra says, "Many of our great scientists have expressed their sense of awe when faced with the mystery that lies beyond the limits of their theories." [20]

° Accessed August 15, 2018. https://www.goodreads.com/quotes/387336-problems-cannot-be-solved-with-the-same-mind-set-that.

Edward Wilson notes, "Although the two great branches of learning, the sciences and the humanities, are radically different in the way they describe our species, they have risen from the same wellspring of creative thought." [137] Yet science and spirituality don't have to compete. They are two different means or languages for telling the same story of Mother Earth. As such, there is room for both lines of thinking. If this is the case, we had better create (or recreate) the connections. Sacred nature can help us do that. Too often life is dominated by technical specialists. Yet the issues and challenges that Earth faces are holistic and require systems thinking. For example, the connections and interactions in a forest or a sacred grove are complex—way beyond our ability to think. [14]

The dominant scientific approaches explain nature based on material and quantitative principles, not as part of a whole, or that nature has spiritual attributes. [55] As a result, nature was not given spiritual values. This opened the way for exploitation and destruction. But we are now seeing a stronger emphasis on the sacredness of nature as this book attests. Yet science itself is not neutral [55] and is increasingly dominated by commercial interests that support economic and development paradigms. The real point is to understand human existence from intellectual, scientific, and spiritual perspectives and so make sense of the world. Scientists such as Planck, Einstein, Bohr, Schrodinger, Pauli, and Bohm tried to understand the world in scientific terms. Even they acknowledge such understanding takes them beyond the realms of *understandable* science!

It is dangerous to continue to think we can solve ecological problems by increasing the computational and technological power we throw at ecology while undervaluing nature and our spiritual heritage. The ancient and spiritual wisdoms are not a panacea for sure, but such wisdom can guide us in how to find more sustainable options grounded in values promoting rather than subverting what is truest and best in humankind. [84] This is what Rachel Carson realized more than sixty years ago with the publication of the book *Silent Spring*, which emphasized that nature and the planet was being assaulted in the name of pest control and intensive agriculture and that war was and is being waged against nature—one that we cannot win as it ignores how nature works. Rachel Carson helped us reconnect with the importance of treating nature for what it is and not to dominate, simplify, and control it. [95] Yet reductionist views led us to commoditize the planet and its services. We created property rights over nature, and markets take precedence over the intrinsic values of land. [49]

Many of us lost our sense of the sacred because of the mistaken notion that nature is separate from God. [40] Spirituality and science are inadequate on their own. Science needs to appreciate the external landscape and embrace a spiritual awakening to nourish the inner landscape. Science equips us to relate to the material world (the how), and spirituality helps us to find meaning (the why) for us to take good care of the earth and live in harmony. [63]

Kepler, Galileo, and Newton reordered nature and the known world into a clockwork so that nature could be understood without reference to the soul. Descartes thought nature could be understood as a clockwork, allowing man to understand and control nature. Here God's promise in Genesis that people should have dominion over nature was being realized through science. [25] Dominion was chosen to mean domination, which is a narrow interpretation. Nature was no longer seen as divine. This approach is rejected by Pope Francis, who says dominion is supposed to be understood in the sense of responsible stewardship. [90] "The Lord God took the man and settled him in the Garden of Eden to cultivate and care for it" (Genesis 2:15). Pope Francis says, "Tilling refers to cultivating, ploughing or working, while keeping means caring, protecting, overseeing and preserving. This implies a relationship of mutual responsibility between human being and nature." [96] This refutes the domination of nature scenario!

Nature Is Much More than Consumerist Values and Materialism

The more industrially developed societies tried to control, dominate, and reshape nature to suit human needs. Thomas Berry notes (see box 3) that present-day religious education, ritual, and sacrament broadly ignore nature. [13] So-called development, science, and technology support a near relentless push in the name of economic growth. As a result, many SNS are undermined as humankind tries to alter the relationship with the earth and nature. [128] Pope Francis paints a clear picture. "The Earth, our home, is beginning to look more like an immense pile of filth." [96] Earth is not only for humankind's benefit. We have no special rights. We are one of the myriads of species making up Earth and Gaia. [70] Gaia is a complex, self-organizing system with the capacity to maintain conditions for life. Life adapts, life remembers, and life learns. [68, 69, 119] So sacred ecology reflects our belief in an underlying structure that links people, and it also asserts that the natural world is a pattern we cannot define. [91]

> **Box 3: Humanity's Dependence on Nature**
>
> "We cannot have well humans on a sick planet. We cannot have a viable human economy by devastating the Earth's economy. We cannot survive if the conditions of life itself are not protected. Not only our physical being, but our souls, our minds, imagination and emotion depend on our immediate experience of the natural world.
>
> There is in the industrial process no poetry, no elevation or fulfilment of mind or emotion compared to that experience of the magnificence of the sea, the mountain, the sky, the stars at night, the flowers blooming in the meadows, the flight and song of the birds.
>
> As the natural world diminishes in its splendour, so human life diminishes in its fulfilment of both the physical and spiritual aspects of our being. Not only is it the case with humans, but with every mode of being. The well-being of each member of the Earth community is dependent on the Earth itself." [11]

Consumeristic and economic drivers underpinning contemporary life are not enough to satisfy us. Otherwise, why is there still so much poverty, stress, suicide, and life pressures at a time when we have everything? Likewise, why do many sacred groves and trees survive despite pressures of high land usage? Why do many rural people still talk about how important cultural and sacred values are together with the environment and nature? As this book and much literature shows, why are there still many hundreds and thousands of sacred trees and groves across the globe? Some have said every village across Africa has a sacred grove. The same might be true for Asia and Latin America.

Without trees, we would not be here. They are life providers—providing wood and paper, cooling the air, binding water and soil, acting as carbon sinks, producing oxygen, and promoting cloud formation. [48] Yet we continue to destroy nature and trees as part of economic growth. All species, humankind included, are of equal importance. It is the interconnections that are important. For example, trees would not be there without fungi. [71] We have plundered Earth's resources because of the shortsighted approaches of economics, commerce, and production. Losing forests means the loss of species and resources not just for food but for health and our lives. [96] What we need, as Rowan Williams (former archbishop of Canterbury) points out, is not conservation for its own sake but as part of conserving humanity. [133] "We seem to be moving towards the idea that rates of growth of money in the bank are autonomous, and the natural world can accommodate this. Or if it can't, we can adjust it. That seems to me the wrong way to go," said Herman Daly. When asked what an economy is, he replied, "I would say that it's a community of people who, through division of labor and exchange, live a life in some mutuality or interdependence. And they depend not only on each other, but [also] on the natural world, the natural community, from which they extract materials and services and to which they have to return wastes." [27] By not taking this into account, we risk the future of humankind as a species. [10] If we put ecology before economy, we might see cures for the various crunches we experience [61] (e.g., the credit crunch, climate crunch, etc.).

Edward Wilson challenges us, "We don't know nearly enough to manage the ecosystems on our own. If we think that we can eliminate those natural ecosystems and substitute prosthetic devices, like creating clean air or water with fusion energy or sustaining the stability of cropland—in fact, [if we think we can] keep the planet in that delicately balanced, highly peculiar state on which humanity depends for its continued existence–then we are kidding ourselves." [134] The more we break nature up, the more we lack a full understanding of the patterns of nature as well as the dependencies within and between ecosystems. As Norman Myers notes, "We don't even have that basic grasp of what makes the planet tick–let alone how to keep it ticking." [118] Fritjof Capra says, "The environment of life, which we thought of as independent, is itself shaped by life … The whole system regulates itself and maintains conditions conducive to life. Gaia, like us, maintains her body temperature, and not only overall temperature, but [also] the composition of gases like oxygen and carbon dioxide, the salinity of the oceans–all these processes are maintained at levels that are conducive to life." [118]

This highlights the importance of understanding shallow and deep ecology. Shallow ecology is anthropocentric and views humans as outside nature. It ascribes usage values to nature. This is how most of us view ecology. Deep ecology does not separate humans from nature. Nor does it separate anything else from it (see box 4). The intrinsic value of all life is recognized, and humans are one strand in that web. [19] The feeling that the world is alive is fundamental to human well-being. We are the first human societies to think nature is not alive, and this alienates us. [72]

Economists regard forests as a factor of production, or as Thomas Berry puts it, "We have turned nature from a community of subjects to a collection of objects," which are exploited as products. [12] Ecologists see forests and nature as the living skin of Earth, which we destroy at our peril. Many spiritual traditions see trees and forests as sacred. Despite this, short-term economics rule with unprecedented technology at its disposal. [37] Nature is the source of our welfare and economic prosperity. But if we are to deepen our commitment to nature's needs, we have to adopt a different mind-set. We cannot simplify nature and expect it to carry on in the way it did as everything in nature's elaborate system is necessary. [53] Pope Francis supports this by saying, "Environmental protection cannot be assured solely on the basis of financial calculations of costs and benefits. The environment is one of those goods that cannot be adequately safeguarded or promoted by market forces." [96] Strong words!

> **Box 4: Deep and Shallow Ecology**
>
> *Shallow ecology* treats problems without tackling underlying causes and without confronting the assumptions that underlie political and economic thinking, as these issues are anthropocentric. The dominant worldview of economics regards nature as a machine. Human beings are separate from and superior to nature in this view and see themselves in charge of nature. The mental and material, the spiritual and physical, are separate, with the mental and spiritual realms excluded from nature. This view led to the belief we have the right to dominate and exploit nature, for nature has no intrinsic spiritual qualities. While we might be concerned about environmental questions, these issues are anthropocentric.
>
> *Deep ecology* does not separate us from nature. Nor does it separate anything else from it. The world is interconnected and interdependent. Humankind should reintegrate with nature and recognize the interdependence of all-natural phenomena, which merge spiritual and material aspects. Such views, which Naess characterizes as biocentric, are often at odds with materialism and consumerism. We can learn from such sources and reconstruct an ecologically sound philosophy of nature. In ecology each species contributes to the functioning of the whole ecosystem and of Earth too. It affects and is affected by those species around it, which makes for ever-changing relationships in the Gaian network.
>
> We are reappraising the assumptions underlying our attitudes about nature and humankind. This transformation is due to revolutions in science, and those associated with the physics of relativity and quantum theory. These ideas challenge basic principles of Newtonian physics and mechanistic worldviews. They force us to think about space, time, and causality. Nature is a constant flux and flow of energy, a network of interactions that cannot be reduced to the activity of discrete particles and a place where human consciousness cannot be separated into a distinct compartment of reality.
>
> Sources: [18, 25]

Mother Earth is sacred to indigenous peoples. The great forests and groves nurture life spiritually and materially. Yet there are problems, and we must change our lifestyles and act. [60] This is why we must try to understand sacred trees and groves and other SNS in a more integrated manner. We rarely look at (i.e., witness, be mindful of) a tree or any aspect of nature, and if we do, we look at a tree from a usage perspective (e.g., sit under its shade, cut it down for timber, harvest other products). [57] Rather we should try to achieve a sense of presence and mindfulness. Similarly, there is no real love of Earth, only our use of her resources. We need to use (not overuse) nature's bounty. We should respect and love nature for what it is in a spiritual and mindful manner.

Spiritual and Cultural Values of Nature— Those Vital Intangible Values

Reverence for trees occurs in all cultures. This was important in ancient times and is resilient enough to stay important for our spiritual lives through the industrial revolution to the present. [138] In Ireland, early spiritual traditions predating formal religion considered important natural features to be conscious and spiritual. For many cultures and spiritual traditions, certain trees are sacred and protected. These can be important for conservation. [79] Everything natural—flowers or trees or animals—are important teachers if we stop, look, and listen to them. [123] For many, we are no longer committed to religions saying that humankind is on Earth as the only divine life and that we are superior to the rest of life. [134] Thomas Berry says, "Our challenge is to create a new language, even a new sense of what it is to be human. It is to transcend not only national limitations, but even our species' isolation, to enter into the large community of living species. This brings about a completely new sense of reality and value." [10]

Many formal religions, especially the Abrahamic ones, do not adequately embrace the sacredness of nature, sacred spaces, and species in their work, though this is changing. Some groups were responsible for, wittingly or unwittingly, the destruction of many SNS. Eastern faith-based organizations and indigenous belief systems better integrated the relevance of nature as sacred in their work and teachings. Thomas Aquinas emphasized, "Faith comes in two volumes: nature and the Bible." [35] Chesterton said, "For him [Aquinas] Man is … rather a thing like a tree, whose roots are fed from the Earth, while the highest branches seem to rise almost to the stars." [22] We cannot be separate from nature. We ought to rebuild our spiritual connections with people and nature while rethinking our assumptions about development, growth, progress, peace, and education.

Religious organizations are taking spiritual aspects of the environment more into account after many years of not doing so. [100] This includes, for example, the World Council of Religious Leaders, Religions for Peace, the Vatican Dialogues, the Uppsala Manifesto, Istanbul Islamic Declaration, and the contributions of the Orthodox Patriarch of Constantinople.[p] These movements acknowledge the environmental roots that religions grew from and the role religious organizations can play in the environmental and climate changes crises. In part, this acknowledges the role religions had in environmental destruction, particularly in the Middle Ages and colonial eras. [92]

The way humankind interpreted sacred texts tended to separate relations between God and creation. Spiritual values stay with God. Material resources are part of creation we can exploit. [105] This false dichotomy characterizes our contemporary world. "Go to church (or mosque or temple) on Sunday, and cut trees on Monday." We are careless and excessive in the way we use (abuse) nature. This is causing nearly irreparable damage to planet Earth (e.g., climate change). As Hildegard of Bingen (1098–1179) said those years ago, "God created the world out of the four elements to glorify his name. He strengthened the world with wind. He connected the world to the stars. And he filled the world with all kinds of creatures. He then put human beings throughout the world, giving them great power as stewards of all Creation. Human beings cannot live without the rest of nature, they must care for all-natural things." [106] To Hildegard, all life is interconnected. So where and why have we gone wrong?

Trees and groves are one key to understanding how we are connected to and dependent on nature through our consciousness. Consciousness, the "knowing together, mutual knowledge, the state of being conscious" (*Oxford English Dictionary*) is not only philosophical or scientific but a reality. This helps us transition from an egocentric to an ecocentric worldview. We need to understand the language of nature and become

---

[p] Sources include the following: https://en.wikipedia.org/wiki/World_Summit_of_Religious_Leaders https://rfp.org/act/protect-the-earth/ http://www.vatican.va/roman_curia/pontifical_councils/interelg/index.htm https://berkleycenter.georgetown.edu/publications/uppsala-manifesto-hope-for-the-future http://www.ifees.org.uk/declaration/, and https://www.patriarchate.org/the-green-patriarch.

ecoliterate (ecological literacy). This is an important but undervalued step to sustainability. [91] Peace and prosperity will prevail when we are alive to this consciousness. [62] Yet consciousness cannot be isolated, labeled, or worked on. It is inclusive and indivisible. [24] As Chopra notes, [24] "There are not two worlds, inner and outer. There is one reality which consciousness conceives, governs and creates."

Whether we agree with these arguments or not, this calls on religions and spiritual groups to examine their purpose regarding nature in the spirit of the Assisi Declarations (see box 5). This gives us courage to rediscover our religious and spiritual foundations in the web of life rather than the continuity of religions by narrow political power and economic interests. If the world religions follow the more familiar route, they will forsake the earth and betray the earth's sacred natural endowment. [38] Peter Marshal states, "Ecological thinking is rising in human minds like sap in spring. What is taking place is not merely a concern with cleaning up our environment but a fundamental shift in consciousness—as momentous as the Renaissance." [75] This

> **Box 5: The Assisi Declarations on the Environment**
>
> In the summer of 1986, a historic event took place in Assisi, Italy. For the first time, representatives of the great faiths came to hear what religion could offer conservation and what conservation had to share with religion. The central message from the Assisi declarations was that ecology needs the deep truths that live within the major faiths of the world if people are to recognize their responsibility for and with nature. "We are convinced of the inestimable value of our respective traditions and of what they can offer to re-establish ecological harmony; But at the same time, we are humble enough to desire to learn from each other. The very richness of our diversity lends strength to our shared concern and responsibility for our Planet Earth" (Father Serrini, Minister General of the Franciscans). The final part of the celebrations concerned the major faiths present issuing declarations, regarding their commitment to conservation—Buddhism, Christianity, Hinduism, Islam, and Judaism. Three faiths joined soon after—Baha'i (1987), Jainism (1991), and Sikhism (1989). As His Royal Highness the Duke of Edinburgh summed up, "A new and powerful alliance has been forged between the forces of religion and the forces of conservation."
>
> Source: Annex 6 in [98]

relates to Lao Tzu's teaching. "Tao as the order of nature, governs their every action. When all things obey the laws of the Tao, they will form a harmonious whole and the universe will become an integrated organism." [126] In Taoism, nature is spontaneous with a natural balance.

Eckhart Tolle says, "When we first go into a natural forest, our thinking mind will tend to see chaos, disorder with little distinction about what is living and what is no longer living. But if we still the mind and be truly present there is harmony, a sacredness of nature and a higher order into which everything is in its right and perfect place—that is the way it is." [123] Such awareness of our consciousness, using the stillness of nature, helps us become aligned with the present moment.

All living creatures are part of the earth, and the stories of indigenous peoples reflect this, including the reference that the earth is the mother of life. The English word *Earth* is derived from the name the tribes of northern Germany gave the mother goddess. The Greeks worshipped Gaia, the goddess of Earth, who brought forth plants, animals, and all creation. The Gaia hypothesis is a powerful call to view the planet as whole. [117] How do the parts function within the whole? As Earth's health is our health, it makes no sense to separate the parts form the whole. [117] For example, what are the effects of trees or a natural forest on our inner state? The response is peace, quiet, and silence. Trees and woodlands are a source of energy and positive effects on our health. [15]

Teilhard de Chardin suggested part of humanity's purpose might be a global brain, the physical embodiment of a planetary consciousness,[q] and he says "Why do we hesitate to open our hearts to the call of the world within us, to the sense of the Earth? The sense of the Earth is the irresistible pressure which comes at a given moment to unite them in a common enthusiasm … The age of nations has passed. Now, unless we wish to perish, we must shake off our old prejudices and build the Earth." [120] This is the same impulse (our minds) that separates us from nature, cuts us off from our being, and affects us as stress. It can feed loneliness and searches for meaning, which underlies much of society. [117] In this

---

[q] Accessed March 19, 2018. http://www.recim.org/bio/dechardin-an.htm#15410.

context, ecology requires us to "involve protecting the cultural treasures of humanity in the broadest sense. It calls for greater attention to local cultures when studying environmental problems." [96]

> **Box 6: First Nation Views on Their Connections with Land**
>
> "One of the things that we as Okanagan people [a *First Nations* American people whose territory spans USA–Canada between Washington state and British Columbia] know is that our very flesh is our land. Our very breath that we take is our land. Everything that is about us is our land. When we refer to everything that is, we have only one word meaning all, everything, the land, the water, the birds, the insects–everything, including ourselves. We say tamihu. And that means everything, including us, has that life force in it," J. Armstrong (Okanagan Elder) emphasizes this and recalls, "Going out on the land was like being with members of the family. I never used to see the differentiation between human beings and the life forms around us. And I think that perspective, in terms of forming relationships to the land, being in love with the land in the same way that you're in love with people, is an essential part of the human being... It's an actual relationship with our land in that way. In that kind of principle, with that kind of attitude, you can't go out and destroy that land unless you're insane, no more than you could destroy your own grandparents."
>
> Most indigenous peoples believe that the earth is alive and that humankind has a responsibility to take care of other creatures. Calamity will result if we are greedy or destructive. They cement this understanding of the physical world not with science but with emotion and experience. "The land is our provider, our healer, our inspiration" (R. Niquanicappo, Cree Indian Quebec, Canada). "We think of ourselves as custodians of the land and the land is not just soil and rock to us. It is the whole of creation—all the land, water, and air and the life everywhere—people too. All things are related and linked together in dreamtime" (P. Gordon, Aboriginal, Bandjalang tribe, Australia). A shaman named D. Manyev from Altai in Russia said, "The whole Earth is sacred and there is a network of especially sacred areas... Each has a guardian who ensures that the local community practise the correct ceremonies to protect these sacred places." Different human cultures hold the earth as sacred. Sacred trees and groves are one part of this interconnected network. They have a shared wisdom of the sacredness of life based on the understanding that the physical world is animated by spiritual forces.
>
> Sources: [50, 54, 117, 118] ; and www.nativeperspectives.net/Transcripts/Jeannette_Armstrong_interview.pdf

Indigenous and First Nation peoples understand how important it is to remember where we are, who we are, and how we fit in the greater whole (see box 6). They developed regular cycles of ritual and ceremony to mark important events and promote balance. Though the form of these celebrations varies, the intention is constant—to honor life, remind ourselves of our place within the whole, and feed the world by giving something back. [117] Indigenous peoples formed their cultures in and around nature. The values may be personal (e.g., the psychological or therapeutic values of visiting a sacred grove) or cultural (e.g., the values linking people) or societal (e.g., the values bringing cultures together). [46] As a result, a large part of the way we change is cultural as increasing numbers of scientists realize that ancient spiritual concepts are a coherent framework, even for many scientific theories. [15]

After three to four hundred years, the religious establishment is still trying to reformulate their theology of nature [81] as Pope Francis makes clear in his encyclical. For a long time, humanity abandoned what was a fundamental principle of religions and spiritual worldviews, namely the order governing humanity and nature. [82] "Allah is the Light of the heavens and the Earth. The parable of His Light is as if there were a Niche and within it a Lamp: The Lamp enclosed in Glass: The glass as it were lit from a Blessed Tree, an Olive neither of the East nor of the West, whose oil well-nigh Luminous, though fire scarce touched it. Light upon Light" (Qur-ān, 24:35). These laws are for humankind, nature, and the cosmos as there is a profound relationship between them. [82] For conservation, Islam has five principles. [29] Most religions and spiritual traditions have similar principles.

> Allah creates everything. Everything is his possession.
> Allah's creation is perfect and well balanced and should not be disturbed.
> By corrupting our ecosystems, humankind is damaging itself. A balanced relationship between humankind and the environment is a religious obligation.
> It is prohibited to corrupt Earth's environment. This is punishable in this world and the worlds to come.

> Wasteful extravagance is a grave damage to the environment. We should avoid this if we are not to deplete Earth's resources. Humankind has the role of the steward and a duty to understand the immense generosity and wisdom of creation.

Why did people consider nature sacred? Was it because they experienced nature's sanctity as something that helped them be more connected with the universe, or did they want to regulate and conserve nature?[r] If we want to revive the sanctity of nature, we need to revive the experience of that sanctity. Lao Tzu wrote 2,500 years ago of the value of returning to the simplicity, stillness, and beauty of nature to achieve inner peace and harmony. [126] Being connected with nature restores our relatedness to the spirit, ourselves, and one another. [46] In the past, people did not understand nature, which was usually held in awe. Now nature is decoded by science. [46]

We should remember to reflect on the patterns of nature. His Royal Highness the Prince of Wales notes that the Qur-ān "explicitly describes nature as possessing an intelligibility and says there is no separation between man and nature; precisely because there is no separation between the natural world and God. It offers a completely integrated view of the universe where religion, science, mind and matter are all part one living, conscious whole." [52] A key teaching of Islam is that there are limits to the abundance of nature and that these limits are not arbitrary. The Qur-ān warns against corrupting the environment and promotes a balance in relations between humankind and nature. [29]

Many have tried to defend the focus on domination by appealing to the dominion God gave to humans. Consider the often quoted passage from Genesis. "Then God said, let us make man in our image, after our likeness. Let them have dominion over the fish of the sea and the birds of the air, and the cattle, and over all the wild animals and all the creatures that crawl on the ground" (Genesis 1:26–28). Pope Francis clarified that dominion means stewardship. "God also said: See I have given you every seed-bearing plant all over the Earth and every tree that has seed-bearing

---

[r] Pers. Comm Manisha Gutman, eCoexist, Pune, India, March 2010.

fruit on it to be your food" (Genesis 1:29). Even so, Christianity is often blamed for humankinds uncontrolled exploitation of nature [130] because of its focus on domination (i.e., control), not dominion (i.e., stewardship). This is exacerbated by humankind's focus on science and a reduced appeal of religion to the millennial generation. This argues for a resacrilization of nature based on ecological principles. [80]

Religion and science seem to be the most potent forces today. If they could unite around nature and the environment, we would solve many challenges. [135] Yet this lack of unity is one underlying cause of degradation. Until recent times, many spiritual leaders representing a large majority of the world's population hesitated to make the protection of creation a key part of their work. [135] David Suzuki's warning is stark. "If we pollute the air, water, and soil that keep us alive and well, and destroy the biodiversity that allows natural systems to function, no amount of money will save us. If all humans disappeared today, the Earth would start improving tomorrow. If all the ants disappeared today, the Earth would start dying tomorrow."ˢ

Sacred Groves in the Context of Much Larger Sacred Landscapes

While this book focuses on sacred trees and groves, I want to set this in the broader discourse on sacred nature. Sites may be sacred to different peoples for many reasons. Sacred species and sacred springs are place-specific. There are also larger sacred landscapes, such as mountains or river systems. These sacred places help us understand, respect, and take responsibility for them as part of the wider environment. This is an opportunity to use sacred natural places to meet, be in silence, bring people together, and bring peace. It is useful to explore sacred landscapes to help us establish a larger worldview of what is sacred. I describe a few sacred landscapes to illustrate their variety, type, and scale. Most sacred landscapes in Europe evolved from Christianity. In other countries these landscapes are associated with different religious and spiritual beliefs (e.g., the Ganges associated with

---

ˢ Accessed December 12, 2016. www.azquotes.com/author/14336-David_Suzuki.

Hinduism and Mount Kailash with at least four faith-based groups). [101] More than 1.5 billion people revere the Ganges and Mt. Kailash.

William Blake said, "The tree which moves some to tears of joy is in the eyes of others only a green thing that stands in the way. Some see nature as ridicule and deformity and some scarce see nature at all. But the eyes of the man of imagination, nature is imagination itself." [121] How we view a landscape is personal and depends on context. A forester may view a landscape differently from a hiker or someone who seeks the deep silence of nature. Though such divisions are not always the case as there are always overlaps.

The Ganges River is a large sacred landscape. Known as Ganga Ma, Mother Ganges, the river is revered as a goddess who cleanses the sins of the faithful and aids the dead on their way. If we consider the size of her life-sustaining force, no wonder the river basin supports half a billion people with thousands of sacred sites along its course. For Hindu mythology, the Ganges was once a river of heaven that flowed across the sky and came to Earth through the hair of Lord Shiva to the Himalayas. The sacred river could restore the dead ancestors of King Bhagiratha and lift them to paradise. All Hindus believe if the ashes of their dead are placed in the river, they will have a smooth transition to the next life or are freed from the cycle of death and rebirth. Hindus believe the Ganges's divine waters purify those who immerse themselves in her. Many cities along the Ganges are the sites of sacred pilgrimages. There are nine large sacred forests (or *āranyas*) that include many sacred groves and trees. [83, 113] But regardless of the religious and spiritual values and beliefs, the Ganges is profoundly polluted. This is an example of instances when spiritual beliefs don't always lead to effective practices.

Mount Kailash and Lake Manasarovar in Tibet are revered as the holiest pilgrimage sites for one billion people of five Asian religions—Buddhism, Hinduism, Jainism, Bön, and Sikhism. [128, 94] Kailash resembles a Hindu temple or a Buddhist stupa. [9] Pilgrims come to Kailash to complete the ritual walk around its base, [7, 83] which is fifty kilometers long at altitudes of 4,600 to 5,600 meters. [94] Both geography and mythology are important in the sacred significance of Mount Kailash. Its grandeur lies not just in its height (6,700 meters) but in its shape of four sheer faces matching the cardinal points of the compass and its solitary placement, free from neighboring mountains. Kailash is the earthly manifestation of the mythical Mount Meru (or Sumeru), the spiritual center of the universe in Hindu, Buddhist, and Jain beliefs. As well as being spiritually important, four of Asia's great rivers—the Indus, Brahmaputra, Karnali and the Sutle—have their sources in Kailash. [74] To Tibetan Buddhists, Kailash is the abode of the meditational deity *Demchog*. For Hindus, it is the main dwelling place for Lord Shiva. [9] Jains revere Kailash as the site where their first prophet received enlightenment. For most Buddhists and Hindus, the journey to Kailash is the most important pilgrimage they make. While there are restrictions on resource usage, the numbers of visitors are now causing degradation. [94] It is interesting to note the governments of China, India, and Nepal delineated the Kailash Sacred Landscape because the area is better defined by ecosystems and cultural linkages than international boundaries. [94]

Uluru-Kata Tjuta (Ayers Rock-Mount Olga, Australia) [17] is a global symbol of Aboriginal struggles for land rights. It is now a model for collaborative indigenous-governmental land management. The area surrounding Uluru is governed by the precedent setting Northern Territory Aboriginal Sacred Sites Act of 1989. Now many sacred places around Uluru are off limits. One traditional elder says, "This place, Uluru, is sacred. Don't say that it is sacred only for a short time. It is a sacred object. We, Anangu [human beings who belong to the Earth], are the keepers of it." [8] The impacts of tourism are now a challenge in terms of how we respect what is sacred. For instance, the Anangu never climb Uluru because of its spiritual significance. Being responsible stewards of the natural environment is key to their lives. The elder goes on to say, "Anangu have not chosen the climb. They prefer that you—out of education and understanding—choose to respect their law and culture by not climbing." [8] The park is a UN World Heritage site for both its natural and cultural heritage. The process of inscription tells a story of different worldviews and how an indigenous sacred area can be part of an international treaty dealing with the heritage of humanity. The Anangu leased the land back to the federal government for ninety-nine years. Since then, they jointly manage Uluru-Kata Tjuta National Park with the National Parks Authority. An important part of managing the park is keeping the traditional rules to guide management yet accommodate visitor interests. The Anangu have a responsibility to protect the environment and its people, and they want visitors to learn about their land and culture. [17]

Mount Everest (Sagarmatha or Khumbu, Nepal) is a sacred landscape linked to the Ganges in India and covers a large area. [116] Sherpa religious beliefs are part of their lives, shapes local land usage and management, and is the basis for managing Sagarmatha National Park. [32] Sherpas conserve Khumbu's SNS through local rites and practices. There are many sacred groves in the Everest region, and all are protected despite external threats. [101] Some are in the World Heritage Site. But the status the Sherpas, the custodians, should be recognized and be a key part of long-term management. [101]

Mount Kenya is a sacred mountain landscape for the Kikuyu peoples as they believe their God lived on the mountain. [77] Everything good came from the mountain. Mount Kenya is shy to them because it is often covered in clouds, and this is a good sign as the people know they will get rain. Mount Kenya itself is a sacred landscape, and many sacred groves occur around the mountain. [86] Some are inside protected areas, while custom protects others.

These examples highlight a key issue. Whose interest counts, and whose interest should count in terms of such SNS? This is true where the interests of economists and those of traditional values clash. Then whose values are more important, and why? Our natural sense of the sacred may be ignored because of materialism. We can no longer fudge the inconvenient truth we are eroding nature's capital, even though we know in our hearts we are living beyond her means. [114] We might acknowledge our dependency on nature but not our spiritual dependency. We might imagine becoming independent of nature if only we can perfect technological substitutes from nature's gifts, [28] which is a delusion!

This Book—Sacred Trees, Sacred Groves, and Spirituality

Chief Seattle of the Suquamish and Duwamish tribes of what is now in Washington state in the Pacific Northwest of the United States made a celebrated speech in 1854 [23] from which the following excerpt is relevant: "This we know: The Earth does not belong to us. We belong to the Earth. The Earth is our mother. What befalls the Earth befalls all the sons and daughters of the Earth … This we know: All things are connected like the blood that unites us. We did not weave the web of life. We are merely a strand in it. Whatever we do to the web, we do to ourselves." This summarizes much of the essence of this book. We are part of nature. What we do to nature, we do to ourselves. Nature is sacred. Sacred groves and trees are visible expressions of that sacredness. This message is also what His Holiness the fourteenth Dalai Lama states. "In the past all of life was based on trees. The flowers gave us nourishment, their leaves and fibers clothed us and provided us with shelter. We took refuge in their branches for protection from wild animals. We used wood for heat, and for canes to bear our weight when we grew old, and to make weapons to defend ourselves. We were very close to trees. Today, surrounded by sophisticated machinery and high-performance computers in our ultra-modern offices, it is easy to forget our ties with nature." [34]

This book contributes to a greater understanding of the spiritual and religious significance of sacred trees and groves to conservation and different religious, cultural, and spiritual communities. I hope the book will help you better understand your relationship with nature and how you can improve it. We now have a greater understanding and appreciation of sacred nature. But conservation and land/water usage disciplines (in government, nongovernmental organizations, and the private sector) have to respect how important SNSs are to reconnecting us with nature and better conserve the resources of planet Earth. This is a calling irrespective of race, color, creed, or discipline.

I focus on sacred trees and groves to show the roles nature plays in our lives and how sacred trees and groves transcend race, color, and creed. Their existence is a testament to their resilience as institutions in the face of often insurmountable pressures. I use language that resonates with different disciplines to better bring us together for the future of the planet. I use the terms religion (faith, belief, creed, or religious conviction) and spirituality (mysticism, holiness, sacred) to separate formal organizations from our spiritual connectivity with God and nature that many of us experience. [6] However, the divisions between religion and spirituality are not clear-cut as table 1 summarizes these terms.

Woods and forests are places for finding peace, silence, solace, beauty, and connectivity as precious values to combat the stresses of life. [5] Trees and groves in religions relate more to their history, a basis for stories and places of poetic and scriptural importance. For some older animist traditions, trees have agency (i.e., the capacity of trees to act independently and make their own choices), can speak, and can influence the lives of humankind. Over time humankind moved from older animist traditions to those of the more formal religions, which focused on the dominion of man and our stewardship of nature. This set humankind apart from nature. Yet we are part of nature, and we are nature. We are all part of Mother Earth. This forms the basis for the inherent spirituality we all feel when we are in nature, in a sacred grove, or along the lake or seashore.

While sacred trees and groves are the focus, the text speaks to broader issues of (a) relating to and managing nature, (b) the importance of nature to seek silence and peace in our stress-filled lives, (c) seeking connectivity with nature, (d) being important conservation assets, (e) being the basis for experiential education, and (f) focusing on peace. Lessons and ideas from the book may help connect us as a powerful force for peace, respecting nature and the fragile earth we depend on. The book offers approaches you may wish to use in your lives. Adapt the ideas, lessons, and experiences that the book offers to our own lives. We don't all have easy access to a formal sacred tree or sacred grove, but we can all have our own personal bit of sacred nature—in the park, a woodland, a river area, in our garden, on our patio, or in a pot. The messages from the book may help you cope with the stresses of life, and in helping you, it will help nature and Mother Earth.

Table 1: Some Definitions of the Terms Religion, Spirituality, and Sacred [26]

Religion	Spirituality	Sacred
• Belief in, worship of, obedience to, submission to a supernatural power or powers considered divine or to control our human destiny. • Any formal or institutionalized expressions of such beliefs. • Attitudes and feelings of one who believes in a transcendent controlling power or powers. • (Thesaurus) devotional, divine, faithful, holy, godly, reverent, righteous, sacred, spiritual.	• Relating to the spirit or soul and not to physical nature or matter, intangible. • Of or relating to sacred things. • Standing in a relationship based on communication between souls and minds. • Having a mind or emotion of a high and delicately refined quality. • The belief that the spirits of the dead, surviving in another world, can communicate with the living world. • (Thesaurus) devotional, divine, ethereal, holy, nonmaterial, other worldly, pure, sacred.	• Only devoted to a deity or to some religious ceremony or use. • Worth of or regarded with reverence and awe. • Connected with or intended for religious use. • (Thesaurus) blessed, holy, divine, consecrated, divine, hallowed, venerable, revered, sanctified.

Sacred trees have spiritual meanings for many of us. The reasons vary from the longevity of some trees (e.g., the yew and baobab trees) to human associations with certain trees (e.g., Buddha attaining enlightenment under the bodhi or fig tree). Sacred groves vary in size. Most are small with a spiritual significance to groups of people as, for example, the place where their God lives or a burial place. These sites are protected and uninhabited with strict rules. The traditional respect for the environment and access restrictions often led to well-conserved areas with high biodiversity value within otherwise degraded landscapes. [110] Trees have an ageless mysticism. Even for the secular-minded, forests are special places for peace and silence—precious values for today. Take a walk in a forest, and feel the silence and peace you become a part of. Many trees live beyond our human lives by hundreds and thousands of years. Some predate formal religions, and most predate formal conservation.

By focusing on sacred trees and groves, I hope will engender positive feelings. Where they give such harmony, people conserve such sacred trees and sacred groves as part of the landscape. For example, placing groves or trees with relation to wind direction or water source protection gave rise to spiritual landscapes in China. [42] This formed one basis for feng (wind) shui (water) in China, where feng shui groves were often the only examples of original vegetation. [42] The Hakka people of south China protect natural and planted forests as they are home of the spirits. [85] If we focus on sacred trees and groves, this gives us a foundation for action and responsibility for nature, and it can inform what conservation and development as well as what spiritual and religious organizations can do.

Governments and funding agencies ought to explore the conservation potential of sacred groves. [112] But conservation managers often undervalue such religious and spiritual values. These sites are treated as idiosyncratic and not in keeping with scientific conservation. They may acknowledge their existence but not their underlying rationale. Yet such areas contain valuable biodiversity and may indicate relic vegetation that survives despite seeming relentless pressures for conversion. Some religions ignore or downplay how important sacred trees and groves are and try to subsume them into formal religion. For example, consider how pre-Christian sacred yew trees and groves became part of Christian graveyards. [138] These yew trees were places of worship for Druids and earlier spiritual traditions well before Christians established churches.

The World Bank's vice president, Dr. Shahid Husain, noted in 1986, "The discounting procedures we use to make judgment about how fast we can or should deplete natural resources are basically moral value judgments. Explicitly or implicitly, we make a moral judgment when we say that this generation, or any generation, has the right to make decisions for the future simply by having an adequate discount rate." [39] This is an indictment of economic models of valuation and the tacit acknowledgment how important other values of nature are. For trees and forests, given ever-increasing pressures, it is time we accept the importance of moral and sacred values as tools for conservation and land usage. It will help people secure their livelihoods and cultural identities and strengthen their spirituality. The book explores these linkages and draws on examples from across the globe, different religious, and spiritual backgrounds.

Through science we seek truth. Through spirituality we seek goodness, and through art we seek beauty. With our heads we think and know the truth—that is science. With our hearts we cultivate and live goodness (the right life)—that is spirituality. With our hands we create and communicate beauty—that is art. Science, spirituality, and art are a continuum. [65] Yet many of us view spirituality with unease as we do not know what it means. This unease matters because spirituality is part of our lives. But as we find it difficult to embrace a coherent expression of spirituality, we say it lacks credibility. [107] It is only recently that religious, cultural, and educational sectors are taking the ecological movement seriously. To the ecologist, survival is only possible if we acknowledge we are a part of the Earth, yet this is still not fully acknowledged by industry and dominant economic growth approaches. [10]

The challenge of our time is to nurture sustainable communities so that their ways of life, business, economy, physical structures, and technologies respect and honor nature's ability to sustain life. We must understand how nature sustains life [21] as nature is not a luxury. We don't realize how nature elevates us both personally and politically. [132] In the book I show the importance and relevance of sacred trees and groves as one way to nurture sustainable communities and how nature sustains us in so many ways. The book covers the following:

> Chapter 1 introduces the scale and scope of sacred trees and groves from conservation as well as spiritual and religious perspectives where intangible values are at least as important as the tangible ones. Though not a focus, I introduce the importance of sacred

landscapes. Many sacred trees and groves occur in these sacred landscapes.

Chapter 2 looks at the long history of sacred trees and groves—a history that predates formal religion and conservation. While we depended on nature in ancient days, we also sought and received spiritual sustenance from sacred nature. The World Tree and the Tree of Knowledge developed from this. I draw lessons for our contemporary world.

Chapter 3 explores the scale of sacred trees on Earth. Though not exhaustive, the chapter provides examples from across the globe of why and how sacred trees are important. I outline various lessons that are important for religious and spiritual traditions and for conservation.

Chapter 4 provides a similar analysis and recognizes an even greater diversity of types and sizes of sacred grove. Sacred groves exist under various political, conservation, religious, and administrative regimes. A series of opportunities and lessons show how sacred groves can be recognized, respected, and managed in our contemporary world.

Chapter 5 shares practical ideas on how we can better respect sacred groves and their custodians as both being important spiritually and for conservation. The conservation movement has examples of indigenous and community-conserved areas (ICCAs). However, the practice of ICCAs ought to build on and respect why such sites are sacred. Hence, there are several principles we can use.

Chapter 6 discusses the spirituality of sacred trees and groves in terms of conservation under the principle of stewardship. It acknowledges the varied roles trees and forests play. Stewardship is common to conservation and spirituality. It is to hold something in trust. This is the basis for our connection with nature and how religious and spiritual groups and the conservation movement can support this. I suggest practical ideas how we can achieve this with the importance of local governance.

Chapter 7 broadens the debate to see how sacred nature can guide us in solving some contemporary challenges humankind face, including (a) children not getting enough access to nature (nature deficit disorder), (b) how nature can improve our health and well-being, and (c) understanding how nature can help create and build peace in our troubled world. I highlight the role sacred trees and sacred groves can play. I provide simple practical guidance to put this into practice.

Chapter 8 summarizes the key messages and practical steps we can take as individuals, communities, and nations. In this way, the importance of sacred trees and groves will be better respected and built upon by religious and spiritual groups, by both the conservation and environmental movements, and by us in our individual and family capacities. We can all plant and nurture a tree somewhere. We can all hold a tree of our choice to be sacred—at least for ourselves.

Generations of people regarded trees as a source of wisdom. Holy men, kings, queens, and many others all consulted trees. They are often sacred as they have the spirits of dead ancestors. Trees are metaphors for many things—youth, old age, fertility, ancestry. [2] We find trees and woody species everywhere on Earth—the obvious exceptions being the true desert landscapes (e.g., Sahara, Gobi) and the Arctic and Antarctic systems. Wherever there are trees, there are sacred trees and often sacred groves. Their presence, longevity, and sacredness transcend race color and creed. Every religious tradition and spiritual group have sacred trees and sacred groves.

Sacred trees and sacred groves are important entry points for diverse groups to connect humankind, nature, and spirit and so help us find solutions for many of humankind's ills. We can all have or find our piece of nature that is sacred to us. It could be a sacred tree or grove or part of our garden or a tree in the park or a potted tree in our home. They help us reconnect with nature, respect how important nature is, and serve as a basis for finding solutions to many of the challenges we face regarding nature, our spirituality, education, health, and peace. Sacred trees and sacred groves are portals for us to engage and reconnect.

Religious and Spiritual Origins in a Time of Natural Resource Dependence and Abundance

CHAPTER 2

When I think that one man alone, relying only on his own physical and spiritual resources, has been able to make the wilderness flower into a land of peace and plenty, I find human nature is to be admired. When I consider the unremittingly generous spirit, the devoted selflessness, needed to bring about this achievement, I am filled with respect for this unlettered elderly countryman who successfully carried out a work worthy of God
—Jean Giono [23]

Our Origins Are in Nature

Nature housed our spiritual and religious origins and made up our livelihoods on which people depended when major religions and spiritual traditions formed. Many people continue to depend directly on nature, and we all depend on nature in one way or other. People developed cultural and spiritual ties relating to important natural resources—trees in particular—that are featured in all the sacred texts. Because many rituals relating to nature and the environment evolved in ancient times, it is more difficult to understand them in terms of modern mind-sets. Such rituals may bear little relation to nature, [42] but they are critical components of our relationship with and dependency on nature. Culture shapes terrestrial nature, and nature and culture go together like subject and object. [16] This helps us embrace the sacredness of nature as the source.

When we document rituals of the past, we must understand the experience created by those rituals and the conditions that shaped them. There may be spiritual experiences in their origins when people depended on nature. For example, in an ancient Hindu ritual, when you touch the ground and your heart, you can feel energy flowing from the earth to your heart. Do we still feel that energy today?[t] It is essential to understand spiritual traditions in terms of how they were formed and their relevance in today's changing world. In early times, the natural world was organic, living, and valued. This changed when material, scientific, and economic perspectives began to dominate. We lost our sense of the sacredness of nature. [14] Now in our materially driven world, the separation between religion, spirituality, and the environment widens. Reconnecting with nature by using sacred trees and groves can help us hold nature as sacred and honor the SNS of all races, colors, and creeds.

Wherever we find trees, they are culturally and spiritually important—whether they are individual trees (e.g., ancient trees or trees where something important happened) or in groves (e.g., where they buried important people). They are Sacred Natural Sites (SNSs)[u]. The resilience of such trees and groves transcend race, culture, and creed. People revered trees, sacred groves, and certain landscapes for thousands of years. [5] Many African myths say that man was born from a tree. [11] The Bible has more than 525 references to trees. Trees are the oldest organisms people will ever see. [41]

Westerners can no longer ignore non-European philosophies of nature. Spiritual beliefs imbuing nature with spirituality are ancient and widespread. The sacred writings of Hindu and the teachings of North American traditions all have a strong sense of Mother Earth. Taoism (verse 8) states, "The best are like water, bringing help to all without competing, choosing what others avoid they thus approach the Tao; dwelling with earth, thinking with depth, helping with kindness, speaking with honesty, governing with peace, working with skill, and moving with time, and

---

[t] Pers. Comm Manisha Gutman, eCoexist, Pune, India, March 2010.
[u] This is a territory or area of land or water or one "of rich and diverse nature" having special spiritual significance to peoples and communities. [62]

because they don't compete, they aren't maligned." [61] So too should we emphasize cooperating with nature, respecting its wisdom, and living under its ways. [14]

Conservation managers undervalue the religious and spiritual values of nature. But the continued survival of sacred trees and groves despite seemingly insurmountable land usage, conservation, religious, and cultural pressures attest to their resilience. [5] Sacred trees and groves transcend materialism. Most formal religions downplay the contemporary importance of sacred trees and groves [22] irrespective of the importance attributed to them in the sacred texts.

Religion can play a pivotal role in stewarding nature as God's creation, as religion once imbued people with conserving creation as a priority. [24] Now religion is affected by shifts from the traditional (values, culture, and spirituality) to the modern world (materialism and economics). There are exceptions as religion is now rediscovering its way regarding Earth by returning to our sacred roots. [24] When the mainstream religions expanded, they absorbed (or tried to) traditional belief and spiritual practices, especially Christianity (perhaps because it is better documented). In Ireland, Christianity absorbed sacred trees found in places of pre-Christian worship, including sacred wells, around graveyards (e.g., yew trees) and groves. [66]

Ancient forests provided people with shelter, food, and medicine and helped shape their consciousness. The Druids of Europe, like the Celts, had close spiritual relations with trees. [10] Most sacred trees of the early Christian era in Ireland were close to wells. [66] Many of the more than three thousand holy wells in Ireland are associated with sacred trees, though the holy wells may be more important. [66] For example, of 210 holy wells surveyed, 103 had sacred hawthorn trees. More than 1,600 Irish towns contain the word *doire* or oak. This shows how important the Irish oak is, [44] which we should not disturb for fear of provoking the fairies. [6] Eastern religions have a similar respect and reverence.

In ancient times we depended on nature as religious and spiritual traditions were evolving. While these ancient spiritual experiences of nature are important, we need to reinterpret them in our contemporary world so that the practices are relevant and something we can develop. The Qur-ān says, "There is not an animal [that lives] on the Earth, not a being that flies on its wings, but [forms part of] communities like you. Nothing have we omitted from the book, and they [all] shall be gathered to their Lord in the end" (Qur-ān 6:38). Humans are spiritual but only religious at times. [46] The Qur-ān reflects the fact that Earth belongs to God with humankind as custodians and that nature is a gift of God. But in the rush for development, many seem to neglect the fact that Earth belongs to God. [54]

Trees—A Key Ingredient for Life, Culture, Spirituality, and Religion

The ancient forests provided shelter, food, and medicine. These forests shaped people's consciousness as they tried to make sense of the world. Many large slow-growing trees were objects of deep reverence, making them sacred. They evoke a sense of the immortal and are at the center of sacred cults. The ancient yews (*Taxus baccata*) found in churchyards throughout northern Europe testify to this mystical aura (see box 7). The Druids of Europe had close spiritual relationships with trees (see box 8) and sometimes still do as some of these systems are being revived. Likewise, the Celts in Europe and Ireland had close spiritual relations with trees (see box 9).

The oak was sacred in Europe and Scandinavia long before the Druids. In the shadow of groves of oak trees in Ireland, St. Columba established the monasteries of Durg and Durrow, whose names originate from the oak. [51] The oak is featured in mystical traditions and folklore from the ancient Greeks to the North American First Nation peoples and from the Norsemen to the Druids. [17] In many English villages, an ancient oak tree may be found on the village green. Where I grew up in Ireland, the village of Castlebellingham (County Louth) had an ancient oak tree on the roundabout, but it died and was replaced. Such ancient sacred trees emanate a sense of power, timelessness, and silence.

The Druids worshipped the oak and invoked it in rituals. The strength and fertility of the oak (*Quercus robur*) made it the symbol of kingship (see box 8). Another tree rich in mythology is the holly (*Ilex aquifolium*). In Ireland, when confronted by the devil, who had killed his servant with a holly stick, St. Colmcille hurled the stick back and cast the devil out of the valley, and that's where the stick grew into a holly tree reputed to still survive. The hazel is associated with wisdom. The yew is the longest living and a guardian tree. It protects the dead. Like the oak, the yew is linked to kingship and war because of its use in making bows and spears. [6]

A similar respect still occurs in Eastern religions. While many traditions relating to trees died out or were absorbed into Abrahamic religions in Europe, this did not occur as much in Eastern religions. For example, the teachings of Buddha still enjoin a reverent nonviolent attitude toward human beings and place a great emphasis on trees. Buddhists should plant and establish trees every few years. [55] As long as Buddhists did this, India was covered with trees. If people had continued to observe this practice, imagine how many trees India would have now! [58]

Trees are the most important of the seven crops of Israel, including the olive (*Olea europaea*), fig (*Ficus carica*) and date palm (*Phoenix dactylifera*). The date is important in the tabernacle ritual. The Bible, Qur-ān, and Thalmud all mention the date. [28; 63] The pomegranate (*Punica granatum*) is the fruit of Israel. It is sacred to Egyptians and Greeks. Muḥammad (Peace Be Upon Him) once remarked, "Eat the pomegranate, for it purges the systems of every hatred." [10]

Box 7: The Yew Trees in Ancient Europe

No other tree represents longevity more than the yew (*Taxus baccata*). The Fortingall yew (Perthshire, Scotland) is about five thousand years old with a circumference of seventeen meters at its base! One of the oldest trees in the world, the area around the Fortingall yew has been sacred for more than five thousand years as a burial ground. It was an important Christian center in AD 7, though the church was built in the 18th century. The yew tree is sacred from before the Neolithic period (4,000–2,000 BC). Yew trees are associated with immortality, and it's hard to stand beside the branches of the Fortingall yew and not think about its history. The tree is much older than the churchyard. Now few large yews grow outside graveyards. A rich yew lore evolved in pre-Christian societies across Europe. Christianity absorbed many of these traditions. The yew's ability of renewal gives it the name "Tree of Life," as it is a symbol of immortality and life after death. In pre-Christian times, people associated such evergreen trees with immortality. A European yew cult was one of the first expressions of reverence, where the yew is a guardian against evil. People use yews as a substitute for palm fronds on Ash Wednesday and still use flowering male branches on Palm Sunday in Ireland as they refer to the yew tree as "palm."

They often built Christian churches on or close to pagan sacred sites, though some churches may be older than the yew trees. Early Christians may have planted yew trees, or the yew trees may be much older. There is no single reason why old yew trees are so common in churchyards. Reasons include being a symbol of eternity, ability to regenerate, and poisonous foliage to deter the grazing of graveyards. Churchyard yews may predate the church or were planted when the church was built. For example, the yew tree in the ruins of the Franciscan Friary at Muckross, County Kerry, in Ireland grows at the precise center of the cloister of the abbey. Was the abbey built around the yew, or the yew planted afterward? The local people believe the Yew came to Muckross before the men of God.

In the crescent of land encompassing parts of the British Isles and Ireland, great yews are found in old churchyards. Many of these trees pre-date Saxon and Norman churches. They were already on holy ground and places of pre-Christian ceremonies. Where Christianity was adopted, some groves were desecrated, though many were integrated. This provided for shelter as the yew groves were sheltered places, and a ready source of wood for construction.

The Doomsday book (1086) mentions the yew. An Irish legend states that High King Lonchobur put yew stakes between the graves of Deirdre and Naoise to separate them. But the stakes grew together and joined the lovers in death. In Ireland, they venerated individual yew trees. Many sacred yew trees are considered immortal, and one of the five mythical trees is the yew. The yew tree has become

> a symbol of resurrection, hope, and wisdom. The yew has been the subject of many poems and stories (e.g., Tennyson's "In Memoriam" or Wordsworth's "Yew Trees"). The yew became the favorite tree of graveyards, and its age is a testament to the transience of memory and the frailty of human experience. The ancient yews (*Taxus baccata*) found in many churchyards through northern Europe testify to its mystical aura.
>
> Sources: [2, 18, 31, 35, 39, 47, 49, 51, 65, 66], and http://www.woodlandtrust.org.uk/blog/2014/12/fortingall-yew/ accessed Feb 2015

For Muslims, the tree reaching beyond the seventh heaven is the symbol of *hakikat* or state of beatitude where a mystic is united with supreme reality. [11] In Islam, conservation of the environment states that all components of the environment were created by Allah for the sustenance of humankind and other creatures on the planet and that there is a meticulous and optimum balance. [32] The Qur-ān makes powerful reference to this "due balance" (Qur-ān 15:19–20). "And the Earth we have spread out; set thereon mountains firm and immovable; And produced therein all kinds of things in due balance. And we have provided therein means of subsistence for you and for those whose subsistence you are not responsible." In addition, Muḥammad (Peace Be Upon Him) instructs us to plant trees even as the world comes to an end.[v] "If the end of the world approaches and one of you has a seedling (or plant) in his hand, if he can plant it before the end comes, let him do it." This refers to the date palm. This implies when we lose all hope, planting must continue, even if we do not personally benefit. [32]

The Bible refers to trees in many places. "Declare a tree good and its fruit good, or declare a tree rotten and its fruit rotten, one or other, for you can tell a tree by its fruit" (Mathew 12:33). "For the Lord Your God is bringing you into a good country, a land of streams and water, of springs, of fountains welling up in the hills and valleys, a land of wheat and barley, of vines and fig trees and pomegranates, of olive trees and of honey … But when you have eaten your fill, you must bless the Lord, your God for

---

[v] Accessed November 2014. https://qbg.org.qa/content/plants-citations-holy-quran-and-hadith-0.

the good country he has given you" (Deuteronomy 8:7–10). Genesis 43:1 mentions "some balm, and honey, gum, and resin, and pistachios and almonds." Abraham planted a grove near Beer Sheva, while oases were sacred because of the trees and water. [51]

> **Box 8: Druids and Sacred Trees** [1, 2, 10, 51]
>
> Druid customs about trees guided people as to how to treat trees and their sacred values, in particular the oak. Contemporary Christianity integrated many Druid customs, though people do not often acknowledge this. Druids burned fires of Scots pine (*Pinus sylvestris*) in the winter solstice to encourage the coming of the sun. From this grew the tradition of burning the Yule log or Christmas tree. Holly, ivy, and mistletoe are part of Christmas festivals, but all have pre-Christian origins. The holly tree was sacred to Druids and, like the yew, represents immortality, with the evergreen leaves symbolizing the tenacity of life. The gift of holly is given at the Roman feast of Saturnalia, close to the winter solstice, and has become a tradition at Christmas. Druids' veneration is strong for large oak trees. Such consecrated trees were often circular or oblong. The oak is one of the most worshipped trees. It was held sacred by the Druids and the Celtic priesthood of Gaul, Brittany, and Ireland. If Druids found mistletoe growing on oak trees, the tree was even more holy.

The Old Testament of the Bible has many references to talking trees. Judges 9:37 described the "tree of the diviners" at Shechem. A mulberry tree (*Morus nigra*) told David (Samuel 2:5) when to attack the Philistines, and God spoke to Moses from a burning bush. [10] The Bible tells us John the Baptist survived in the desert by eating locusts and honey. Here locust refers to the locust beans of the carob tree. [58] The Talmud often mentions the carob (*Ceratonia siliqua*), while the Judas tree (*Cercis siliquastrum*) is the tree on which Judas hanged himself after informing on Jesus.

Our Future in Nature: Trees, Spirituality and Ecology

Box 9: Sacred Trees and the Celts of Ireland [6, 20, 31, 30, 35, 40, 66]

Our ancestors in Ireland respected trees. Brehon Law protected them. Of particular importance is the link between sacred trees and royal inauguration sites. Rival tribes in Ireland destroyed trees sacred to their enemies. Even today *lone bushes* occur beside the remains of these forts, and people now regard them as the abode of the fairies. Trees dominated the views of the Celts of Ireland and the forces they represented. There is a long tradition of tree veneration. Galatians conducted rituals at a *drumemeton* (or oak sanctuary or sacred oak grove) on the east of the Celtic world. The city of Derry (Northern Ireland) means Oak Grove. The tree lore was well developed in Ireland. Certain trees were magical—the yew (*Taxus baccata*), oak (*Quercus robur*), hazel (*Corylus colurna*), hawthorn (*Crataegus monogyna*), alder (*Alnus glutinosa*) and mountain ash (*Sorbus aucuparia*). The sacred sites of pre-Christian Ireland are *nemeton* or groves of trees. These played important roles in the lore of Druids. Individual revered trees are called *bile,* and they include the oak, yew, and ash. Ancient Irish chiefs performed inaugural ceremonies under sacred trees.

Trees are associated with the early Christian churches (*cill*) as they are found on pre-Christian sacred sites. Many early Irish saints are associated with trees and sacred groves. St. Kevin threatened "hell and short life to anyone who should burn either fresh or dry wood from his forest forever" in the pre-Christian sacred groves of Glendalough, many of which still exist. These trees are now found on monastic grounds. Sacred Irish trees feature in many poems (e.g., the "Dindshenchas"). The ancient texts of Irish law contained information on trees. This is the *Bretha Comaithchesa* (Judgment of Neighborhood) from about AD 8. It includes a section on damage to trees. They divide the twenty-eight main trees into four classes of seven trees each because of their economic worth, based on which special fines were levied for interfering with those trees. The most precious species (oak, hazel, holly, yew, ash, pine, and apple tree) formed the *Airig Fedo* or the nobles of the wood for chieftain trees. The other three classes were *Aithig Fedo* (commoners of the wood), *Fodla Fedo* (lower divisions of the wood), and *Losa Fedo* (bushes of the wood). There was high esteem for trees in Ireland. Maybe there are lessons for contemporary respect for trees in Ireland.

The early Irish alphabet (from about 600 BC), the *Ogham* or *Beth-Luis-Nuin,* has twenty-five letters, each with its own name of a tree, plant, or natural element. People used the tree alphabet till about AD 700, and they hid it in the monasteries of the early Celtic church. Its use was symbolic relating to Celtic spirituality and philosophy. Of the twenty-five letters, trees account for seventeen. They include birch (B), rowan (L), alder (F), willow (S), ash (N), hawthorn (H), oak (D), holly (T), hazel (C), apple (Q), ivy (G), blackthorn (S), elder (R), silver birch (A), white poplar (E), yew (I), and beech (Ph).

Olive branches are emblems of peace and friendship. There are many accounts in the Bible of its uses as food and its symbolic importance. It is said the Angel Gabriel carried an olive branch and was a symbol given to the Virgin Mary. It is still the oil of consecration in the Catholic church. [10] Just like an olive, which yields its oil only when pressed, so too do we yield what is best only when pressed in the millstones of life. [52] In Hebrew, the Menorah was lit with "clear oil of crushed olives" (Exodus 27:20), and "only with olive oil which is a light unto the world" (Yalkut Shimoni verse 1,378). When the angel of the Lord told Sarah she would bear Isaac, "Her face shone like the Olive tree." [28, 63] The olive, the most mentioned fruit in the Bible, is slow-growing and long-lived. [30] For example, some olive trees in the garden of Gethsemane are more than two thousand years old. The Bible (Exodus 27:20, Judges 9:8–9, Romans 11:24) and the Qur-ān (23.18) mention the olive.

The pomegranate shows how individuals may be empty yet full of good deeds. "Your lips are like a scarlet strand; your mouth is lovely. Your cheek is like a half pomegranate behind your veil" (Song of Songs 4:3). Pomegranates are divided into compartments. A person can do many good deeds; however, these are isolated acts, and they have little effect on character. People may have many virtues and be full of good deeds, yet they remain spiritually hollow. The pomegranate is our capacity to overreach and act in ways surpassing our internal states. [52]

The date represents our capacities for peace, tranquility, and perfection, which can blossom in our souls when we are at peace with ourselves and achieve a sense of harmony. Thus, the psalmist sings, "The just man shall flourish like the palm tree, like a Cedar of Lebanon shall he grow. They that are planted in the house of the Lord shall flourish in the courts of our God. They shall bear fruit even in old age" (Psalm 92:13–15). While the olive and date describe two different spiritual personalities, they both exist in every person. [52]

Tree worship played important roles in Neolithic and Bronze Age cultures. Old trees became objects of folklore and places of historical importance. There are many well-known ancient oak trees in England, [35] including the Conqueror's Oak in Windsor Park, where William of Normandy was sheltered, and the Abbots Oak near Woburn Abbey where they hanged the abbot in 1537 when Henry VIII dissolved the monasteries. Perhaps the most famous oak is in Sherwood Forest, where Robin Hood is said to have lived. [21] The literature about ancient trees is more available in Europe and with the main religions. There seems to be less literature on sacred trees in ancient times from the Americas, Asia, and Africa. The religions of the world offer important links for people, conservation, and spirituality as more than 5.77 billion people follow a particular belief. That's about 76 percent of the world's population.[w] For these formal belief systems, trees are an important component, so it is important that people become more aware about and act on that importance in their contemporary lives.

The World Tree, Tree of Life, and Tree of Knowledge

> Sorrow is knowledge: They who know the most
> Must mourn the deepest o'er the fatal truth,
> The Tree of Knowledge is not that of Life.
> —Lord Byron [12]

The World Tree, Tree of Life, and Tree of Knowledge are often confused, yet may mean different things. The Tree of Life is not the same as the Tree of Knowledge, which is associated with Christianity and the expulsion of Adam and Eve from Eden (Genesis 3:24). The sacred fig tree (*Ficus religiosa*) is both. It was sacred for hundreds of years before the Buddha attained enlightenment under a fig tree. This is also called the Tree of Enlightenment.[x] Many creation myths focus on the tree as a central element where the tree was a symbol of power, wisdom, fertility, and life. [11] In Europe, the sacred tree symbolized how important trees are to humankind. *Yggdrasil*, the World Tree (and the Tree of Life) of the Norse sages, kept Earth safe for the coming of humankind. [58] It was the axis of the world where the Nordic god Odin sacrificed himself. [53] *Yggdrasil*, an

---

[w] Accessed May 2018. https://en.wikipedia.org/wiki/List_of_religious_populations.
[x] M. Shanahan wrote an excellent book on the history of the fig tree. [56]

enchanted and great ash tree (*Fraxinus excelsior*), is a guardian tree and was sacred to the Norse gods of Odin, Thor, and Loki, with roots extending through the universe. [10, 29] In many African myths, man was born from a tree. They called the great hero of the Hottentot in Namibia, *Heitsi-Eibeb*, meaning Great Tree. [11] While in nearly treeless deserts, the date palm became the Tree of Life for early Semites and Assyrians, [3] which helps account for the importance of the date palm to Christianity and Islam.

Trees are linked with wisdom—the Tree of Knowledge. This is the talking tree in many parts of Africa where elders meet. [11] With formal religion, popular traditions and spiritual practices relating to nature and trees lost significance as sacred trees were considered unimportant. [66] Yet the tree as a religious and spiritual symbol dates to at least 3 BC. [53] Trees are at the center of the world, as they are part of three cosmic zones—the underworld, the earth, and the sky. [53] People associated trees with fertility as Artemis is the tree divinity with many breasts who is mother of the earth and embodies powers from which all life originates. The tree is a complex of roots, trunk, branches, and leaves, showing a strong coherence and practical efficiency as expressed by the cosmic tree and the Tree of Life. [7]

For many societies trees symbolize a bridge to heaven, ascension to the sky world. [15, 53] Some use an inverted tree to show that life extends from above (heaven and sky) downward (earth, roots, and underworld). "Imagination is a tree. It has the integrative virtues of a tree. It is root and boughs. It lives between Earth and sky. It lives in the Earth and in the wind. The imagined tree imperceptibly becomes the cosmological tree, the tree which epitomized a universe which makes a universe" (Gaston Bachelard).[y]

Since ancient times, trees played important roles in religious beliefs as they were a symbolic power. Trees and forest groves were God's first temples. The Celts practiced religious rituals within sacred groves, and the magical and spiritual role of trees were important during Greek and Roman times. But while people venerated individual trees and groves, the people of the Bronze and Iron Ages also had real or imagined fears of forests. Such fears

---

[y] Accessed June 2018 https://www.azquotes.com/quote/779707.

of the forest had different motivations than revering trees, though the two are linked. [38]

The tree, a symbol of nature and life, is important as part of wider religious and spiritual symbolism. Tree worship relates to their seeming immortality compared with man's short life. The image of the great tree with its roots far into the underworld, with a pillar-like trunk containing blood-like sap, and with branches reaching into the heaven became embedded in human consciousness. [38]

Trees played important roles in creation stories across the globe—Norse, Kung, Iroquois, Christian, Sumerian, Germanic, and Korean peoples. Russians equate the Tree of Life with the cross of Jesus Christ, which they call the new life-bearing tree. [59] Speaking trees, the Tree of Knowledge, the Tree of Life express the spiritual quality of trees. [34] In Korea, sacred groves are important as the conduit between the sky gods and goddesses, the earth and humanity. The deities enter the leaves of certain species, journey down the trunk, and travel underground through the roots, coming to rest in man-made shrines.

The book of Genesis refers to the Tree of Life and Knowledge. "Out of the ground, the Lord God made various trees grow that were delightful to look at and good for food, with the Tree of Life in the middle of the garden and the Tree of Knowledge of good and bad" (Genesis 2:9). From the earliest records, trees are at the center and are often seen as the world axis. [13] The Tree of Life is a unifying image and transcends race, culture, and time. In Genesis, the Tree of Life was unattainable, and the Tree of Knowledge was forbidden. Yet two thousand years before Genesis was written, the fruits of the Sumerian tree offered wisdom and eternal life. [13]

The components of trees are spiritually significant. The roots anchor it to the ground and supply it with water and nutrients. The trunk, branches, and leaves make up its body. The fruit has the seeds by which the tree reproduces itself. The spiritual life of man also includes roots, body, and fruit. Roots represent faith. Trunks, branches, and leaves are our intellectual, emotional, and practical achievements. The fruit is our power of spiritual procreation. Roots are the least glamorous yet the most crucial. Buried underground and invisible, a tree cannot survive without roots. [13] In a similar way, faith is the least glamorous of our spiritual faculties, yet it is the foundation.

The symbol of the Tree of Life has within it a paradox. The tree draws its strength from the earth through its roots, while humans draw their strengths from the divine in the heavens. But trees actually draw sustenance from heaven in the form of sunlight for photosynthesis. This paradox is acknowledged in the upside-down representations of the Tree of Life. In the Vedic texts and the Upanishads of the Hindus, the universe is a tree upside down. The Laplanders sacrifice a prize animal every year to the god of vegetation, and they place a tree beside the altar with its roots in the air and crown to the ground. In Australia, some groups use a magical tree in ceremonies, which they plant upside down as a symbolic gesture. In Africa, the Baobab is the upside-down tree. [11; 64] Its shape, longevity, and water storage abilities made it the Tree of Life for many societies. It is sacred to all, and it is the subject of creation and other stories (see box 10).

In the Kabbalah, the spiritual text of the Hebrews, there is a diagram of the world in the form of a tree called the Tree of Life. Ten pomegranates of different colors come from the tree and are the *sefiroth,* which are aspects of God. [10] As a result, there is confusion whether the Tree of Life was a fig tree (*Ficus carica*) or a pomegranate tree (*Punica granatum*). The World Tree varies with different areas and groups. The Bodhi or Bo (*Ficus religiosa*) World Tree of the Buddha represents Buddha's universal wisdom and is connected to his birth tree. [51] For Hindus, the World Tree is a banyan (*Ficus benghalensis*) [27].

> **Box 10: The Tree Where Man Was Born** [37]
>
> "The tree where man was born, according to the Nuer of Sudan, still stood within man's memory in the west part of South Sudan and I imagine a great Baobab thrust up like an old root of life in those wild grasses that blow forever to the horizon" (Peter Matthiessen).

The five mythical trees of ancient Ireland (ash, oak, yew, apple, and hazel) are World Trees and grow in the center of the world. Their branches and trunks reach to the heavens. This is a channel for communicating with the divine. The roots reach deep in the soil, connecting the realms of death and spirits. [66] The Tree of Life is featured in early Irish literature and lore [66] and grows in paradise gardens, where it is the last retreat for the souls of the dead. In Africa, these trees are baobabs. In many countries the Tree of Life is the fig tree. Some trees symbolize abundant life, e.g. the olive tree (*Olea europaea*) and baobab (*Adansonia digitata*) as there are many values attributed to these trees both real and mythological. [19]

The Tree of Knowledge in the Earth People philosophy [z] gives the knowledge that forms nature. The Tree of Life symbolizes people and their interactions with creation. If people follow the Red Road or a spiritual life, the Tree of Life will bloom, and the people will prosper. If people follow the Black Road or materialism, the tree will wither. [9] First Nation American people (one of the Earth People groups) may say *Chanunpa*. *Cha* is wood. *Nunpa* is two. The wooden bowl is the world, and the stem is the Tree of Life, which is man.

The original Tree of Knowledge in the garden of Eden was an apple tree. A serpent entwined the tree, and its movement was like the rise of sap in the tree. Fruit and seed follow flower and leaf, which mirrors the continuum of life in fertility. [45] Other authors feel that the fig tree was the Tree of Knowledge in the garden of Eden. [56] But the three Abrahamic religions (Islam, Christianity, and Judaism) agree that the fig tree has been part of the human story for a very long time. [56] Many creation myths feature the fig tree, which is why the fig is sacred to so many.

In Scandinavia, they plant certain trees to symbolize the World Tree (*Yggdrasil*), and they provide porridge as a gift in the festive season to remind people to express gratitude for what trees give us. By taking care of trees, we take care of the World Tree. The care tree is a figurative expression of interdependence and represents nature. [33]

---

[z] Accessed April 2018. http://sittingowl.com/philosophy.htm and http://www.markaronson1.com/earthpeople.htm.

Mpafa (*Ziziphus mucronata*) is the most important tree in the bush in South Africa according to Zulu elders. It feeds all living creatures at different levels, and no one is in the way of anyone else. Giraffes nibble the leaves from the top. Lower down the tree water-buck browse, and still lower, impala browse. Still lower down, porcupines eat the bark, which lets out resin and attracts butterflies, insects, and birds. The baboons eat the red berries, which pass through them, and the seeds fall onto the earth and germinate. The Mpafa is the Tree of Life because it gives life to so many. [13]

Blake reminds us that every tree is a Tree of Life. "The tree which moves some to tears of joy is in the eyes of others only a green thing that stands in the way. Some see nature all ridicule and deformity … and some scarce see nature at all. But to the eyes of the man of imagination, nature is imagination itself." [aa] For Emily Dickinson, not the Bible but nature became her treasured book of revelation. Trees are our ancient mothers. We can create our personal or community World Trees. They can be in a forest or a sacred grove. It can be an individual tree in our garden or a small tree in a pot.

What Can We Learn from Our Ancestors about Conservation and Religion?

Before, during, and after the establishment of formal religions, trees and sacred groves played key roles in the spirituality of humankind. People depended on nature for their sustenance, spirituality, and religions. There are many references and quotations in the religious texts affirming how important nature is. Yet in current religious teaching, their importance appears to be downplayed and at worst, ignored. The conservation movement exacerbates this with language that largely excludes rather than includes people. This is one reason why conservation is not as successful as we think. [48]

[aa] Accessed April 2018. http://www.faena.com/aleph/articles/a-letter-from-the-young-william-blake-in-defense-of-the-imagination/.

Religions ought to engage with conservation organizations in an integrated manner and with other religions and indigenous spiritual traditions. This will help bring faith and spiritual-based groups together for peace, awareness, and education. This calls for humility in being open to learning from others and from ancient and traditional cultures. Nature is not what it is to the scientific mind—an external object to be studied—but a living part of their being. [26] If we respect, understand, and use religious and spiritual learning based on our experiences with nature, trees, mountains, rivers, the seas, and the wind, why are we not responding religiously and spiritually to these realities? [8] The answer relates to our egos and the mistaken notion that we control the earth. If religion was better grounded in the practical realities of ecology, this will build on humankind's role to steward and fulfill our obligations for Mother Earth.

Religious and spiritual people had more important roles in ancient times than they do now. They were societal gatekeepers. The institutions with their rules of practice helped conserve and manage nature, around which community life revolved. But people misinterpret the term dominion to mean control, not stewardship. Many now refute this, including Pope Francis. Such control was one reason for so much destruction of nature. Many religions in their formative times tried to destroy or absorb preformal religious rites. As Christianity became the dominant religion throughout Europe, missionaries, saints, and kings cut sacred groves to consolidate power. [57]

Many indigenous and First Nation peoples are connected to nature. For example, Standing Bear of the Lakota people in North America said, "The Lakota was a true naturist—lover of nature. He loved the Earth and all things of the Earth … The soil was soothing, strengthening, cleansing and healing … Wherever the Lakota went, he was with Mother Earth. There was a great unifying life force that flowed in and through all things … the flowers of plants, blowing winds, rocks, trees, birds, animals–and was all the same force that had been breathed into the first man. We learned to do what only the student of nature learns and that was to feel beauty." [9, 14] In First Nation of America tradition, God, the source of life, is the root of the tree, while the trunk and the branches symbolize the early communities that grew spiritually close to the creator. The leaves represent people. They had a reverential respect for nature. This can help us regain our spiritual respect of nature. But it cannot come from thinking about nature. It comes from being in nature. [60] David Orr says, "We cannot win this battle to save species and environments without forging an emotional bond between nature and ourselves as well—for we will not fight to save what we do not love." [46]

Conservation and spirituality were closely linked in early times and still can be. Population and pressures about land use were low, and the dependency on natural resources was high. They were close to nature, which allowed for spiritual and religious practices to evolve around important natural features (e.g., old trees and forest groves). Women took the side of nature as they collected food, water, and building materials. The ecofeminist view is if Earth dies, humanity will die with it. [25] Yet at some point in history, the essential contributions of women became devalued. This was due to how food became commercialized and commoditized. Food and other natural products moved from the sacred and the home to profit and business. [4] Women are changing their attitudes toward nature from the inanimate to the living and spiritual. Vandana Shiva says we can be that change. We used to eat five hundred species of crops, but now eight dominate.[ab]

The connection to and stewardship of nature are concepts I will return to, and I will show people how to reconnect and become responsible stewards. Science together with an increased perceived separation from nature led to material and consumptive worldviews. I use the term *perceived* as the perception we are or can be separate from nature is an illusion. The perceived separation is exacerbated by our separation from the sacredness of nature so that nature seems like a giant clockwork machine. Many peoples connected with nature know how illusory this is. The spiritual aspects of nature and trees are very much alive. They transcend race, color, and creed, and they occur all over the world.

We can no longer separate nature from spirituality or say nature lacks spiritual values. [43] The Western world has separated nature and reduced

---

[ab] Accessed August 2018. https://www.youtube.com/watch?v=ER5ZZk5atlE.

nature to parts for far too long. This is domination, not stewardship. People thought using science would help them gain power without thinking of the ethical, spiritual, or environmental consequences. Maybe this why international policy and implementation responses are weak. With them, we are subject to technology, finance, and economic growth. [50] Yet at the local level, there is often a huge respect for nature and Mother Earth despite policy that seems to go against that—policies that foster degradation and conversion all in the name of economic growth and human well-being.

Sacred Trees—Diverse in Every Culture and Country

CHAPTER 3

When I want to celebrate, I always plant a tree.
— Wangari Maathai, Nobel laureate[ac]

Truly trees are beings. We feel that to be so. Hence their silence, their indifference to us is almost exasperating
—John Stewart Collis[ad]

Trees are Earth's endless effort to the Listening Heaven
—Rabindranath Tagore [72]

Sacred Trees—Celebrating Diversity

Increased population and land pressures call for different conservation approaches so that we have a greater respect for how important cultural and spiritual values are. Over the past century, utilitarian values and scientific views of nature dominated. Yet people keep many sacred and cultural values despite changes in worldview. It is useful to explore this in scale and scope to show how important our spiritual links with nature are in terms of our daily lives and for conservation.

[ac] Accessed May 2017. www.greenbeltmovement.org.
[ad] Source: [1]

Ancient trees are resilient. They are cut and abused, and they still regenerate. For example, people cut some of the thousand-year-old giant sequoias of California. From their stumps, new trees grew, which are now more than fifty meters tall. [30] But we still ignore the resilience of such trees, and this further disconnects us from nature. Now we must move to more balanced approaches that integrate, not reduce, approaches that respect diversity and complexity, not simplify it. [31]

There are examples everywhere emphasizing the religious and spiritual importance of nature, which survive despite how dominant the scientific views of nature are, together with unprecedented land usage and population pressures. Trees play an important role because of their longevity, size, and shape. In industrialized urban societies, where people are removed from their ties with nature, they lost many of these values and the associated knowledge. Now there are emerging moves to rediscover them. In many rural societies, where nature plays a more important role, there is still—maybe—a strong culture, detailed knowledge, and institutional base relating to the religious and spiritual values of nature. Formal religion or traditional spiritual groups often house such knowledge and experience.

For example, Kajedo Wanderer was a Findhorn gardener for thirty years and was the custodian of the trees. "It was in the company of trees that I felt closest to the greater mystery of life—God," he recalled. [14] How we interact with the land and soil requires us to be kinder, more sensitive, and better tuned into working with the earth. The simple idea that "anyone can dig a hole, put a tree in it, water it, and nurture it" transformed Wangari Maathai's life, and it can transform ours. This simple gesture combats soil erosion and desertification, retains rainwater, provides firewood, and restores biodiversity. [7]

Much knowledge about sacred trees is private and hidden. As it is not technical, people view it as unimportant or backward. The areas covered may not be large in conservation terms to be sustainable. However, if sacred trees and groves are integral parts of social and ecological landscapes, they are part of connectivity within those landscapes and part of a landscape's resilience. Such connectivity is a network as ecosystems are networks. [8]

Such connectivity, relationships, and interdependence are key concepts in ecology. Capra believes deep ecology is the ideal bridge between spirituality and science. [9] Sacred trees and groves are important parts of such multifunctional and interconnected landscapes. Who does not feel a sense of the spiritual when walking in a natural forest or a sacred grove or standing in front of a thousand-year-old tree? Sacred trees and groves are important for many intangible reasons, including the following:

- as residences for spirits;
- they can be important keystone[ae] species such as the universally revered fig tree;
- adorned to identify them as sacred;
- as part of tree ordination;
- as symbols for birth, marriage, and death (the cycle of life and renewal);
- as a result of tradition where important events took place at or close to a certain tree;
- for various utilitarian reasons; and
- as monastic trees.

Trees were important in ancient times as (a) places for warriors to gather before battle (e.g., an old yew tree in Castle Avenue that is linked to the Battle of Clontarf in 1014 in Ireland despite the tree dying in 1993); (b) places of strength and symbols of victory; (c) a living witness to significant events (e.g., battles, conflicts, and memorials to those who died); [82] and (d) a means to resolve conflict (e.g., the trees under which Pokot and Turkana pastoralists in Kenya discuss issues and resolve conflict).

[ae] A keystone species is a species that has a disproportionately large effect on its surroundings relative to its abundance. Such species are described as playing a critical role in maintaining the structure of an ecological community, affecting many other organisms in and around the ecosystem and beyond and helping to determine the types and numbers of various other species in the community. A keystone species is a plant or animal that plays a unique and crucial role in the ways an ecosystem functions. Without keystone species, the ecosystem would be dramatically different or cease to exist (https://en.wikipedia.org/wiki/Keystone_species).

All civilizations viewed trees as sacred, though many more industrialized countries have lost such knowledge. The tree is God's (or the deity's) home, or it is the God himself as happened in early Buddhism. Trees may be associated with the divine because of some incident. For example, Buddhism revolves around Buddha's enlightenment under the bodhi tree. It is the convergence of shade, life of the tree, and silent reflection that facilitated the Buddha's awakening. Here, meditation relates to the silence of our minds, which we can attain under a tree or in a grove. This is a moment of respite, an opportunity for transformation, and the ecological conversion that Pope Frances speaks of. [55]

There are many examples of sacred trees in religious texts, and these may associate the branches of certain trees (e.g., the palm, olive, and laurel) with the gods. We use trees in worship, for example the branches of the bilva (wood-apple tree, *Aegle marmelo*) to celebrate Lord Shiva. The Tulsi (holy basil or *Ocimum sanctum*, see box 14) is a symbol of Laksmi, the Hindu goddess of prosperity. [16] Individual sacred trees can express nature's spiritual linkages with humankind [11]. For example, Nepal has trees and groves that are sacred and worshipped [42] across the landscape as people planted and/or protected them. [34]

As space for conservation reduces because pressures from humans and land usage, sacred trees and sacred places become more important conservation assets. Many sacred trees represent times when forests were more encompassing, and so they can be a basis for restoration. Others are repositories of biodiversity (e.g., the fig or baobab trees, which are both keystone species). So we should respect the sacredness of such trees and groves. The historic desecration of many sacred trees and groves or subsuming them into religion is no longer acceptable given the universality of spiritualism.

We lost our senses of reverence, mystery, and the sacred as we no longer hear the voices of nature. The tree became its utility and economic value. We take large ancient and sacred trees for granted rather than respecting and honoring them. [52] These attitudes became more prominent with the industrial revolution, but such use of trees started long before. For example, the Greeks and Romans had massive wooden fleets and required much timber for their cities. We should accept that trees (and all living beings) have rights to be what they are. Humans have rights, but within the larger context of the planet Earth. If our rights are sacred, then we accept that the rights of other animals, plants, and trees are sacred. [3] Wangari Mathai says, [41] "Trees also have spiritual meaning. I come from a tradition where our ancestors prayed and made offerings to trees. My people were particularly respectful of the fig tree. To them it was a symbol of the power of God—a gift that God gives. In most other traditions round the world, trees have always been symbols of plenty. In the Bible it's a symbol of knowledge. So, a tree is a wonderful gift."

All life on Earth has value and the right to exist. Nature has rights. Trees have rights. When we understand this and recognize the rights of trees and of nature, we are colleagues. [39] Trees are not just artifacts or things people plant, beginning in the nursery and ending as timber. There were trees long before nurserymen. A single five-hundred-year-old oak tree is a world of special complex habitats for which ten thousand hundred-year-old oaks are no substitute. [58] Sacred trees have strong spiritual meanings because of their longevity. Much of the cultural and spiritual knowledge about individual trees is old. Yet this knowledge and spiritual identity is important in contemporary life. Wangari Maathai said, "Trees heal the land and break the cycle of poverty and violence."[af] Many sacred trees are symbolic. The roots are deeply embedded in place in an extensive underground network while the branches spread wide and high in the sky. [38] This is a great illustration of balance and harmony where outward and inward growth complement each other.

Spirits Reside in and around Trees for All Sorts of Reasons

To conserve trees for spiritual reasons is common in many rural and some urban areas. In India, when they felled primary forests, they left majestic trees standing as sacred. In Bambara villages in Niger, there is usually

---
[af] *Daily Nation Newspaper*, Kenya, April 25, 2010, p. 12.

a tamarind tree (*Tamarindus indica*) where the spirits live. Among the Galla in Kenya, a priest consecrates a certain tree. [56] In parts of China, some sacred trees were inscribed with the message "If you pray, you will certainly be heard." The Herero people of Namibia have a sacred tree called *Omumborombongo*, which is their ancestor. The Ashanti of Ghana had a very important sacred tree in Kumasi and the fall of that tree in 1874 was a bad omen. Soon afterward, the British captured Kumasi. [56] Even now there is a sacred grove of 0.5 hectares in the center of Kumasi—a city of more than three million people. The grove's survival there is a testament to its spiritual importance as the land has tremendous economic value. The baobab (*Adansonia digitata*) has cultural associations in Africa and Madagascar because of its shape, longevity, uses, and residence of spirits. [40, 56] In Keren, Eritrea, they consecrated a baobab tree in 1881 as a shrine to the Virgin Mary. [77] It is hollow inside, and this is a place of worship for both Christians and Muslims. In a main shopping street of Hanoi (Vietnam), between two shops stands a fig tree that remains untouched and sacred despite being in the heart of the city.

The tamarind is associated with spirits in India as a symbol of solidarity. [63] The Nile tulip tree (*Markhamia lutea*) is important to the Bagisu of Uganda as a shrine for the spirits, circumcision, and grave-making. The Tulip tree is used to make poles for shrines to the ancestral spirits. [51] While in Zimbabwe, the ancestors conserved groves and trees to foster the relations between people and creation. [67] Certain big trees contain spirits. In some places when people tried to cut them, their hand would be paralyzed, or they would become ill because the trees were where the spirits rested. [66] Shrines for traditional ceremonies occur in thickets or under a big tree in Zimbabwe. [10]

In Ireland (as well as the Isle of Man and Celtic areas), they associate fairies with solitary whitethorn trees (*Crataegus monogyna*). It is considered a meeting tree and symbolizes repentance.[ag] These fairies are earth fairies. People say nothing evil as they fear retribution. The old belief that any damage done to the meeting tree will bring misfortune has not died out.

[ag] Accessed June 2017. http://www.wildflowersofireland.net/plant_detail.php?id_flower=116#glos.

It is often impossible to get workmen to remove thorn trees for a new road or footpath. There are many fairy thorns in Ireland, and many believe in them, so they cannot be cut. [68] In Ireland, people dislike the term fairy and prefer the term little or wee people, and they use the term lone bush. [82]

Apart from fairy thorns, there are other revered thorns that overhang holy wells. They are connected with fifth- and sixth-century saints. People tie rags on them as it is a custom to leave articles of clothing on a branch. Some wells were places of pilgrimage at the time of the early Christian missions to Ireland, and they were also pre-Christian sites of veneration. Pilgrims to such wells hang crucifixes, rosary beads, or pieces of cloth on the thornbushes to acknowledge the cures they get.

Judaism supports the awareness that trees communicate sacred knowledge. Adam and Eve tasted the forbidden fruit of the Tree of Knowledge in the garden of Eden while the Lord appeared to Moses in a burning thorn. Abraham settled near a sacred grove of turpentine and oak trees. The prophetess Deborah lived under a sacred palm tree when the children of Israel came to her for justice. [82]

Rowan (*Sorbus aucuparia*) trees were among the most sacred species in Celtic mythology during pre-Christian times, especially in Scotland and Ireland. They protected the home and farm. The idea of trees as protectors has continued, and people plant them close to homes.[ah] If you cut a branch of a rowan tree and put it on the roof with a piece of timber, the roof will be safe from storms for twelve months. [45] There are examples where ill-thought tree cutting, usually for commercial reasons, was done without considering whether the trees or place were sacred, as box 11 illustrates.

The ancient peoples of the Holy Land revered the cedar of Lebanon (Tree of the Gods, *Cedrus libani*). It is the national emblem of Lebanon. These trees have clung to life in scattered groves in the mists of Mount Lebanon. [52] Hindu people regarded the cedar or Deodara (*Cedrus deodara*) as the Tree of the Gods in India. Other cedars are sacred, including *Cedrus*

[ah] Accessed March 2017. http://www.wildflowersofireland.net/plant_detail.php?id_flower=226.

brevifolia (cedar of Cyprus), *Cedrus atlantica* (Atlas or Algerian cedar). In the Bible, cedars are symbols of power, dignity, and sincerity. In Judaic mythology, the cedar was the main tree of the garden of Eden. They used the cedar of Lebanon to build King Solomon's temple and was a place of pilgrimage for centuries. Psalm 104:16 says, "Well watered are the trees of the Lord, the Cedars of Lebanon, which he planted." The Maronite church elders hold a feast of cedars every August where they bless the trees and ask God to protect the groves. [26, 40, 56, 76]

> **Box 11: Don't Tamper with Trees** [24]
>
> "Beware, beware the hawthorn,
> Lest it strike you down,
> For if you take an axe to it
> You'll rue that you were born."
> (Extract from "Fancy" by John Keats)
>
> Some years ago a logging company sent tree cutters to fell teak trees in part of the Beng forest in Côte d'Ivoire. Well trained in their trade but ignorant of the landscape, they cut several teak trees that served as the abodes of forest spirits. They made no offering to these spirits. The local people say the spirits of these trees were angry because of the loggers destroying their homes. They did not ask forgiveness before or offer any compensation afterward. In cutting the trees, some loggers were injured and others killed by the trees they were felling. The survivors interpreted this as the forest spirits' revenge. So loggers were fearful of the forest spirits and refused to work. The timber companies focused on short-term gain with little thought of sustainability or the forest itself!

Sherpa sacred forests in the Mt. Everest part of Nepal may have evolved from Sherpa and Tibetan beliefs about spirits known as Lu. Lu live in trees near springs and forests. Often they build a small shrine at the base of the Lu tree. The Lu trees are old juniper trees (*Juniperus recurva*), but they can be willows (*Salix triandra*), rhododendrons (*Rhododendron arboretum*), or firs (*Abies pindrow*). While many have shrines at their bases, others are unmarked but recognizable.

In Māori culture in New Zealand, *Hinewaoriki* and *Mumuhnunga* are two of the eight deities that produced large trees. [70] From the *Hinewaoriki* came the *Kahikatea* (*Dacrycarpus dacrydioides*) and Matai trees (*Prumnopitys taxifolia*), and from the *Mumuhunga* came the Tatora tree (*Podocarpus totara*). [70] The Kauri (Lord of the forest, *Agathis australis*) and Totara trees are sacred to the Māoris. The Kauri tree possesses a spirit related to the Māori. If the Māori cut a tree (perhaps for canoes, meeting houses, or shrines), then they would perform spiritual ceremonies beforehand. Giant Kauris are sacred and protected by *Tane*, their supreme being. Protecting the forests protects the home of Māori ancestors and maintains a vital part of Māori culture. Māori believe the Totara tree has a spirit and a common ancestry with the Māori people. The Totara is an elder of living Maoris. Māori people never fell Kauri or Totara trees without a ceremony where they ask for forgiveness. [40, 56, 74] Totara is the greatest Māori tree because of its splendor and the red color of its timber, which is the color of royalty. [74]

Now these ancient sacred trees of New Zealand are under threat. *Tāne Mahuta* is New Zealand's largest living being and most sacred tree. But the forty-five-meter-tall two-thousand-year-old Kauri tree is under severe threat from the devastating Kauri dieback disease, which is spreading largely unchecked through the northern part of North Island. Thousands of Kauri trees, many sacred, are dead or dying.[ai] In Māori mythology, *Tāne* brought trees and birds to Earth. The Waipoua forest, home of *Tāne Mahuta* and other majestic Kauri, is one of the worst affected areas. Yet Kauri dieback occurs meters from *Tāne Mahuta* despite the best efforts of a prevention program since 2009.

Te Kawerau ā Maki, a Māori tribal group with customary authority over the land of the Waitākere forest, placed a *rāhui* (temporary closure) over the forest. But a *rāhui* is not enforceable, and it was ignored. It seems that the Kauri trees' right to live and flourish is of lesser value than recreational tourism. Kauri dieback infection rates increased from 8 to 19 percent in five years. It looks as though government agencies tasked with preserving the intrinsic values of native species are prepared to let this happen. This is a situation where competing values don't balance. The government funds less than NZD $2 million per year for Kauri dieback. Yet the response to recent agricultural biosecurity threats was NZD $54 million. For the

---

[ai] Accessed July 27, 2018, Mathew Hall. https://theconversation.com/lord-of-the-forest-new-zealands-most-sacred-tree-is-under-threat-from-disease-but-response-is-slow-100447?.

survival of *Tāne Mahuta*, the Kauri forests should be closed, and funding should be boosted for implementing a dieback management program.

The Universally Revered Fig Tree

For many societies in Africa and Asia, the fig tree (*Ficus sycomorus, F. religiosa, F. thonningii,* and other species) is holy. [56] In India, when they cut forests, they left fig trees standing as sacred groves. The fig is the fruit of the Tree of Knowledge of Good and Evil. The fig shows our capacity for deep involvement in our endeavors. [60] There are about 750 species of fig, all of which have had an inordinate influence on humankind, shaping our world, influencing our evolution, and nourishing our bodies. [64] The genus *Ficus* is a keystone genus for biodiversity and [25] is sacred in all religions. It is referred to in the Bible (Genesis 3:7; Judges 9:10–11; Amos 7:14; Mark 11:13, 20; Luke 13:6–9) and the Qur-ān (95.01). Given its importance to religious groups and spiritual traditions, figs are also important conservation assets. Fig trees could be one means to restore degraded forests, help stem biodiversity loss, and serve as a bridge between scientific and faith-based worldviews. [64]

People pay homage to the fig tree in every religion and culture where it grows naturally because of its shape, aerial roots, longevity, and fruit. In Eastern culture, this cosmic tree is the center of the universe and part of traditional beliefs. [27] The Vedic people called *F. religiosa* an abode of the gods. [64] The fig tree is the tree of creation, particularly in the tropics. It is the bridge to safety for Tibetan Buddhists. [4] Buddhism states trees have souls as spirits live in the bodies of trees and speaks. [4]

Prince Siddhartha (Lord Buddha) was born under a sal tree (*Shorea robusta*) in full bloom. That is one reason the tree is sacred individually and in groves. [57] Siddhartha attained enlightenment under a bodhi tree in north India. Lord Buddha's death took place in a grove of sal trees in full bloom. The bodhi or peepal tree (*Ficus religiosa*) is a classic representation of the axis of the world and the Tree of Life. [5, 43] Lord Buddha once said, "The forest is a peculiar organism of unlimited kindness and benevolence that makes no demand for its suffering and extends generously the products of its life activity; it affords protection to all beings, offering shade even to the axe-man who destroys it."[aj]

The greatest bodhi tree, the Sri Mahabodhi tree of Anuradhapura in Sri Lanka, is dated from 245 BC. It coincided with Buddhism's arrival in Sri Lanka. [48] This revered tree grew from a cutting brought to Sri Lanka from Bodhgaya on the northern parts of the Ganges in Gaya in Bihar state of India. From that tree they took cuttings to many places, including the royal park at Anuradhapura. They planted a branch in a special enclosure to mark the king of Ceylon's conversion to Buddhism. This is written about in the *Mahavamsa,* the great historical record of Ceylon. The tree still lives. The old shell is gone, but the growth from the original roots and branches is still visible. [45, 64]

Ficus carica (common fig) is the first plant mentioned in the Bible where the prophet Amos was a "shepherd and dresser of Sycamores" (Amos, 7:14). The ancient Greeks believed the fig was a gift from the gods. [64] Prophet Muḥammad (Peace Be Upon Him) declared the fig tree as being sent from heaven. "If a Fruit ever descended from Paradise, I would say that this is it, as heaven's fruits contain no pips. Eat from it as it relieves hemorrhoids and treats gout." [64]

The sycamore fig (*Ficus sycamorus*) embodied various Egyptian goddesses (e.g., Hathor, Nut, Isis). They often buried the pharaohs in coffins made from the sycamore fig, which speeds up their return to the womb of the mother tree goddess. [64] These are described in hieroglyphs dating back to about 2400 BC.

Peepal or bodhi (*Ficus religiosa*) is one of the most important sacred trees for Indian religions and indigenous faiths. Hindu saints plant peepal and banyan trees in and around their hermitages, and they practice penance under them. The banyan (*Ficus benghalensis*) is the World Tree for Hindus as it sheltered the infant Lord Krishna. [25, 56] In Hong Kong, *Ficus*

[aj] Accessed March 1, 2019. https://todayinsci.com/B/Buddha_Gutama/BuddhaGutama-Quotations.htm.

microcarpa is home to spirits, and two of these trees became wishing trees. People threw oranges into the crowns of the trees, to which they had attached wishes they had written down. [64]

> **Box 12: The Giant Fig of the Maasai** [44]
>
> "The Giant Fig, which looks like a small grove in the distance, is at least as old as man's recorded history on this plain. Its spread is not less than 150 ft, the size of six ordinary figs, and it is a true Tree of Life. The tree has a Maasai hearth built into its thick base. One day I would like to sit under this tree that has drawn so much fat wood and fleshy leaves out of near desert, and stare for a week or more into the emptiness. One understands why these monumental figs take on a religious aura; they are thought to symbolize the sacred mountains and the old ways of close kinship with Earth and rain, nature and God" (Peter Matthiessen).

Fig trees are sacred to many groups in Africa. People revere them for their size, area they cover, and association with spirits. [50] The most important species of fig in Kenya Kenya are *Ficus thonningii, F. sycomorus, F. sur,* and *F. exasperata*. [50] The Maasai of East Africa conduct rituals under a sacred *F. thonningii* tree or oreteti in Maasai (see box 12) or mugumo in Kikuyu. Leaders of the Akan of Ghana create a sacred place by planting a fig tree. Wangari Maathai inspired the Plant for the Planet movement,[ak] and her mother told her, "Don't pick any dry wood out of the fig tree, or even around it. Because that's a tree of God! We don't use it. We don't cut it. We don't burn it." [41] The Kikuyu people of Kenya have a grove of sacred fig trees at the center of their creation story. [64] The mugumo tree is sacred to the Kikuyu because the original parents of the Kikuyu—Gikuyu and Mumbi—prayed to God under a mugumo tree. [41] It was because Wangari Mathai said, "People talk too much, we are no longer talking, we are working," that the school children of Plant for the Planet started the campaign "Stop talking. Start planting." [19] As a Chinese proverb notes, "The best time to plant a tree was twenty years ago. The next best time is now!"[al]

[ak] Accessed December 2017. https://www.plant-for-the-planet.org/en/home. See chapter 7 for more details.

[al] Accessed February 2018. https://sayingimages.com/tree-quotes/.

Wangari Maathai claimed some missionaries felled mugumo trees to replace the "God of the tree with the God of the church." While there were incidents of missionaries felling mugumo trees, many were more understanding. It was unlikely that converts would harm sacred fig trees without upsetting the elders. There are also cases of missionaries protecting mugumo trees. Other missionaries found in sacred fig trees opportunities to align the Kikuyu faith with Christianity. These missionaries saw Kikuyu sacrifices at fig trees as similar to Christian ones. They built some churches beside sacred fig trees where Kikuyu elders made sacrifices to their god *Ngai* when the rains failed.[am]

Trees Adorned

Many societies adorn trees with strips of cloth and other items. People adorn the arbor tree (a black poplar) of Aston-on-Clun in Shropshire (England) with multicolored flags. In northern Scotland, a woodland has thousands of rags above the holy well of St. Boniface. [45] The Celts hang cloth on special trees for fertility. There are many trees adorned in Ireland and the practice is being revived. [45, 82] People adorn trees across the globe to express praise, for prayers, and various other reasons. Such trees may be solitary with special features, or they could be particular trees where certain things happened. People adorn trees as a token of veneration for different purposes (see box 13). Some are wishing trees and adorned with rags and ribbons (e.g., the Wishing Tree in Dungiven, County Derry, Ireland). [82]

Residents of Gobi region in Mongolia worship tamarisk trees (*Halaxylon ammodendron*). While people in the Khangai region praise the silver birch (*Betula platyphylla*), cornelian cherry (*Cornus mas*), and juniper (*Juniperus chinensis*) trees. Such trees can be adorned with scarves or *hadach*. [79] Many Mongolians praise single or peculiar trees (called *Udgan Mod* or sacred). People praise them by placing *hadach* or offerings at their base. It is taboo to cut them. In some places, it is sacrilege to even approach

---

[am] Accessed July 2018. https://underthebanyan.blog/2018/04/11/when-happened-when-christian-missionaries-met-kenyas-sacred-fig-trees/.

them. The birch is considered to be faithful to man and livestock because it is commonly used. Children are taught that if they cut growing trees, the trees cry milky tears, resulting in reduced milk yields. People offered prayers to trees so there would be no forest fires. [75]

The most famous black poplar tree in Shropshire, England, is the Arbor tree (*Populus spp.*) of Aston-on-Clun. People decorate this old hollow poplar, which is more than 250 years old with multicolored flags attached to long poles and nailed to the tree. Every year on May 29, people dress the tree with new flags, and a celebration takes place. This is a reenactment of a historic wedding and procession to the tree. Local children dressed in costume meet the bride and groom. People dance by the tree with sprigs of oak. At one time they took cuttings from the tree to give to village brides. The remarkable thing about Arbor Day is that the ancient practice has survived as the ritual has its roots in early pagan fertility rites. The following lines are from the poem of the "Ballad of the Arbor Tree" by Tom Beardsley (1956):

> In Aston Clun stands a tree
> A Poplar dressed like a ship at sea,
> Lonely link with an age long past
> Of Arbor trees, I am the last.

Box 13: Adorning Trees in Veneration—Some Examples [5, 18, 20, 45, 56, 64, 68, 69, 73, 80, 82]

1. Arbor Day in England refers to dressing a tree with flags, a custom that survives from ancient times when they worshipped Bridget, the goddess of fertility, who later became St. Bridget. The goddess had a tree for a shrine, and they hung emblems and prayers on the tree.
2. In parts of the Middle East, travelers can find a solitary tree by a spring covered with red handkerchiefs put there by women who are barren.
3. Trees are adorned for festivities and dancing (e.g., the Dancing Tree in Cloncurry, Kildare, and the Great Ash of Laois in Ireland). In County Offaly, St. Kieran's Bush is a hawthorn tree covered in pieces of cloth.
4. In temples, people associate trees with many ceremonies. They crown and decorate trees. They offer prayers. People kiss trees. They have religious processions, and sacrifices are offered.
5. In Clareen (east of Birr, Ireland), there is a small whitethorn bush called St. Ciarán's tree, which, despite church reforms, is still held in veneration and adorned in cloth rags. Those who hang rags offer prayers for special intentions. When the rags rot, their prayers will be answered. The bush at Clareen is linked to the holy well nearby and is associated with the monastic settlement of St. Ciarán. The thorn is not old, but villagers confirm this is the same bush they dressed for more than forty years. It's likely the present thorn replaced older ones. There is a tree adorned with cloths that "could not be burnt" in Fore Abbey, County Westmeath, Ireland. Rag offerings were and still are an important means to honor a sacred tree and obtain a cure or have wishes fulfilled.
6. In Siberia, Yakuts hung pieces of iron and brass on a fine tree as a basis for chanting to the spirits of the forest, while the Slavs of Russia offered prayers to hollow trees and adorned certain trees with pieces of cloth.
7. Adorning trees with prayers, white pieces of cloth, or religious pictures is common in Celtic society. These trees occur in Ireland and the Isle of Man. In St. Brigid's well in Kildare, Ireland, there is a single-prayer rag tree or *clootie*. Researchers carried out a survey in 2001 on May bushes that people adorned with pieces of cloth, eggshells, or string in County Offaly, Ireland. They noted thirty-two such May bushes.
8. North of Inverness in Scotland, you enter Black Isle near the village of Munlochy. Here people covered the woodland with thousands of different sized and colored rags above the holy well of St. Boniface, known as the Cloutie Well. It has attracted those who want answers to prayers over many centuries. Such offerings are where people place objects (e.g., pieces of cloth) on trees without any intention to recover or use them. This place is like St.

> Ciaran's bush. The difference is the sheer numbers of rags decorating the trees.
>
> 9. In north India, married women tie colored threads on a Banyan tree (*Ficus benghalensis*) as they pray for well-being.

Trees Ordained

In the struggle of the Karen in Wat Chan, Thailand, a Buddhist monk used the ritual of *Buat Pa* (or forest ordination). In Buri Ram Province, southeast Thailand, the Buddhist monk (Phra Pachak Kuttijitto) ordains trees as monks to protect them from illegal logging. He wraps them in the sacred yellow cloth of Buddha. He realized that you "cannot take the forest out of Buddhism, as the Buddha reached enlightenment in the forest" and that "we must take only what we need and we must remember ... impermanence." In another place he asked villagers to donate an area for a *khet paaphiyathan* or land of forgiveness, where they forbid tree felling. [23] This was and is a common practice as part of the struggles for legal recognition of community forests. It uses two Buddhist concepts—*buat*, which alludes to the ordination of monks, and *pa*, which is an abbreviation of *paaphiyathan* or a religious forest where no one can violate trees or animals. In these areas Buddhist monks wrap the largest, oldest trees with the sacred orange cloth of Buddhism. No trees are cut as local people working for illegal loggers feel this act would be like killing a monk. This moral dimension of a community forest helps villagers reconstruct their rights as protectors and negotiate with the state for greater legal rights. [23] In both Cambodia and Thailand, monks wrap monastic robes around trees. This means they are ordained into the monastic lineage. Since their culture does not see sanctity in nature as much as it sees sanctity in the monks, this helps change people's perception of forests. [6]

Trees as Part of Birth, Marriage, and Death

In Kenya, people plant mugumo (sycamore fig) trees to honor deceased male relatives or clan ancestors. These trees are sacred, and to cut them is taboo. [37] Ramogi sacred hill and forest (283 hectares) in western Kenya is where the Luo settled and is named after Ramogi, the sacred Luo ancestor. [50]

People plant trees at the birth of a new era as a symbol of marriage or birth. Amongst the Sioux of North America and the San and Hottentots of South Africa, when people marry, they first marry trees. The Dravidian people of southern India marry two trees. [5] Many people plant trees at the birth of a child as a symbol of the tree growing with the child. [56] In parts of Nepal, they practice tree marriage (with peepal, neem, or sacred basil). [35] In Jimiti in Odisha State of India, a banyan and a peepal were married to raise awareness about trees. [64] The Warramunga of north Australia believe some trees harbor a child's spirit. People plant trees during marriages, while in some societies, couples walk around certain trees. The Arucans of Malaysia carry their dead deep into the forest and place the body on top of four wooden pillars, beside which they plant an Indian Pavett tree (*Pavetta indica*). Throughout Anatolia in Turkey, a tree is planted when a child is born or when there is a wedding or a burial.

In West Africa, the sausage tree (*Kigelia africana*) relates to many beliefs because of its large fruits that look like enormous bags hanging from the end of long stalks and is a fertility image. Women nursing children hang strips of fabric on the tree to ask for protection and many children. [63] In western Kenya, they never cut the sausage tree as the fruit is buried with the deceased, which in turn makes the tree sacred. [50]

In the Islamic region of the north African Maghreb, there are important Moroccan sacred sites. Local people use the surroundings of these tombs as burial grounds and shelter patches of forest vegetation in a cultivated area. These sites are similar to the Kayas in Kenya. Here the vegetation cover reflects the fact that most sacred areas occur in marginal lands. [49]

There are close links between cemeteries and trees in West Africa. Cemeteries are often found in baobab forests. Baobabs and their configuration help identify long-abandoned cemeteries in the West African landscape. The island town of Diop in Senegal, which served as a main port, grew around a large baobab in the main square. A cemetery on a separate island has a dozen baobabs. There are tall iron crucifixes in the middle of these baobabs. The cemetery is remarkable as there are Muslim and Christian graves. The two mature baobabs in the burial ground still rise above the cathedral. [61] Like in Senegal, baobabs close to Morondava in Madagascar are sacred to the Malagasy people. [48] There are similar baobabs in Kenya (e.g., in Gedi Malindi) or wherever baobabs grow in Christian and Muslim cemeteries. [77]

People plant trees in cemeteries and conserve existing trees. This is one reason that you find yew trees in church cemeteries. In Ireland, trees can reflect the souls of those buried beneath or close to them. [82] For the Celts, people planted trees at the birth of a child. Then there would be connections between the child and the spiritual and physical parts of the child's being. [71] Many trees commemorate special occasions. We plant trees to mark occasions or celebrate. For example, my wife and I planted a podo tree (*Podocarpus falcatus*) when we were married in Eldoret, Kenya. That tree is now more than twenty-five meters tall.

In the documentary *My Passion for Trees*, Dame Judi Dench says, "My life now is just trees." She has her secret woodland in Surrey, England, where she has been planting trees for more than thirty years. Every time a friend dies, she adds a tree for him or her, including one for her late husband. She follows trees throughout the year, and she uses a stethoscope to listen to what's going on inside them. She delights in hearing their popping noises, the sound of the water traveling up through the xylem tubes to the leaves as they drink. Maybe we can follow this example and plant a tree for every friend or family member who dies. We can plant trees in a hedgerow, in a green belt, or in fields set aside for woodland. "I think of my trees as part of my extended family," says Judy Dench. So should we all. [an]

[an] Accessed August 2018. https://www.thetimes. Countyuk/edition/comment/without-our-great-woods-we-arerootless-k9wqhkdq5 and https://www.youtube.com/watch?v=YCQ62deoq_8.

Trees—Sacred Because of Tradition

Trees are often associated with wisdom. Many African societies designate a special tree as the talking or palaver tree (or the meeting place for the elders). In Senegal, palaver trees are large, and one may be a baobab or kapok. Here people discuss issues of common interest in a peaceful and constructive manner. Farther north, palaver trees are likely to be baobabs because of their longevity. Some of the oldest baobab trees are historical landmarks that predate human settlement and have names. Senegalese oral history mentions baobabs as the location of battles or markers of political boundaries. Besides the baobab and kapok trees, cola trees, acacias, and other trees have important historical roles in the identities of people. A variety of large trees mark many of Senegal's important precolonial settlements and royal capitals (e.g., coronation trees, tree altars, tree cemeteries, and trees that marked the central places and squares of capitals). [61]

In India, tulsi (*Ocimum sanctum*, see box 14) has a special significance for women. In Bhutan, the cypress tree (*Cupressus corneyana*) is an important sacred species. [81] This together with other sacred species make up part of larger sacred landscapes in Bhutan. *Ficus religiosa* and *F. altissima* are also important sacred trees. People believe the Hindu trinity of Brahma, Vishnu, and Shiva live amongst sacred peepal and banyan fig trees. Their trunks represent the connection between the invisible and visible world. [42]

Almost every village in Xishuangbanna Dai Autonomous Prefecture of Yunnan Province (China) has sacred trees for rituals and ceremonies. Some predate Buddhism. People worship these trees through rituals, and they plant trees for individual rituals. Families plant *Ficus religiosa* as a sacred tree for family activities and are found close to villages. [32] There are about 558 Buddhist temples and most have a temple forest. The following trees (of more than a hundred species) occur in temple gardens: There are ritual plants including Buddha trees, plants related to Buddhism (*Alstonia scholaris*, *Ficus racemosa*, and *Ficus religiosa*), and the leaves of the *Corypha umbraculifera*. They use these trees to care for Buddhist sutras, and there are more than fifty thousand examples of Buddhist sutras protected in

Xishuangbana. Second, people make statutes from the wood of *Tectona grandis*, *Artocarpus heterophylla*, and *Gmelina arborea*, and they use the oil from the seeds of *Mesua ferrea* and *Aleurites moluccana* to light the temple. Third, plant offerings include flowers such as *Nympaea lotus*, *Hedychium chrysoleucum*, *Crinum asiaticum*, and fruits of *Anona reticulate*, *Citrus grandis*, and *Mangifera indica*. Monks use these to make offerings at Buddhist ceremonies and eat as food. And finally, there are ornamental plants such as *Butea monosperma*, *Cassia fistula*, and *Michelia alba*, which beautify the temple and the village. [28]

Frankincense (*Boswellia sacra*) and myrrh (*Commiphora myrrha*) are two trees producing important resins, and both were gifts at the birth of Jesus Christ. They were also used for burning incense for John the Baptist's elderly father, and they were mixed with wine as a drink when they crucified Jesus, [17] where "they tried to give him wine drugged with myrrh, but he would not take it" (Mark 15:23).

Box 14: The Sacred Tulsi (Holy Basil, *Ocimum sanctum*) Plant of India [15, 22, 42, 47, 59, 62]

Tulsi (*Vrinda*, holy basil, *Ocimum sanctum*) is a woody herb that has a unique position in India because of its spiritual and medicinal properties. There are many stories about tulsi in the ancient Vedic texts, the Puranas, where Lord Vishnu tricked Tulsi (the wife of the demon Jalandhara) into being unfaithful to her husband. In return, Vishnu assured Tulsi that she would be immortal, and out of her ashes grew the tulsi plant. The Nairs of Kerala connect the plant with Lord Shiva. The plant is holy in India and cultivated in every Hindu house and temple. Every morning women worship the plant and eat two to three leaves.

Tulsi means the incomparable one and has been worshipped for thousands of years as the divine Mother on Earth. Tulsi flourished as a symbol of reverence for nature inherent in the ancient culture of India. The sacredness of tulsi reawakens the longing in people around the world to honor the divinity of Mother Nature. The spiritual leader Ama said, "May the tree of our life be firmly rooted in the soil of love. May good deeds be the fruit on that tree. May words of kindness form its flowers and may peace be its fruit. Let us grow and unfold as one family united in love. Oh Tulsi, you are born from nectar, you are eternally dear to Lord Keshava [Hindu name of Vishnu]. It is for Lord Keshava that we collect your leaves. Oh, beautiful Tulsi, grant us the blessing of serving the Lord."

Tulsi is part of the Vishnuyamal Tantra, and they nurture and worship the plant for three months. On the eleventh day of the bright half of the month of Karttik (which is 23/10/2019 to 21/11/2019), they perform a marriage of tulsi. The symbol of tulsi is silver, while that of Vishnu is gold. The marriage occurs under a tulsi tree. The goddess Lakshmi is identified with Tulsi through worship. She blesses devotees with riches, happiness, children, and virtues. Women devotees are blessed with long life for their husband and children. When a Hindu is dying, people place tulsi leaves in his or her mouth, believing the person will go to heaven after death. Prayer beads are carved from the wood of tulsi.

Hindu ceremonial dinners begin with tulsi leaves. No Hindu meal is complete without one to two tulsi leaves. The Hindus take oaths by tulsi leaf and holy water in their hands. Tulsi is Tulsi Mata or Mother Tulsi. It is said the area about 3.2 kilometers around a tulsi plant becomes pure. Brahma lives on its branches and several other gods and goddesses live on its leaves. This plant is the meeting point of heaven and earth. Virgins pray to tulsi to find worthy and suitable husbands.

> Religion teaches us to worship God within nature. Through the stories of Sri Krishna's life, the tulsi plant and the cow have become dear to the people of India, who protect and look after them. Each house has a tulsi plant growing in the front yard. People loved, worshipped, and protected nature as the visible form of God. The tradition of worshipping tulsi is a powerful practise that helps re-establish harmony between humanity and nature.

Monastic and Temple Trees

In parts of China, people protected holy hill forests and plants in temple gardens. But by the 1960s, many holy hill forests and temples were destroyed and planted with cash crops. Since the 1980s, many are being restored, and the number of species is increasing. The recovery of plant diversity helps conserve traditional cultures, and it also benefits and beautifies the environment. [53] Sacred temple sites in northwest Yunnan are diverse with at least 447 temple sites, including Tibetan, Chinese, and Taoist Buddhist temples, Islamic mosques, and Christian churches. There are various religious plants found in Tibetan and Buddhist temples. The Buddhist temple gardens in Xishuangbanna Di Autonomous Prefecture use more than forty species, [28] and the Tibetan Buddhist temples of Lijiang County, China, use more than twenty-six species. [53] It is likely the maidenhair tree (*Ginkgo biloba*) survived here because it is protected in temple grounds where they cultivated it for thousands of years. [13] The maidenhair tree is 270 million years old, and its family is 350 million years. It is a living fossil. [52]

The holy hills and religious plants in these areas of China show the role of culture in conservation. Establishing the connection between culture and conservation is important but not simple. Conservation based on cultural and religious values may be more sustainable than those based on legislation. [28] Cypress trees found in sacred sites show the influence of Tibetan Buddhism. The maidenhair tree, magnolia (*Magnolia delavayis* and *M. wilsonii*), and sabina (*Sabina chinensis*) represent evidence of the Chinese Han culture, while the castanopsis (*Castanopis delavayi*), oak

(*Quercus aquifolioides*), and tsuga (*Tsuga forestii*) relate to local beliefs. Local people conserve these trees as they also grow outside sacred groves. [53]

Ancient trees have always been sites for worship and used as shrines. The only church built inside a tree that remains in use after eight hundred years is an oak tree at Allouville-Bellefossein in Normandy, France. It is called the Chapel Oak (or Le Chêne Chapelle[ao]), The chapel is dedicated to the Virgin Mary and dates from 1669. [48] The tree is about 1,200 years old as it was a large oak well before William the Conqueror's time. Two chapels were built one above the other in the huge trunk of the tree, which is still alive. [21] In west Lithuania, there is a two-thousand-year-old Stelmužė oak tree, one of Europe's oldest oaks. The tree is dedicated to the sky deity *Perkūnas*, god of fertility and the guardian of law and order. The Baltic people revere this oak tree. The tree is witness to prayer, celebration, healing, and sacrifice. Now a younger forest encloses the oak grove. [48]

In Ireland, they often held Mass near a sacred tree, bush, or well (e.g., the Mass tree in Killarney, County Kerry). This evolved because of the persecution of Catholics after Cromwell's conquest. [82] Mass trees were ancient oaks, while Mass bushes were whitethorn or holly trees (e.g., the Altar Bush at Ballylurgan, County Antrim). Maybe it is time for more open-air interdenominational services. This could help us reconnect with nature and conserve old (and new) sacred sites. The Church of England offers such guidance for trees on church lands. [12] Other faith-based groups provide similar advice.

Other Reasons for Trees Being Sacred

The Bible (Psalm 1:3), the Qur-ān (16.11), and Thalmud [26, 76] mention the date palm. The pomegranate (*Punica granatum*) is the fruit of Israel and is sacred to Egyptians and Greeks. Muḥammad (Peace Be Upon Him) once remarked, "Eat the pomegranate, for it purges the systems of every hatred." [4] The Bible (Song of Songs 8:2) and the Qur-ān (6.99; 6.141) mention the pomegranate. The Hadith and Sunnah mention the toothbrush tree

---

[ao] Accessed September 2018. https://en.wikipedia.org/wiki/Ch%C3%AAne_chapelle.

(*Salvadora persica* or siwak). "If I had not found it hard for my followers or the people, I would have ordered them to clean their teeth with Siwak before every prayer." [2] The Bible mentions trees as sources of food (Genesis 1:29), while the Qur-ān refers to using the olive for food and fuelwood as a divine product (Qur-ān 36:80 and 56:72). In many parts of Africa, trees are sacred because of their products. For example, the Kaya forests of Kenya are sources of fuelwood, herbal medicines, wild fruit, and vegetables. [50]

The olive (tree of peace, *Olea europaea*) was sacred to the early peoples of the Near East, the Egyptians, Greeks, and Romans. The Greeks believed the olive was a gift from the goddess Athena, while the Romans believed the olive had links with the goddess Minerva. The Olympic Games vases were filled with olive oil and given as prizes, while the victors received olive wreaths. The tree is a symbol of joy, peace, compassion, and prosperity. Religious and ceremonial uses of olive oil are emblems of goodness and purity. The most famous olives are in the garden of Gethsemane in Jerusalem. [26, 40, 56, 76] Yet these and many olives in Italy are now threatened because of a bacterial disease [54] despite surviving thousands of years.

The baobab (*Adansonia digitata*) has many cultural associations contributing to its conservation. [40] Like the fig, the baobab is sacred in all places where it grows naturally and is a keystone species. In certain societies in eastern Africa, spirits may live in the baobab. [56] It is the Tree of Life because of its water storage abilities, which assisted the migrations and expansion of peoples in Africa. The San of the Kalahari use hollow stems of grass to make long straws to reach the water inside. In Sudan, people hollow large baobabs to collect rainwater. The baobab marks the central shrine of towns in Senegal. Many of these baobabs are in compounds of important sheikhs. Trees played important roles in configuring Sufi shrines as markers, memorials, and monuments. [61] Some of these ancient baobabs are now dying because of climate change.[ap] This may be due to drought or a lack of regeneration. If there is regeneration, it is often eaten by livestock. This does not bode well for their future. Some of these baobabs are national monuments (e.g., in Botswana, South Africa).

[ap] Accessed June 12, 2018. https://www.nature.com/articles/d41586-018-05411-7.

Joseph of Arimathea brought the Glastonbury thorn (*Crataegus oxyacantha praecox*) to England when he was spreading Christianity. Joseph and twelve followers climbed a hill to survey the land, and he "thrust his staff in the ground" to signify the journey's end. His staff took root, and they built a church. The thorn tree only flowers on Christmas day, the sixth day of January (old calendar). The original tree was cut in the seventeenth century, but two thorn trees exist as cuttings [56] and were planted in other locations in England. The oldest thorn is on Wearyall Hill overlooking Glastonbury, the traditional place of Joseph's first planting. The trees now growing are not old as they are from cuttings. The thorn is like the Christian message—the same church through the ages represented by different people. The Glastonbury thorn is the same tree but represented by different specimens. [45, 82]

The turning of a saint's or spiritual leader's staff or walking stick into a tree is common. For example, St. Kenelm in England planted his staff, and an ash grew from it. [29] A tree grown from the Glastonbury thorn forms the story associated with the village of Appleton Thorn, which is near Warrington in Cheshire.[aq] The tree grows at the crossroads in the center of the village and the sign by the tree reads, "This thorn tree is an offshoot from the famous Glastonbury thorn in Somerset." Over the centuries the custom of bawming the thorn grew, which means decorating the tree with flowers and ribbons and people dancing around the tree. They revived the present ceremony in 1973, and it is held on the third Saturday in June. [45]

In England, the Green Man signifies irrepressible life of renewal and rebirth. The Green Man is the sacrificial figure of the old woodland spirit who is killed by the new spirit of spring. The custom of the maypole originates from these beliefs. In Britain and Europe, people worshipped the maypole as a fertility symbol of the vegetation god. It is a persistent practice that preserves the folk memory of a sacred marriage to promote the fertility of the land. [45]

Despite being a pre-Christian tradition, bringing hawthorn (*Crataegus monogyna*) inside a home brings bad luck and is dangerous in contemporary

---

[aq] Accessed May 27, 2018. http://calendarcustoms.com/articles/bawming-the-thorn/.

Christianity in the British Isles. There is a story of the death of one church warden after he did not listen to local advice about the prohibition of removing yew or hawthorn trees from a graveyard.[ar] My mother forbade us to bring any hawthorn into our home in Ireland in the 1950s.

In Xinjiang in northwest China, the Uygur people consider trees to be the main protector of the environment. As far back as AD 3, the first forest regulation of China was in the Loulan Ancient Kingdom of Xinjiang, which forbade tree cutting. The Uygur have many proverbs, poems, and legends referring to forest and tree protection. If you cut one tree, you must plant ten trees. The forest is a reservoir. It cannot only store surplus water, but it also releases water. The Uygur plant trees around their homes for protection when they settle. They worship ancient trees that symbolize rainfall and peace. As a result, many ancient trees are well-preserved in Xinjiang. [78]

When looking at trees associated with Wales, the tree that comes to mind is the ancient churchyard yew, where large dark yews are found on circular mounds in the churchyards. Many are older than the churches, and some were inhabited since the Bronze Age. Yet there is no agreement why they are there. In pre-Christian times, people planted yews on or near burial sites. People think that circles of trees have supernatural properties to keep out evil. Placing a sprig of yew on graves symbolizes everlasting life and is still carried out in parts of Wales. On Ash Wednesday, the ash from burned yew twigs is smeared on the forehead to show penitence. Using leaves to symbolize everlasting life is still a custom. In Pennant-Melangell, four ancient yews encircle the pre-Christian churchyard. In the village of Nantglyn (several miles southwest of Denbigh), a sacred yew tree has stone steps and a pulpit for outdoor services within its hollow trunk, which is eight meters in diameter. [45]

In Sweden and Norway, there is a tradition of planting a sacred tree at the center of the yard in the family home. They refer to this in Sweden as *Vårdträd*, and in Norway as *Tuntre*. This tradition predates Christianity and the Viking era. Even today these sacred trees occur in the cultural

---

[ar] Peter Barrett pers. comm., April 2004.

landscape of Scandinavia. [33] People distinguish these sacred trees by where they find them (center of the yard) and age because reverence increases with the age of the tree.

In Senegal, Gambia, and western Sudan, certain trees served as sites for the public administration of justice and displays of royal prerogatives. Other trees mark sites of coronations, religious functions, and rituals conducted by traditional leaders or Muslim clerics. They used a variety of trees for different public functions. These trees had individual names. For example, the baobab was a site for circumcision, or these trees were also important to the elders. [61] The Turkana in Kenya name people after trees. Important trees were important customary meeting places. The neem tree became sacred in India as a conscious decision by Hindu society linked to its utilitarian and intangible values. [27]

For Lebanon (cedar of Lebanon or *Cedrus libani*), Canada (maple or *Acer saccharum*), and Chile (monkey puzzle tree or *Araucaria araucana*), trees are national monuments and are part of the national flags. The monkey puzzle tree is sacred to Pehuenche Indians of south-central Chile, as the people feel these forests have their own spirit. The canelo tree (winter's bark or *Drimys winteri*) is sacred to the Mapuche people and is a hardwood tree found in the rainforests. It is important for healing and religious rituals, and it has symbolic significance.[as] The Mapuche people worship the canelo tree as a symbol of peace.

In Ireland, several family coats of arms feature trees. The oak is the most prominent tree in Irish heraldry. [82] Trees represent liberty. For example, the Tree of Liberty in France was planted after the French Revolution, or in Ireland, they planted many trees of liberty to commemorate the 1798 rebellion and independence.

[as] Accessed January 2018. https://www.etsy.com/listing/277478260/sacred-mapuche-tree-leaf-dye-organic.

Edmund Barrow

What Can We Learn from This Diversity, and What Can We Do?

Individual trees all over the world are revered as national monuments and as homes to spirits. They are used to conduct ceremonies, to honor deceased people, to bury the dead, and to name children. They can make up parts of marriage ceremonies. They can serve as meeting places, and they may be planted at the time of the birth of a child. The reasons vary and resulted in the spread of sacred trees across the landscapes as people planted and protected them. Most of these trees are large and long-lived. They are a focus for people to honor the spirits and a visible expression of their importance for various ceremonies. While the examples cited allude to this importance, they are not exhaustive, but they show the widespread importance of individual trees across our planet. It is important from both the context of conservation, for example, different species, rarity, age, or species which contain a lot of biodiversity; and that of religions and spiritual groups (variety of spiritual practices associated with the main faith-based groups). Table 2 shows some trees mentioned in the Qur-ān and Bible. Table 3 shows how different religions respect some species. The Bible mentions at least forty-eight tree species. [17]

Table 2: Trees in Islam, Christianity— Mentions in Sacred Texts [36, 46, 64]

	Islam	Christianity
Trees (general)	19	23
Grape	12	6
Olive	6	12
Date	22	8
Fig	1	13

Table 3: Examples of Trees Important to More than One Spiritual Tradition [13, 36, 46]

	Islam	Christianity	Judaism	Hindu	Buddhism	Traditional belief systems
Fig (different species)	✓	✓	✓	✓	✓	✓
Date Palm	✓	✓	✓			
Olive	✓	✓	✓			
Baobab						✓ (Africa)
Tulsi	✓			✓		✓ (India)
Crown of Thorns	✓	✓	✓			
Pomegranate	✓	✓	✓	✓		
Almond, Apple, Walnut		✓				

Trees are natural symbols for social institutions. Trees can be social agents for progress and moving on from colonial legacies. Sacred trees can support partnerships between the state and community. The status of sacred trees and groves reflects institutional changes over time and how they relate to modern institutions. This means we need to bring what is valuable and useful in such institutions into our present world. [65] To visit such ancient and often sacred trees and to be in their shade is to pay homage at a mysterious shrine. [52]

Sacred Groves—Places of Mindfulness for Religion, Spirituality, and Conservation

CHAPTER 4

The groves were God's first Temples.
—William Bryant [63]

There are no unsacred places; There are only sacred places and desecrated places

—William Berry [5]

No one ... can escape the cold fact that we are a single humanity.
—Nelson Mandela [59]

Sacred Groves Underestimated and Undervalued across the Globe

Sacred groves occur across the world, and they were important to people for thousands of years. Now there are fewer sacred groves in Europe or North America. However, many still occur in Africa, India, Asia, and Latin America. In Africa, a senior climate negotiator suggested every rural village has a sacred tree or grove, and many villages have more than one. In Europe and North America, many sacred groves were destroyed or are no longer used because of industrialization, [129] the settlement of North America, and the rising importance of formal religion, which tended not to support traditional beliefs. Across Africa, Asia, the Australia-Pacific region, and Latin America, many sacred groves still exist, though modernity has taken its toll as over three-quarters of the world's forests were cleared along with sacred groves in order to feed consumerism. Every year an area the size of Austria is cleared of forests from the Amazon to Indonesia so that humankind can keep consuming. [50] Sacred groves have their legends, lore, and myths, which are integral parts of the groves. They are an inextricable link between present and past in terms of biodiversity and spiritual and cultural heritages. [45]

Sacred groves are usually uninhabited, have strict rules, and are part of a landscape with well-defined geographic features that delineated and protected by societies through traditional arrangements. [90] The reasons for sacred groves vary, ranging from fear and respect for God and ancestral spirits to more utilitarian uses. Traditional respect for the environment and access restrictions often led to well-conserved areas with high biodiversity in degraded environments. [97] Sacred groves became sacred over time as they often buried people in forested areas. Such areas became respected as burial sites or as residences of the spirits. After that, they became sacred with rules and norms that legitimated the grove. These groves might be a formal religious graveyard (e.g., some sacred yew groves in Europe). In other cases, customary spiritual norms and traditions enhance their sanctity.

Sacred groves serve various purposes (e.g., as sites for the induction of young men and women, cultural education, and burial grounds). Taboos and customs control access to and the usage of groves, with control resting with specific members of the community. [51] Sacred groves vary in size, location, and rationale. There are many more sacred groves than we think as most are neither documented nor recognized. For example, Japanese Shinto and Buddhist sacred groves are common and cover more than 110,000 hectares. Ghana has more than two thousand groves; however, China has four hundred sacred village groves in one province alone, and most are more than a hundred hectares. Nepal has hundreds of documented groves, while in India, estimates suggest there are between a hundred thousand and 150,000. [14, 32, 43, 62, 70, 96]

Sacred groves are mostly undisturbed areas and vary in size from less than one hectare to more than five hundred hectares. They occur in the old and new worlds as well as in temperate and tropical lands. While they may not be large, many are rich in biodiversity (see box 15). Their continued existence is a testament to their importance. People may collect dry wood, fruit, honey, and other products. In some areas, they allow cattle to graze. But tree cutting is forbidden without the deity's permission. In the Western Ghats of India, this permission is obtained through a ritual known as kaul. [43]

> **Box 15: Why Sacred Groves Are Important**
>
> - Consider the sheer age and numbers. Some conserve important biodiversity as a by-product of spiritual and religious values.
> - Many are examples of remnant flora, and so they are important historically and ecologically.
> - Traditional and religious management systems are important for conservation.
> - Their numbers create connectivity and could be a focus for restoration through ICCAs.
> - The fauna and flora are more than species collections. They are interconnected, have complex interactions, and are imbued with a sense of the sacred.
> - They serve as entry points for livelihoods and conservation.

Sacred groves are more associated with India than anywhere else. Many of these groves predate the Vedic age, but many are now part of post-Vedic Hinduism. [88] Though not as well documented, sacred groves are common in Southeast Asia, Africa, and South America. They may be the last refuge of endangered species. They are storehouses of medicinal plants. They may contain wild relatives of crop species that can improve cultivated varieties. They may provide water for nearby communities, and they may help in soil and water conservation. [56] These groves are islands of biodiversity and a source of germplasm for restoration. [89] They can be at the heart of local ecological governance and restoration. The revitalization of their importance will provide a boost to conservation, community, and spiritual imperatives.

The scale and scope of sacred groves is a testament to their resilience in the face of high population and pressures about land usage. The truth is that we have little idea of the number and area of sacred groves. There are 209,444 formal protected areas (Categories I-VI) in the world. [115, 116] Yet few sacred groves are recognized. The literature indicates there are more than 150,000 sacred groves, though there are probably many more that are not documented! Sacred groves and natural sites are the world's oldest protected areas—the Yellowstone model is only 140 years old—and some groves are thousands of years old (e.g., the garden of Gethsemane)! Because of the reverence people attached to sacred groves, this discouraged encroachment or exploitation. While many groves still survive, the pressures on them increase, both internal because of social change and external because of conversion or commercial pressures. Without greater efforts from religious and conservation groups, it is questionable how long these groves and the cultures that uphold them can continue to survive.

Many sacred groves were degraded or destroyed. The threats include changes in attitudes, sociocultural practices and values, the erosion of religious beliefs and traditional values, and conversion because of land and population pressures combined with in-migration and a loss of a sense of place. This resulted in habitat degradation, encroachment, conversion, and exploitation. These threats are human-induced, and now we can add climate change. [45, 77] Sacred groves are being lost because of social and religious changes and because of the destabilization of cultural and ecological equilibrium by external pressures. [104] But this should be put in context. Most ancient woodlands were cut more than forty times since their origins, and each time regrowth occurs. Ancient woods are complex, the result of interactions between trees, wildlife, and human activities over long time periods. [85] In his classic work *The Golden Bough*, James Fraser identified sacred groves as relics of past ages in the social evolution of religion.

Sacred groves are a category of landscape created, worshipped, and protected by local people for cultural and spiritual reasons. The sacred grove may contain sacred items (e.g., sacred trees, wells, and springs), sculptures or images of God, religious buildings, and artifacts. They are fragments of landscapes and ecosystem types. [82] The four categories include the following: (a) those discovered when clearing agricultural land (e.g., because of settlements), (b) those used for ritual reasons, (c) those associated with a specific event (e.g., a battle), and (d) those used as burial grounds. In southern Ghana, people differentiate groves associated with burial places as homes of ancestral spirits and groves as the habitat of nature spirits. [15] There are several characteristics of sacred groves, [27] including being (a) an abode of a supernatural power; (b) an area of natural tree vegetation; (c) an area that's well delineated spatially; (d) a place related to historical, cultural, and spiritual issues; (e) an area managed through various rules and taboos; (f) places protected from interference through local sanctity; and (g) areas that have values not restricted to specific religions, landscapes, or territories.

In his essay "Tapovan (Forest of Purity)," Rabindranath Tagore writes, "Indian civilization has been distinctive in locating its source of regeneration, material and intellectual, in the forest, not the city. India's best ideas have come where man was in communion with trees and rivers and lakes, away from the crowds. The peace of the forest has helped the intellectual evolution of man. … The culture that has arisen from the forest has been influenced by the diverse processes of renewal of life, which were always at play in the forest, varying from species to species, from season to season."[at] This is a basis for ecological sustainability and democracy, and it is an important rationale for sacred groves, where the forest is a source of knowledge, freedom, beauty, joy, art and aesthetics, harmony, and perfection. [105]

This chapter explores the extent and reasons for sacred groves. The analysis is not exhaustive, but it shows the scale, scope, and importance of sacred groves. This helps us understand the resilience of groves as to why they still exist and why they are important to people in an era where materialism holds sway. Understanding why and how they continue to exist and thrive provides insights into how management can be better recognized and respected from both conservation and spiritual perspectives and from the

---

[at] Accessed July 27, 2018. http://www.yesmagazine.org/issues/what-would-nature-do/vandana-shiva-everything-i-need-to-know-i-learned-in-the-forest.

perspective of people's lives. I divide up sacred groves into several broad but often overlapping categories. I draw out a variety of lessons useful for the increased recognition of such sites in future areas of both spiritual and conservation importance.

Home of the Spirits, Mother Earth, and Ancestors

Sacred groves occur close to villages. They are usually old, and their origins are often lost in time; however, people share the knowledge about them through the generations. People associate groves with places where certain trees dominate. There is often a prohibition on cutting or using trees and wildlife. Even human presence is only allowed during ceremonies. Sacred groves are important relic areas of natural vegetation in often degraded landscapes and are a basis for restoration.

Sacred Groves of Ghana[au]

Sacred groves in Ghana are examples of ICCAs, though the primary rationale is sacredness, not conservation. There are three categories of indigenous strategies to conserve biodiversity in Ghana as sacred groves, namely (a) protection of ecosystems or habitats (e.g., groves and rivers, royal burial grounds), (b) protection of a certain animal or plant species (e.g., totem or taboo species), and (c) the regulated exploitation of nature (e.g., close seasons for harvesting or hunting).

People used to set aside small patches of forest that are protected through customary law. Such areas still exist in Ghana and are known as *Abosompow* or *Asoneyeso* (shrine), *Mpanyinpow* (ancestral forests), and *Nsamanpow* (burial grounds). Many are small, less than one hectare in size, and protected because they support sacred or taboo species. The Boabeng-Fiema Monkey Sanctuary is an example as the grove supports black-and-white colobus monkeys, which are sacred to the people. Interestingly, in PDR Lao, there is an example of a sacred grove because of Rhesus macaque monkeys—the Monkey Forest of Donmuang Village. The forest is eleven

---

[au] Sources: [3, 43, 70, 76, 113, 114]

hectares and home to about a thousand monkeys. [30] There are similar rules governing the grove as in the Boabeng-Fiema Monkey Sanctuary!

Some Ghanaian groves are more than three hundred years old. Others are burial sites that became sacred with time. UNESCO implemented a project (1993–97) in Ghana on conserving groves in the north. These groves survived degradation because the Dagomba people respected the traditional beliefs that they were the abodes of gods or places of initiation. There are between two thousand to 3,200 sacred groves in Ghana. They are under traditional authorities (priests, chiefs, or clan heads), but responsibility rests with the community. For example, Nkodurom grove, which is about five square kilometers, has been conserved for more than three hundred years. It and its associated shrine are close to Paakoso village near Fumesua, off the Accra-Kumasi road. Authority lies with the Ashanti king, though functionally, it is with the chief. Rules governing such groves include the following:

- There is no hunting as they protect animals.
- If an animal is accidentally killed, pardon comes from the fetish priest.
- No burning of bushes in the grove is allowed as this destroys the abode of the gods.
- There is no cutting of trees for any purpose, including cooking. If a tree has to be harvested for specific reasons, prior permission has to be sought from the custodians.
- Strangers can only enter the grove if accompanied by someone appointed by the custodians.
- Access is prohibited except for authorized people to perform customary rites.

These groves have no written rules and no legal status. But people observe the unwritten rules. The traditional guards receive no payment. The sacred groves survive because of the strong traditions of the local people together with their spiritual, religious, and cultural attachments. The relative power of the deity determines use. For example, in the Nanhini village, no one can enter the grove of the goddess Numafoa or ignore her taboos.

Shai Hills National Park is important culturally for the Shai people. It is their spiritual home. The National Parks authorities allow people into the sacred caves in the park for ritual needs. For this, there is a Park Management Advisory Board composed of one-third park staff and two-thirds from the community. It provides a good example of how a protected area authority can be sensitive to local cultures and traditions concerning sacred groves. If only more would do the same. While in Kumasi, a city of more than 1.5 million people, there is a small undisturbed sacred grove in the city center. It's conserved because it is sacred, yet the land value is huge in dollar terms.

Sacred groves are often the only remnant forest amidst degraded forests, farmlands, and urban areas. The erosion of traditional beliefs threatens their survival. The number of groves has shrunk because of encroachment or development. This is due to Western education, religion, in-migration of people who show little respect for local traditions, and the lack of legislation to reinforce traditional rules. A management strategy for groves could include a national inventory of groves and their biodiversity, legislation to reinforce traditional regulations, and capacity building to improve local people's capacity to manage their groves.

Commercial deforestation, mining, and urban expansion destroyed many sacred groves and put others at risk. Ghana's National Environmental Action Plan does not acknowledge the existence or significance of sacred groves. As a result, local traditional groups work with nongovernmental organizations to conserve sacred groves and raise awareness about their importance. To save the Guako Grove on the outskirts of Accra, Friends of the Earth Ghana implemented education campaigns and restored the grove. The Ghana Association for the Conservation of Nature works with local communities to manage sacred groves. Such initiatives acknowledge the value of spiritual and religious beliefs for management. These groves are important genetic resources for restoration.[av]

[av] For example, see https://www.iucn.org/theme/forests/our-work/forest-landscape-restoration, and visit http://www.forestlandscaperestoration.org/ for detailed descriptions of forest landscape restoration.

Social Values of the Nyangkpe Sacred Groves of Cameroon[aw]

The Nyangkpe society of the Manyu people of southwest province Cameroon have institutions for their sacred groves. Decision makers of Manyu villages are the village chief, traditional council, traditional societies, and representatives from institutions and groups involved with the Nyangkpe and its groves. The most visible trait of Nyangkpe sacred groves are the virgin pieces of forest. Recent ceremonies involve laying yellow and black palm fronds along the entrance to the grove to show the abode of departed ancestors. The community invokes these spirits from time to time to resolve problems. For example, conservationists witnessed instances where the Nyangkpe suspended activities of commercial (and local) loggers by laying a yellow palm frond to expropriate the tree for short periods of time. Where the status of a place is in dispute, they place the Nyangkpe insignia on the site, even if it is the property of nonmembers. They make it Nyangkpe property temporarily, pending resolution. Nyangkpe groves emphasize the continuity of life in terms of the interactions between the living and the dead, whose spirits live in the grove. Protected area managers should incorporate such knowledge and institutions in management.

Like Nyangkpe, the Osun-Osogbo sacred grove close to Osogbo City in Nigeria is one of the last areas of virgin high forest in south Nigeria. The people dedicate the seventy-five-hectare grove to Oso-Igbo, the Yoruba goddess of fertility, protection, and blessings. It is a World Heritage Site and one of the few existing Yoruba sacred groves. They hold an annual festival at Osogbo in the first week of August.

Sacred Groves in East Africa[ax]

The Kikuyu and Mbeere peoples of Mt. Kenya have many sacred groves or *matiiiri*. They are under the control of the elders and are focal points for local concerns. In the 1930s, there were more than two hundred such groves on hilltops or along ridges, varying between 0.25 to 3.0 hectares

---

[aw] Sources: [44, 66] and http://whc.unes Countyorg/en/list/1118.
[ax] Sources: [2, 10, 53, 54, 64-66, 71, 79, 99, 109, 119, 125, 126]

and comprising of large spreading trees. They allow no cutting, clearing, or cultivation except branches to propagate new sacred trees. The cultural significance of these practices is being eroded by formal religions and land tenure privatization, and there are much fewer now.

The Loita Forest in southwest Kenya is sacred to the Loita Masai. It is their spiritual center. Not only is the forest important for sacred rituals, but it is also a source of medicine and dry season forage. The Loita Masai imbue their sacred forest with an elaborate mythology, and the springs and streams emerging from the forest symbolize enduring hope. In the center of the forest is the Cathedral of the Seven Trees, which is a sacred place where the Masai Laibons or prophets bring offerings to *Enkai* or God. *Enkai* entrusted his cattle to the Masai and passed them to the earth through the *Oreteti*, the link between sky and earth. There are many important ceremonies performed within or at the edges of the sacred forest. Especially revered by the Masai is the wild fig tree (*Oreteti, Ficus sycamorus*).

Ridge elders and medicinal specialists use the forests in Ruwenzori National Park, a World Heritage site in west Uganda, for sacrifices to the forest spirits. They make shrines from the Afromontane dragon tree, *Draceana afromontana*. The location of these shrines relates to historical occurrences. This caused tension as park authorities forbade people to conduct sacred rites. But this changed with collaborative management agreements between the communities and park management, and thus, they allow people access their sacred sites.

Kipumbwi village, on the coast of Tanzania in Tanga region, started before Arabs arrived in the eighteenth century. The elders brought the spirits from their original home (Mombasa) to a sacred site in the mangrove forest called Kwakibibi. People believe the spirits are still there. Nobody enters without the consent of three elders (two men and one woman) who are responsible for its management. Only Kipumbwi and neighboring villages used the site. Now people come from Arabia, mainland Tanzania and Pemba to worship. If they succeed with their prayers, they bring something to leave at the site (e.g., a white goat, red or black cloth, or rice).

In the biodiversity-rich Eastern Arc Mountains of Tanzania, the Zigua and Gweno people live and occupy part of the North Pare Mountains. In Handeni district, there are 660 traditionally protected forests in a pilot study of twenty-three villages. Most of these forests are sacred. There is an average of twenty-eight forests per village with an average size of seven hectares. They use the sacred groves for various reasons, including making rain, sacred hunting, burial, training forests for boys and girls, and as boundary forests with neighboring clans. Many of the rules make good conservation sense—no tree cutting, grazing, lodging, or walking through the forest except to collect certain things. This means in these twenty-three villages, about 196 hectares of sacred groves are conserved per village or more than 4,500 hectares for the twenty-three villages in Handeni. Overall, Handeni district has more than 1,400 sacred groves of between two to five hectares. In 1982, cultivation surrounded 18 percent of these groves. By 1997, the figure was 69 percent, which shows the pressures for land usage that these groves face. There is a similar story in the South Pare Mountains, though they are not as well studied or as extensive. It's interesting that the Ziqua are Muslim and that they all accept these traditional beliefs. Yet the colonial government and early missionaries took a negative attitude to sacred groves. They destroyed many and even cut trees to build churches!

Sacred groves are important for cultural and spiritual reasons in East Africa. But small sacred groves may be very numerous. However, the survival of these sites is contingent on the power that the management institutions (for example, the council of elders or religious leaders) have to protect them in the face of powerful economic and external interests and pressures for land usage. Sacred trees and groves symbolize community identity, their history, and their sense of place.

Sacred Controls on Trees and Woodlands in Zimbabwe[ay]

The Karanga people of southern Zimbabwe have sacred controls governing access to and use of certain trees and woodlands. Particular trees and groves are sacred because of their association with ancestral spirits who

---

[ay] Sources: [12, 17, 61, 66, 69, 123]

provide links between people and God (*Mwari*). The Karanga protect all large trees regardless of species as they believe this is the resting places of spirits. Sacred groves occur on hills and may be ancient burial sites. There are strong taboos preventing tree cutting in graveyards. Forests and woodlands growing along rivers and around springs or river sources are sacred. Woodlands where certain tree species dominate and groves of wild loquat (*Uapaca kirkiana*) are often sacred. Access and use controls for such trees are strict. Only spirit mediums can enter the most sacred sites. In other sites, people can enter, but they must observe strict rules as to what they can do, say, or wear. For example, people use one hand to collect fruit in wild loquat sacred groves, place the fruits in a natural container, and make no negative remarks about the quality.

There are incidences where spirit mediums ensure ancestral prohibitions on tree felling in sacred groves or *marambatemwa* (places that resist cutting), where they bury chiefs and respected people. These can cover large areas. They are subject to rules, one of which is a ritual tree-planting ceremony. Shona society protects large trees, though the custom is not as strong now. In precolonial times, protected woodlands could be as large as eighty-hectares and occur on sacred hilltops. These sites protect graves and the people leave trees to shade the ancestral spirits. The Shona revere these ancient groves where human, natural, and spiritual worlds intertwine.

Sacred Groves of Nepal[az]

In Nepal, nature sustains life, and life-cycle rituals involve sacred species and groves. This includes tree marriage. This is one way that people attain religious merit. Other ways include not degrading grazing lands, planting trees around water points, planting sacred trees, establishing a sacred grove, and making pilgrimages to sacred sites. Sacred groves (*dharmic ban*) in Nepal are larger than 0.1 hectares, and religious and spiritual rituals are the basis for management. A survey of twenty-six groves in three districts showed 65 percent were less than one hectare with 8 percent larger than four hectares. Their size depends on their popularity, how important the deity is, the number of sacred sites in the forest, and the ratio of forested to

---

[az] Sources: [13 40, 41, 86]

agricultural land. Many of Nepal's sacred groves occur on hilltops (*Thaan*) and are sites of deities together with places where forest shamans dwell. They perform rituals, many of which are good for forests. For example, tree worship, tree planting, and protecting forests that contain sacred sites all help conserve the groves and contribute to forest conservation.

Sacred groves in Nepal have their origins in Hinduism. Many sacred groves in Nepal are close to temples. The monks maintain them, and they do not allow tree cutting. Social arrangements for managing sacred groves conform to local systems of forest management. This is important for natural resource governance. Differences between systems of managing groves compared to other common property forests relate to the objectives and the important roles priests have. These groves go through cycles of decline and regrowth because the emphasis is on protection, not managing for regeneration.

Sacred groves have spiritual and educational values. Their presence reinforces how important conservation and respect for nature is in the teachings of Hinduism and Buddhism. Sacred groves are an important part of the cultural heritage of Nepal for spiritual and recreational reasons. Much of the social life of Nepalese villages revolves in and around sacred groves, as they provide a reminder of the conservation messages of Hinduism and Buddhism. But the increasing influence of Western culture threatens the effectiveness of this symbolism.

Sacred groves provide forest products for domestic and ritual purposes. Some groves do not have a sacred site, yet they produce products for rituals such as funeral pyres. People do not manage sacred groves for conservation, though conservation may be an important benefit. If a sacred grove is old, it can be an important reservoir of natural vegetation and play an important role in conservation. For sacred plants, protection for religious purposes assists their conservation.

Edmund Barrow

Conserving Biodiversity through Sacred Groves in India[ba]

There may be between a hundred thousand and 150,000 groves in India. The truth is that we don't know. Many are forest fragments in agricultural landscapes. These sacred groves predate the Vedic age and date back several thousand years to pre-agrarian periods of hunter-gatherer societies. The Vedic peoples subsumed many of the sacred rights and groves and integrated them into post-Vedic Hindu rituals. Hindu deities replaced many pre-Vedic sacred groves, with local tradition being challenged by westernization, for example, because of the loss of values by younger generations. Sacred groves are tracts of undisturbed forest preserved since ancient times around sacred or temple structures or set aside as abodes of local deities and spirits. Many occur on hills.

Sacred groves occur all over India, though four regions are best known. There are (a) Khasia and Jaintia hills in Meghalaya state, (b) Western Ghats of Maharashtra and Karnataka; c). the Aravalli hills, and (d) the Sargu, Chanda, and Bastar areas of central India. Sacred groves have different names—*Sarna* (Bihar), *Oran* (Rajasthan), *Deorais* (Maharastra), *Ki'Law Lyngdoh* and *Ki'Law Kyntang* (Meghalaya) and *Kavus* (Kerala). The Meghalaya area is best known for sacred groves. It also has high biodiversity and endemism values.

Sacred groves reflect India's long history of nature worship. They dedicate sacred groves to local deities or ancestral spirits and protect them through social traditions incorporating spiritual and ecological values. However, pressures of the modern world are depleting and weakening the traditions that protect them. Conservationists and local communities recognize that traditional knowledge and sacred practices are important in conservation.

Many of the sacred groves in the west Ghats of Maharashtra are more than two hundred years old and have diverse peoples around them. In a survey of forty groves, thirty are less than one hectare, and only one is larger than five hectares. For fifteen groves studied, they found 223 species of trees, and the species richness varied between ten and eighty-six per grove.

[ba] Sources: [8, 9, 25, 31, 49, 56, 77, 81, 83, 84, 90, 94]

They often harbor a rich vegetation and may be the only representative of the forest in near pristine condition in many parts of present-day India. The hill regions of western Maharashtra region—known as Ghatmartha (Crest of the West Ghats)—is rich in sacred groves, which vary in size from five to ten hectares. The groves are important as they are often the only source of forest products. Some groves contain rare plants. A grove known as Dhuprahatra in Varandha Pass in Bhor Taluk has two rare and magnificent dhup trees (*Canarium strictum*).

Groves in forest reserves are less defined than on village lands, though the surrounding forest may be degraded. Simple temples may occur in the depths of forest patches located on hills or at the origin of a stream. Most villages in India have a grove close to a temple. Many of these groves are comprised of sal trees (*Shorea robusta*). Indigenous peoples refer to sal groves as *Sarnas* or *Jahiras*, and several deities live in them.

In Jharkhand (*Jhar* meaning forest and *khand* meaning area) in north India, the people protect a large area of forest for the spirits and against droughts, floods, and crop failures. They do so by maintaining the balance between society, the natural world, and the supernatural. The local view of the forest is utilitarian, but they enrich this with the moral values of reciprocity, restraint, and prudence. Sal (*Shorea robusta*), honey (*Madhuca longifolia*), and Bengal quince (*Aegle marmelos*) trees are sacred, as the spirits live in these trees and the forest. The Jharkhand *Adivasis* or indigenous peoples keep patches of original forest that they dedicate to their deity.

The forests of Gandmardhan in Orissa feed twenty-two streams and are sacred because Hanuman gathered medicinal herbs to save Laxman's life. A bauxite mine was proposed, and this mine would destroy the sacred forest. There was resistance by the people, not because they did not want development but because they wanted to conserve the sacred. The Ministry of Environment and Forests recognized the area—and especially the summit—as one of the holiest sites of the local people. They lodged a successful complaint, which led to mediation that halted the project. The Ministry of Environment and Forests blocked the company in 2010, and the Indian Supreme Court gave the decision over the mine to the twelve villages of the area. The villages voted against the mine. The Ministry of Environment and Forests blocked the plan again in 2014.[bb]

People of Uttara Kannada have various traditions for nature conservation, including protecting individual sacred plants and animals (e.g., fig trees or monkeys such as the Hanuman langur). But British colonialists and Indian managers (following independence) undermined these traditions. For example, the plywood industry harvested *Ficus nervosa* as a preferred species. As a result, they cut many sacred groves to supply timber. Fisheries managers poisoned sacred ponds to remove indigenous fish and restock them with exotic carp for export. Yet the effectiveness of traditional conservation is still visible as many Hanuman monkeys survive and thousands of fig trees dot the countryside because of their religious significance. The only remaining natural stand of Dipterocarpus (*Dipterocarpus indicus*) is in a sacred grove as is the last large patch of a Myristica (*Myristica fatua*) swamp. Sacred grove conservation is a benefit based on traditional values, not conservation. This shows that even small areas conserve significant biodiversity.

The Holy Hill Forests of the Dai in South West China[bc]

The Dai are an indigenous group in southwest China's Xishuangbanna region of Yunnan Province with a long tradition of conservation. The holy hills (or *Nong*) are areas of forest where the gods live. The plants and animals inhabiting the holy hills are sacred. The origins of the holy hill forests lie in pre-Buddhist beliefs. The Dai believe the spirits of great and revered chiefs go to the holy hills. Wherever there is a forested hill near a Dai village, it is holy and part of Dai culture. The Dai perception of the relations between people and their environment is comprised of five elements—forest, water, land, food, and man. Water comes from forests, which feeds the land, and food comes from the land.

[bb] Accessed June 2019. http://www.facing-finance.org/en/database/cases/bauxite-mine-in-orissa-india/.

[bc] Sources: [35, 38, 80, 82, 100-103, 127]

There are two types of holy hill. *Nong Man* are natural forested hills of between ten and a hundred hectares, and these are sacred to one village. *Nong Merg* occur where several villages form a larger community, and these holy hills are much larger. They believe the forests are the cradles of humankind. The trees on the *Nong* hills cannot be cut. Nor can you build houses there. You do not want to antagonize the spirits and gods. The Dai keep the sanctity of these hills and present regular offerings. For example, near the village of Mar-yuang-kwang, the holy hill covers fifty-three hectares. There are 311 plant species in this small area, which makes it an important asset for biodiversity. These hills conserve large numbers of endemic or relic species of local flora, including a hundred species of medicinal plants and more than 150 useful plants of economic value. They listed 268 plant species (ninety-two families) in twenty-eight holy hills, with 15 species listed in the China Plant Red Data list.

Many Dai sacred forests have more biodiversity than formal protected areas. The holy hill forests reflect nature as the counterpart of the village. The spirits live on certain holy hills, and all the animals and plants are companions of the spirits. The holy hills are under strict protection as all its resources are sacred. Violations anger the spirits, who can unleash retribution in the form of floods or fires. Neighboring non-Dai people respect the sanctity of the holy hills. In 1984, researchers listed 257 holy hills in Xishuangbanna covering approximately fifty thousand hectares (average 125 hectares); however, many are degraded, and they covered only 1 percent of the area as of 1957.

The use of cultural values is important for conservation, especially traditional beliefs about sacred forests. The Dai and other indigenous ethnic minority peoples in the Xishuangbanna Biosphere Reserve have established harmony and a balanced relationship with nature through using traditional knowledge and cultural beliefs. But indigenous approaches of natural resource management were established for low population densities, large areas of forest cover, rich biodiversity, and a subsistence economy. Now there are more complex challenges (e.g., markets and globalization, population expansion, environmental degradation, and a decline in biodiversity). So it is important to promote the wider use of indigenous knowledge, culture, and local practices in conservation. This can be achieved through greater community participation to manage and protect these sacred forests.

The holy hills connect nature reserves with other forms of land usage. This is relevant today as people cleared forests for rubber plantations in the Mao era. Today sacred forests provide services for local people (e.g., water and soil conservation, food, medicinal plants, and natural fertilizers). In a Naxi village in Lijiang County (northwest Yunnan province), villagers preserved a sacred coffin forest since 1913, and only villagers older than fifty can select a tree there. Holy hills are often the only remaining areas of rainforest found outside the Xishuangbanna National Nature Reserve. Now they are being integrated into the larger biodiversity corridor because they are well adapted and are found in the lower, more tropical foothills that are richer in biodiversity.

Sacred Groves as Part of Community Forests in Thailand[bd]

Sacred groves are connected to and influenced by Buddhism in Thailand, occur near temples, and have trees such as *Ficus religiosa, Dipterocarpus turbinatus,* and *Dialium ovoides*. They manage them to serve the temple for economic, ecological, social, and religious functions. All ethnic groups in north Thailand support sacred groves. The law of King Mengrai, the first king of Chiang Mai (AD 3), mentions sacred groves. The law, known as *Mangraiyasatra*, stated that violation of sacred forests was an offense. Surveys of sixty-six community forests in north Thailand show that most communities have sacred groves. Forests in areas of spirit worship (*Hor Phi Chao Ban, Phi Khun Nam*) and Pagoda (*Phra That*) occur on hills in north Thailand. Other forests serve as graveyards, grazing areas, watershed forests, and public lands.

Communities protect watershed forests (*Pa Ton Nam*) as sacred. The groves are at the head of watersheds where people draw water. These sacred groves are where communities believe the spirits of the watershed (*Phi Khun Nam*) live as the guardians. There is an annual ceremony where they

---

[bd] Sources : [11, 26]

worship the spirit of the watershed in gratitude. They reserve sacred groves for ceremonies, and these occur where a community reserves a shrine for its guardian spirits, for a cremation ground, or for a pagoda containing Buddha's artifacts. Often these groves are in a national forest reserve, while others are in conservation forests. This can result in confrontation between local communities and government over access. At present villagers have no legal rights to protect their groves since they are natural forests or are part of a forest reserve or a conservation forest. Legal recognition of the indigenous communities and their sacred groves is essential for their continued existence.

Marginalized villagers and minorities resort to rituals when faced with threats of oppression. For instance, the Karen people opposed a sawmill. They used ethnic symbols and reinterpreted them to articulate their rights to the forest. The struggle of the Karen at Wat Chan used the ritual of *Buat Pa* (or forest ordination) to legally recognize community forests. This ritual is a respected, successful, community-based conservation measure. Karen leaders claim their forests have more green areas than those under state control because of their spiritual attachment.

To attract attention, the Karen carried out extensive ritual performances that now make up a social movement. Early in 1996, through this network, local organizations started a large-scale campaign to promote restoration. They organized this to mark the fiftieth anniversary of the king's accession to the throne to highlight their interest in forest conservation. In 1996, when the Thai government set up a committee to revise the Forest Bill, a Karen leader took part. In 2007, the Thailand Community Forest Bill was passed.[be] This took more than eighteen years, and in theory, it gave legal recognition to the collective rights and local control of community forests to the local people. But there were still challenges, and the bill lapsed without it being promulgated by the king. It was not approved as the people challenged it on constitutional grounds as being against the people.

[be] Accessed February 2018. https://rightsandresources.org/en/blog/the-thailand-community-forest-bill/#.Wumh7SBRXIw.

Sacred Groves of St. Francis of Assisi in Italy[bf]

St. Francis was fond of the Valley of Rieti in Latium and performed miracles there. There are at least four forested sanctuaries of the Franciscan order—places of peace and tranquility amongst woodlands and natural springs. It is in the Sanctuary of Santa Maria della Foresta that St Francis (in 1223) wrote the *Canticle of the Creatures*. Ancient trees (oaks, chestnuts, hornbeams, firs, larches, and holly) cover the hills. These sites link sacred, cultural and biodiversity values in the landscape. Cultural and spiritual aspects interact with ecology and nature as St. Francis, the patron saint of ecology, would have liked. These sites are UNESCO World Heritage sites. It was here St. Francis called the animals and plants his brothers. It is here he taught his followers how important forests and nature are. As a result, the spiritual and natural heritage of the forest are inseparable and revered. At La Verna, Saint Francis spent long periods in prayer in the sacred beech forest where he received the stigmata in 1213. These forests are a testimony to the relationship between spiritual values, culture, and nature, which supports conservation, spiritual and international respect, and management since those times.

Sacred Groves—The Kayas on the Coast of Kenya[bg]

Kaya forests are ten to four hundred hectares in size and found on the coastal plains and hills. They are relic patches held sacred by the Mijikenda people and are an integral part of their culture. The word Kaya means homestead. These forest groves sheltered the fortified villages of the Mijikenda people. Kayas owe their existence to the beliefs, culture, and history of the nine coastal Mijikenda ethnic groups. During the twentieth century, people moved outside the groves, and their Kayas came to mean the forest groves that survived and that the people protected. Within local society, conflicts may occur between the elders who still revere the Kayas and the youth who see the Kayas as an economic opportunity.

[bf] Source: [16]
[bg] Sources: [28, 29, 55, 67, 68, 72, 74, 93, 96]

There are fifty-two Kayas in Kwale and Mombasa counties and thirty-nine in Kilifi. Over the past fifty years, many of the Kayas reduced in size as people registered and sold common property land as individual title. It accompanied a decline in knowledge and respect for traditional values because of rising demands for forest products, land for agriculture and mining, and a loss of cultural values. Agricultural encroachment reduced the forest sizes. For example, Kaya Chonyi is one-fifth of its original size. Others they cut for hardwoods, or some fell prey to hotel development and settlement schemes.

Kayas contain more than half of Kenya's rare shrub and plant species, and more than 50 percent of Kenya's rare plants occur along the coast and within sacred groves. There is increasing concern over the fate of the Kayas. Between 1996 and 1999, the government declared thirty-nine Kayas as national monuments (under the Kenya Antiquities and Monuments Act) with nearly two thousand hectares protected. Eleven Kayas are on the World Heritage List.[bh] They emphasize traditional uses of Kayas for cultural activities and their management by the council of elders. Giving Kayas legal recognition supports formal recognition in a way that supports local culture. This provides some protection as they defined the boundaries of their forests. But the act is weak, and conserving the Kayas needs enhancing to protect them against powerful outside interests. To secure the status of the Kayas, some things can be done to (a) strengthen statutory protection to handle cases of forest destruction, (b) strengthen and support local institutions (e.g., giving the Kaya elders' committees and conservation groups legal status), (c) develop management and coordination bodies at local levels, and (d) set up sustainable funding mechanisms.

There are rules governing access to and use of Kaya forests, including (a) non-Mijikenda people cannot enter unless agreed to; (b) sacred sites are out of bounds to those who are not initiates; (c) if you visit the central clearing, you must ensure that a Kaya elder accompanies you; (d) no modern clothing is allowed, including shoes, wristwatches, shirts, and trousers; (e) you must not stray from the traditional paths; (f) you must avoid sensitive sacred sites pointed out by the hosts; (g) livestock grazing

---

[bh] Accessed March 2017: http://whc.unes Countyorg/en/list/1231.

is not allowed inside the Kaya; (h) people who die in the Kaya are buried there, while those who die outside are buried outside; (i) people cannot fell trees inside the Kaya but are allowed to collect fuelwood from specific places; (j) poles for building can be collected from certain areas; and (k) forest burning is prohibited.

The most important part of the Kaya forest is the Kaya or central clearing. This is at the center of the grove, and visitors approach by well-defined paths. At a secret spot near the central clearing, a powerful protective talisman of the Mijikenda is buried, and it must have come from their original home. The graves of great leaders are kept apart and treated as shrines. All members of the Kaya, including women, can visit and use the site under the elders' guidance for ritual and ceremonial purposes.

The biggest problem facing the Kayas is tourism. Hotel and residential housing resulted in Kayas being destroyed. Local communities tried to protect their Kayas from land grabbers, but they have lost faith in their elected leaders' commitment to Kaya conservation. Hotel and residential development threaten Kayas close to the beaches. Powerful people violated the Antiquities and Monuments Act with little appreciation for the importance of Kaya forests to the Mijikenda or for conservation. The elders are not strong enough and cannot prevent such exploitation, especially when the government takes little heed of their concerns. They said, "How can we [the community] campaign for the preservation of sacred forests or any forest at all, if our leaders grab the only remaining forests?" (*Standard Newspaper*, September 9, 1995). Community elders protested about the fifteen hectares of the twenty-hectare Diani Kaya that was allocated to local dignitaries. In their letter to the Home Affairs Ministry (on March 24, 1995), they protested by saying, "Attached is one of the many letters we got from the authorities assuring us that our Kayas will not be cleared." Until they are strongly protected in law, Kaya forests and their traditions and culture are at risk. The same applies to many sacred groves.

Other Examples of Sacred Groves

Many people worship Maria Lionza, the forest goddess of Venezuela. The forest home of Maria Lionza is a forty-thousand-hectare tropical rainforest and is not degraded by slash-and-burn agriculture because dire misfortune would befall anyone who cuts or burns her trees. The forest was gazetted in 1960 as the Maria Lionza National Monument and is one of the best protected areas in Venezuela. [32] In a similar manner, the Tanimuka and Yukuna Amerindian tribes in northwest Amazonia have sacred palm groves in headwater regions and wetlands. [92] Hunters and gatherers avoid these groves as they are linked to the ethnic origins of these peoples.

Europe had many sacred groves, but many disappeared. Kozmin Copse in Russia's Kanin Tundra, with its sacred birch and fir trees, is an exception where people make offerings. [39] The birch is sacred to the eastern Slavs of Russia, and the white birch (*Belaya bereza*), typical of the Russian north, often occurs in churchyards. [84] In Ireland, St. Flannán's Shrine (Inagh, County Clare) shows how an ancient grove has contemporary interpretation. An ancient sacred ash tree with a shrine to St. Flannán dominates the sacred well. People adorn the trees with small objects and religious statues. [129] In Syria, forests retreated from mountains (because of degradation, grazing, and cultivation), but small forest patches still occur, surrounded by agricultural land that mark a saint's burial ground. [18]

The Kasepuhan community in the Mt. Halimum area of West Java, Indonesia, believe their forests are the sources of life and recognize three forms of forest—ancient, exploited, and sacred. Local leaders have to approve any exploitation of the sacred forests or *leuweung titipan*. Cultivation is allowed if they receive permission from the ancestors through religious leaders. Many of these sacred groves are in nature reserves managed by the government. [1]

In Bhutan, *Nye* are special places attributed to enlightened Buddhist masters and are important spiritual centers. They occur in various places, for example, springs, hills and forests. [128] As a result, Bhutan has many sacred groves. *Nye* is an important traditional and spiritual institution that can be built on by conservation, spiritual, and religious traditions for both conservation and spirituality.

Sacred groves and grasslands surround the Sacred Mount Fuji in Japan. Only people who completed certain rites can move from the grasslands to the groves. [75] The trees provide a spiritual aura as people prepare to visit the mountain and the ancient trees. As a result, there are many important Shinto shrines surrounded by sacred groves. [75] This is why Shinto shrines found elsewhere (e.g., in cities) are surrounded by sacred trees.

In one biosphere reserve (Ysyk-Köl) in Kyrgyzstan, 194 sacred sites occur, and 103 are sacred groves. [95] People visit these sites for various reasons, including health, fertility, wealth, power, knowledge, and accepting their spiritual calls. This involves a pilgrimage to the site combined with prayer and ritual. Like many sacred groves, they are important in terms of local culture and for conservation.

New Zealand nominated Tongariro National Park as a cultural landscape in 1993, even though it was already a natural World Heritage site. Tongariro is the most sacred area for the Māoris of New Zealand. Because of the religious and cultural associations the Māori have for the area, Tongariro was the first sacred site nominated as a cultural landscape under the World Heritage Convention. [97]

Most villages in Sierra Leone have at least one sacred grove maintained by secret societies that enforce sanctions and limit exploitation. There is a secret society of women that associates with some sacred groves and uses them for education. An area of sacred forest between a quarter and half of a mile wide surrounds every village. Some of these groves are reminders of resistance to enslavement or colonialism. They conduct ceremonies inside the groves focusing on the reasons for the grove's existence, rules governing access, exploitation of forest resources, and cultural taboos. [51]

Mongolia reinstated and reconsecrated many sacred sites as part of restoration after the communist era (1924–89). Certain trees, groves, animals are sacred and part of sacred landscapes. [111] For example, the

Khan Kentii Strictly Protected Area (1.2 million hectares) is part of these sacred landscapes and includes 10 percent of Mongolia's forests.

In Lao PDR, one of the two Ramsar sites, Xe Champhone, is not protected under law. Research carried out in ten villages show twenty-four customary protected areas, nineteen of which are sacred. [30] All the villages surveyed—except one—had a sacred grove, and half of the villages had a sacred lake. Customary law in the villages is similar and governs the use of species and ecosystems relating to hunting and collecting forest products unrelated to timber. It is interesting to see that the government took on most of the customary rules and institutions when the area was gazetted as a Ramsar site, and there are few real or potential conflicts between customary and statutory law.

The coastal Wazaramo people in Tanzania have myths telling of *Mwen Mbaga* (owner of the forest), to whom all trees belong. [48] Discussion about the ritual uses of the forest are taboo because of pressures to abandon traditional beliefs by Islam and Christianity. [22] But forest guards confirm that people visit the sacred groves containing graves within Pugu Forest and that they leave trees for the spirits to live in. A small burial grove near Pugu Forest still has sanctity and is the only known location for the endemic species *Stephanostemma stenocarpum*. [22]

For Tolawa and First Nation American peoples on the Pacific coast of the United States, redwoods are sacred protectors of the forest and guardians of the spirits of the ancestors. [52, 83] The giant sequoias were protected from logging as they are part of sacred groves. After long periods of loss, indigenous communities are standing up for their lands, rights, and culture. The Cree of north Quebec in Canada are suing the federal and Quebec governments and twenty-six forestry companies because of outsider interference destroying their traditional ways of life.[bi] Their boreal

---

[bi] Accessed January 2018. http://montrealgazette.com/news/local-news/waswanipi-cree-of-northern-quebec-make-last-stand-to-save-their-forest and http://www.cbc.ca/news/canada/north/cree-and-quebec-sign-agreement-to-resolve-dispute-over-forestry-practices-1.3149770.

forests are important for use and survival, and they serve as sanctuaries for cultural and religious values.

Sacred Groves around Wells and Springs

Many sacred groves evolved because of place and location as part of a sacred spring or well or as part of an important watershed. A spring might become sacred over time together with its surrounding vegetation, usually a forest that became part of the sacred spring. The spring might assume spiritual significance because it continued to provide water in dry times, or the spring rises under the roots of a tree. Whatever the reason, it was the spring (or part of watershed) that became sacred and then encompassed the surrounding vegetation.

The people of Dawan (Belu District, West Timor, Indonesia) protected a special landscape for their sacred groves. This landscape relates to springs and is the main reason for conserving these forested areas. Despite their size (one to two hectares), they conserve a high species diversity and are the last resort for some endangered species. The high degree of endemic species found in these small sacred groves highlight their importance for conserving West Timor's sacred sites. The traditional knowledge associated with these sites helps protect them from degradation. The Dawan believe their ancestors or God created *Fatus* (sacred sites) to provide water. [108]

Sacred Groves Providing Goods and Services—India

The Mawsmai sacred grove of the Khasi people lies in the Cherrapunji region of Meghalaya in north east India—one of the wettest areas on Earth. It is a relic rainforest containing once widespread climax vegetation. Even today they protect the grove for religious and cultural reasons. But too much rain combined with human disturbances make for a major stress on this fragile ecosystem. As a result, deforestation has eroded the landscape of Cherrapunji, except for the relic grove. The community banned shifting agriculture in and around the area through their traditional institutions. Although Cherrapunji is an extreme case, hundreds of sacred groves in India form islands of biodiversity in seas of degraded landscapes. Many are being lost because of modernization. So understanding how sacred grove ecosystems function becomes even more significant for restoration.

There is a vast diversity of India's sacred groves. Some contain few trees, while others are large. Some overlap larger forests or are deep within forests, while others are islands in open plains. Karnataka has 1,500 sacred groves that are called *devarakadus* or *devarkans*. In the smaller groves, there is no tree cutting, while larger groves often function as resource forests. Kerala has two thousand sacred groves. The quality of these is the basis for a network contributing to conservation and connectivity, with local community ownership. [7] These networks support higher biodiversity than each single patch. [112]

The Bishnoi manage sacred groves or *orans* in the desert regions of Rajasthan in India. [91] This practice is a religion of environmental conservation and an offshoot of Hinduism. [20] Burying rather than cremating the dead became the custom of the Bishnoi to protect trees from being cut for cremation. Khejarli is a Bishnoi village (Jodhpur district, Rajasthan).[bj] The name comes from the *Khejri* trees (*Prosopis cineraria)*. In 1730, in Khejarli, a woman named Amrita Devi was cooking with her three daughters when there was a commotion. Men sent by the king came to cut their sacred *Khejri* trees. Amrita Devi called on the men to stop, saying they are sacred trees and must not be cut. Willing to sacrifice her life for the trees, she offered her head and was beheaded. Amrita's daughters followed her example and sacrificed their lives. One of the Bishnoi announced that for every *Khejri* tree cut, one villager would sacrifice his or her life. Old people and young people alike—men, women, and children—stepped forward to sacrifice their lives for the trees. By the end of that day, 363 *Khejri* trees were cut, and 363 Bishnoi had given their lives. The next morning the king arrived and was shocked to learn how the people were killed. Honoring the courage of the Bishnoi, Maharaja Abhay Singh apologized and vowed that everyone would respect their beliefs. He issued a royal decree that

---

[bj] Accessed July 2018. https://en.wikipedia.org/wiki/Khejarli.

was engraved on a copper plate on a monument, ordering that cutting green trees and hunting animals within the boundaries of Bishnoi villages was prohibited. If an individual violated this order, he or she would be prosecuted and receive a severe penalty. Even members of the ruling family would not shoot animals in or near Bishnoi villages.

Although the Bishnoi paid a huge price for saving the trees, this incident inspired and continues to inspire others to fight and protect trees and wildlife. Old people embraced trees to prevent them from being cut. This was the origin of the Chipko movement. [20] The word Chipko, meaning "hug a tree," became their slogan. As an *Adivasi* (indigenous person) woman from the Jharkhand Save the Forest Movement said,[bk] "Forest is Our Mother. Our life sustains her. Our spirituality is tied to the trees."

Despite sparse vegetation and limited water, the Bishnoi landscapes support higher densities of human and animal populations than any desert region in the world because of the Bishnoi conservation practices. [20] Their laws ban killing animals and felling trees, especially the sacred *Khejri* tree, which is important for fodder, fruit, and fuel for the people (by only cutting branches). Only a few sacred groves are documented, but they are large (thousands of hectares) as the trees are widely dispersed in the dry landscapes. The Bishnoi, given their concern for conservation and sanctity of life, support conservation as an important benefit of land usage and social practices. Where the massacre took place, they built a temple besides the monument, and a special *Khejri* tree nursery was set up. [23]

Monastic (Church, Temple, and Monastery) Groves[bl]

Forest groves evolved as part of temples, mosques, monasteries, and churches. Now many are sources of important biodiversity. Monasteries protected patches of forest and trees for hundreds of years. They planted

---

[bk] Accessed July 2018. http://womensearthalliance.blogspot.com/2013/04/the-original-tree-huggers-lets-not.html.
[bl] Sources: [14, 28, 32, 43, 55, 62, 67, 70, 93, 96, 98, 117]

trees as part of the sanctity of the monasteries to connect them to the saints the sites commemorate. In Thailand, Buddhist temples are built in forests. There are about thirty-seven thousand temples in Thailand, and most have a sacred grove varying from 0.5 to 8.0 hectares or more.

Monastic Forests in Ethiopia[bm]

Ethiopia and Eritrea illustrate how important monastic forests are. Monastic forests have been important for a long time and are repositories of relic biodiversity. These forests provide many of the daily requirements for the monastery priests and staff. They became islands of natural forest biodiversity in seas of deforested landscapes. Table 4 summarizes the uses of monastic forests in terms of forest products and services. Species diversity ranges from thirteen to ninety, and between one and twelve species are common across more than one monastic forest.

Table 4: Production and Service Roles of Trees in Ethiopian Monastic Forests [4]

Forest Products	Forest Services from the Monastic Forests
• Construction materials for churches • Wood for sacred objects (e.g., drums, crosses) • Food and fruit • Charcoal for services • Poles for Meskel bonfire	• People respect the forests as God's place and a resting place or sanctuary for saints. • Microclimate around the areas is improved and soil erosion reduced. • Church schools can learn and be taught under the shade of trees. • There is a sweet aroma for the church provided by the trees. • Church forests or trees justify land ownership. • Trees around churches symbolize that God created Adam, placed him in Eden, and how God appeared to Abraham under a tree and for life after death. • Church forests are used as symbols or examples in teachings of the Gospel. • Church forests or trees are a national heritage.

Sacred monastery lands of the Ethiopian Orthodox Tewahedo churches survive as islands of natural forest biodiversity because the church has a

---

[bm] Sources: [4, 98]

long tradition of conservation. Ethiopia has more than thirty-five thousand churches and monasteries, with some more than 1,600 years old. Many have groves rich in biodiversity. At least fifty of the ancient monastery grounds (older than two hundred years) contain important forest vegetation and occur in the central and northern highlands.

In the Gamo Highlands of south Ethiopia, there are sacred groves which are burial grounds and relic natural forests. The Gamo people believe natural objects can be sacred. Their sacred groves are home to spirits. They serve important spiritual functions, and are important for conservation. For example, 152 plant species (of which nineteen are endemic to Ethiopia) occurred in a sample of 2.24 hectares.

These monastic forests are places of worship, and they provided many requirements for Christian life. The references to them in the Bible reinforce this fact, and the religious connections between tree planting and the church relate to the scriptures. "Along both banks of the river, fruit trees of every kind shall grow; their leaves shall not fade, nor their fruit fail. Every month they shall bear fresh fruit, for they shall be watered by the flow from the sanctuary. Their fruit shall serve for food, and their leaves for medicine" (Ezekiel, 47:12). As a result, the church has a long history of planting trees and conserving them. It is teaching and advising clergy and people about the importance of trees, conserving existing trees, supporting the planting and care for trees, and taking care of indigenous trees.

Large and old trees—for example, cedar (*Juniperus procera*), sycamore (*Ficus sycomorus*), and yellow wood (*Podocarpus latifolius*)—are sacred, and they allow no usage, except for church services. For some trees, people cannot use the dead branches. Within a certain radius of the church, the wood and leaves may not be used, and the land may not be farmed. "You shall not destroy its trees by putting an axe to them. You may eat of their fruit, but you must not cut down the trees. After all, are the trees of the field men, that they should be included in your siege?" (Deuteronomy 20:19).

Ethiopian practices about groves cite the Bible to conserve trees and emphasize that sacred trees express human commitment to God. They provide important benefits for the church. Monastic forests also show the church's tenure over them. Until the 1974 revolution, the state recognized church ownership of land, buildings, and sacred groves. During the revolution the state confiscated many Ethiopian churches' useful lands, and it has been difficult to recover these lands since the end of socialism in 1991. Monastic forests are important repositories of flora and fauna and may be the last sanctuaries for some endangered species. They can be a source for restoration and learning. But the quality and area of most monastic forests are declining. Those who aren't followers and do not agree about the ownership of monastic forests exacerbate this issue. It is important to devise conservation plans to promote restoring indigenous species, foster awareness about conservation, and promote sustainability through training and improved management.

Other Christian Monastic Landscapes and Forests in Europe[bn]

Many European countries established protected areas on sites of former or existing monastic lands. Such lands can be ICCAs. Most would be category-V or VI protected areas. Their experiences over long time periods in adapting to and overcoming environmental and other such crises still apply today. Europe should consider these Christian monastic sites as SNS or sacred groves for those that contain forests. [122] Christian monasteries and their lands thrived in Europe and the Near East for many centuries. Some are 1,800 years old, and many had positive impacts on the environment and natural resource management. [57] Now these monasteries are undergoing a renaissance as people seek lifestyles close to nature.

There are some Christian and monastic territories that date back to the beginnings of Christianity and even further back for some Eastern religions (e.g., Buddhism). Most monasteries and their landscapes are old (six hundred to 1,800 years old). There are two types of monastery—those for community life and those for the isolated life of hermitages. Both types

---

[bn] Accessed September 2018. [58] http://ayla.culture.gr/en.

still survive. Their values are like those of sacred groves found in other parts of the world.

We find monastic settlements in different landscapes—mountains, forests, islands, dry areas—and in different parts of the globe. For most of these, the monastic communities managed large areas of land with high biodiversity and agrobiodiversity values. There were tens of thousands of such monastic communities between the tenth and sixteenth centuries. While there are no current inventories of these monasteries (like many ICCAs), estimates show that thousands still exist in Europe. Thus, they are significant conservation assets and important in religious terms.

Many of the forested monasteries contain old-growth trees. Like many sacred groves, they are repositories of species important for restoration, many of which may be endemic. Two examples are Sainte Baume (Holy Cave) of Saint Marie Madeline in France and Sacro Eremo delle Carceci (a forested landscape where St. Francis of Assisi retreated to). The Santa Creu Hermitage at the Holy Mountain of Montserrat in Catalonia, Spain, has been inhabited for more than 1,400 years. Now it is a nature reserve within Montserrat National Park.

Monastic communities are some the oldest self-organized communities with a continuous conservation record. Most predate formal protected area and conservation movements by hundreds and even thousands of years. Their records show there was a focus on ecological integrity and landscape diversity. Further, they contributed to sustainability of both the land and societies bordering them. This made them centers for peace. Their sustainable management by these monastic communities has been key to well-conserved landscapes. Monastic communities and their landscapes are one specific type of ICCA. They are one category of community with similar landscape and conservation objectives. This further makes the case for more engagement between the conservation movement and monastic custodians. We have much to learn for conservation from the long-term practices that monasteries adopted for community conservation and protected area management.

Sherpa Sacred Forests of the Mt. Everest Region Nepal[bo]

Sacred trees and groves are an integral part of the Khumba landscape (Mt. Everest area of the Nepal Himalayas). They express the historical depth of Sherpa Buddhist faith. Trees dot the villages and fields believed to be the home of *Lu* or spirits that particular family's worship. They pass the knowledge of the trees, spirits, and shrines through the generations. Sacred groves surround temples. Monks set apart other forests called *Lama Nating* (Lama's forests) because monks sanctified them as places where no trees can be cut and no cutting implement taken in. Revered local religious leaders established the largest sacred groves in the Khumbas. Phurtse is the most famous of the Lama's forests. The sacred trees and groves are striking elements of Sherpa village landscapes and represent a gesture of faith in a land where trees are so useful yet so scarce. People still protect them despite increased land and population pressures, and this supports conservation in this landscape.

Buddha's Sacred Forest on Sri Pada Peak in Sri Lanka[bp]

Sri Pada (or Adam's Peak) is the highest point in the west shoulder of Sri Lanka's Central Mountains. The peak is important for conservationists, spiritual leaders, and the public because of its commanding position and the sacred footprint of Lord Buddha on the rock summit. This enhances the spirituality of the Peak Wilderness area. The sacred footprint (*Sri Pada* or *Siri Pathula*) is on *Samantha Kuuta Parwathaya*, the highest mountain peak in the area. Those who live in the villages treat the forest as living and sacred. Local beliefs use the teachings of Lord Buddha, who said, "The forest is a peculiar organism of unlimited kindness and benevolence that makes no demand for its sustenance and extends generously the products of its life activity: it affords protection to all beings, offering shade even to the axe-man who destroys it."[bq]

[bo] Source: [21]

[bp] Source: [120, 121]

[bq] Accessed September 2018. https://www.goodreads.com/quotes/148391-the-forest-is-a-peculiar-organism-of-unlimited-kindness-and.

Three million people climb Adam's Peak every year between the full moons of December and May. This is a tradition for pilgrims who have to respect certain rules (e.g., bathing in the holy waters of the *Seetha-Gangula* stream and wearing clean clothing). There are important reasons for Buddhists, Hindus, Muslims, and Christians to conserve this sacred mountain. Buddhists believe the sacred footprint is the imprint of the left foot of Lord Buddha. Muslims believe it is the footprint of Adam, who stood on the peak for a thousand years after being cast out of paradise. The peak is also called Baba Adam-Malai or Father Adam's Mountain. Christians believe it is the footprint of St. Thomas, who brought Christianity to Sri Lanka. Hindus believe it is the footprint of the Lord Shiva. Such beliefs make it possible to embrace all ethnic and religious groups under a common interest to safeguard and revere the sacred footprint and the area.

Local communities living close to the area have a practical and spiritual understanding. "Siripa Adaviya [the sacred forest area] is superior to all manipulated systems and full of great powers. This is a huge living organism and it has produced habitats for flora and fauna. … It provides food, water, and shelter, and regenerates materials season after season and sustains conditions to support all living beings. Its superiority cannot be explained but should be understood. The sacred mountain forest has sustained itself through natural processes and every plant and animal within it can be found to be useful," said a local inhabitant who has lived in a cave in the forest for more than fifty years.[br] While the Sri Lankan government created wilderness areas and national parks, it has yet to set up ways to better conserve sacred groves or declare and safeguard sacred mountain forests. Yet hundreds of monasteries and shrines occur in forests that were established through ancient rules for conserving nature and culture and reflecting the serene philosophy they tried to instill into local lifestyles.

Shinto Shrines in Japan[bs]

Shinto and Buddhist sacred groves cover more than 110,000 hectares. The Kasugayama Primeval Forest outside the city of Nara is a home of

---

[br] Source: [120]
[bs] Sources: [24, 33, 42, 66]

the Shinto gods and is protected from hunting and tree felling. Japanese ancestors cut forests to develop *Hitozato* or agricultural land but kept forest shrines. Shinto shrines occur all over Japan, and they are surrounded by trees and woodlands. These are called *Chinju no mori*. This refers to forests that keep the atmosphere peaceful. The forests relate to the worship of gods by local people, their shrines and temples irrespective of religion. Some shrines occur in the heart of cities (where there are similarities with the groves and trees in Kumasi, Ghana, and Hanoi, Vietnam). These shrines are important way beyond their monetary value.

Many Shinto shrines and their groves are part of Japan's *Satoyama* cultural landscapes. The *ujiko*, a committee of shrine parishioners, manage rural Shinto shrines. They play important roles in connecting the sacred with daily life through ceremonies and festivals. This committee makes and implements the rules that govern the groves and shrines. Some of these groves occur on farm lands or on hills and mountains. Yet local people still protect them in the face of strong development pressures. But the younger generation, in-migrants, and tourists are not so interested in preserving such groves—a familiar pressure in many countries.

Relevance of Monastic Groves in Our Contemporary World

We assume sacred groves are static forms of vegetation. But they are dynamic, and they change with changing societal and settlement patterns, migration, and tenure. So we require a better understanding of the ecological, social, and symbolic factors for adaptive and comanagement. [73] While nature has receded from landscapes because of agriculture and development, churchyards and monasteries escaped these pressures. These places combine spirituality with the opportunity to experience nature. The words to best describe how people felt in their monastic or church forest were peace and tranquility. [47]

In north Russia around Lake Kenozero, there are forty-five documented sacred groves. [84] Because of their cultural significance, these groves are part of Kenozersky National Park. It is likely these groves predate the orthodox church. While in China and Hong Kong, feng shui forests helped people locate their villages at sites with good *qi* (vital energy) and have a balance between the *yin* and the *yang*. Many of these forests occur behind temples and shrines. [33] There are about six thousand feng shui forests in China, which play important roles for conservation and connectivity. [60]

Because of Ireland's history, there are many natural places associated with trees and wells where they celebrate Catholic Mass. For example, one such place is an ash in a field in Lahardan Upper (County Tipperary) known as *Crann Beannaithe* (the Blessed Tree). At Craigagh in Cushendun (County Antrim), a Mass site occurs on a secluded hillside enclosure made up of rock outcrops, dry stone walls, and tall trees. [106]

The Garden of Gethsemane in Jerusalem is the site of Jesus's nightlong agony, his betrayal by Judas, and his arrest. There are at least eight ancient and gnarled olive trees between nine hundred and two thousand years old. Those trees might have been there at the time of Jesus's betrayal. In addition, the garden of Gethsemane and its olive trees have survived the turbulent history of Jerusalem. [66]

In the Margareb countries of northwest Africa, areas surrounding Muslim saints' tombs and cemeteries of local Muslim communities are holy forests. Everyone knows the cultural and spiritual importance of these Marabout forests. The noncommercial values of the sites' biodiversity and spiritual resources predate formal conservation. Within the sacred area, they protect trees, not as objects of veneration but because they are important for the identity and social organization of the people. Some of the oldest trees in Tunisia occur in Marabout sites. Marabouts are interesting from a gender perspective. In Morocco, women healers practice at Marabout sites and have great power. The Marabout sites still play a central part in North African community life and harbor a rich diversity of species. Though these sites are small, they are important culturally and spiritually.

The TKF Foundation[bt] sparked a national movement with local roots and support more than 130 urban parks in the United States through a program called Open Spaces Sacred Places. [110, 124] This created accessible,

---

[bt] Accessed Sept 2018: http://naturesacred.org/about-us/.

open, green spaces to help people and communities find solace, respite, and renewal. Like many scared trees and groves, such places have important restorative effects in reducing stress and becoming more serene. Many of these Open Spaces Sacred Places were created as memorial or celebration sites and then became places for community ceremonies. They contribute to both sacred nature and local identity and cohesion. Many of the qualities people find in sacred groves are like those found in these urban spaces—stillness, reconnection, reverence, mindfulness, and silence.

What Lessons Are We Learning, and What Practical Action Can We Take?

We see a great diversity of sacred groves in scale, numbers, area, type, and objectives. They survive despite land and population pressures that would have resulted in their conversion under normal circumstances. The fact they are not converted is a testament to their resilience as well as their cultural and spiritual importance to local villages, communities, and people across the globe. This importance is part of or transcends formal religion. At an individual level, they may not be extensive, though some are. The sheer number of groves in different countries and different ecosystems and managed under different conditions is important in itself. Many groves contain important biodiversity, some endemic, and in other cases, these are relics of more ancient vegetation types. They are important local and global forest conservation assets. It is important to reemphasize the underlying rationale for sacred trees and groves is their sacredness. Conservation is a benefit. [43] But that is not an excuse to ignore their importance in conservation. There are many ways to conserve. Setting them aside as national parks or forest reserves is one way, and ensuring they are ICCAs is another. Yet we must respect that such trees and groves are protected by the cultural norms of neighboring communities. [17] There are reasons sacred groves are important conservation and forest assets.

    a) Their sheer age (e.g., the sacred yew groves in Europe, old sacred trees and groves in India, and the redwood or bristlecone pine groves in the United States) make them important.

b) Some conserve biodiversity as a benefit of their spiritual values (e.g., the Boabeng-Fiema sacred grove in Ghana).
c) Many are remnant communities of flora and fauna, and they are often important historically and ecologically because such areas may be surrounded by areas of converted or degraded lands.
d) The traditional and religious management systems, while important for managing sacred sites in a religious and spiritual sense, are also important for conservation.
e) While not large, the number of sacred groves contributes to connectivity and can be a focus for natural forest and landscape restoration.
f) The number of groves found all over the world is important. They are all protected areas, though only a few are formally recognized.
g) They also serve as a key point of entry for linking rural livelihoods to conservation.

Making way for development caused the destruction of many sacred groves. Government often ignores communities' customary management systems while allowing commercial forestry or gazetting national parks. Some groves have large numbers of tourists and pilgrims (e.g., in India or the Kayas in Kenya). Other groves are part of formal religions (e.g., Hinduism and Christianity). Of greater concern is the loss of traditional wisdom and practices because of the increasing influence of Western urban cultures and an expanding market economy. As a result, the youth no longer learn respect for local traditions and the cultural importance of sacred groves. This relates to the fact that most of us lack a sense of place as modern technology and lifestyles separate us from place. We no longer understand where our food comes from or where our waste goes. Attachment to place grows when the boundaries of a person and place are indistinguishable. [78]

People are starting to see (or see again) how important traditional wisdom is and integrate this into modern systems of awareness and education. New sacred grove management plans can restore power to local communities. Awareness campaigns can educate people about the value of conservation and stimulate the revival of traditions. But without greater efforts from religious and conservation groups, it is questionable how long these groves and their institutions can survive. Some groves contain important keystone and endemic species that have been conserved because of their sacredness. [88] Some Kaya sacred groves were destroyed, many reduced in area, and they suffered significant ecological change because of the extraction of certain trees. [72]

This highlights an opportunity. Conservation may be easier to achieve through connectivity and integrated landscapes. So we can combine approaches—community-reserved hillsides, sacred groves, national parks, conserved riparian areas together with farmland. Recognizing connectivity and negotiated trade-offs will help in the optimal use of ecosystem services. This will be more sustainable though more difficult to achieve than alienating more lands for national parks or converting such land for agriculture. Sacred groves have various ownership and management regimes. So context is important, and solutions need to be local. We need support for sacred groves and their conservation as a culturally sensitive approach for community conservation. [77]

Sacred trees and groves do not have much legal protection. They exist based on their local importance. Some were included and given increased protection as national parks (e.g., Shai Hills in Ghana), while others were designated as National Monuments (e.g., Kaya forests in Kenya). A review of thirteen new forest laws provided mixed results in terms of legal recognition of such sociocultural uses and values. Only four countries in Africa—Lesotho, Tanzania, Mozambique, and Kenya—have legal provisions for sacred groves and sociocultural values to empower local communities to manage them. [73] However, implementation of such policy and law is another challenge. Other countries afford greater legal protection for SNS, including sacred groves. These include many Australian national parks being handed back to traditional Aboriginal owners. [107] Perhaps the most famous of these is Uluru Kata Tjuta National Park.[bu] As a result, many sacred groves are now part of national protected area systems[bv]

[bu] Accessed July 2018. http://www.environment.gov.au/resource/20th-anniversary-handbook-brief-background-uluru-kata-tjuta-national-park.

[bv] For the sake of this discussion, this also includes forest reserves, world heritage sites, and other forms of national or international official recognition.

across the globe—something we could expand, provided the protected area authorities respect the rights of grove custodians. Canada, the United States, and New Zealand now have more supportive legislation, but it does not appear that land claims and protecting such sacred groves has become any stronger. [114]

SNS and groves are at the heart of ecological governance. Revaluing how important sacred places are promotes connection with nature. However, if we continue to degrade our ecosystems, we will compromise their natural resilience. [37] This can help us reemphasize the role of ecosystems in maintaining climatic, hydrological, and energy equilibrium. This is one of the central lessons that understanding sacred sites teaches us. [36] From the analysis of sacred groves, there are important lessons for religious, spiritual, and conservation groups. From the perspective of religion, it calls for us to

1. acknowledge and understand the value of sacred trees and groves in terms of the spirituality of local people irrespective of religious denomination or spiritual tradition;
2. understand and appreciate the variety of social institutions responsible for management;
3. understand that sacred trees and groves can be important for peoples' lives (because these practices survived despite formal religious efforts to either destroy or subsume them);
4. take responsibility and address the environmental crisis, in particular for trees and forests, as religion and conservation are intertwined and the security of sacred groves cannot be isolated from wider society and the land usage of which they are a part;
5. appreciate that spirituality can be expressed in different ways, many of which formal religions still appear to find difficult to recognize and respect;
6. uphold and support local indigenous technical knowledge to conserve groves, which may represent ancient relic forests;
7. engage with conservation organizations for the better management of sacred groves;

8. integrate and make sacred groves a part of education and awareness and experiential learning, as many younger people may not have the same values for sacred groves; and
9. redefine religious responsibilities with respect to the environment and for forests and trees.

From the perspective of conservation, it calls for us to

1. acknowledge that the variety and range of tree species held sacred by one or more societies, spiritual groups, and religions is important;
2. understand that, while conservation is not a primary goal, many groves conserve biodiversity, which may represent relic populations and may be endemic;
3. recognize sacred groves provide important ecological services;
4. integrate spiritual and religious perspectives into conservation principles and practice, including landscape connectivity and restoration;
5. use sacred groves as one basis for enhanced sensitive ecotourism;
6. respect sacred groves as one form of ICCA;
7. manage sacred groves so they can adapt to external, economic, and land use pressures with our support in terms of policy and governance;
8. understand traditional and local institutions that manage sacred groves as one way to improve conservation, thus enhancing conservation and respecting spiritual traditions; and
9. engage more with different religions for the better conservation of such sacred sites.

Sacred groves offer an alternative view of conservation based on spirituality and the norms and taboos of local people rather than formal protected areas. [77] There are key lessons we can learn about conserving and managing sacred groves. They link nature and culture and serve as anchors for cultural identity. Sacred groves can be effective for conservation as they are part of local and traditional belief systems. They are of great value for conserving areas of high biodiversity value, sanctuaries for rare or threatened species, and indicator sites showing potential natural vegetation in areas prone to degradation, and they could be important for restoration. [97] So it is important to better support sacred groves to reduce the further destruction of forests. Since the 1950s, the world's forests reduced by 33 percent at a rate of fifteen football pitches per minute. [37] With each tree felled, who knows what else we are losing in terms of biodiversity, especially in the tropics.

The changing views of sacred groves as institutions call us to better understand social organization. For instance, African sacred groves cut across multiple social processes, ranging from the localized division of labor by gender, age, and kinship to regional politics of global economics. To explain how sacred groves are important institutions and threatened ecological patches requires us to transcend sectoral and pastoral divides and acknowledge that the important social issues change with time. [104]

While trees and groves became sacred over many hundreds and thousands of years, we can have our own sacred tree, planted or natural, be it a tree in the garden having special meaning or a patch of garden used for silence and meditation or a potted tree used as a focus for mindfulness, silence, and peace. These you can make personally (or corporately among family) sacred, a focus for your attention, a place to be silent and at peace. We can make these spaces. It does not have to be tangible. It can be a memory, a story that resonates, or a picture. We can bring the sacred aspects of nature, the majestic presence of trees and groves, and the silence and peace they bring us into our own spaces and our own minds.

If we want to save sacred groves, we must save the people who belong to them. But if we want to save those people, we must save the land people belong to. The two are interconnected. [6] Rather than more technological breakthroughs, we need a homecoming that requires more local knowledge, a more competent and empowered citizenry, and more reflection on what is important and what is not. [78] And if we are to save both people and land, solutions must be local and the work local with, one hopes, political and policy support. In the next chapters, I will explore how we can achieve this in practice through community conservation and stewardship, a term that religions and conservation groups and organizations use.

Conserved Areas—Whose and for What Purpose in the Context of Sacred Trees and Sacred Groves?

CHAPTER 5

You are your environment, and your environment is you.
—Wayne Dyer [24]

Role of Conserved Areas for Sacred Trees and Sacred Groves—Takeover or Synergy?

If we rely on biodiversity to justify conservation, this can be a mistake. It ignores other values, namely those related to culture and sacredness. So integrating scientific and indigenous scientific knowledge and practices is important, including those intangible values that influence conservation. As a result, conservation may be a benefit of other social processes. Conservation focuses more on the science. Yet humankind has lived with, evolved from, and depended on nature for millennia. Over the past few decades, community conservation has moved conservation from the more scientific and protectionist focus to various forms of community involvement. This is a sound basis to frame sacred trees and groves. Respect for and legitimation of sacred trees and groves combined with designating them as ICCAs is a practical way to do this. It embraces species and groves from the perspectives of religious and spiritual traditions (sacredness) and from conservation (biodiversity, endemism, and connectivity) perspectives.

Sacred groves are sacred to those people who live with them, view them as sacred, and protect and manage them. Some sites are secret. So we require ways to ensure the continued respect for and stewardship of such sites and species by the people who hold them sacred. One step is better documentation and recognition. We should make sure local management and institutional structures are respected, recognized, and legitimated in conservation, land use, and policy and law. This chapter frames these points. I suggest ways sacred trees and groves can be legitimated and respected in both local and national policy and law. The key framing arenas include the various forms of ICCA.

Sacred groves are important for biodiversity, though the areas may not be large. Yet in many countries they are very numerous. For example, in two groves in Kerala, India, they found four threatened species. [59] In Nepal, in one valley, sacred groves have up to 150 useful plants that are otherwise absent or rare. [48] But there is little real emphasis on how important sacred groves are as repositories of biodiversity. The reasons relate to scale (not big enough) and lack of connectivity. Still, sacred groves contribute to ecosystem conservation because of customary ownership, their numbers, and connectivity in the landscape.

Sacred trees and groves are one form of ICCA and one form of community conservation. Community conservation as a practice and approach to conservation stems from the recognition that conservation areas and values will survive only if they address human concerns. [3, 31, 44, 51, 52] While most concerns are utilitarian, many areas are important culturally and spiritually. If local people do not support them, the future of such areas is insecure as the temptation to exploit them may be irresistible [21, 49] as has happened with Kayas and other sacred groves.

While the Rio +20 process did not make much progress, some governments moved to create a new worldview of nature. Ecuador stands out as the first country to include the rights of nature (see box 16, which is translation from Spanish) in its constitution. [68] Bolivia has since done likewise.[bw]

[bw] Accessed May 2018. The Guardian - Bolivia Enshrines Natural World's Rights With Equal Status for Mother Earth.

There is increasing convergence as faith-based and spiritual groups seek to bring SNS into protected areas to ensure their survival. [23] If protected area authorities adapt and cater to the needs of the custodians of these sites, this can support both conservation and spirituality. This is achievable if we work with local communities. Community conservation tools enable local people to be effective stewards. Managers of protected areas ought to use more inclusive models to integrate local people's interests, to not displace resident people, and to have a high degree of local participation in planning and management. [14]

> **Box 16: Ecuador Constitution—Chapter 7 on the Rights of Nature**
>
> Art. 71. Nature or *Pachamama*, where life is reproduced and occurs, has the right to integral respect for its existence and for the maintenance and regeneration of its life cycles, structure, functions and its evolutionary processes. All persons, communities, peoples and nations can call upon public authorities to enforce the rights for nature. To enforce and interpret these rights, the principles set forth in the Constitution shall be observed as appropriate. The state shall give incentives to natural persons and legal entities and to communities to protect nature and to promote respect for all the elements comprising an ecosystem
>
> Art. 72. Nature has the right to be restored. This restoration shall be apart from the obligation of the State and natural persons or legal entities to compensate individuals and communities that depend on affected natural systems. In those cases of severe or permanent environmental impact, including those caused by the exploitation of non-renewable natural resources, the State shall establish the most efficient mechanisms to achieve the restoration and shall adopt adequate measures to eliminate or mitigate harmful environmental consequences.
>
> Art. 73. The State shall apply preventive and restrictive measures on activities that might lead to the extinction of species, the destruction of ecosystems and the permanent alteration of natural cycles. The introduction of organisms, and organic and inorganic materials that might definitively alter the nation's genetic asses is forbidden.
>
> Art. 74. Persons, communities, peoples, and nations shall have the right to benefit from the environment and the natural wealth enabling them to enjoy the good way of living.

Many community conservation initiatives try to improve the integrity and conservation status of protected areas, where conserving biodiversity and natural habitats are the main drivers. This led to a stronger understanding of community needs and aspirations and a greater emphasis on their involvement. [10] Community conservation does not just support conservation, but rather it is a political, social, and cultural obligation in its own right. We recognize natural forest management and restoration of degraded natural systems also requires us to consider the ecological, socioeconomic, and cultural dimensions and the interactions between them. [67]

Sacred trees and groves are important for community conservation and focus on the sacred values but this can also include use. The sheer scale and number of sacred groves and natural sites requires more strategic recognition. SNS, of which sacred trees and groves are an important subset, have a range of strengths and weaknesses (see table 5) that need to be considered so that they can be integrated in community conservation, ICCAs, and protected area movements.

From a conservation perspective, conservation and protected area agencies can provide greater respect of, recognition for, and legal and policy support to SNS as there are threats that [27, 83, 87]

- disconnect people from nature and from their spiritual traditions because of urbanization;
- create a homogenous global community because of internet and other media with people who are less appreciative of traditional and spiritual values;
- include pollution, noise, unplanned development, deforestation, and degradation;
- make the case for sacred groves as conservation assets at national and global levels;
- document losses of sacred groves and the reasons for this loss (threats and pressures);
- downplay roles of traditional beliefs by religions that reduces the importance of sacred groves;
- become tourism sites that dilute the relevance of the sacred sites;

- undervalue their contemporary importance because of changes in belief systems and modern education, which can undermine customary stewardship;
- make the custodians less able to adapt to a fast-changing world (socially, culturally, spiritually) and send the message that they might be replaced, often with little effect, by formal government institutions;
- instigate a lack of learning about how custodians collaborate to understand and conserve sacred groves;
- are more vulnerable if they are not part of formal belief systems; and
- communicate that sacred trees and groves are rarely protected and could be degraded, converted, and settled.

Sacred groves contribute to social and spiritual well-being and offer refuges for species that might go extinct in changed landscapes. Their management can strengthen community cohesion, which can further enhance conservation. For example, the influence of religious beliefs on forest conservation in Nepal is significant. It gives rise to institutions for co-management and provides messages for forest conservation in Nepalese society.

Poverty means a lack of food, but it also means a lack of access to food. Poverty also relates to spiritual poverty and emphasizes how important sacred trees and groves are to help people reconnect with their spirituality as "the world has enough for everyone's need, but not enough for everyone's greed" [bx] (Mahatma Gandhi). Our problem results from the few seizing the gifts of Mother Earth. [43] There are three relevant messages from the Millennium Ecosystem Assessment. [53]

1. Ownership and local governance are key. Local communities will conserve if they decide how they use nature and can take a fair share of the benefits.
2. If we create the enabling environment that communicates how important nature is, this will translate to nature receiving

---

[bx] Accessed January 2017. https://www.goodreads.com/quotes/427443-the-world-has-enough-for-everyone-s-need-but-not-enough.

greater protection. This is particularly important for government and business decision making and not leaving it to the weak environment sector.
3. We must consider natural costs in economic decision making as protecting nature's services will not be a priority as long as we see them as *free and limitless*.

Table 5: Sacred Natural Sites (SNS) Strengths and Weaknesses [45]

Strengths and Opportunities	Threats and Weaknesses
1. High conservation value, an indicator for restoration.	1. Inadequate recognition by government and public. Policy does not integrate SNS.
2. Sustainable protection as ICCAs resonate with traditional systems and values.	2. Secrecy of the sacred may cause nonrecognition.
3. Model sites for management as SNS reflect a more holistic view of nature interactions and can be part of protected areas.	3. Arbitrary selection of many sacred sites, and maybe too small, but ecological features are not the sole consideration for SNS.
4. Conserve local and traditional knowledge at species and ecosystem levels.	4. Artificial ecosystems as SNS may not be pristine or shaped by human hands.
5. Culture and cultural diversity as SNS are reference points for cultural, religious, and spiritual identity.	5. Cultural change as SNS are subject to changing values, and sites may lose or gain value. Cultural values disappear as younger generations no longer share the same values as their elders.
6. Ecotourism, if sensitively applied, can benefit people and nature.	6. Economic benefits as custodians of SNS are not strong enough to resist external forces.
7. Sacredness as a value in itself should be respected as culture and biodiversity are intertwined.	7. Traditional ecological knowledge is the basis for SNS, but validation of SNS only done when deemed useful to *science*.

Community conservation [31] provides an overall way to recognize and respect sacred trees and groves. That way, they are no longer a sort of add-on, not important for conservation and land use. At a community or custodian level, such trees and groves are important. Formal religions now acknowledge the relevance and importance of these trees and groves. To complete this triangle, conservation and land use has to integrate how important sacred trees and groves are. This chapter sets sacred trees and groves in relation to protected areas and ICCAs. I summarize some arguments for community conservation on how sacred trees and groves and other SNS are recognized for the critical roles they play in conservation and as important livelihood components for people.

Species Diversity—Important Conservation Benefits from Sacred Groves

Table 6: Species Diversity in Seven Kayas in Kenya

Kaya	Forested Area (approx.) in Hectares	No. of Species	Percentage of Rare Species
Jibana/Pangan	250	354	19.8
Kinondo	30	112	14.3
Dzombo	295	361	10.0
Kivara	130	170	3.5
Muhaka	130	278	9.0
Mrima	290	271	9.2
Rabai	850	425	4.7

Species diversity, endemism, and rarity are not major objectives of sacred trees or groves. Yet table 6 regarding the Kayas of Kenya [69] and table 7 about species diversity in West Timor [77] are examples of the impressive diversity sacred groves can have. There are similar examples in many places. Sacred trees can be keystone species (e.g., the fig and baobab trees). Many groves may be the only remnants of forest types that were once widespread (e.g., the monastic forests of Ethiopia).

Xishuangbanna Province in southwest China covers 0.2 percent of China yet supports 16 percent of higher plant species and more than 23 percent of China's animal species. For the Dai custodians, humanity is part of a unified whole that the sacred Dai forests illustrate. To take care of the environment is a Dai virtue. [30] Positive biodiversity effects are benefits of religious and spiritual behavior. Sites are often less disturbed because they are based on culture and traditional belief systems. On five Dai holy hill sites, they found 105 to 122 species of plants in 0.15-hectare survey plots. This emphasizes how important the holy hill forests are for conservation [30] and creating connectivity in the landscape.

Edward Goldsmith challenges us, "Modern ecology has become highly reductionist. Most of its practitioners insisting that one can only understand the functioning of an ecosystem by examining its parts in isolation from each other." [26] Conservation is more than conservation science, which argues that most sacred groves are not large enough. This might be valid if one is looking at sacred groves in isolation. Yet they are parts of cultural landscapes, and there may be many sacred groves. We can achieve connectivity through combinations of land use (e.g., riparian and catchment conservation, a sacred grove and a reserved forest being part of a landscape) together with land for agriculture.

Table 7: Species Diversity in Ten Sacred Sites in West Timor

Sacred Grove Name	Species	Genera
Wemean	22	21
Alkani	39	32
G. Mandeu	30	27
Simulu	24	22
Laran Tetun	26	21
Nualain	21	15
Raihuli	47	44
Lahurus	26	23
Webot	31	28
Takirin	38	33

Conservation should build on the conservation values of sacred groves, not criticize their size and viability. This moves the discourse from more Western conservation science approaches to embracing the spiritual and cultural importance of nature wherever sacred trees and groves occur. Though groves may be a small part of the interconnected whole, they may be key elements out of proportion to their size and are an important link between social, cultural, ecological, and biological perspectives.

For example, a sacred grove in southwest Madagascar, when compared to aerial photographs taken in 1949 and satellite images from 1989, shows it is well conserved considering how degraded much of the nation's forests are. Traditional rules govern access to the grove and maintain ecological, social, and moral relationships. The conservation of these groves is due to local communities containing intrusion. The state and community agree how to conserve the groves. [62] In Madagascar, community rules allow for the use of traditional rules. [74]

Community Conservation—The Framework to Support Sacred Groves

Sacred groves are a form of community conservation. Community conservation is a broad spectrum of management arrangements[by] and benefits from partnerships for being involved in natural resource management by local people. Because of their collective location and activities, such people are well placed to shape the present and future status of these resources. This enhances conservation and the well-being of local people and communities. [7] There are three categories of community conservation:

1. Protected area outreach enhances the biological integrity of parks by working to benefit local communities and enhance the role of a protected area in local planning. For example, consider a national park with a sacred grove inside its boundaries where park authorities allow customary users access as in the Shai Hills National Park in Ghana. But there are still evictions from protected areas, and not all people are allowed to access their sacred sites, which is no longer acceptable.
2. Collaborative management is based on agreements between local communities or groups of resource users and conservation authorities for access to nature's bounty under some form of statutory authority. For example, there might be a collaborative agreement for customary users to access their sacred groves inside a

---

[by] For example, consider Integrated Conservation and Development (ICDP), Community-Based Conservation (CBC), Community-Based Natural Resource Management (CBNRM), Community Wildlife Management (CWM), Collaborative (or Co-) Management (CM), and Protected Area Outreach.

protected area and have secure rights. The collaborative agreements for sacred groves in Ruwenzori National Park in Uganda can serve as examples.

3. Community-based conservation turns over control and responsibility for sustainable natural resource management to the community. Most sacred groves are forms of community-based conservation and are often managed for hundreds of years.

Table 8 summarizes the different types of community conservation in terms of land and resource ownership. Some examples of sacred grove arrangements illustrate the different categories and how they fit with the knowledge and institutions for managing sacred nature. This determines the rights and responsibilities that can accrue within the different institutions involved. Resources refer to an area of land and its resources (e.g., community forest, a sacred grove, a national park), or it can refer to a bundle of resources—access to papyrus, fuelwood, water, resources required for sacred ceremonies. It can also relate to one resource (e.g., a sacred tree species).

Table 8: Ownership as the Main Determinant of Rights and Responsibilities

	Total State Ownership of Area and/or Resources	**Collaborative Management Arrangements**	**Community- or Land User-Based Ownership**
Ownership of resource or land (*de jure* or *de facto*)	State-owned land (e.g., national parks, forest and game reserves), but which may contain a sacred grove.	Communities with specific rights to resources (e.g., grazing, forest products, etc.), though land is state-owned. Many parks and reserves contain sacred sites and sacred species, which may be ignored during gazettement.	Private land through customary or modern law. Many sacred groves fit here. Private could be a community, a whole village (e.g., Dai forests), or a religious group (e.g., Ethiopian monastic forests).

Some components of management	State agencies decide type and level of use, by whom and under what circumstances, objectives of Government and sacred site complementary.	Agreement between state and user groups or individuals for management of area and/or resource(s) that are state-owned.	Conservation as part of land use and rural economies. Most sacred groves fit here.
Type of community conservation	Protected area outreach. Where the protected area authorities allow access to sacred grove.	Collaborative management, where agreement for access to a sacred grove is part of a collaborative management agreement.	Community-based conservation, where sacred groves belong to a group or community.
Sacred trees and groves	Where a grove or a SNS is part of a state's protected area or part of one (e.g., Mt. Kenya).	Sacred grove inside a national park (e.g., Shai Hills in Ghana). Communities with agreements to visit and practice their rituals.	Most sacred groves are community- or group-based (e.g., Kaya forests and sacred groves of India). Many lack formal recognition.

Source: Adapted from [7]

An example from Russia is interesting where traditions of protecting sacred sites are strong in the cultures of Russian indigenous peoples. Some are in national parks (e.g., Kenozesky National Park in Arkhangelskage District). The Pomor people living close to the White Sea protect sacred sites as part of the national parks. Park managers respect the traditional attitudes to these sanctuaries. Sacred groves are part of some Zapovedniks' territories and are strictly protected state nature reserves (protected area category I). Even here, management does not contradict existing traditions but protects such groves from encroachment. [28]

For community conservation, different arrangements suit different tenurial, institutional, and cultural mechanisms based on different objectives. Tenure regimes determine the nature and scope for community conservation and the role conservation plays in the landscape and for users. [7] This framework for community conservation in terms of sacred trees and groves

- is functional and based on *de facto* or *de jure* ownership of a resource or resources;

- recognizes the state, through its conservation system has rights and obligations to conserve important biodiversity in a strategic manner;
- recognizes the state can enter a range of benefit sharing arrangements from its protected area system (to support sacred groves in a park);
- allows for collaborative management arrangements for the more sustainable and fair use of resources within conservation areas;
- assumes that where land is held either *de jure* or *de facto* by rural resource users or communities, such people have prime rights to and responsibility for conservation as part of land use;
- allows for flexibility as arrangements can change with changes in tenure or resource status;
- allows for a wide range of arrangements from top down (e.g., the park allowing people to collect thatching grass once a year) to arrangements based on partnership to ones that empower rural people to use their resources in a manner that they see fit; and
- shows where and how cultural and sacred aspects of nature can fit into the community conservation framework.

Collaborative management evolved due to the uses rural people made of nature inside official protected areas under customary arrangements. It tries to redress the balance between negotiated rights of access and agreed responsibilities for conserving. There are many sacred trees and groves in reserved areas (forest reserves and national parks). Conservation authorities should allow communities and custodians access to such sites based on at least collaborative management agreements. At present, such arrangements are informal and at the discretion of the warden. For example, consider the arrangement regarding the sacred groves in Shai Forest in Ghana. Active recognition through collaborative agreements will increase how important sacred groves are in government-controlled land and show their relevance in contemporary conservation.

Community-based conservation is natural resource management by, for, and with local communities. [58] Advocacy for community-based conservation relates to how important areas outside direct state control, including sacred groves, are. It relates to the impotence of state agencies to respect such conservation areas where authority is vested in community custodians and institutions for sacred groves. Community-based conservation offers the potential for cost-effective local management based on social institutions and sanction. This is combined with an enhanced motivation to conserve nature when benefits are created, including those derived from sacred trees and groves. Most sacred groves are part of community-based conservation, yet few are recognized. The Kaya forests are an example of formal recognition. Many groves are based on different management objectives than those of conservation even if they support conservation. For example, research on sacred groves in Uganda revealed that informal rules and regulations alone are not necessarily sufficient to stand up to the effects of increased population and market pressures on forest resources. [5]

Devolving authority for conservation to the local level is the basis for community conservation as sacred groves show. But this tends to run counter to government conservation management. This resulted in resistance to devolve authority to lower levels. [57] Yet centralization undermines the potential for ethical action at the local level and increases the potential for mischief. [64] We must address issues of local organization and good governance. This involves sharing responsibility and authority between stakeholders involved in management. We need guidelines for designing accountable institutional linkages for stakeholders to negotiate access to and gain control over their resources. Such community conservation guidance is important for respecting and managing sacred groves as good governance is closely linked with tradition, culture, and heritage.

Whose Protected Areas—Intent or Tenure?

A protected area is a geographical area that is recognized and managed through legal or other effective means to achieve the long-term conservation, associated ecosystem services, and cultural values. [22] So there are different forms of protection for areas of conservation importance, based on the IUCN categories. [32] The IUCN categories are based on decreasing levels of restriction of land and resource use based on management. Sacred sites are rarely recognized though this is changing. But the IUCN categories do not really address issues relating to which management institutions are more important and the different types of political control there are. For example, Mt. Kenya has a variety of sacred groves, a national park, and forest reserves. Parks and reserves tend not to recognize important sacred sites or allow custodians access. While a global protected area network (mostly state-owned) is good for conservation, it can come at a cost to indigenous and local communities as it often ignores their rights and the biodiversity they manage (e.g., sacred groves). [71] If we focus more on equity and less on livelihoods, this will address how conservation should be managed and by whom.

Intent and effectiveness of objectives and management are key, not just their legally defined conservation status. [28] Yet the protected area movement focuses more on state-owned national parks (category II) and less on other categories. The present protected area framework recognizes that biodiversity conservation may not be appropriate for all situations and cultures. So ICCAs should be an active part of formal conservation areas [34] in terms of local action, not only global rhetoric. We need clarity as to what conservation areas are. In the context of this book, where do the hundreds of thousands of sacred groves and SNS fit, and why?

For protected area categories, scientific criteria prevail. They select sites from ecological perspectives and assign greatest value to protecting biodiversity. This is not always true as many early protected areas were declared based on the whims of leaders or were important hunting areas. This leaves cultural and spiritual values, even if acknowledged, at the periphery. Even now, despite the increasing literature attesting to the cultural and spiritual values of nature, there is still a reluctance to recognize protection for cultural values at a national level. [28] But some protected area authorities appreciate sacred groves in terms of conservation, while spiritual traditions may recognize the security that protected area status can offer. The trick is to balance achieving the long-term objectives of both. We need to integrate sacred groves into conservation planning, [82] which means integrating these values into protected area management, land use planning, and conservation training. And the protected area movement needs to formally recognize and respect sacred trees and sacred groves at the local level.

However, we cannot be romantic traditionalists as the uncritical espousal of traditional management systems is as unfortunate as dismissing it. Traditional uses and controls worked under different pressures and livelihood patterns. The social cohesion that was present in the past is being eroded together with time-tested strategies that benefited local people. Customary relationships and usage patterns are being replaced by often selfish consumerist ethics. [6, 9] Traditional knowledge and institutions are not a panacea for resolving problems of how rural people and communities engage with, benefit from, respect, and manage nature. But it is important to build on what is useful and valuable from the traditional knowledge and institutional base and integrate modern knowledge and institutions. [8]

Sacred trees and groves offer refreshing perspectives. The sheer number of sacred groves together with their universality shows that the sacredness of nature transcends materialism and consumerism and can be a vehicle for peace, silence, and spiritual renewal. It is important to recognize such conserved areas if we are to achieve connectivity and sustainability. The scope to reserve more state-owned national parks is increasingly difficult to justify because of increasing land usage and population pressures. Yet only very few of the many ICCAs for whatever purpose (sacred, dry season grazing, or water) are recognized or registered under the IUCN protected area categories.

Many sacred groves have clear boundaries, though management varies with different ethnic groups and communities. Most sacred groves are secondary forests, but some are near pristine. Groves vary in size from 0.001 to more than a thousand hectares and make up one form of ICCA. For example, the area of sacred groves in a Naxi village accounts for 1 to 13 percent of the collectively owned land in Lijiang County in northwest Yunnan, China.

Why should conservation integrate people and culture? It reduces conflict with local and indigenous peoples. Too often, creating national parks resulted in forced evictions and hostility that causes conflict and the social and physical breakdown of local communities. [54] We can recognize and integrate local people in protected areas as the US Parks Service shows (see box 17), or Shai Hills in Ghana. But this requires institutional willingness, and involving government does not always work. In India, for example, state management of sacred groves sometimes led to increased exploitation by elites. The assumption that sacred groves are community resources ignores there are may be different meanings for different groups. Further, forestry policy is use-based, which can contradict religious and spiritual uses. [74] If we combine the technical and spiritual importance of sacred groves, we can respect and manage for these requirements, and then winning more and losing less is more likely. And we won't need to evict people to achieve conservation.

Over the past decades, governments faced declining budgets, structural adjustment, retrenchment, population and land use pressures, and other macroeconomic forces. We have to make the case for conservation, on conservation grounds, and on how conservation relates to livelihoods and the economy. One way is to secure rural people's rights through community conservation. This is relevant for sacred trees and groves to bridge the formal conservation of lands with how important such areas are as cultural assets for people as table 9 summarizes. Sacred groves can help conservation argue for its role at the national level.

Box 17: How the US Parks Services Recognizes Local Communities [16]

New areas are being added under the US National Park Service. They embrace lived-in landscapes where management depends on partnerships. Called non-traditional units or partnership areas, they include long-distance trails, wild and scenic rivers, heritage areas, and corridors. Such partnership areas represent most new designations proposed to the US Congress. There are twenty-three national heritage areas in seventeen states encompassing an area of 440,000 square kilometers with a population of forty-five million people living in and around them. The growing role of and benefits from such partnership approaches include

- helping the National Parks Service reach new constituencies and build relationships to enhance public support for conservation;
- helping broaden the impact of the National Park Services and partners;
- offering valuable lessons for sacred groves; and
- fostering a stewardship ethic among the public.

Table 9: Evolving Approaches to Planning and Management of Protected Areas [11]

As it was, protected areas were	As it is (or should be), protected areas are
• planned and managed against local people, • run by central government, • set aside for conservation, • developed separately, • managed as *islands*, • established for scenery and wildlife, • managed for visitors and tourists, • about protection, and • viewed as a national concern.	• run with, for, and by local people; • run by many partners; • welcoming of social and economic objectives; • planned as part of national or international systems; • developed as networks; • set up for scientific, economic, and cultural reasons; • managed with local people in mind; • concerned with restoration; and • viewed as an international and local concern.

Community-based approaches are gaining impetus by the greater focus on devolution of government services. Governments are devolving responsibility for managing nature as a local government responsibility is becoming important in national policy. But is this enough, or do we want more formal recognition of how communities conserve their lands? We can recognize different ICCAs based on management in all the different IUCN categories (see table 10), and this provides one means for formal recognition.

Despite promoting community conservation, little significant transfer of power seems to have taken place except in certain cases. As the dominant land owner, the government remains the dominant stakeholder. There has often been a reluctance to carry out decentralized policies, except at the level of rhetoric, [7] though there are exceptions. More insidious is the commonly held belief by many technical experts that rural people and communities are not able to manage their natural resources [56] despite many examples to the contrary. The examples of this book show how local people manage sacred groves.

Embracing and respecting the rights of peoples and cultures combined with their active involvement, participation, and ownership is central. [66] Such integrated action is what Edward Wilson terms consilience, [86] which refers to agreeing to approaches that embrace diverse sectors, including science and the humanities[bz] (e.g., environmental policy, ethics, biology, and social sciences). This helps form the basis for a truer participatory democracy. But centralized approaches die hard! We still believe in hierarchical societies, not networked ones, which are increasingly the reality. [38] The technical and hierarchical domains still dominate major sectors (e.g., economics, forest management, protected areas, biodiversity, and agriculture). Landscape mosaics and connectivity are two examples of local networks where sacred groves can be an important component.

Table 10: Some Examples of Sacred Groves in Different IUCN Protected Area Categories

IUCN Category	ICCA type & Examples of Sacred Sites/Groves
Categories 1a & 1b: Strict Nature Reserve and Wilderness Area	Sacred or otherwise no-use groves, lakes, springs, mountains, islands, etc. have no use except on particular occasions (e.g., a once-a-year ceremony). Many sacred groves are in this category (e.g., the garden of Gethsemane, cedar groves of Lebanon).
Category 2: National Park	Community declared sanctuaries (can also be for ecotourism use) (e.g., in Ghana, India). Sacred groves as part of national parks.
Category 3: Natural Monument	Natural monuments (caves, waterfalls, cliffs, rocks) protected by communities for religious, cultural, or other reasons. Consider the Kaya forests in Kenya, many of which are national monuments.
Category 4: Habitat, Species Management Area	Wildlife populations, sea turtle nesting sites, watershed forests, community-managed wildlife corridors and riparian vegetation areas, shaman forests, some sacred groves in Ghana, watershed forests in Thailand.
Category 5: Protected Landscape or Seascape	Sacred and cultural landscapes and seascapes such as the Himalayas, Ganges, and Mt. Kenya, which include many sacred groves.
Category 6: Managed Resource Protected Area	Resource reserves (community forests, grasslands, waterways) that are under usage and communal rules to assure sustainable harvesting through time (e.g., Monastic forests and some sacred groves in India, Ghana, and China).

Source: Adapted from [40]

[bz] https://en.oxforddictionaries.com/definition/consilience.

Sacred nature behooves us to think and act in a more integrated manner, show greater consilience, and empower custodians and communities to take on their rights and responsibilities. Trends in conservation stress how important cultural and spiritual values are and see biodiversity as one way to conserve cultural and spiritual aspects. But sacred groves and protected areas are not the same. Religious and spiritual aspects may not be compatible with conservation, [76] even though conservation is often an important benefit. The goals may differ. For conservation, norms ought to be shaped and determined by people's actions toward sacred groves [76] as well as their rights and responsibilities.

Indigenous and Community-Conserved Areas (ICCAs)—Recognizing Sacred Groves

ICCAs are diverse in terms of ecosystems, reasons for conserving, and types of community. Sacred groves are an important subset of ICCAs. Many sites are important for the churches, mosques, and temples of mainstream religions and for indigenous spiritual traditions. ICCAs sometimes include landscapes of wild and domestic biodiversity and provide crucial ecological and cultural linkages. If all sacred groves of the world were recognized as ICCAs, the number would increase by more than a quarter of a million! ICCAs include [42]

   a) territories of indigenous peoples managed for sustainable use and cultural values;
   b) territories of nomadic peoples who manage their resources for customary use and under customary regulations (e.g., pastoralism);
   c) sacred spaces from forest groves and wetlands to entire sacred landscapes;
   d) catchment areas where communities derive their livelihoods (e.g., community forests);
   e) nesting sites and important habitats of wildlife, which are also important for communities; and
   f) landscapes with mosaics of different natural and agricultural ecosystems that communities use for diverse reasons and are culturally important.

For ICCAs, local communities are the most important decision makers. [42] Whatever the management objectives are, conservation is achieved directly or given as a benefit. So why should we focus attention on ICCAs[ca] and on sacred groves in particular? They are far more important than governments give them credence for. ICCAs conserve large portions of the planet's biodiversity—about 12 percent of Earth's terrestrial surface. But documentation underestimates the scale, and I doubt whether this includes many sacred groves. [42] ICCAs and sacred groves can integrate people and conservation and reduce hostility. They contribute to connectivity and provide important environmental benefits. In this way, we can meet conservation and livelihood security goals.

ICCAs offer an opportunity for greater recognition of sacred groves. ICCAs are "natural and/or modified ecosystems, containing significant biodiversity values, ecological benefits, and cultural values, voluntarily conserved by indigenous peoples and local communities, through customary laws or other effective means."[cb] [41] When categories V and VI of the IUCN categories were approved in 1994, this provided the space for the full recognition of SNS. [22] Now SNS are one form of legitimate nongovernment-controlled protected area [85] or ICCA. But having such ICCAs recognized is not enough. We need to understand the reasons that communities conserve sacred trees and groves. These reasons may include

- cultural, religious, and spiritual reasons;
- concern for nature, future generations, and long-term sustainability;
- ecological benefits (e.g., groundwater supply, soil, water conservation, and soil fertility);
- economic benefits from ecosystem-based activities such as ecotourism;
- increased social cohesiveness and awareness about rights and responsibilities, knowledge of political processes, and influence on local and regional decision making;

[ca] See www.iucn.org/themes/ceesp/CCA.index.html for a set of case studies.
[cb] https://www.iucn.org/content/indigenous-and-community-conserved-areas-bold-new-frontier-conservation https://en.wikipedia.org/wiki/Indigenous_and_community_conserved_area.

- enhanced ecological, social, political, legal, and administrative ability;
- recognition by wider society, including acceptance of local and indigenous knowledge systems;
- increased local employment, resulting in lower migration; and
- creating just and egalitarian societies with decision-making power within local communities. [28]

There is a global ICCA registry[cc] similar in structure to the World Database of Protected Areas. [20] To register an ICCA requires free, prior, and informed consent. There are benefits from registration—greater recognition, respect, and reduced conflict (e.g., around extractive mining). By 2016, there were 167 registered ICCAs, of which 35 percent (or about sixty) had sacred nature as a key aim, and more than 70 percent have conservation as a core objective. [20] ICCAs are an opportunity to recognize and respect the many hundreds of thousands of sacred groves across the globe. But this needs careful documentation in terms of biodiversity values and free, prior, and informed consent by the custodians.

ICCAs include ecosystems with minimal to substantial human influence. They can embrace traditional practices such as sacred groves or new initiatives taken up by communities in the face of new threats or opportunities. Some ICCAs are small. Others are large stretches of land and waterscapes. Three features define ICCAs, namely (a) a community closely connected to a well-defined ecosystem (or to a species and its habitat) culturally and/or because of survival and dependence for livelihoods; (b) community management decisions leading to conservation and associated cultural values, even if the main aim of management may be different (perhaps related to livelihoods, water security, and/or the safeguarding of cultural and spiritual places); and (c) the community acting as the major decision maker and implementer regarding management. So community institutions enforce regulations and have clear rights and responsibilities. [15]

ICCAs fit well with stewardship, and many sacred trees and groves have similar criteria. Conservation recognizes the importance of ICCAs, [41] and

---

[cc] Accessed September 2018. http://www.iccaregistry.org/.

table 7 provides examples of how sacred groves can be part of the different IUCN protected area categories. We ought to support such stewardship and adopt new ways of managing conservation areas as government-owned and -managed is not enough. [65] So it is important we respect and recognize the relevance of ICCAs and sacred groves. They are a real interface between ecology and culture and are responses to challenges and opportunities that communities face. ICCAs are one key to the future of life on Earth. [42] Given the scale (numbers, area, geographic spread), sacred groves are a great fit with ICCAs. As a recent study pointed out, [79] this offers opportunities to formally recognize and respect ICCAs, including sacred groves, at national, regional, and global levels as an important conservation strategy rather than a continued focus on state-owned protected areas and forest reserves.

Sacred groves help address two shortcomings of formal protected areas. [13] First, as they exist, protected areas do not cover certain habitats. Second, sacred groves can be recognized and respected together with their custodians as local people often resent formal government-imposed arrangements. Custodians of sacred groves can conserve and manage their groves in various habitats, many of which are biodiversity-rich. They do not require direct government involvement. Rather they need government to respect, recognize, and implement enabling and supportive policies so that the threats sacred groves and their custodians face can be addressed. [13] For example, a single sacred grove on its own may not conserve in the long term. But if it is part of a connected network, such groves can be very important. Education and awareness for government, protected area authorities, conservation and land use agencies, and local people can help in the greater recognition of sacred groves for all. This increases the value of local institutions and custodians for sacred grove management.

Fitting Sacred and Spiritual Values in Place

Managing cultural and spiritual values brings into perspective the interactions between local people, protected areas, and conservation and land use agencies. Western scientific approaches to conservation categorize, describe, and split nature into conservation and land use, while traditional approaches are integrated and networked. [28] So the dominance of Western notions of conservation—science-based—needs to give way to a more integrated understanding as our own existence falls into three categories of consciousness—material objects and events, subtle objects and events, and consciousness itself. Trees, mountains, and clouds belong in the first category. Dreams, ideals, and aspirations belong in the second. The self belongs in the third. The essence of human nature is to reach beyond what we know about ourselves. [18] Spirit of place is one way to describe this uniqueness. It is the distinctive feeling we can discover if we stop rushing for long enough, center ourselves, and tune into our surroundings. [72] This is what sacred trees and groves do so that we can experience subtle events and see ourselves in the trees.

By including cultural landscapes in 1992, they made far-reaching changes to paragraph 24 (b) of the World Heritage Convention. [80] To have relevant legislation at national, provincial, or local levels and/or a "well-established contractual or traditional protection as well as of adequate management and/or planning control mechanisms" is essential when sites are nominated. [80] For the first time, traditional management and customary law are acceptable forms of protection for a cultural site, [28] which further supports the recognition of sacred groves and other SNS.

Government policies encourage more devolved governance. This creates an enabling framework and pressure for the improved and local management of sacred groves. With emphasis on devolution, lower-level accountable units have the responsibility to manage their natural resources. This means local people are the key players in conservation. Sacred trees and groves are an example of how relatively small areas of land are managed at the grove level, can be respected at the local and administrative levels, and result in greater connectivity.

Edmund Barrow

Getting Governance Right—The Importance of Local Institutions

Conservation is more than ecology. It is a social construct, and governance is key. Institutions and governance relationships are crucial to the long-term recognition and respect for sacred groves and trees. Conservation is one part of landscape management, yet landscapes demonstrate a complexity of management institutions. The challenge is whether or not these institutional systems can resolve the conflicts that may arise between different organizations with different mandates at different levels (e.g., a sacred grove managed at the custodian level but in a national park managed by a protected area authority). The whole spectrum of societal values ought to be represented. [28]

How sacred groves are managed relates to the complexity of institutions found. There is complexity (types of rules, guidelines, institutions) surrounding different sacred groves and the institutions (some of which may be secret) that have evolved. I analyze how institutions fit with institutional theory to suggest how we can better respect and recognize sacred trees and groves and their institutions. The sacredness of groves is not just culture. It is not just trees, plants, vines, or springs. The institutions and the hearts and souls of people responsible for sacred groves are filled with sacredness. [74]

Institutions for natural resource management may be obvious or hidden, and they may or may not be linked to formal administrative institutions. Most institutions that mediate sacred trees and groves are not formal. If the institutions are not analyzed, the real managers may lose institutional power to either government structures or outsiders. Yet many of these institutional arrangements survive, not by statutory decree but by the ability of their proponents to support and negotiate rules and procedures with community members and outsiders. It is one reason why the institutions for sacred trees and groves are so resilient and robust. The respect for the sacred allows these institutions the power and respect at the local level. But many of these institutions' power bases are being eroded by the role of the state, globalization, and commercialization. We need to recognize such institutions and the sacred groves they manage. Yet institutions for sacred trees and groves are still resilient as they have survived the onslaught of desecration by some formal religions, being converted to other forms of land use, including being gazetted as protected areas and being politically and scientifically ignored. This shows the robustness of the spiritual and cultural institutions responsible for sacred groves combined with local respect and reverence for such sites.

Ouadi Qadisha in Lebanon illustrates how important it is to get the institutional arrangements right. The Ouadi Qadisha (Holy Valley) and the sacred forest of the cedars of God (*Horsh Arz el-Rab*) in Lebanon were first nominated as a World Heritage site in 1993. This recognized the sacred cedars of Lebanon as important. But the nomination failed because the site was too small to keep its integrity and did not meet some criteria. But the cedars could be part of a nomination for a wider cultural landscape for the Qadisha valley. They did this in 1998 and linked it to management plans that embraced government and local custodians agreeing as partners. Now about 375 remaining cedars are protected, though they once covered most of Lebanon. [60] Two trees are more than three thousand years old, and ten are more than a thousand years old. [4] The Qadisha valley is the center of Maronite creationism, and the valley has the world's largest concentration of hillside hermitages and monasteries dating back to the origins of Christianity. There are three Maronite monastic communities who share the custodianship of this holy natural site. [47] The cedar forest is known in ancient texts such as *The Epic of Gilgamesh*, which refers to and describes the cedars as sacred. [28]

There are various cultural and sacred values, including institutions, that may be more important than they are visible. Such values are increasingly acknowledged as vital for natural resource management and include rules and management norms for sacred groves and trees. Many of these rules make conservation sense (e.g., control of access, restricted use, and not allowing the cutting of trees). For community forest and sacred grove management, decentralization works better if they are compatible with traditional authority structures. Yet there is still a widespread lack of official recognition for such customary institutions. This relates to a perceived reduction of official administration power. Conflict between customary and formal government structures is common, except where formal structures build on customary institutions. This is the case for some pastoralist systems and with some institutions for sacred forest groves.

Many people misunderstand the role of local and customary institutions in natural resource management. There may be a wide range of institutions within a community, both traditional and modern, for controlling access to and defining responsibilities for natural resource management, including those of sacred trees and groves. Their roles may not be obvious and may be undervalued. Many conservation authorities and agencies only recognize and work with institutions seen as official (e.g., village governments in Tanzania or local councils in Uganda). Some of these official institutions take power and authority from customary institutions with which rural people may be better able to relate. So where official institutions evolved from customary ones, they can be stronger (e.g., the Kaya forest institutions in Kenya as part of their gazettement as national monuments and how Shai National Park in Ghana recognized the importance of the sacred sites in the park).

Community conservation requires institutional rules and authority relationships as to who decides what in relation to whom. [25, 63] Where a community has no or weak rights and responsibilities over natural resources, developing strong local institutions is less likely. Often resource users don't have the authority or incentives to enforce rules for effective community conservation. [25] Such considerations are important for the institutional arrangements for sacred trees and groves.

Traditional resource management can be romanticized though indigenous groups have generations of experience of living with nature. These groups have spiritual relationships with the environment that are insightful, protective, visionary, and reverent. [39] For some, traditional institutions play a strong role (e.g., the manner in which they gazetted the Kaya forests in Kenya). The Kaya elders are the primary custodians of the sacred forests. This is why they can maintain some control over the land, timber, and non-timber forest products of their sacred forests. [61]

Understanding the institutional dynamics at community and sacred grove management level is key, not to mention how they are recognized and respected. The rules for community conservation govern access, set up the mechanisms for usage, and empower communities to include or exclude. Many of these arrangements are unseen and unheard by development agencies, yet they are vital for community cohesion, social responsibility, and management. Box 18 summarizes some key attributes for successful community institutions, [70] and we could measure sacred grove institutions by these attributes.

> **Box 18: Some Attributes of Successful Community Institutions**
>
> a) Build on existing motivation.
> b) Be representative and legitimate.
> c) Be resilient to changing conditions.
> d) Be able to apply effective rules, mutual obligations, and sanction.
> e) Have a balance between customary and statutory law.
> f) Have negotiated goals.
> g) Have conflict resolution capacity.
> h) Demonstrate equity in distribution of benefits and social justice.
> i) Have political efficiency to build relationships.
> j) Have the capacity for layered alliances.
> k) Have the confidence to coordinate external interventions.

In Ethiopia, levels of protection for monastic forests range from strict taboos on resource extraction to limited exploitation for religious purposes such as tree felling to fulfill Monastic needs. [12] Religious beliefs inform the social constructs of power, which shape ecological relationships. Even though various processes tried to undermine the links between Ethiopian sacred groves and community belief systems, the groves do not become irrelevant, which is a lesson for planners. [62]

Local institutions for resource management are resilient, and no more so than those responsible for sacred groves and trees across the globe. But the legitimacy of many of these institutions is not formal, which is a key for robustness and sustainability. These include both systems of usage rights and regulations and the authority to govern such rights. In most countries these institutions are informal and exist in parallel to formal ones. There is a great potential to strengthen local institutions and better integrate them with formal structures to be a stronger basis for management by the custodians. In addition, institutions for sacred groves are part of wider networks. They are part of ecosystems, food webs, and networks of organisms. [17] Such networks are part of life, and sacred groves are part of such networks as nature is a complex of different networks at different scales providing different services. [19] These networks are the webs of life. This complexity and differences of scale make these networks part of the web of life. Diverse and resilient social and ecological networks are what makes planet Earth the way it is. [19]

Sacred groves correspond to certain forms of social organization, and many of the challenges facing groves relate to their misfit with contemporary management (e.g., the secular and religious institutions of a country or of conservation and forest authorities. Most sacred groves are community institutions and should be legitimate sources for ownership. This explains their persistence during periods of social change as they shape ecological dynamics as part of broader ecological networks. [74]

For sacred groves in Buganda (Uganda), historical events and beliefs determined roles and responsibilities. One clan member is elected by the spirits as the guardian of the grove. The elders and clan leaders monitor the sacred grove users and enforce rules. The people respect these guardians, yet there are no written rules regulating use. Community members are taught the dos and don'ts at an early age. Transgressors may have to return illegally harvested produce to the forest, slaughter an animal to appease the spirits, or pay fines. Such rules help prevent exploitation, ensure conservation, and enhance respect for the sacred. [5]

Herman Daly said, "The natural world is the envelope that contains, sustains and provisions the economy" and not the other way around. [29] We have to be part of the fragile ecological web as members of the planetary community and share in Earth's resources. [75] Earth democracy enables democratic participation and the worth of all species, peoples, and cultures. We need to protect ecological processes as a human right together with rights to, for example, water, food, health, and education. Earth democracy relies on the cultural space to express ideas and aspirations. [36]

Pope Francis calls for a reinvigoration of existing and customary institutions to enhance cooperation and community organization. [66] The institutions and organizations that manage sacred groves and sacred nature should be better recognized and respected. But these institutions require the political clout to be heard at local and national political and policy levels. We cannot forsake sustainable management for short-term political and economic gain. The reality is the environment cannot be assured solely by market economics or based only on costs and benefits. [66]

Secure Rights and Responsibilities Are Vital for Sustainability

Tenure refers to various systems of land rights, which may or may not be secure. Security of such rights is critical for conservation since it determines the linkages between responsibility and authority over land and nature. [55] This is true for sacred groves. Security of rights takes various forms from statutory-defined individual titles to *de facto* customary rights of access and use to resource users who gain rights to natural resources owned by another. Having the rights is one thing, but being able to have those rights recognized and respected is another issue. For sacred groves and trees, custodians and local people may have the rights, but they may not be respected or known and may be difficult to enforce. The long-term security of such sites could be enhanced by providing them with the status of legal subjects or juristic personhood. [78] Some SNS are now legal subjects, including sacred rivers (e.g., the Ganges), sacred mountains (e.g., Kailash), and groves (e.g., Kayas). This may help strengthen the recognition for sacred groves. Juristic personhood could be an additional tool for ICCAs to enhance the spiritual governance of sacred groves.

Frameworks for community conservation differ depending on ownership, policy, and legal frameworks of countries, institutions, and the objectives of land users. Use, which includes sacred use, is the real determinant of ownership. If this relates to responsible authority, use may be sustainable. But if the distant state has the authority and there are no perceived local benefits, use may not be sustainable. Distant state ownership is no longer a valid form of local management. But the state has an important role in regulation, arbitration, overall enforcement, and setting the enabling policy. As sacred groves and trees are locally managed, the custodians need to be able to enforce their rights. This means support and recognition by local and national government.

Ownership is one way to assess how secure sacred groves are. Establishing a framework for the community conservation of sacred groves based on resource and land ownership will allow for the following:

a) We will have clarity in understanding of who owns what land and resources. Who has secure rights to the sacred groves? Are the rights enforceable? Is it the whole village or a subset?
b) We will have communities and conservation authorities to work for more secure rights and responsibilities for land and resources (e.g., securing rights for custodians of sacred groves) through local or national legal and policy recognition (e.g., the Kaya forests).
c) We will set a legal framework for negotiating rights and responsibilities for different interest groups. We require clarity regarding sacred groves and trees in terms of who is responsible and how that relates to others in the community who use the grove.
d) We will readdress past inequities where many sacred groves were subsumed in national parks or reserves, including Shai National Park (Ghana) and Mt. Kenya National Reserve (Kenya).
e) We will have greater participation and collaboration between conservation authorities and local people. Sacred groves and trees offer a space for enhanced relationships between local people who have direct responsibility for sacred groves, government, and external agents.
f) We will recognize that participation is not everything. Representation (who represents who and why) can be contentious. This is particularly important for marginalized groups. Otherwise, they may be left out of discussions.
g) We will have a firm *de facto* or *de jure* basis for participation in conservation. Here sacred groves and trees offer a space for local empowerment.

Tenure dynamics underpin whether *de facto* or *de jure* rights to land and resources determine who has security of rights and responsibilities or not. Trees and forests may be private or communal. A sacred grove might belong to a community, a subset of the community, or several communities. It is essential to understand who has these rights and responsibilities even if time-consuming. We can only understand this when there is trust between and within communities and between communities and external agents. Tenure is likely to be stronger in traditional communities with a strong sense of identity and cohesion compared to fragmented ones where outsiders live (or people from different ethnic groups). So sacred groves and trees are likely to be more respected where there is a strong sense of identity. [84]

Common property registration can give sacred groves respite in terms of security. Simple delimitation can do this as demonstrated in Mozambique and Ivory Coast. It can be more complex (e.g., new categories of tenure for group-owned property) as demonstrated in Uganda and South Africa. Perhaps more consideration is given by the Tanzania Forest Act (2002), which provides not only for a community to create and declare community forests but for subgroups of the community to do so as well. [1] In Tanzania, there are opportunities for sacred groves to be established as community forests by groups within the community with strong traditional ties to the forest.

Where ethnic differences occur, they can play out as resource conflict. For Ethiopian monasteries, their forests were in places where such conflicts played out. Members of different ethnic groups cut trees and claimed property rights in the forest. They threatened, intimidated, and occasionally killed monks. Ecological destruction and violence resulted from the government's policy of ethnic territoriality. Not having a clearly defined forest policy determined the fate and status of these sacred sites [12] as the policy decisions did not consider their importance.

While quick to take rights and responsibilities over natural resources away from rural people, reversing this has taken much longer. This is the case where many sacred groves became part of state gazetted parks and reserves.

Authorities are reluctant to lose power, and state bureaucracies may resist such changes. Together with entrenched attitudes amongst government, technical experts and educated elites who think they know what is best for rural people. However, literature and experience show how important it is to build on community and customary structures for improved management. From the examples in this book, local people and their institutions can and do manage sacred groves and trees with efficiency and sensitivity.

Having Power at the Right Level Is Key

Sacred groves are places of power because they represent social order and can be focal points for resolving conflict. To maintain social order is the essence of politics, and sacred groves are places where political power can be contested and reinforced. Because the political *status quo* shifts and is subject to renegotiation, the political roles of sacred groves are dynamic. In Africa, sacred groves were symbols of power, place, and ownership. But far-reaching changes because of the colonial and postcolonial nation-states shifted the locus of power to new institutions. [74]

Power is at the center of decision making, and nature is where such decisions play out. How people manage sacred groves together with their ability as custodians to defend such lands offer us guidance by (a) focusing the locus of rights and power at the local and landscape level; (b) ensuring sacred groves have meaning (spiritual, cultural, and material) to us; and (c) supporting management with strong institutions that, if not representative or democratic (and most sacred groves institutions are probably not), then they are at least consensual with community support.

The ability to decide is crucial for taking on roles and responsibilities. Without that ability or the power to implement decisions, little will change. But power and control often lie outside the locale or village. However, we cannot separate responsibilities from rights. This is empowerment—the ability to decide and act on peoples' rights and responsibilities regarding sacred groves and trees. This power has to be combined with legitimacy for stewardship. We cannot sidestep questions of power and justice. We need to tackle them. Otherwise, they will be replaced by self-interest, greed, and anger. [2] Nor can we subsume good community work to rapid one-off participatory approaches.

In all institutional arrangements, power is key. Those with power are more visible and represent the community to outsiders. The weaker or marginalized are neither seen nor heard. Without a proper understanding of community relationships, the weaker may be further disenfranchised to the benefit of the powerful, both internally and externally. Many sacred grove custodians had such power in the past, but because of changes in power dynamics and the changing and reducing importance of sacred groves, many custodians lost power. Understanding power and decision-making dynamics is crucial to understanding institutional complexities. Too often, projects focus on creating new institutions rather than understanding and building on existing ones. Sustainable institutions that meet people's needs and expectations are important for sustainable management and development, [81] and their role in sacred groves is no exception.

There is a variety of stakeholders of different socioeconomic status affecting and being affected by different types of power within a community. Social ties, linkages, and obligations are at the core of these relations. These are key areas to understand in terms of how people manage and respect sacred groves both internally and externally. Responsible community involvement recognizes the rights and responsibilities of different interest groups and tries to assure equality. At an individual level, social inequalities can lead to differential power balances that alter with changing situations, commercialization, and external influences. For sacred trees and groves, we may know the interests. The interest *per se* is not so important, but the way different peoples negotiate those interests and how they occur within a community or a wider group along with the understanding whether some groups are marginalized and others strengthened is important.

Power linked to recognition and position can relate to administrative power (e.g., chiefs and government officials), political power (e.g., elected councilors, political leaders, and civic organizations), economic power (e.g., shop owners and traders), religious power (e.g., religious leaders), power related to education (e.g., teachers), and traditional power (e.g., elders, clan leaders, and custodians). They represent a community to the outside world because of their positions. As communities take on responsibilities for natural resources, the politicization of natural resource management increases, and local elites will vie for more power. It is in this institutional and social mix that the institutions responsible for sacred groves and trees have to make their case and position themselves in the wider social and institutional arenas. The ability of sacred grove institutions to have their rights and responsibilities and manage their sacred groves varies and depends on the type of grove and institution as the following examples illustrate:

a) Sacred yew trees in Europe occur on church property and authority over the sacred grove lies with the church.
b) Ethiopian monastic forests are under the Ethiopian church. But the power of the church waned during the Dergue era, resulting in the degradation of many monastic forests.
c) The elders with overall responsibility for Kaya forests in Kenya had their authority enhanced when the Kayas were gazetted as national monuments. But the National Monuments Act is weak. Powerful interests could abuse the act (e.g., those who want to convert Kayas into hotels).
d) When Shai National Park was gazetted in Ghana, the traditional authority that had responsibility for an important sacred grove within the national park lost power. They then achieved a negotiated outcome between the traditional authorities and park management.

Power struggles occur between traditional authorities, political leaders, and elected representatives, which can disrupt community-based processes such as the preservation of sacred groves. If traditional authority is eroded, people may fight to keep their power or reestablish the authority they lost. [35] Compromises may be required, so each group is accommodated, including traditional leaders as *ex officio* members of local government. The modern power shifts can cause changes in management, and customary knowledge, rules, and norms may be lost or downgraded.

Liberalization and democracy are being promoted without the matching behavioral ethics. Commercial interests may force sustainable use into unsustainable exploitation. This happened to some Kayas when they were destroyed to make way for tourism, and it happened with the extraction of high-value timber from sacred groves in India and West Africa. While these power struggles may be acknowledged at the level of rhetoric, they are not acted upon as they are difficult to address and do not lend themselves to quick-fix solutions. If the poor are not to be further marginalized, we need a greater understanding of power struggles to ensure greater equality and to better understand sacred grove institutions.

We may miss important aspects (e.g., sacred grove custodians). So we need to support communities to negotiate with outsiders. This means seeking ways to create situations where we win more and lose less and where customary rules and knowledge become part of improved management. How we respect sacred groves and trees depends on how respected the institutions are and their networks at the local levels.

Some Key Principles for Sacred Trees and Sacred Groves

Conservation approaches are starting to value the relationship between local environmental knowledge and communities and between scientific and spiritual perspectives. Conservation might be more efficiently achieved through connectivity, combining community-reserved hillsides or sacred groves with a national park or a community-conserved riparian area. To recognize connectivity in the landscape and the negotiated trade-offs to use the environmental services may be more sustainable than alienating further lands. This argues for decentralizing rights and responsibilities for sacred groves and the formal recognition of those rights and responsibilities at higher levels. Responsible decentralization gives local customary institutions, such as those responsible for sacred groves, greater responsibility.

It is ironic that many of the more successful sacred sites and groves are successful because they cut out middlemen, which are government conservation agencies in most cases. [33] Local respect and sanction were sufficient when such sites were sacred. While local respect and sanction may have worked and still does in many places, it is now more difficult for sacred grove custodians at the local level to withstand globalization and local or external political pressures.

Decentralized rights and responsibilities for sacred groves to practical institutional levels combined with recognizing those rights and responsibilities is key for sustainability. Yet much decentralization devolved power to lower levels of government rather than empowering existing local institutions. This deconcentration of government power, while administratively tidy with clear and simple reporting lines, may usurp or downplay how important local institutions are. An understanding of these institutions will enable a greater synergy between decentralized government institutions and existing customary institutions, such as traditional spiritual leaders. It will reduce institutional conflict, create the space for greater community cohesion and improved natural resource management, and allow for greater recognition of and respect for sacred groves.

Contemporary thinking on integrated ecosystem management (see table 11, adapted from [50]) has people as its focus and makes direct links to landscapes. Ecosystem and landscape management lend themselves to decentralized approaches. The ecosystem approach recognizes how important conservation is at a landscape level and the trade-offs needed combined with decentralized governance systems. This is a true opportunity for the greater recognition of sacred groves. The ecosystem approach [73] embraces cultural and spiritual significance and mosaics of land uses in the landscape. This creates greater connectivity and enhances community cohesion and responsibility.

Table 11: Traditional and Modern Thinking on Natural Resource Management

"Traditional or Formal" Management	Ecosystem "Management"
• Use values. • Commodity production (maximum sustainable yield). • Single species models and management. • Determined based on science. • Top down—government- and expert-based. • Scientific monopoly on data and analysis. • Social equals level of resource use.	• Use and land ethic values. • Multiple species, habitats, interactions, and discontinuities. • Humbler science that accepts uncertainty. • Adaptive and regional management of biodiversity. • Bottom up—collaborative. • Scientific and local knowledge are important. • Social equals active, engaged user groups and communities.

Conservation and Spirituality/Religion Must Work in Partnership

How important sacred groves and trees are may be more relevant to people who have a spiritual or religious connection. Yet the biodiversity values of sacred groves and trees also speak to conservation, the environment, and landscape planning and use. Such values may be less important for religious and spiritual communities. Likewise, those concerned with conservation may not see how important sacred values are. But both groups have more in common than their differences. This includes the desire to maintain such areas and the institutions to manage them with their rules. It offers a great opportunity to work together to support the values of sacred groves through recognition and security of rights. This is also important for conservation, landscape management, and connectivity.

Neither economics nor science will save protected areas. Rather it is people who care about the sense of connectedness between people and nature. Those intangible values cannot be reduced, boxed, and understood. This ill-guised dominance of economics is unpacked by David Suzuki, who says, "My Prime Minister regards the economy as our highest priority and forgets that economics and ecology are derived from the same Greek word, oikos, meaning household or domain. Ecology is the study of home while economics is its management. Ecologists try to define the conditions and principles that enable a species to survive and flourish. Yet in elevating the economy above those principles, we seem to think we are immune to the laws of nature. We have to put the eco back into economics."[cd]

We have to link rights, benefits, and management responsibilities. But these may differ for different stakeholders. The poor and marginalized often need access to nature to meet contingencies. It is essential to embrace the rights and responsibilities for sacred groves and trees. This means greater recognition of sacred grove management institutions to ensure that they can maintain and strengthen their rights. We can cause high-risk situations if we remove or privatize such resources from common property regimes because access may be denied or costed. For communities to better manage their groves and trees and to allow local institutions to manage them, it is necessary to

- create the incentives for governments to devolve,
- build and develop the capacity of existing community institutions for sacred grove management,
- establish and formalize linkages between customary institutions with those of government,
- ensure equality and make certain that local institutions do not exclude the weaker and less powerful,
- recognize the rights and responsibilities of different interest groups so they are not marginalized,
- make sure community institutions can take on their rights and responsibilities,
- ensure government make policy and practice commitments for the greater involvement of communities and internalize this so that it is not a donor or trial activity,

---

[cd] Accessed June 2018. www.azquotes.com/author/14336-David_Suzuki.

- ensure that custodians and communities have the power to decide, and
- show that government transaction costs reduce with increased community management.

We all need to change the way we think about Earth as we are not in charge of the planet. Nor is it for our sole benefit. For too long we have behaved badly toward Mother Earth. [46; 66] As the human and natural environments deteriorate, tackling environmental issues and the causes of social inequity and poverty is an imperative. As Pope Francis succinctly puts it, it is "both the cry of the Earth and the cry of the poor." [66] Such ecological approaches must also be social. If we are to work with traditional knowledge and institutions and nurture and support local empowerment, this takes time beyond the normal politically driven three- to four-year project cycles. But results will be greater and more sustainable. [37]

There are very many sacred groves and trees, but they are little known beyond the locale. That is changing as interest in sacred nature increases within religious and spiritual traditions. There is a growing understanding of sacred nature as important for conservation. Sacred groves and trees can help us connect with nature. They are important for bringing different spiritual traditions together for a common cause, which helps bring greater peace and harmony in our troubled world. Sacred groves and trees should be an integral part of religious and spiritual groups and also amongst conservationists.

The importance of sacred groves and trees is clear in terms of scale (numbers and area), scope (nearly every country, as where there is a tree, there is a sacred tree/grove), and relevance (for religious and spiritual groups and for conservation). Their importance has to be tangible, recognized and respected by diverse and different groups. We need the means to engage and link sacred groves into both formal conservation and religious and spiritual group conversations, approaches, and implementation.

Religion, Spirituality, and Conservation in the Stewardship of Sacred Trees and Sacred Groves

CHAPTER 6

When you're are in nature there is such joy
—Gurumayi Chidvilasananda [17]

Let us stand together to make our world a sustainable source for our future as humanity on this *planet*.

—Nelson Mandela [67]

Stewardship—The Key for Management

Sacred groves and trees speak to two largely different though sometimes connected audiences. The basis for sacred groves and trees is spiritual and religious and may have little to do with conservation. Yet many sacred groves and trees are important conservation assets even if conservation is a benefit. We can focus on what reinforces how important the spiritual basis for sacred groves and trees is and how relevant they are for conservation and landscape management. Then we can create strong synergies between the two groups–spiritual and religious, conservation and land use. There are differences between these audiences, but there are also similarities, overlaps, and even a coming together in thinking and practice. At the local level, there are overlapping values and interests.

Sacred trees and groves might not seem relevant to conservation. However, there are very many sacred groves and trees, and we find them everywhere. They may not be large, though they may be components of much larger sacred landscapes. They may or may not contain important biodiversity, though many do. They survive and thrive despite seeming insurmountable land and population pressures as in India and China. Irrespective of race, color, or creed, we need ways to recognize and respect sacred groves and trees and their importance as conservation and landscape assets. This will help us better secure those rights and responsibilities that assured the survival of sacred groves and trees to the present day.

One reason for this seeming lack of connection is that we tend to separate environmental values into three categories—anthropocentric (human welfare concerns and direct use), biocentric (moral standing related to awareness and the capacity to strive to certain ends), and ecocentric (values derived from the ecology of communities and interdisciplinary relationships). As such, there are three interconnected dimensions that are imbued with consciousness—the human world, the world of nature, and the world of spirit and ancestors. [39] The religious traditions of west Asia (Islam, Judaism, and Christianity) view nature more in anthropocentric terms. On the other hand, Eastern religions (Buddhism, Hinduism, Shintoism, and Taoism) and most indigenous and traditional peoples relate to nature in more ecocentric terms. [34] World religions and spiritual groups ought to redefine their purpose for nature and the environment, perhaps in the spirit of the Assisi Declarations (see box 5). This can give us the courage to rediscover our religious and spiritual foundations in the web of life with sacred trees and groves being important guides. The religious view of nature requires understanding again what nature is and who we are as human beings because we cannot discuss nature without discussing the image we have of ourselves. [74] As Zaghloul El-Naggar notes, "Man is clearly and irrevocably interwoven into the fabric of his environment. By corrupting its ecosystems, he is clearly damaging himself." [24]

Given the importance of nature in the sacred texts, formal religions, in particular the Abrahamic ones (Christianity, Islam, and Judaism) could do more to embrace and promote the sacredness of nature, sacred trees, and sacred groves. They could promote the role of spiritual values of the environment in wider society as nature is not a regular part of teachings despite the many references in the sacred texts. This is an important role for religions and spiritual groups. It is happening at a more global level, but it has yet to really inform conservation and religious practice at the local level in different societies.

While nature will take care of herself, we human beings have to alter our attitudes and the ways we use (and abuse) nature. Scientific literature on climate change attests to nature taking care of herself in terms of Gaia. [65, 66] Likewise, materialism and science neither satisfies nor provides us with a more integrated understanding of ourselves or nature. The intangible values—those cultural and spiritual values that we ascribe to things we cannot measure with our scientific minds—are a core part of our lives. Some great physicists recognized these values in their quest to split the atom. This sense of oneness is the key characteristic of spirituality, and this awareness of the fact that we are connected to nature is strong in deep ecology. [14] Now scientists are starting to acknowledge the earth is self-regulating and made up of all life. [64] Many spiritual leaders are coming to this conclusion. I was moved to see that the spiritual leader Gurumayi Chidvilasananda emphasized this by saying, "Earth will take care of herself. Pray for humanity." [3] We have to alter our attitudes about nature so we are more nurturing and are better stewards of nature. Then we might just be part of that *care*!

We need a vehicle common to religion and spirituality for conservation and land use. Stewardship is one such vehicle. It resonates with these different groups. It will help us know we are part of nature as nature flows through everything and everyone. To become one with nature means to become one with oneself. [1] The source of our consciousness is nature. We are intelligent because nature is intelligent. [83] The health of humankind is linked to the health of our ecosystems, forests, and trees. Ecological health embraces the relationships and dependencies amongst living and nonliving things, including humankind, as everything is interconnected. [93] But still, we often think we are separate from nature. That's a delusion.

Ernst Schumacher said, "To strive for smallness means to try to bring organization and units of production back to a human scale ... simplicity, from a Christian point of view, is a value in itself." [94] There is an increasing convergence between the languages and practices of spirituality and our daily lives. Such a convergence helps us survive, thrive, be at peace and know we are not separate from nature. So, it is best not to challenge nature, since, as Gurumayi Chidvilasananda says, "the universe is constantly pulsating, constantly expanding and contracting, creating and destroying. And the Universe hears you." [17]

As the patron saint of ecology, Saint Francis of Assisi's work is loved for aesthetic and religious reasons. [31] In the spirit of Assisi, he said, "It is our duty to contribute to the growing awareness of the relationship between man and nature according to God's plan rediscovered and preached by Francis: use, not appropriation; respect not exploitation," [86] "Then shall all the trees of the forest exult before the Lord, for he comes to rule the Earth" (Psalm 96:12). This is a call to use trees and groves to reduce conflict and foster peace. There are similar examples to St. Francis of Assisi in Islam and in other religious and spiritual traditions. St. Francis's views of spirituality about nature transcend religion (see box 19). This *image of goodness* can help us interpret the interconnections between spirituality, nature, and ourselves, where God inhabits all things and all our religions should be of the heart and spiritual. Living in harmony with nature is good in itself. It includes simple and compassionate ways of living, being fair and kind to all beings, and having a culture of nonviolence, respect, and reverence for the life. [54]

This chapter explores stewardship as a central means to bring together spirituality and religion along with conservation and biodiversity for the common cause of that image of goodness. But it also has benefits for other sectors (e.g., being part of education and awareness, peace and nonviolence, and landscape and land usage planning). We need practical tools and approaches to support the spirituality of nature in our quest for improved conservation and for a greater understanding of spirituality and conservation, which will help us enhance our education systems and serve as a vehicle for peace.

> **Box 19: St. Francis of Assisi and Nature—That Image of Goodness** [19]
>
> When the people fell silent, and standing reverently in attention, a flock of swallows, chattering and making a loud noise, were building nests in the same place. Since the people could not hear the blessed Francis over the chattering of the birds, he spoke to them, saying: "My sisters, swallows, it is now time for me to speak, for you have already spoken enough. Listen to the word of the Lord, be silent and quiet until the word of the Lord is finished". And those little birds, to the astonishment of the people, fell silent and did not move until St Francis finished the sermon. St. Francis regarded creatures and natural phenomena, as a manifestation of what he called an "image of goodness." Francis saw the patterns in nature and followed in its footsteps. To understand nature is to enter a dialogue with God. The Canticle of Brother Sun is a poem to God's presence in the world, and to the wonder of existence:
>
> > "My Lord, be praised for our sister, Mother Earth
> > Who nourishes and watches over us
> > With fruits abundant as her variety of flowers.
> > My Lord, be praised and blessed
> > We give thanks, and with humility serve you."
>
> In this Canticle, the prayer represents the entire cosmos. The prayer shows God inhabits all things. Francis saw the world (nature) as an eternal act of self-revelation and man's role in it as interpreter, not exploiter. Francis is contemporary as he wanted to take control of his own spirituality. That he aligned himself with the Church does not negate his desire to create a spirituality based on the principles of early Christianity rather than institutional religion. For St. Francis, we can only approach God through a pure heart, not that of systematic knowledge. His religion was a religion of the heart.

Stewardship—The Basis for Connecting and Reconnecting

From the perspective of sacred trees and groves, stewardship is key to integrating conservation and religion/spirituality. Stewardship is to hold something in trust for another. [79] It combines managing nature sustainably with the understanding that nature is more than use and economic values. Localism and stewardship are linked as it helps in solving problems of the networked nature of the twenty-first century—more local community, more interdisciplinary, less central and sectoral, local but not national or international economics. [45]

Religious and spiritual as well as conservation and land use groups can embrace stewardship as the glue for more coordinated action to conserve the world's valuable natural heritage. Stewardship implies present and future responsibility and acknowledges the many and varied roles trees and forests play in our lives. Stewardship and conservation are similar. They focus on use, not overuse. They recognize interdependencies in the natural world, and they also emphasize future generations. Stewardship helps humankind learn how to live side by side like the trees of the forest. [73]

Stewardship comes from impeccable religious and spiritual fundamentals. We bear the responsibility to develop, not deplete. We want to use, not abuse. We want to act with prudence, not greed, and we want to pass the world to our children in a better state than that in which we found it. [31] We nurture attitudes of stewardship in the religious texts through the four virtues of simplicity, moderation, frugality, and gratitude. This sets the tone for ethical discussions about our relationships with nature. [5] Different groups and peoples express stewardship in different ways. Amongst Aboriginal groups in Australia, they look after country, [36] while Andean Quechuas speak of caring for Mother Earth. Indigenous and local peoples have much to teach us about stewardship. Table 12 shows qualities of stewardship in terms of harmony with nature.

Table 12: What Do We Mean by Indigenous? [26]

The Indigenous Way of Life: Harmony with Nature.	Western Progress: Domination of Nature
Everything has a spiritual value. The spiritual and physical are united.	Everything has monetary value. Spiritual and physical are separate.
Emphasis is on the laws of nature. Nature reflects the Creator.	Emphasis is on the laws of nature. The creator is in man's image.
Feelings are important.	Feelings are rational and logical.
Society is based on cultural extended family. We remember our roots.	Society is based on the nuclear family. We forget our roots.

Cosmology is spatial and timeless.	Cosmology is linear and time-oriented.
Education is experiential. Teaching comes from nature and elders.	Education comes from the mass media and salaried professionals.
We base knowledge on culture and tradition.	We base knowledge on science.
Technology serves people and nature.	People and nature serve technology.
Material wealth is shared and given away.	Material wealth is hoarded and consumed.
Behavior is cooperative.	Behavior is competitive.
Justice and equality are achieved by cultural ways.	Justice and equality are achieved by legislation.
Society is egalitarian. Women and men have equal freedom and power.	Society is patriarchal. Women emulate men.
Leaders put people above themselves.	Leaders put themselves above people.
The balance of nature is maintained.	The balance of nature is destroyed.

In the Bible, stewardship refers to humankind's responsibility for husbanding God's gifts. Too often Christians misapply God's words to Adam, "God blessed them, saying: be fertile and multiply; fill the Earth and subdue it. Have dominion over the fish of the sea, the birds of the air, and all living things that move on the Earth" (Genesis 1:28). Dominion means rule and authority, but the real implication is care or good stewardship of nature and humanity. [79] Dominion is not domination, and we have dominion because we are made in the divine image.[44]

Stewardship is firmly embedded in Islam as Allah created humankind and other creatures of the earth for a purpose. "He [Allah] is the One that has made you inheritors in the Earth" (Qur-ān 35:39). The human being is God's vice regent of the planet, caretakers of the environment, not the plunderers. So we have to live and act in ways that do not upset the balance of nature. The Qur-ān (32:4) states, "It is Allah Who has created the heavens and the Earth and all things on it in balance." Islam emphasizes, "Any mishap exercised on the surface of our planet will be accounted for in this world and in the world to come." An Indonesian Imam who spoke at the last World Conservation Congress in Hawaii (2016) was explicit in explaining that Islamic teachings have not yet fully understood and articulated what it means that God made man his khalifa on Earth, his steward. Rather than placing humankind in a position of privilege over other species, God made man responsible as stewards for his creation. In this, humankind finds religious meaning through care of the physical world and conservation of its integrity and species. Each species is a sign of God's existence. The Qur-ān warns against corrupting the environment and advocates for a balanced relationship between humankind and ecosystems as the basis for conservation. [24] If humankind disrupts this balance, it will bring disaster to all the earth and humankind. Like Islam, all religions, faith-based groups, and spiritual traditions have similar texts that call us to use but not overuse. They talk of sustainability, stewardship, and conserving ecosystems.

Stewardship of nature links the social and environmental pillars of sustainable development. It enriches our meaning of sustainable development by emphasizing the importance of the spiritual, intangible, and other cultural aspects of how we live. So religious and spiritual organizations ought to reaffirm how important the stewardship of nature is as a core part of human spirituality and translate this into action.

From the perspective of sacred groves and the twelve principles of the ecosystem approach, [96] we should devolve societal choice and management to the lowest appropriate level (see box 20). Some choices relate to sacred nature, sacred groves, and sacred trees. In this way, we can make links between the ecosystem principles and sacred groves and trees. It offers a more integrated stewardship approach than most practices of sustainable forest management, [92] which focus more on technical forest management and less on cultural and sacred values. These are principles of ecological literacy (ecoliteracy) as nature sustains life by creating and nurturing communities. So sustainability is not just an individual property but the property of a web of relationships. [13] Failure to develop ecoliteracy is a sin of omission. Not only are we failing to teach the basics about the earth, but we are also teaching stuff that is wrong. Ecoliteracy forces us to address root causes, not just the symptoms. [78]

> **Box 20: Convention on Biological Diversity's Twelve Principles of the Ecosystem Approach–A Summary** [92, 96]
>
> 1. Objectives of management of land, water, and living resources are a matter of societal choice.
> 2. Management should be decentralized to the lowest appropriate level.
> 3. Ecosystem managers should consider the effects (actual or potential) of their activities on adjacent and other ecosystems.
> 4. To recognize potential gains from management, we have to understand and manage ecosystems in an economic context. Management should reduce market distortions adversely affecting biodiversity, align incentives to promote conservation, and internalize costs and benefits to the extent workable.
> 5. Conserve ecosystem structure and function to maintain ecosystem services as a priority of the ecosystem approach.
> 6. We must manage ecosystems within the limits of their functioning.
> 7. The ecosystem approach should be undertaken at appropriate spatial and temporal scales.
> 8. To recognize the varying temporal scales and lag effects that characterize ecosystem processes, objectives for ecosystem management should be long term.
> 9. Management must recognize change is inevitable.
> 10. The ecosystem approach should seek to balance conservation and use.
> 11. The ecosystem approach should consider all relevant scientific, indigenous, and local knowledge.
> 12. The ecosystem approach should involve all relevant sectors of society and disciplines.

Sacred groves may be small, but there are many. There are many more sacred trees and groves than we recognize. As many of these sites support conservation, understanding how important partnerships and alliances are is essential—among local communities, government, nongovernmental organizations, and the private sector. Sacred groves represent conserved landscapes as a practical means to achieve conservation on private and community lands. So we require stewardship, education, and leadership to embed the values and characteristics of sacred groves as part of capacity building. This will help reconnect people with place and build a greater understanding of conservation stewardship and its potential benefits to society. [12]

Stewardship considers our needs and responsibilities about ecosystems and culture. ICCAs offers us practical ways to achieve stewardship and is one solution to humanity's troubled relationship with the earth. These could be crucial components of conservation practice as the Convention on Biological Diversity has recognized. [50] Different groups advocate for this more integrated view of nature—deep ecologists, religions, political groups, and conservationists. This relates to Karl Barth's view of nature. [108] "He [man] is not set up as Lord over the Earth, but as Lord on the Earth which is already furnished with these creatures. Animals and plants do not belong to him; they and the whole Earth can belong only to God."

Teilhard de Chardin combined evolutionary theory with Christian theology in a synthesis of nature and consciousness [18] where there is no separation between nature, our spirituality, and us. This is really what stewardship is all about. Such connectedness benefits us all as we affirm we are part of nature. When we connect with nature, it can fill us with gratitude, appreciation, respect, and beauty. [101] The example of Tu B'Shevat (the fifteenth of Shevat) in Israel celebrates the start of a new year for trees (January 20, 2019) when early blooming trees in Israel emerge from winter. They mark the day by eating from the seven kinds of the Torah (wheat, barley, grapes, figs, pomegranates, olives, and dates).

Until recently, many religious groups shunned involvement in environmental issues at a local level. This is no longer acceptable given religious origins and present-day pressures. Nor can we ignore acknowledging and understanding the importance of nature in spirituality as only animist or pagan. We should foster a greater acknowledgment of spiritual values wherever they are from as part of action by religious and spiritual groups so that they respect and steward the earth.

Formal religions, especially the Abrahamic ones, can do more regarding the role of spiritual values of the environment. Nature is not normally part of everyday religious teaching despite the many references in important religious texts. This is due in part to changing spiritual requirements of people to cope with contemporary life and because we are more removed from nature. But if we are to conserve the rich cultural, spiritual, and natural heritage we have on this planet, it will not be enough to address technical and economic aspects alone. We should reinforce our cultural and spiritual links with nature that many of us still have. This calls for an important role for the major religions and spiritual groups of the world to play in stewardship. It is happening, as there have been high-level global meetings between religious leaders, conservationists, and scientists. Pope Francis's call in his encyclical [85] is a phenomenally strong plea for the stewardship of Earth and nature by us—as individuals, as communities, as nations, and as religious and spiritual traditions.

The sacredness of trees and groves shows the importance of something deeper and more spiritual. Margaret Mead said, "Never doubt that a small group of concerned citizens can change the world. Indeed, it is the only thing that ever has." ᶜᶜ We can be that change. There is the ancient truth that we are better off cultivating our own gardens and focusing on family, friends, and our own world rather than expecting too much from politics and diplomacy. [91]

There are differences between religious and spiritual groups as well as conservation and land use. But these differences should not cause conflict. We should build on the synergies and common areas to resolve our many challenges. The two seemingly different perspectives (conservation and land use as well as religion and spirituality) do not have to be so different. Stewardship enables us to integrate the practical with the sacred values of nature. With the environmental crisis as it is, these views must come together to conserve, respect, and manage such sacred areas together with the knowledge and institutional systems that support them. The stewardship of sacred trees and groves will help us better respect and understand the spirituality of nature. [35]

A real impetus for ecological sustainability and social justice stems from ethical, aesthetic, and spiritual visions. Love of nature and the intrinsic value of life is a basis for environmental and social justice movements. Mahatma Gandhi's founded his political philosophy on spiritual values,

---

ᶜᶜ Accessed March 2018. https://www.brainyquote.com/quotes/margaret_mead_100502.

saying, "You must be the change you wish to see in the world."[cf] Stewardship is a key quality for such change if we want to attain a broader worldview than being limited to ecology, sociology, and economics. We want to live in harmony and live on Earth without destroying it. [52]

Stewardship embraces development (economic, social, and material) and the religious and spiritual (internal, personal, and spiritual). Spirituality on its own is not enough, and development without spirit is inadequate. [51] We have separated the secular from the spiritual, yet we are all spiritual—whether or not we choose to acknowledge it. Such a separation is artificial. Yet the emphasis is on development and economic growth at the expense of all else. This is based on the false premise that humans are superior to all else and that everything is there to serve economic growth. Religion and spirituality ought to underpin development to help us seek a quality of life of elegant simplicity. [51] In stewardship we can all find common ground. As Edward Wilson puts it, "An enduring environmental ethic will aim to preserve not only the health and freedom of our species, but access to the world in which the human spirit is born." [113]

Religious and Spiritual Perspectives on Stewardship

From a spiritual perspective, we can express stewardship in differing ways. But it comes back to caring for the earth, using but not overusing, and holding nature in trust for future generations. "Culture is like a tree. If the green branches–a people's language, legends, customs–are carelessly chopped off, then the roots that bind people to their place on the Earth and to each other also begin to wither" (Mariano Lopez, Tzotzil Indian, Chiapas, Mexico [49]). The Andean Qyechuas speak of caring for Pacha Mama or Mother Earth and have many traditions about stewardship. The reasons relate to survival and responsibility to future generations. Aboriginal peoples see their deep and abiding commitment to looking after country as a legacy for their children and future generations. [36] Stewardship is

---

[cf] Accessed March 2018. https://www.brainyquote.com/quotes/mahatma_gandhi_109075.

much more than preservation as it includes rational sustainable use. [49] We have much to learn from indigenous and local peoples with generations of experience of cohabiting with and managing nature. Their legacy of stewardship has approaches and techniques that are similar across many cultures and spiritual traditions. We can use these techniques to better define contemporary spiritual views of nature that are right for our times, relevant to our needs, and also practical and implementable.

Stewardship pictures human beings in harmony with nature and focuses on the interdependence of the elements within nature. [69] "Then God said—Let us make mankind in our image, after our likeness, and let them have dominion over the fish of the sea, the birds of the air, and over the cattle, and over all the wild animals of the Earth, and all the creatures that crawl on the ground" (Genesis 1:26). "This is a sign I am giving for all ages to come, of the covenant between me and you, and every living creature with you" (Genesis 9:12). These quotations are at the heart of stewardship. But the terms subdue, rule over, and dominion are contentious. [25] Pope Francis is clear. Dominion is stewardship, not domination. [85] In the biblical context, stewardship refers to humankind's responsibility for husbanding God's gifts. The Qur-ān says, "Then let man look at his Food, [and how we provide it]: For that we pour forth water in abundance, and we split the Earth in fragments, and produce therein grain, and grapes and the fresh vegetation, and olives and dates, and enclosed gardens dense with lofty trees, and fruits and fodder–a provision for you and your cattle" (Qur-ān 80:24-32).

For many, challenging humankind's dominant position on Earth is an anathema. If we replace domination with stewardship, this emphasizes that we are one species amongst many. Yet some still state that our basic right is to subdue and be masters of nature. [48] Of all the misjudgments that emerged from religion, one of the most harmful is the view of the earth for our sole use. It is to the credit of various religious and spiritual groups that they reject this and stress a more benign attitude about the earth—one of caring stewardship of God's creation. It was in the first papal encyclical on climate change that Pope Francis formally repudiated dominion (June 2015). He said (para. 67), "Nowadays we must forcefully reject the notion that our being created in God's image and given dominion over the Earth justifies absolute domination over other creatures ... and has to do with God's loving plan in which every creature has its own value and significance." [85] A very clear statement! But domination doctrines still persist, often there to deny challenges such as climate change, the fair sharing of nature's benefits, and equality. [48]

If human communities live in ways that disturb due balance, it will bring disaster to people and planet. [46] The inconvenient truth (for many) is we share the planet with the rest of creation for a good reason. We cannot exist in or own the balanced web of life around us. We can only be stewards. Islam has always taught this, and to ignore this lesson is to default on our contract with creation. [41] These ethical views see people as better off because they are stewards of nature. Such separation occurs when we destroy the environment for short-term gain. Here, the Taoist understanding of nature emphasizes cooperation with the rhythms of nature rather than imposing our will. In the words of Lao Tzu, "In the age when life on Earth was full ... rulers were simply the highest branches on the tree and the people were like deer in the woods." [70]

Stewardship speaks of a harmony and a deep unity at the heart of creation, which the Russian Orthodox church refers to as *Sobornost*,[cg] where we are part of creation and nature, not the dominators. While stewardship is a step beyond dominion and domination, it still assumes people are the sole living species capable of husbanding God's gifts and still implies a superiority of humans. But it is important to know how we depend on nature. This has to inform the way we conceive of and perform our roles in nature.

Stewardship and dominion have similarities with sustainable development and conservation (see box 21).[ch] Achieving sustainable development will only succeed if the social, economic, and environmental pillars are addressed. In our material world, the economic pillar dominates.

[cg] Accessed May 2018. https://en.wikipedia.org/wiki/Sobornost.
[ch] See https://sustainabledevelopment.un.org/content/documents/11803Official-List-of-Proposed-SDG-Indicators.pdf.

Stewardship relies more on the links between the social and environmental pillars than on economics, but it allows us to connect the three pillars. No matter what religious and spiritual texts say about man's right to make use of nature, they emphasize man's responsibility for nature. Economist Herman Daly points out, "Sustainable development will require a change of heart, renewal of the mind and a healthy dose of repentance. These are all religious terms and that is no coincidence because a change in the fundamental principle in which we live is a change so deep that it is essentially religious whether we call this or not." [76] This requires a transformation founded on a worldview to enable humankind to live sustainably and to resacralize nature as part of this transformation so that we recognize the interconnectedness of all life. [62] For this to happen, three core values emerge as being essential—emphasis on quality of life and not more possessions, a shared humanity that emphasizes fairness and dignity, and environmental sustainability for a flourishing natural world.

Good policies depend on good economics. But good economics depends on good care of nature. Fritjof Capra said, "The great challenge of our time is to create sustainable communities, designed in such a way that they respect nature's inherent ability to sustain life. To do so, we need a new technological understanding of life, new values and a new way of thinking in terms of relationships, networks, psychical processes. This thinking is not taught in our schools, nor in our universities and the corresponding values are not embraced by our political leaders or businesses." [58]

Religious, spiritual, and conservation groups can embrace stewardship. This is the glue for action to conserve our natural heritage and will help us rebuild or develop cultural and spiritual relations with sacred trees and groves. But even if we agree to such approaches as stewardship, there are challenges to translating them into practice. [88] These challenges include multiple stakeholders with differing perceptions and being able to consider different practices and traditions. For example, if a sacred grove is designated as or within a formal reserved area, this can popularize a site in a manner the custodians may be unprepared for or that visitor activities may be inappropriate in—the climbing of sacred rocks (e.g., Uluru in

Australia), entering sacred caves or forests, bathing in sacred rivers, taking part in sacred ceremonies, or entering sacred areas without permission.

> **Box 21: Stewardship and Sustainable Development**
>
> **Stewardship**: hold something in trust for another; use the world we have been lent as temporary custodians, but we must leave it in good order for our descendants; use not overuse; recognize the interdependence in the natural world; emphasize how important future generations are; include relations between organizations and human resources.
>
> **Sustainable Development**: meeting the needs of present generations without compromising the ability of future generations to meet their needs.

Land encroachment, agriculture, hunting, tourism, and mining all impact sacred groves. Other anthropogenic pressures such as pollution, climate change, fires, floods, erosion, and conversion exacerbate this. To balance material and immaterial values is a challenge and depends on whose values matter at what level. As a result, modern and traditional systems may conflict in terms of whose knowledge counts. For modern management, science is the basis. Yet traditional custodians may have greater confidence in knowledge passed down through the ages. For example, mobile pastoralism is both a sustainable land use strategy and a cultural practice that is often spiritual. Many pastoralist communities have sacred groves and sacred trees.

Stewardship enriches our meaning of sustainable development by promoting the importance of spiritual, intangible, and other cultural values. Yet the spiritual and religious aspects of stewardship are neither fully recognized nor appreciated in the sustainable development discourse. Box 22 provides a summary of the Sustainable Development Goal indicators that might be relevant for this book, though sacred nature is not mentioned. While the Sustainable Development Goals are the current global discourse, we still do not really know how we might secure our fragile and tenuous presence on Earth or what we might have to do. The term sustainable is much more than smart technologies or smart economics and much more to do with being good stewards! We have to be more aware of the connections that bind us to life and all life to come. This will transform how we view the world, our roles, and how we might use the earth more sustainably. [78] Sacred groves and trees offer insights how this might be done.

Religious and spiritual groups ought to acknowledge and reaffirm the importance of stewardship as a core component of spirituality and so display leadership. This requires action as part of spiritual work that resonates with sustainable development. Environmental leaders can combine hope for the future of the planet with a commitment to the flourishing of each person, creature, and place. But leadership and stewardship will be flawed if results are more important than people and if leaders stop listening. [10]

Box 22: Sustainable Development Goals Indicators Which Sacred Trees and Groves Could Contribute

Indicator	Key content of indicator (shorthand)
1.4.2	Secure rights to land
4.7.1	Education for sustainable development
12.8.1	Similar to 4.7.1
12.b.1	Sustainable tourism
13.2.1	Climate change, especially adaptation
13.2.2	Climate change, especially adaptation
15.1.1	Forest area
15.1.2	Biodiversity protected by ecosystem type
15.4.1	Mountain biodiversity protected
15.5.1	Red list index
15.9.1	Aichi targets progress

To imbue politics with spiritual values, we need governance based on stewardship. The responsibility of government is to make sure we sustain nature and culture in the interests of future generations and the millions of other species. Governance here has nothing to do with control and everything to do with service and trust. [53] Politics without spirituality has proven to be a failure, and it is time to bring politics and spirituality together [52] in stewardship. The United Nations, government, and conservation agencies have been reluctant to engage with religious and spiritual groups, though there are exceptions. We should acknowledge the complementarity between these knowledge systems and address different but related aspects of human experience. [21]

Spirituality and ecology complement each other. Early in the twentieth century, Albert Schweitzer highlighted a desire to develop reverence for life, rediscover the world as sacred, and feel the wonder of the miracle of life. Reverence for life summarizes the common goals of religion and ecology. Ecologists deal with life but could use more spiritual approaches. Religions know about reverence, but tuning into the web of life that sustains us is also important as Mary Evelyn Tucker claims, "religions enter the ecological phase." [84] We can relate to planet Earth as tourists or pilgrims. As tourists, Earth is a source of goods and services for use, enjoyment, and domination. As pilgrims, we treat Earth with reverence and gratitude. We think of it as sacred and recognize the intrinsic value of life. Pilgrims are more likely to be good stewards than tourists. Satish Kumar says, "Sacred Earth is a gracious host to all pilgrims, but are we prepared to be gracious pilgrims rather than mere tourists?" [55] Are we pilgrims or tourists? Nature is neither neutral nor materialistic. It is part of God's creation. While humankind may think we are the top of the pyramid, we still have to be careful stewards, not the thoughtless exploiters, converters, and degraders [28] that we seem to be. Stewardship implies respect, love, and responsibility for nature as being the keys for our relationship with Creation.

Conservation Perspectives on Stewardship

"We, the undersigned, senior members of the world's scientific community, hereby warn all humanity of what lies ahead. A great change in our stewardship of the Earth and the life on it is required if vast human misery is to be avoided and our global home on this planet is not to be irretrievably mutilated." [107] This warning came from a group of the world's scientists to humanity in 1992. The declaration was signed by more than 1,700 senior scientists from across the globe, including more than half of the living Nobel Prize winners. Former World Bank chief economist Joseph Stiglitz put it another way. "[Gross domestic product] [100] has failed to capture what makes a difference in people's lives and contributes to their happiness, such as security, leisure, income distribution and a clean environment as it is clear that capitalism has failed to deliver a better quality of life for all through materialism, humanism and utility maximization." Bhutan's prime minister, Jigme Thinly, puts it clearly when he said, "In Bhutan personal spiritual fulfillment is not just a spiritual pursuit: it is government policy. My role is to create the conditions that will help our people find happiness." [4] The great thing in Bhutan is people from all spheres of life support the principles of gross national happiness. I don't think we can say the same of gross domestic product.

Many have reiterated these types of message from diverse backgrounds (e.g., the Brundtland Commission, the Rio+20 Declaration, the Sustainable Development Goals, and the Climate Change Convention). All emphasize stewardship if we are to avoid human misery or the extinction of *Homo sapiens*. So we need to present ourselves to Mother Earth as she presents herself to us, namely in a positive and stimulating manner, not one of domination. We need to be much more courteous to Earth [7] and think beyond sustainable development to one of restorative development [30] in order to restore local communities, the environment, and local and not global economic models. This might give us a stronger and more effective local framework for both people and planet. [30] But at present, humankind is progressing to self-destruction. We are progressing too fast without the proper checks and balances, and in the end, this will destroy us as a species. [90] However, an increased emphasis on stewardship will help us progress to reconnect with nature and respect the sacredness that nature is.

In the previous section, I explored the term stewardship from religious and spiritual perspectives. While stewardship is much stronger than other terms, we are more than nature's stewards. We are a part of nature. Though there are differences of emphasis, stewardship and sustainable development have many similarities (see box 21). There are similarities with conservation in caring for Mother Earth. Many sacred trees and groves are important areas for biodiversity and nature conservation. So it is important that conservation, like the different religious and spiritual groups, take a more proactive and responsible role regarding the stewardship of sacred trees and groves. Sacred groves are important for conservation yet have been largely unrecognized by conservation organizations in practical terms. So making links with the ecosystem approach can help us relate sacred trees and groves to implementing the principles of the Convention on Biological Diversity.

Many sacred groves are under a different form of more restrictive management (e.g., state-owned national parks and reserves or forest reserves). Under such management systems, the ability to negotiate for the recognition and respect for sacred groves and trees is more difficult and is often left to the discretion of the protected area manager. Yet many sacred groves and trees contain high degrees of biodiversity. So sacred groves can be sanctuaries and gene pools for rare and endemic species, and these can provide a basis for ecosystem restoration to create greater connectivity. We can make improvements based on the traditional ecological knowledge custodians have. To integrate traditional ecological knowledge with modern science is one key to understanding broader landscape processes. This strengthens the argument for sacred groves as ICCAs. Their management can be sustainable as it is community-owned, but their rights (to land and natural resources) need to be formally recognized.

Sacred groves are reference points for cultural, religious, and national identity and can support endangered cultural systems. At the interface of culture and nature, sacred trees and groves offer opportunities for ecotourism. For example, visitors can experience new cultures and learn about nature. It provides space to experience human-nature relations from different cultural perspectives and to build bridges for intercultural dialogue, understanding, tolerance, and peace. Culture and nature shape landscapes. Yet those within conservation and land use often undervalue and misunderstand such cultural landscapes. It is here local people have important stewardship roles, in particular those closest to the resources.

Stewardship refers to the essential role individuals and communities play in the careful management of their natural and cultural wealth for present and future generations. Stewardship is nuanced and can mean different things to different people in terms of conservation. "My husband's and my philosophy are that none of us really ever own the land—we only hold it in our hands for a very brief time and what we do with the land is our gift to the next generation. And some day, we'll be held accountable for what happens to this land" (Lynne and Del Sherrod, ranchers in Colorado).[ci] Stewardship reflects efforts to create, nurture, and enable responsibility for landowners to conserve and use their lands, [71, 105] and it taps into human qualities to care for home, the surroundings, and the environment. It offers ways to cultivate local involvement and reach beyond contemporary conserved areas. By fostering individual and community responsibility, stewardship puts conservation in the hands of the people most affected by it (see box 23).

Community-based conservation and stewardship are similar with issues ranging from exploiting tangible benefits to conservation and nurturing a conservation ethos. Both involve approaches to give people rights and responsibilities. If proponents of cultural and biological diversity become allies, this may save both nature and culture. [11] Community-based conservation will not always result in benefits for nature and people, and the results are longer term and [71, 72, 105] will be sustainable and locally owned.

Stewardship fosters individual and community responsibility for nature and is one way to extend conservation beyond protected areas to address the needs of the wider landscape, connectivity, and community interactions. Stewardship is helpful where managing larger landscapes, not protection, is the aim. For example, *Nye* in Bhutan is an important customary and spiritual approach

> **Box 23: Some Examples of Conservation Stewardship** [115]
>
> These examples include
>
> 1. protecting open spaces and fragile natural areas in the face of development, especially where planning controls are weak;
> 2. conserving biodiversity through habitat protection;
> 3. maintaining landscape integrity in times of changing land use and declining rural economies;
> 4. sustaining traditional land uses important for ecological, economic, and scenic values;
> 5. conserving and managing sacred groves and natural sites as part of wider landscapes;
> 6. protecting individual sacred trees as part of local culture; and
> 7. enhancing the ability of government agencies to manage protected areas through partnerships.

[ci] https://www.nps.gov/mabi/learn/historyculture/lynne-sherrod.htm.

for conservation, but they are not recognized as formal protected areas, [115] though they are examples of ICCAs. *Nye* can be important for protected areas and for creating biological corridors and connectivity in Bhutanese landscapes as 50 percent of the land is a network of protected areas.

Stewardship draws on many disciplines, but mostly from natural and social sciences and law. This is a challenge where different sectors take responsibility for a forest, a park, and/or a river. Stewardship is about adaptive management, builds on traditional management, and takes an integrated landscape view. This can address compatible objectives of conservation, development, culture, and spirituality and help maintain connections to the land. It offers ways of extending the reach of protected areas to address conservation more broadly, cultivate local responsibility for sustainable management, and offer the potential to conserve heritage at ecosystem and landscape levels. [109]

Human centered values are important as conservation moves to address cultural diversity, quality of life, and social justice. At the community level, stewardship integrates social, cultural, and ecological values by (a) strengthening the ethical core of conservation to include social issues and caring for people; (b) providing tolerance, respect, and new ways of working together; (c) respecting cultural traditions, historic places, and the values of people; and (d) preserving a strong sense of place. There are three common threads of conservation stewardship (see box 24)—a sense of place that is complex and multifaceted; community-based conservation that is comprehensive, collaborative, respectful, and self-sustaining; and a foundation for commitment and passion. These provide enduring inspiration and lead to respect for the land. [71, 105]

Box 24: Conservation Stewardship—A Sense of Place, Belonging, and Caring

Conservation stewardship is a sense of place that includes the landscape, people, built environments, culture, and ecology that contributes to the uniqueness of place. Stewardship links past, present, and future conservation. In cultures with a long history of being in one location, heritage and feeling connected to the land and the landscape are strong. Community-based conservation relies on collaboration, respects traditional knowledge and practice, emphasizes local self-determination, and attends to sustaining stewardship as an integrated approach to natural resource management. It has the following components:

a) Commitment and passion—Successful stewardship draws on feelings and respect for peace (land, human, and community), values, ethics, and spiritual traditions. Stewardship is rooted in deep personal connections to the land and special places, such as sacred groves, with a sense of moral responsibility for future generations. It reflects a powerful convergence and direction for conservation that reconnects people with place and with one another. "If I die, my children are going to judge me not by the money I make, but by whether I have kept the forest in good condition" (Village Elder from Melanesia in S. Pacific).

b). Stewardship creates and supports resilience, allowing a system to respond to shocks that come in a complex world. Change can be incremental or rapid. Resilience involves the capacity to handle changes without destabilizing the systems.

c). The promise of conservation stewardship

- is a sense of place that is complex and dynamic;
- embraces community-based conservation to integrate conservation into people's lives and community;
- requires conservation to be inclusive and reflect the values and importance of conservation to society;
- lays important groundwork to strengthen the fabric of community life and enhances civil society;
- helps people reconnect with nature, which is essential for respecting and protecting the land; and
- is grounded in scientific knowledge and personal passion. Rachel Carson says, "I sincerely believe that for the child, and for the parent seeking to guide him, it is not half as important to know as to feel. If facts are the seeds that later produce knowledge and wisdom, then emotions and the impressions of the senses are the fertile soil in which the seeds must grow." [15]

Source: Adapted from [71, 105]

While not about sacred trees and groves, the following example from India highlights the fundamentals of stewardship. Vandana Shiva talked to an eighty-three-year-old farmer in India who had developed twenty varieties of rice. [102] She asked him if he would try to patent them to control them and make money. "How could I own them?" he replied. "They are my friends. They are my partners. I have to be a good friend to them and they will then be good to me. But without my treating them as friends, they will never feed us. We are in a partnership of species." In India, there is even a word meaning a partnership of species and a word for Earth family, which refers to all species together. [102] This example has salutary lessons for us all.

Stewardship approaches have similarities with entitlements, [60, 61, 95] which, as a concept, evolved around food availability and poverty, but these are important in community conservation and for sacred groves and natural sites. An absolute lack of resources may be the reason for people not being able to access the resources they require. Resource availability and access are interconnected as is local governance. Conflicts over access intensify when resources become scarce. [61] This has a relevance for sacred groves because many survive in areas of high land use and population density.

Entitlements arise through *mapping*, and endowments or a person's initial ownership of land or labor becomes a set of entitlements. As a result, we should understand how different people derive entitlements from their endowments and improve their well-being or capabilities. [95] This is important in how we recognize sacred groves, their management, and how such entitlements are negotiated and respected. For example, an entitlement may refer to a community's sacred grove. The community has customary rules. These are endowments that can strengthen the community's capacity to steward their grove. Entitlements refer to the rights and resources of social actors, (e.g., to land, labor, alternative commodity bundles, and their ability to defend their entitlements). [61]

An emphasis on effectiveness of entitlements as to who has what rights and responsibilities highlights two issues. Resource claims may be contested. Within existing power relations, some actors' claims are more likely to prevail as the management of risks faced by sacred groves attests to in many places. For example, Kaya forest management in Kenya was not powerful enough in the face of political support for tourism development. Then actors, such as sacred grove custodians, can gain legitimate and effective control over a resource bundle (i.e., the sacred grove) and defend those rights.

Aldo Leopold, as a spiritual scientist, said, "We abuse land because we regard it as a commodity belonging to us. When we see land as a community to which we belong, we may begin to use it with love and respect." [63] This statement embraces the core aspects of stewardship—a sense of place, respect for nature, sustainable use, community-based approaches, and commitment. Friendship, an aspect of stewardship, is not only toward humans but to nature. Satish Kumar says, "I am a friend of my place and of my garden. I'm a friend of trees and flowers. I'm a friend of the bees. I'm a friend of even the earthworms and the slugs and snails. The weeds are my friends. Friendship is a term people use mostly for human relationships, but I use the term in a broader sense." [59] Lao Tzu says, "Water is altruistic because it supports life, is modest and humble because it always takes the lowest ground. Water is adaptable and flexible because it can stay in a container of any shape. Water is transparent and clear." This saying uses the metaphor of water to explain the ideal form of leadership. [106] Such approaches to leadership and friendship are intertwined with stewardship and sacred space. [104] Stewardship is important for conservation. Its focus is local, —looking after place. It is community-based, blends local and scientific knowledge, and is not dominated by science and expert management.

Importance of Stewardship for Religion and Spirituality

The only conservation action likely to be effective is based on the principle we are responsible for our actions beyond our own individual and physical well-being. We cannot sit and do nothing, saying it is God's will. God holds us responsible for what we do. When we accept the freedom given to us—to not only destroy nature but live in harmony with it. We see our only action has to be a change in our state of being. [74] Care for creation and care for the poor are one. These are the two pillars of the encyclical that Pope Francis conveyed.

Pope Francis calls this an integral ecology, which he bases on respect for creation and a renewed emphasis on our mutual interconnectedness with one another and with nature. As a result, we have one complex global crisis that is social and environmental. [77] Pope Francis stresses care for creation and care for the poor. The two go hand in hand. Creation embraces nature, and the poor represent key groups to work with. It is a stark reiteration of the Rio Earth Summit (more than two decades earlier), where protecting the environment is "an integral part of the development process and cannot be considered in isolation from it." Yet development and economics still treat conservation as nearly separate. Christians and Muslims ground the ecological foundation for protecting nature in a shared view of creation. [22] The role of humanity is that of nature's caretaker, which corresponds to Judeo-Christian notions of stewardship. [46]

The example of *Hima* (or protected place) in Jordan is illustrative. It refers to protecting areas of land in wider landscapes from encroaching demands and is an example of stewardship. Hima existed before Islam; however, with Islam, its function changed, and it became more dedicated to the well-being of the community who lived around it. [29] People manage the natural resources of the Hima for times of scarcity. [47] These set-asides for the protection of the welfare of people existed from the time of the prophet Muḥammad (Peace Be Upon Him), who laid down some of the rules of Hima. *Harim* is like Hima and refers to a zone that people may not use or develop unless they get permission from the state. *Harim* relates to natural wells and springs to ensure they are free from pollution. [46]

The key difference between an ungoverned common property regime and a resilient commons is the stewardship of the community managing the resource. [80] A key challenge to the long-term sustainability of such institutions as Hima is that national law, policy, and institutions do not adequately recognize or respect them. [82] For example, in the 1960s, there were about three thousand Hima in Saudi Arabia of between ten and a thousand hectares. Few of these still exist because of modernity. [47] Lebanon is reviving Hima. But in Lebanon and may be in other countries, it is more of a community conservation strategy and not sacred. It seems clear the traditional institution of Hima needs to evolve to embrace contemporary pressures and aspirations.

Religions can engage more (see box 25) as they used to have a strong influence on societies and cultures. That they might have performed with bias, prejudice, limitations, and corruption is undeniable. But religions are and can be movements for liberation, peace, and moral cohesiveness. We cannot ignore the power and potential of religion. We can expand human-centered religious ethics to include biocentric and ecocentric aspects. Most religious traditions should reevaluate their roles in nature. [23]

Box 25: Religions Promoting Tree Planting

Forest Monks promote tree planting in Thailand to show respect for nature. In India, the Badrinath Temple in the Himalaya's takes its name from *badra* (juniper tree), which is the form Lord Vishnu's wife Lakshmi took to protect him from a snowstorm. It is a very important Hindu site and visited by half a million pilgrims per year. But the slopes surrounding the hills and valley are degraded. They hold tree planting ceremonies, and pilgrims planted about twenty thousand trees for religious merit in the first ceremony and the chief priest blessed the trees. They repeated this and extended the planting to other sites. The reasons pilgrims planted such trees included reestablishing the sacred forest of Badrivan, sacred plants and herbs needed for religious practice, worship and service to a deity (e.g., Hanuman or Lord Vishnu), religious duty or dharma, selfless action or kharma yoga, and the restoration of a healthy environment for religious practices and goals.

In the United Kingdom, the Alliance of Religion and Conservation stimulated the Sacred Land Project—the largest religious campaign on ecology ever undertaken in the United Kingdom. The project will conserve—and restore where necessary—ancient woodlands belonging to historical monuments and churches. They can replicate such restoration where pilgrimage sites exist, irrespective of religion. Society can support and reinforce the sacredness of such sites. They can recognize the sacredness of certain trees and groves. Societies could support local folk songs, stories, legends, rituals, and festivals relating to sacred trees and groves. This will reinforce the younger generation's bond with the natural world.

Sources: [6, 32, 99], and http://sacredland.org/ accessed May 2018

Everywhere, people kept spiritual and religious linkages with trees because of their age, presence, and timelessness, not to mention the sense of peace and tranquility they imbue. These are common characteristics across contemporary and historical examples. These include revering individual old trees and groves of trees often on hills or in parts of a forest where people live close to. Though sacred groves may be small, there are many, especially in some countries. There are many more sacred groves and trees than acknowledged by conservation organizations and governments. Many sacred groves conserve tree species from bygone days, and their presence can support conservation as some of these trees are keystone species.

"Learn a lesson from the way the wild flowers grow. They do not work; they do not spin. Yet I assure you not even Solomon in all his splendor was not arrayed like one of these" (Mathew 6:28–29). Trees are not separate from but are one with life. This quotation from Jesus (and similar quotations in other sacred texts) draws our attention to the power of nature to help us reconnect. Becoming more mindful changes our view of Earth as humankind is inseparable from nature. [103] As Eckhart Tolle puts it, "When we go into a forest that has not been interfered with by man, our thinking mind will only see disorder and chaos all around. Only if we are still enough inside and the noise of thinking subsides, can we become aware that there is a hidden harmony here, a sacredness, a higher order in which everything has its perfect place." [103]

Sacred trees and groves make up an important natural and spiritual heritage, both from a usage sense and in spirituality. Hassein Nasr says, "The fact is we are murdering creation is what has got to stop and to stop it, we must first realize that we are responsible for our actions. As God holds us responsible." [75] Religions often ignored sacred trees and groves. So we must steward such trees and groves in terms of our spirituality. Islam considers man to be a vice regent on Earth and a trustee for its ecosystems. [24] When we understand nature as creation, its stewardship calls for greater inter- and intra-faith harmony and reaching out to the environmental movement.

Everyone has innate spirituality and believes in some form of God or consciousness or whatever term we use. So there is much common ground to work together to steward Mother Earth. Different faiths and spiritual traditions have to put stewardship into practical action. Conserving sacred groves and sacred nature is one expression of action and a good example to build on. We can no longer entertain a worldview that separates humanity and the divine as well as community and nature. We can overcome this [75] by (a) challenging sciences' monopolistic claims to provide the only true knowledge on every aspect of our relations with society and nature; (b) understanding the philosophical shortcomings of modern science and understanding that this is making the planet uninhabitable; (c) addressing the fundamental challenges of planet Earth for ourselves, our families, and our greater family of all animate and inanimate life; and (d) applying traditional religious and spiritual wisdom in our contemporary world as our ancestors did.

For Christianity, we are seeing a growth of eco-congregations where local churches sign up to environmentally responsible practices for their individual and community lives in England. [112] Such examples help us to be more aware of our common origins. We all share our future on the planet, and we will need a reinvigorated reverence for life on Earth. [85] We can also reconnect with nature, and here Earth Jurisprudence[cj] offers us some lessons [68] to (a) be humble when we work with nature, carve its wood, till its soil, and teach children; (b) treat nature as sacred with humility; (c) practice generosity through giving and receiving as nature does; and (d) be patient as nature is. Everything happens in its own good time. Restraint helps us maintain the natural balance of abundance and use.

To be good stewards of our trees and forests calls us to live within the four principles of humility, generosity, patience, and restraint. Then we will live

---

[cj] This is a philosophy of law where the universe is the primary lawgiver. Earth jurisprudence is a philosophy of law and human governance that is based on the idea that humans are only one part of a wider community of beings and that the welfare of each member of that community is dependent on the welfare of the Earth as a whole. [20]

in harmony with nature. For religious and spiritual groups with respect to sacred trees and groves, this calls us to

1. improve our understanding of people's spiritual and religious views of nature, trees, and forests as to what this means for religion and spirituality and also support a fuller appreciation of nature;
2. understand customary and local institutions and their cultural practices as they are responsible as custodians for such sites;
3. acknowledge and understand the value of sacred trees and groves in terms of the spirituality of local people irrespective of religious or spiritual belief;
4. implement plans and agreements concerning nature and religion, including the Assisi Declarations, to address integrating environmental issues in spiritual work;
5. appreciate the variety of social institutions responsible for managing such areas and how we can transfer the knowledge and institutions of SNS between generations;
6. take increased responsibility to address conservation and environmental challenges, in particular for trees and forests;
7. engage with conservation organizations to better manage, recognize, and respect sacred trees and groves so that the different IUCN protected area categories acknowledge them;
8. redefine and reemphasize our religious and spiritual roles and responsibilities for the environment and in particular for forests and trees, including the role of education;
9. connect communities with nature, sacred trees, groves, and celebrate tree folklore;
10. act with humility, affection, neighborliness, cooperation, and loyalty;
11. recognize the multiple dynamics in spirituality because spirituality and culture are not static;
12. promote dialogue among faiths, religions, spiritual groups, and the secular world around common values and approaches toward improving human well-being;

13. develop and implement conservation stewardship education and leadership because then stewardship becomes one basis for securing local customary governance systems; and
14. understand the interface between religion/spirituality and ecology, especially where more than one faith or spiritual tradition has an interest (e.g., Mount Kailash).

Importance of Stewardship for Conservation and Land Use

The inspirational book *Silent Spring* was concerned with the biological damage we are doing to the world and ourselves. But Rachel Carson's book is also an indictment of our perception of our place in the larger scheme of things. For Carson, our ecological thoughtlessness is matched only by our lack of philosophical maturity, and she concluded that "the control of nature is a phrase conceived in arrogance, born of the Neanderthal age of biology and philosophy, when it was supposed that nature exists for the convenience of man." [16] Carson's critique suggests that what we need, regarding our ecological problems, are not bigger and better technical solutions but a rethinking our fundamental attitudes concerning our place in the larger scheme of things. [27]

At the heart of the ecological crisis is a failure not only to understand the essence of humanity's place but to know the forces driving human nature and determining the choices we make. [2] The knowledge and institutional base of why sacred values are important for people requires a greater understanding from a conservation perspective. This links spiritual knowledge about biodiversity to use values and provides a stronger rationale to advocate for conservation. But we still lack basic knowledge and information about many sacred sites (see box 26). It is also essential to understand that economic and use values are not the sole drivers for conservation and livelihoods. Nor are they always the most important. We need to house conserving sacred groves and trees with the custodians who retain spiritual linkages to them. Too often conservation authorities gazette areas in ignorance of important cultural, religious, and spiritual values.

> Box 26: Information Requirements for Sacred Trees and Groves with Respect to [8, 43]
>
> ➢ assess contribution to biodiversity;
> ➢ have inventories to understand spatial extent and formal recognition;
> ➢ understand sociocultural belief systems that help conserve;
> ➢ understand institutions and rules for management;
> ➢ how to integrate and recognize groves in different protected area categories;
> ➢ take long-term approaches to conservation as many groves are older than formal protected areas; and
> ➢ provide legal and policy tools supporting communities to manage their sites to raise the profile of groves at national and global levels.

It is best to work at a broader landscape level that includes an array of uses and systems. Many of these uses may be the responsibility of diverse sectors. Together they form a landscape that integrates and respects diversity. Here sacred trees and groves have their niche as one means to enhance connectivity. They help integrate complex overlapping forms of ecological, social, political, symbolic dynamism in sacred groves and their landscapes and also enhance their conservation potential. Sacred groves can make significant contributions to resilience. Yet conservation organizations and governments tend to oversimplify diversity and mitigate risk with blueprint approaches. This can lead to tension between conservation and people whose lands they seek to conserve. [97]

Some government agencies and conservation organizations are starting to better recognize the importance of sacred trees and groves. IUCN is at the forefront through its commissions of specialist groups. This resulted in various publications. [87, 110, 111, 114] But we require more in terms of practical action and enhancing the evidence base for conserving these special sites. Some countries recognize their historical values or the physical characteristics of trees and groves and have tried to protect them. For example, Senegal has established a procedure for identifying and classifying remarkable trees.

What conditions are necessary for conserving sacred groves? Community autonomy and institutional self-sufficiency is essential. Community interests in grove conservation should, if possible, converge with those of the state. When local rules do, community and state conservation benefit. It is then possible for local communities to manage their resources. Rules should be compatible with local livelihoods. [38] Many conservationists emphasize ecosystem integrity. While important, this must go hand in hand with the integrity of human life and spirituality. We can become the stewards of nature we desire to be, but this requires humility, not arrogance, and it implies having the right attitudes to be attentive and mindful of life and our earth. [85]

It will take more than conservation science to respect and conserve sacred groves and trees. For many conservationists, sacred groves are not large or interconnected enough to be important despite evidence to the contrary. We ought to embrace ethics, values, spirituality, and religion to better conserve such areas, [32] while demonstrating to conservation science how important sacred trees and groves are in the landscape. It is this coming together for a common cause of religious and spiritual leaders with conservationists and land use managers that is likely to make a bigger difference than any on their own. Stewardship is the glue to bring these partners together for a common cause.

In wider landscape management, sacred groves can play important conservation roles to create connectivity with other forms of conservation (e.g., reserved areas, national parks, ICCAs, and human land use, including farmlands, hillsides, and river edges). Trees—those ancient, sacred teachers—are the best carbon sequestration mechanism available and offer us lessons in enlightenment and humility just as the bodhi tree did for the Buddha those millennia ago. [40]

An example from Karnataka in India illustrates how important mosaic landscape approaches are, [9] where a forest reserve borders a tree-covered cultivated landscape comprising coffee cultivation and sacred groves. They farm coffee under indigenous shade trees. The size of the sacred groves did not influence species richness. Rather the distance between the sacred grove and the forest was more important. The biodiversity in the sacred groves is also influenced by the indigenous trees found, in this case, as part of shade coffee. To better conserve biodiversity, the integrity of the indigenous tree cover in the landscape is important as part of connectivity. Such informal (and even formal) networks of nature are important for conservation and species richness. Sacred groves can be an important part in these mosaics. With increasing land use and population pressures, such approaches to connectivity become important irrespective of the size of sacred groves. The land use types in mosaics are important where agroforestry with indigenous species is more successful than a monocrop for instance. The fate of conservation may well depend on these mosaic landscapes and ecosystem remnants. Sacred groves may be one important component of this together with their custodians.

Conservationists have to move on from utilitarian and preservationist values of nature. The literature on community conservation provides strong arguments for such a shift. But much of the scholarship on community conservation relates to how rural people can or cannot use nature and the economic benefits they provide, or they are concerned with protected areas, especially state-owned national parks, to conserve the world's rich natural heritage. This is important but not enough, given ever-increasing pressures on land and resources. The active understanding and integration of religious and spiritual values in nature is both a challenge and an opportunity for conservation, religious, and spiritual groups to work together.

Even small sacred groves can be arboreta for seed stock through proactive conservation as happened in Ethiopian monastic forests, which are reservoirs of biodiversity for restoration. But we require inventories of sacred trees and groves in terms of their scale and extent and their biodiversity composition. Often the reasons for protecting the spiritual connections between people and Earth and for conservation are inseparable. Many sacred groves survive without government protection as local respect and sanction is strong enough.

Local respect and sanction may work, but it is difficult for those responsible for sacred sites at the community level to withstand globalization together with local or external political pressures. National parks included many sacred sites with little concern for the sacred grove custodians. This happened in Kenya (Mt. Kenya and Mt. Elgon) and Ghana. Unscrupulous business interests and politicians converted other sacred groves. For example, some Kayas along the Kenya coast were cleared, and the land was privatized for developing tourism. Policy and legal support are required to formalize their status and still keep such sites for the people and by the people in a manner that is defendable. Sacred groves are expressions of the interdependence of ecology and culture. But we ought to be cautious in linking conservation, indigenous knowledge, and culture in ways that may imply enforced primitivism, which is unacceptable. [43] We need to be careful when trying to integrate traditional knowledge with conservation. Such knowledge is vital and living, and changes with changing circumstances. This is an important building block for improving management and long-term sustainability. The value of this knowledge is stronger in stable and homogenous societies compared to communities comprised of a mix of peoples with often differing interests and views.

Schumacher realized we can only apply Buddhist economics on a human scale if we recognize the principles of right livelihood and human well-being. [56] Goethe said, "If we want to behold nature in the living way, we must follow her example and make ourselves as mobile and flexible as nature herself." [33] Thomas Berry proposed a name—the ecozoic era. Humanity can repair the damage done on Earth and bring about an era that respects nature and that is self-renewing and ecologically sustainable. [57] The ecological age fosters an awareness of the sacred within each of us where to destroy a living species is to silence a divine voice. [7] Eckhart Tolle highlights an exercise we can do (see box 27). [103] Then we can embrace the three Rs of

1. *redesigning*, meaning to have new ways of operating and innovating to be more on doing good, shifting from the take-make-waste economic paradigm to a regenerative approach supporting the web of life;

2. *reconnecting* with our relationship with nature and reestablishing our bond with ourselves, neighbors, and the web of life through education and responsive leadership; and
3. *rekindling* wisdom so we work with the grain of nature and the rules of life on Earth to sustain and thrive by practicing wise approaches to life that draw on symbiosis, ecological thinking, culture, systems thinking, business inspired by nature, and indigenous wisdom. [42]

Historically, conservation belittled how important sacred trees and groves were. *There are too small to be viable. There's no connectivity. They don't conserve important species.* These arguments are being refuted as (a) we can recreate connectivity using a mix of land uses; (b) many sacred sites contain endemic species, which shows their conservation importance; and (c) sacred groves offer real opportunities for ICCAs. Western conservation approaches are starting to value these relationships between local environmental knowledge and communities and between scientific and spiritual perspectives. Recognizing connectivity and the trade-offs to use the environmental services may well be more sustainable than alienating further lands from people.

This calls for conservation authorities to move from mechanistic views to more integrated approaches and interact more with different religions and spiritual groups regarding how we manage sacred groves at the practical level. This requires more ethical and spiritual approaches to create bonds between conservation and spirituality. [81] Forest and conservation authorities

> **Box 27: Being Present with Nature**
>
> "Chose an object close to you—a plant or a tree, or even a pen or a cup. Explore it visually with great interest. Without straining, relaxed but alert, give your attention to the plant or tree—explore every detail of it. After a few minutes, let your gaze wonder more widely; listen for any sounds—but don't differentiate between good and bad (don't judge). Feel the aliveness of the tree or plant. When you really look and listen in this way, you may perceive a subtle sense of calm—a stillness in the background. When consciousness is no longer totally absorbed by thinking, some of it remains. It is formless, unconditional, original state. That is inner space."

could engage in a range of activities for improved sacred trees and grove management, including to

1. improve our understanding of people's spiritual and religious views as to what this means for conservation to recognize and value the diversity of the world's cultures and spiritualities;
2. understand traditional, customary, and local institutions with their rules and norms and how we can strengthen these institutions for improved natural resource management;
3. use traditional, customary, and local institutions as a basis for restoration;
4. implement community protocols to enhance the management of sacred groves, [98] which will empower custodians with rights-based approaches;
5. implement the contents of agreements concerning environment and religion regarding improved policies and practice (e.g., the Convention on Biological Diversity);
6. develop and implement conservation stewardship education and leadership approaches;
7. use stewardship as the basis for securing local level and customary governance systems;
8. develop and implement plans of work to integrate religious and spiritual values into forest and conservation management;
9. better understand the biodiversity and conservation values, including their mapping, and promote the integration of scientific knowledge with traditional management;
10. make sure protected area authorities respect how important sacred trees and groves are;
11. support communities in their quest for greater statutory recognition of their sacred trees and groves through improved, stronger tenure and governance arrangements;
12. assist custodians to form civil society organizations and be part of informal local networks so that we recognize their stewardship; [89]
13. reconnect people with place and nature to build a greater understanding of stewardship and its benefits to society, which also fosters respect for diversity;

14. strengthen the ability to practice effective stewardship and encourage new forms of leadership at the community level;
15. promote equity and conservation that supports the vulnerable and disadvantaged groups, whose cultures and spiritual values maybe ignored or discriminated against;
16. redress past inequities where many groves were reserved as parks or forest reserves, which might include restitution or various forms of comanagement; and
17. celebrate the contributions of stewardship as SNS can conserve both culture and nature.

Sacred Groves and Nature—Key for Education, Health, and Peace

CHAPTER 7

> Adopt the pace of nature: her secret is patience
> —Ralph Waldo Emerson[ck]

> Education is the most powerful weapon which you can use to change the world
> —Nelson Mandela[cl]

> Reconciliation is a spiritual process which requires more than just a legal framework. It has to happen in the hearts and minds of people
> —Nelson Mandela [70]

Importance of Learning from Nature

What do sacred trees and groves have to do with peace, education, health, and reconnecting with nature? In our contemporary world, we are increasingly separated from nature despite our dependency on it. Though we may not realize it, we desperately need ways to reconnect, respect,

---

[ck] Accessed May 2018. https://www.brainyquote.com/quotes/ralph_waldo_emerson_106883.
[cl] Accessed June 2018. https://www.washingtonpost.com/news/answer-sheet/wp/2013/12/05/nelson-Nelson_Mandelas-famous-quote-on-education/?noredirect=on&utm_term=.80a1eeae2df2.

and understand the wisdom and peace that emanates from nature. For example, people are least happy at work or when they are sick. People are happier outdoors in green natural habitats than in urban environments. [113] Children bond with nature by being present and innocent. [8] This is being lost as children spend less time in nature. Pierre Rabhi notes, "Today, in Europe, people are sad. There's no joy left. Nature is joy; a political party isn't. Nature concerns everyone … So, our task is to move ecology from a political level to the level of consciousness. That's why it's so important for each individual to feel that he or she is a child of Nature." [53] Then we can bring nature back to the center of our lives. Sacred trees and groves offer a strong focus and means to show how important nature is for education and health, help bring peace to our troubled world, and help us reconnect with nature.

We now see what in our hearts we always knew. Humans need nature not only to survive and thrive, but it plays multiple roles in our lives—as teacher, health provider, spirituality teacher, and resource provider. The time is right to reassess the roles of nature in our personal and national lives. Nature should be upfront in public policy, not just environmental policy. We can no longer set questions of outdoor space in urban and rural planning to one side or in a box labeled green issues! [90] This relates to how important place is in education, something we overlook. Place is very relevant for coping with problems of education becoming overspecialized, combined with the destruction of local community, especially in urban areas [82]. The importance of place should be part of curricula which study such relationships.

We have much to learn from nature. [67] We can use nature to learn from and experience beauty and peace. Forests and trees are places of rest, silence, recreation, and reflection, and sacred trees and groves even more so. Because of their age, they are places of folklore, history, legends, and sacredness. Forests give us materials and inspiration, and they are places for learning, awareness, and peace. Maria Montessori suggested that we should drop lecture-based education and head for the farm and nature, where students can learn by doing. [113] Lessons of being with nature include recognizing the energy connecting us to the whole, falling in love with the outdoors, remembering how to play, knowing nature is home, and knowing nature is more complex than we know. [34] But sacred earth has the last call as there are nonnegotiable limits in Gaia we should respect and beyond which we cannot go. [36] Humility, respect, and a willingness to learn from nature will help restore that balance. [66]

Our education systems have conditioned us to think working the land and working with nature is not good. It won't make us millionaires! Rather we should be in offices in front of computer screens. This dramatic loss of nature-based exploration in our children's lives and in our own happened so fast we hardly noticed it, much less corrected it. [113] We must move from this perception of nature and retool education to being experiential. Paulo Freire pioneered experiential learning, saying, "Education is suffering from narration sickness." [30] He criticized education for being too passive. The educator is the guide and feeds information to the student with little real dialogue or learning by doing. [32] In learning by doing, student and teacher learn together. They solve problems together, and solutions become avenues for learning. Such approaches bring more people into nature and should attract stronger policy support, especially given all the current environmental crises (e.g., plastics, climate change, etc.). As an example, David Orr recollects, "I had a high school diploma, a bachelor's degree, a master's degree and a PhD and presumed myself to be educated. But 11 years of living in a small valley in the southern Ozarks [USA] in the 1980s showed me how little I knew and how little I could ever know, but also the importance of striving to know." [82] I had similar experiences in the twelve years I worked with Pokot and Turkana pastoralists in Kenya. They were far more knowledgeable than I am, and they taught me about nature and living in dry risk-prone environments.

This chapter offers some ideas and guidance on how we can connect and reconnect with nature—wherever we are, whatever we are doing, and in whatever life circumstances we find ourselves. Sacred trees and groves are examples of sacred spaces to do this and of what we can do. We need to set our loss of connectivity with nature in context of the challenges we face because of our separation from nature—a subject called *nature deficit disorder* by Richard Louv. [60] This causes many disorders (e.g., a lack of peace and the increased violence). Even the shootings of innocent children in schools within the United States may be linked to this phenomenon. For millennia we were connected to and dependent on nature. It is only in the last fifty or so years, especially the last two decades, that our separation from nature increased because of urbanization and being confined to the classroom or office. Many children are not exposed to nature as they want to stay indoors with their electronic devices. [63] Urbanization exacerbates this as 55 percent of humanity is urban, including more than 50 percent of the world's children.

Many of us are passionate about the environment because of early and deep experience with nature—experiential learning. This is how we became conservationists or environmentalists, which might not have happened if we were only exposed to technical and scientific approaches. [82] I grew up on an organic farm in Ireland, and through my father's enthusiasm, I became passionate about trees and nature—a passion not dimmed by a scientific training.

The word education comes from the Latin word *educator*, meaning to lead or bring out what is there, to unfold what is dormant, and to make explicit what is implicit. If we compare a student and a seed, a tree is in the seed. [49] A gardener or a forester cannot teach the seed how to become a tree. The forester provides the right conditions for the seed to become a tree. Pupils and students have the potential to be who they are, but the potential is implicit. The work of the teacher is to inspire and create the conditions for students to discover themselves. [49] Julius Nyerere had a comparable definition as having the "purpose to transmit from one generation to the next the accumulated wisdom and knowledge of the society, and to prepare the young people for their future membership of the society and the active participation in its maintenance or development. This is true, explicitly, for all societies." [81] But most contemporary education systems lack the means to connect, reconnect, and better appreciate and understand nature as the basis for life. Education has to be more proactive in terms of awareness and understanding of nature as part of a more integrated understanding of what nature means for us. I suggest different approaches and ideas to achieve this, which can include sacred trees and groves as entry points.

We can use sacred trees and groves as places for building peace. Parks for Peace have been around for some time (see box 28). The role sacred trees and groves can play expands this to be more accessible—be it at the level of an individual, family, community, or nation, where sacred trees and grove are havens for and conducive to peace and nonviolence. We can reconnect with nature in our own ways depending on our circumstances. But we need to commit to do so and appreciate the real value of what Herman Melville says, "Silence is the consecration of the Universe … Silence is the only voice of our God." [75] Sacred trees and groves offer us space for that silence.

In contemporary education systems, particularly in the West, when do we pay attention to traditional and spiritual values of nature and conservation? Do children experience nature? Or is nature gleaned from books and films? How is sacred knowledge concerning nature viewed or applied? And where does this fit within the greater scheme of things (e.g., conservation, culture, religion, development, education, or poverty reduction)? One way is to integrate these subject areas into formal training curricula for forestry and natural resource management and into formal theological studies and education curricula. This will help bridge the gap between the sacred, social, and scientific.

Fundamentalism increased in all the major religions over the twentieth and twenty-first centuries and continues to do so, which is sad. Extreme nationalism, patriotism, or religiousness is everywhere. The desire to be right

> **Box 28: Peace Parks**
>
> In Nelson Nelson Mandela's words, "I know of no political movement, no philosophy, and no ideology that does not agree with the peace parks concept as we see it going into fruition today. It is a concept that can be embraced by all. In a world beset by conflict and division, peace is one of the cornerstones of the future. Peace Parks are building blocks in this process, not only in our region, but potentially in the entire world." Peace parks are large ecological regions straddling the boundaries of two or more countries, encompassing one or more protected areas and multiple resources for use. These areas are not just national parks but can include private and state land. Ten peace parks exist in Southern Africa, and there are more in formation.
>
> Source: http://www.ecology.com/2012/02/10/peace-parks-southern-africa/ Accessed June 2018

trumps compassion and kindness. Confucius said, "What you do not want done to yourself, do not do to others."[cm] He equates religion with compassion. The focus is compassion, not theology, not going to heaven, not defining what you mean by sacred, and not being right. It is about human-heartedness, the exercise of compassion and peace. [3] Awareness and education about nature and sacred groves will help us know how connected we are and how we can be more compassionate.

The survival of humanity depends on ecoliteracy, which is our ability to understand the basic principles of ecology and live by them. David Orr coined this, and it is the first step in sustainability. The second step is ecological design or ecodesign. [16] Ecoliteracy should be a central skill for politicians, business leaders, and professionals in all spheres of life, not just conservation. We need to embed ecoliteracy from the preschool stages to primary and secondary schools to colleges, universities, and the continuing education of professionals. [17]

When we interact with our environment, we experience it all at once. Consider a familiar experience as an example. A view out of the bedroom window or a favorite painting can help us know if something is out of place. We sense it at a glance, without knowing what is different. This is experiential. It is intuitive, not technical. It highlights the difference between knowing about something and knowing it. [89] Indigenous peoples are strongly connected with the world around them. In the West, we have separated ourselves from our natural world, and then we think we know.

"There are some can live without wild things and some cannot. Like winds and sunsets, wild things were taken for granted until progress began to do away with them. Now we face the question whether a still higher standard of living is worth its cost in things natural, wild, and free. For us of the minority, the opportunity to see geese is more important than television, and the chance to find a pasqueflower is a right as inalienable as free speech." Aldo Leopold never lived to see these words published. This passage opens his classic collection of nature writings in the *Sand County Almanac*, [42, 56] but it highlights experiential and not book knowledge.

[cm] Accessed May 2018. https://www.brainyquote.com/quotes/confucius_136805.

The 1986 meeting in Assisi, Italy, was the only religious environmental movement that brought together diverse religious views and common areas of concern about the environment at that time. Today there are many religious, educational, and environmental programs that are becoming action-oriented (e.g., the Interreligious Network for Climate and Ecology and the United Religious Initiative) or using the environment to build bridges (e.g., Le Sommet des Consciences).[cn] But few have links with the major environmental movements, and perhaps more tellingly, few feel these movements had anything they required. [83] At the local levels from villages in Mexico to megacities such as Shanghai, faith-based organizations developed environmental programs. They work in 8 percent of the habitable surface of the planet and about 15 percent of the planet Earth is sacred (mountains, forests, rivers, cities, pilgrimage routes, etc.). They involve 50 percent of all schools. (In Africa, according to UN figures, it rises to 64 percent.) In a recent meeting on an environmental education toolkit for East African faith-based schools, the Alliance of Religions and Conservation team leader pointed out, "The usual one starts with telling the children how dreadful everything is and what was gone wrong. Our one—for Muslim and Christian schools—starts by saying thank you to God for creating such a fabulous, beautiful, complex and exciting world." [83] If we do not celebrate, why should we bother?

Satish Kumar said, "Walking in the wild is my meditation, walking in nature is my prayer, my peace, and my solitude. I come here for fresh air, the smell of wet grass, the coolness of water and the purity rocks." [111] Being mindful and present and not having preconceived ideas about what we do helps us refocus traditional attitudes. This helps us conserve, renew the vitality of communities, and take on our responsibilities for the planet. [39] But what is missing is a level of spiritual education and transformation in us. This is largely absent in modern society. Spiritual education empowers us to refine our character and contribute more constructively to civilization. At this level, we can build in effective responsibility and accountability. This is why UN Environment should engage more with religious and faith-based groups to reinforce the spiritual foundations of

---

[cn] See https://www.ice-network.net/ ; https://www.uri.org/ ; http://www.whydoicare.org/fr/le-sommet-des-consciences.

society. [22] Then we can focus on ethics and the responsibilities of states, leaders, and the public for the common good of Earth.

We can sum up ecology as follows: Everything is connected. Deep inside, we know this to be true, but such interconnections are often an anathema to consumer notions. Nature is like a close-knit human community designed to help you stay sane. To experience this, take a walk in a park, tend a garden on the patio, or care for a pet. [74] Just being in nature gives us an emotional lift. A walk in the park or garden can restore you. It is something we take for granted, though we know it to be true since we started to spend time in nature. Research provides proof that walking in nature and spending time under the leafy shade of trees causes changes in the brain that can lead people to beneficial states of attention. This can help you be more reflective, which reduces stress. To be in nature produces a restorative experience. [24] The biologist Edward Wilson writes, "The more closely we identify ourselves with the rest of life, the more quickly will we be able to discover the source of human sensibility and acquire the knowledge on which an enduring ethic, a sense of preferred direction, can be built." [109]

Nature Deficit Disorder—When We Do Not Get Enough of a Good Thing

What we have done to the world, we will hand to our children, who could live amidst ruined infrastructure and the ruins of the nature. [8] This need not be. One thing we can do is focus more on experiential learning from and about nature and better connect with nature. We can still learn from those who are in close connection with Mother Earth—the indigenous peoples and others who live close to the land, including farmers, fishers and pastoralists. [8] David Suzuki says, "We can't blame children for occupying themselves with Facebook rather than playing in the mud. Our society doesn't put a priority on connecting with nature. In fact, too often we tell them it's dirty and dangerous."[co]

[co] Accessed September 2017. www.azquotes.com/author/14336-David_Suzuki.

Our Future in Nature: Trees, Spirituality and Ecology

Some of us were lucky to grow up in nature and respect nature's gifts. We even assume our future generations will receive the same. [62] I grew up on an organic farm in Ireland in the 1950s. I could walk in the small wood we had, lie amongst the blue bells, catch tadpoles, fish in the river, make straw houses, and climb trees—memories I still vividly remember and treasure, memories that had a strong influence on my future. Our children were lucky to grow up in nature in the 1980s when we worked in northwest Kenya and did similar things—walk in the forest and play in the river. We could learn from nature and take that learning into our lives. But now, as Richard Louv notes, children prefer "to play indoors as that is where all the electrical connections are." We are cut off from nature. We think we are part of and have done nature from our televisions, which is not experiential. [112] If we remain so removed from nature, we will lose that sense of love to conserve and protect nature.

There are risks from learning and playing in nature, but rules and litigation will not solve them. There are risks of staying indoors too long. There are threats to our judgment and values of place and to our ability to experience awe and wonder, and there is a lost sense of stewardship. In the immediate term, there are serious threats to our psychological and physical health. [63] Richard Louv says, "It is clear that nature serves as a blank slate and inspires creativity in a child by demanding visualization and full use of the senses. Given a chance, a child will bring the confusion of the world into the woods, wash it in the creek and turn it over to see what lies on the unseen side of that confusion." [62] Nature gives itself to children and to us, but we have to be open to that giving and receiving.

Nature deficit disorder means that human beings, especially children, spend less time outdoors, which results in various behavioral problems. [60, 61] These include the diminished use of senses, attention difficulties, and higher rates of physical and emotional illnesses and stress. Miyakazuki explains, "Throughout our evolution, we've spent 99.9% of our time in nature; our physiology is still addicted to it. During everyday life, a feeling of comfort can be achieved if our rhythms are synchronized with those of the environment." [113]

We can weave nature experiences into our classrooms and nature therapy into our health care. Yet it rarely happens because education curricula do not allow it or health care does not embrace natural remedies. We should make nature a necessity for education and health care. This makes the case for working with and not against nature. In nature everything is more positive, and we are more connected. [113] If children play in nature, they have less instances of obesity, attention deficit disorder, depression, suicide, alcohol and drug abuse, and bullying. [4] And it contributes to less violence and greater peace.

Reduced exposure to nature is due to parental fears, restricted access to natural areas, electronic devices, and increasingly, electronic media. People can but often don't spend time outdoors (e.g., outdoor education or forest schools). Physical activity and exposure to nature are good for health with positive impacts on mental health and well-being, which reduces sadness and negativity. The causes of nature deficit disorder include the following: [60, 102]

- Parents keep children indoors for safety. We overprotect children and disrupt their ability to connect to nature, climb trees, etc. This is the leading cause of nature deficit disorder.
- The loss of natural surroundings in a child's neighborhood make it difficult to access nature.
- Many nature areas restrict access with "do not walk off the trail" signs. Environmentalists and educators add to this by telling children, "Look, but don't touch." This may protect nature, but at a cost of our children's relations with nature as experiential learning requires touching and doing.
- Poor and minority groups are disproportionately exposed to environmental risks (e.g., pollution).
- Growing up in urban areas with few green spaces affects how people perceive nature.
- Children are more vulnerable to the negative effects of environmental toxins. For example, large numbers of children in the United States suffer from asthma, cancer, and learning disabilities.

- Children spend more time and have more reasons to stay inside because of computers, video games, and television. The average American child spends forty-four hours a week with electronic media.
- The lack of exposure to nature in childhood years often continues into adulthood. This creates a vicious cycle resulting in increased alienation from nature into adulthood. When was the last time you walked in the woods or dug the garden?

The "Look, but don't touch because nature is fragile" attitude of much environmental education may alienate more than it enables us to embrace nature. We need spaces to do this—much as John Muir and many like him (e.g., Rachel Carson, Aldo Leopold, Edward Wilson) had and as I did (climbing trees, rafting, picking wildflowers). Environmental education needs to (a) allow children to experience and explore and (b) focus more on practical experience, not just books and lectures. Such nature experience as a child correlates with adult environmental values and behaviors. [100] Because of these changes, children (and adults) change their interactions with nature. Children disproportionately suffer long-term developmental consequences because of limited nature exposure. [102] This contributes to various effects, which we can relate to a lack of exposure to nature. Such effects include the following[cp]:

- Children have less respect for their natural surroundings. This may become a bigger problem in the future due to, as Richard Louv says, the "increasing pace in the last three decades, of a rapid disengagement between children and direct experiences in nature ... has profound implications, not only for the health of future generations but for the health of the Earth itself." [60] It may result in shorter life spans than a child's parents.
- Attention disorders and depression may develop or be exacerbated because children who do not get adequate time in nature are more prone to anxiety, depression, and attention-deficit problems. Walking in nature and being silent and quiet is calming and stress-reducing.

[cp] Accessed September 2017. https://en.wikipedia.org/wiki/Nature_deficit_disorder.

- With a greater understanding of attention deficit disorder and other mood disorders, lower grades in school seem to relate to nature deficit disorder. Outdoor classrooms and experiential education can reduce this.
- There are positive effects of treating nature deficit disorder. Richard Louv says, "Everything from a positive effect on the attention span to stress reduction to creativity, cognitive development, and their sense of wonder and connection to the Earth" is possible. [60]
- Regardless of race, ethnicity, and socioeconomic status, early childhood experience in nature has positive influences on lifelong attitudes to nature. [102]
- More outdoor experiential education and access to nature results in children who have greater self-esteem, are better at solving problems and asking questions, and have reduced stress, aggression, and risks of obesity. There is more of a motivation to learn. [63, 102]
- The negative impacts of pollution and the lack of access to nature in education, cognitive functioning, and mental health has serious implications for environmental success. [102]

Much of our current environmental crises and nature deficit disorder relate to our increased separation from nature. So we need to shift from our anthropocentric (i.e., humankind first) worldview to an ecocentric one (nature first). It moves us from self-interest to the common interest. [50] We can achieve this through more time in nature. Trees and woodlands can help us do so. But with the majority (55 percent as of 2017) of humanity living in cities, they no longer care or understand what trees are cut to build their homes as there is no connection. For many indigenous peoples, because the connection is deep this is like killing our children. [88]

Our education systems support the fragmentation and reductionism of knowledge. This starts in school and goes through our education though there are enlightening exceptions. As a result, many of us lose sight of the whole, the earth system, and we don't appreciate our interconnectedness with nature. Then our solutions (technical but not social) are too simplistic (e.g., monocrops of trees for carbon sequestration or gazetting more protected areas without addressing the real needs of people) to address the complex challenges we face. Our education systems have to go beyond simple technical remedies. The *silver bullet* does not work! Pope Francis said, "Ecological culture cannot be reduced to a series of urgent and partial responses … Otherwise, even the best ecological initiatives can find themselves caught up in the same globalized logic. To seek only a technical remedy to each environmental problem separates what is in reality interconnected, and to mask the true and deepest problems of the global system." [85] Education has to combine the technical, social, and spiritual. These are the ingredients for the future and the paradox of the present.

A child today knows about the Amazon rainforest (TV knowledge) but does not know the last time he or she explored the woods in solitude or lay in a field listening to the wind and watching the clouds move (see box 29). Young people in schools can recognize more than a hundred corporate logos, but they can hardly name any plants and animals. [82] Take them into the woods, and few can name ten trees. [46] Parents still cite various reasons why children spend less time in nature than they did (e.g., diminishing access to natural areas, competition with electronic entertainment, and time pressures, including increased homework and longer school hours). Yet children as young as five show reduced symptoms of attention deficit disorder when they engage with nature! And it's free.

Box 29: What Nature Means to One Schoolgirl

"When I am in the woods, I feel like I'm in my mother's shoes. There was a big waterfall and a creek on one side of it. I'd dug a hole there and sometimes I'd take a tent or a blanket and just lie down in the hole and look up at the trees and sky. I just felt free; it was like my place and I could do what I wanted. I used to go down there every day. And they just cut the woods down—it was like they cut down a part of me." [62]

Schools using outdoor classrooms and experiential learning produce students who are better problem solvers, critical thinkers, and decision makers. They are more engaged in class and more open to conflict resolution. Time in nature stimulates children's creativity. Separation from nature causes a failure to bond with and have a caring relationship with nature. With less exploration of nature, future generations are unlikely to be as interested in conservation as past generations. [98] Everything natural—trees, plants, rivers, animals—provide important lessons if we stop, look, and listen. [107] We don't take that time in our stress-filled world. Yet we can be alert and present to a plant or tree or flower. Just observe and be the witness. This helps us be conscious. [107]

To be in nature is effective for improving our health. It encourages us to be more active, less stressed, and calmer. Children become less hyperactive and concentrate better. They are more creative and independent when they play. Children develop a lifelong connection with nature, but this has to start before the age of twelve. [11] Regular contact with nature promotes the ability to concentrate and reduces stress, in particular with direct experience (e.g., walking in a forest, visiting a park, or gardening). With or without policy support, such examples and initiatives are becoming more widespread in urban areas.

As Richard Louv puts it, "The future of children in nature has profound implications not only for the conservation of land but also for the direction of the environment movement. If society embraces something as simple as the health benefits of nature experiences for children, it may be able to re-evaluate the worth of the environment." [63] This will be a potent force for policy and political support. Rachel Carson had similar words. [18] "It is our misfortune that for most of us that clear-eyed vision, that true instinct for what is beautiful and awe-inspiring is dimmed and even lost before we reach adulthood."

Education for Awareness about and Reconnecting with Nature

How can we hope for greater environmental awareness in education and life if 75 percent of millennials work more than forty hours per week and 25 percent have two or more jobs? [97] In the United States, elementary school children have seen a 146 percent increase in time spent on homework. In fact, 37 percent of Japanese millennials say they can never retire, and one student per hour commits suicide in India because of perceived academic failure and economic anxieties. [97] Given this, how can children and millennials connect with nature? It leads one to question the rationale for education—to prepare people for jobs in industry, business, etc., not preparing them for life and experiencing nature.

Ecological education changes our assumptions and goes beyond discipline-centered curricula and the confines of the classroom. This implies working toward the real purpose of learning—values and not theories, consciousness and not the abstract, questions and not smart answers, and conscience and not technical efficiency. [82] As a result, those now being educated have to repair the damage done to Earth over the past 250 years of industrialization while at the same time reducing economic inequities. These are indeed heavy challenges!

Children of the Plant for the Planet movement have a delightfully simple rationale for their tree-planting and respect for nature. "We do it because trees are the lungs of the world. There is no life without trees. They are also a beautiful symbol." [28] Such community-based approaches to trees help children and adults understand how important working and learning together is and how valuable participating and knowing our efforts count too as "it all counts, every tree planted counts." We need to be at peace with nature through the use of science, [114] the support of religious and spiritual bodies, and our actions to respect and restore trees. To achieve this, we should (a) move from the general (systems) to the specific (experiential), (b) reach out to other disciplines to solve challenges in an integrated manner, (c) focus on solving problems as the Plant for the Planet movement does, (d) think about our own education by following our hearts, and (e) commit to the plan. [114]

William Wordsworth said (verse 4, "The Tables Turned") wrote, "Come forth into the light of things, let nature be your teacher," while John Muir noted, "The clearest way into the Universe is through a forest wilderness." [76] David Suzuki adds, "Unless we are willing to encourage our children to reconnect with and appreciate the natural world, we can't expect them to help protect and care for it." [103] When asked what people feel when they are in nature (in a forest, along a seashore, on a mountain), the feelings are similar—peace, silence, stillness, grace, connectedness, well-being, harmony, and wholeness. [68] Yet gone are the days when children roamed across the countryside and explored nature. So how can we expect children to grow up conscious of the environment? With practical experiential approaches to nature and trees in particular, children can get in touch with their own inner selves, discover their links with nature, and learn a greater respect for life. [13]

> **Box 30: Being Mindful of a Tree** [45]
>
> When we say we see a tree (or flower, bark, or person), do we see them? Or do we see the image the world has created? When you look at a tree, do you see it, not only with your eyes and minds but totally and completely? Try looking at an object (a tree, a branch, or the bark) without making associations or using your knowledge.
>
> Try this and see what happens when you observe the tree with your being, all your energy and all your mindfulness. You will notice there is no observer or observed. There is only consciousness and mindfulness. If we have a relationship with and are mindful of a tree, we can have a relationship with humankind. We can look into the quality of the tree, touch it, and feel its solidarity and its rough bark. We can hear the sounds of the tree—not the sounds of the breeze or wind, but the tree's own sound. This sound is part of the universe.

"Nature is the greatest teacher even greater than the Buddha," said Satish Kumar's mother [47] in 1944. She said, "The Buddha may have been the greatest among human teachers, but he received his enlightenment while sitting under a tree. In that moment he realized the interdependence of all existence and how life is designed in such an intricate and symbiotic manner that millions of forms live with each other in a harmonious and miraculous way. No-one manages nature. Nature needs no rulers, yet the laws of the universe and the health of the Earth are maintained. The Buddha learned all that whilst observing nature. So, the tree was his true teacher." Nature can teach us if we but listen. We learn about nature, not from nature. We must show love for the tree and for nature, but in our contemporary world, we would rather turn the tree into profit. For the Buddha, the tree is sacred. For Western civilization, it is a commodity!

We can sit under a tree and be silent and present. We can notice the sounds of silence, the stream, the birds, and the rustle of leaves. This helps us be aware to the aliveness of the world. [107] We can focus on a tree, a stone, or the sound of a stream. Focus without thinking what you are focusing on, without commenting or judging. Just be mindful and present (see box 30). It puts you in a place of a deepening inner peace.

Education in the early years is one foundation for reversing the destruction of the planet and our pursuit of economic growth. [105] Bhutan infuses their education with the human ecological values of their policy on gross national happiness, something other countries could learn from. Thinley, the prime minister of Bhutan noted that we should separate true happiness from feel-good moods. True happiness cannot exist while others suffer, and it requires us to live in harmony with nature. So too, gross national happiness is a development path embracing sustainable and economic development with conservation, good governance, and the wisdom of Bhutan's profound and ancient teachings. Finally, education is the glue that holds this together so that we are no longer ignorant of how to conserve nature. [105] In a similar way, the African author Sobonfu Somé said, "We must try not to educate our children away from the spirit, so they don't have to work so hard trying to reconnect when they grow up. When they know they already have spirit, then everything else becomes understood. And it makes life easier for them." [29]

Teachers should be facilitators and sources of knowledge. We should bring the class out of the classroom and learn by doing what our natural world is. If young people graduate with a sense of care for nature and one another, this will help us live in harmony with nature and our neighbors. [105] This is a challenge to put into practice in education systems, syllabuses, and how we train teachers.

We have to find ways for children to experience nature and meet nature on their own terms. It used to be part of growing up, but that is less and less the case now. Such experiential learning is encompassed by more and more rules. [100] Environmental education should be at the forefront, but it has assumed a "Look, but don't touch" mentality and is rule-bound. Yet many indigenous peoples show a deep knowledge of the natural world around them through experience. For example, eight- to ten-year-old Mayan girls in Central America know the names and uses of a thousand different plants! [101] How many in the developed world could name ten? Rachel Carson pointed out, [18] "The lasting pleasures of contact with the natural world are ... available to anyone who will place himself under the influence of the earth, sea, and sky, and their amazing life."

Our education systems ought to encourage environmental responsibility so we care for creation as a daily imperative [85] and look toward sustainability, not degradation and exploitation. In this way, we sow the seeds for stewardship when we are young and most receptive. Sacred nature shows what we can use for education—both in conservation and spiritual terms. This supports a move, as Pope Francis says, to "ecological conversion, and the ecological conversion needed to bring about lasting change is also a community conversion." [85] That way, we are passionate about and committed to the stewardship of nature at whatever scale is appropriate. But our education systems teach children to avoid getting their hands dirty as such work is undignified and less important than fiddling on a computer.[cq] So we should sit under a tree and learn from nature rather than an artificial light and learn book and computer knowledge. As Rachel Carson puts it, we should be "exploring nature with your child is largely a matter of becoming receptive to what lies all around you—it is learning to use all your senses." [18]

Education systems do not prioritize learning about nature. Nor is nature experience encouraged, though there are exceptions. So what is education for? Is education for the needs of the industrial and business world, academic ability,[cr] or more for our own experience and personal growth? Children between six and twelve show a strong desire to explore woods and climb trees, dig tunnels, collect earthworms, and so forth. The great environmentalists (e.g., Edward Wilson, John Muir, Rachel

---

[cq] Accessed November 2017. https://www.youtube.com/watch?v=VAz0bOtfVfE. TED Talk, "Education with Hands, Hearts and Heads."

[cr] Accessed November 2017. https://www.ted.com/talks/ken_robinson_says_schools_kill_creativity/transcript.

Carson, Aldo Leopold, and Wangari Mathai) did just that. They had firsthand experience with nature—getting their hands dirty, feet wet, and clothes messy. [100] My wife used to take her school class into nature in the outskirts of Nairobi, Kenya. They experienced nature—the soil, the leaves, the earthworms (and other insects)—and they planted trees. The parents of these children often questioned why their children came back so muddy, happy, and full of what they had learned about and from nature. And many of those children, now adults, still vividly remember those experiences.

Nature has been our school since before formal education. Friedrich Fröbel started a school in 1837 in Germany for children to absorb nature through their senses and let curiosity guide them. What Fröbel believed, the Finns put into practice, and science is now affirming [113] that nature enhances a child's cognitive and emotional development. Through exercise and exploratory play, we improve our mental skills. As nature changes our brains for the better, we need to bring the lessons into urban areas. In urban areas we should try to be close to nature—in schools, green parks, and trees on avenues. [113]

As learning is social, we cannot limit education to the formal sectors. Collaborative learning is both a social and an individual journey where the whole is greater than the sum of the parts. [23] It is part of a lifelong journey that can happen anytime, anywhere, or with anyone. We should foster such inquiring minds throughout life and particularly in the early stages. A good starting point is to see how a learning society can support ecoliteracy and place-based education, which could [23] in turn (a) create learning communities, (b) help people learn from experience, (c) foster a new worldview, (d) help people think systemically, (e) embrace diversity, and (d) focus on whole-person learning. Environmental educators can focus on experiential learning and enable children to climb trees, catch frogs and insects, paint their faces with charcoal, and explore and question their experience. There are increasing examples of this happening in schools and camps. [100] I still remember building straw houses, climbing trees, hiding in the ditches, and making our own rafts on our farm in Ireland.

The Youth Voices Curriculum Sourcebook was developed as part of the IUCN World Conservation Congress Hawai'i 2016 to reach the younger generations.[cs] It aims to integrate nature into teaching and learning, help reconnect children with nature, and inspire their passion and action for conservation. The sourcebook suggests ideas to enliven classroom experiences, launch practical fieldwork, and engage students in out-of-school activities. The sourcebook helps articulate IUCN's #NatureForAll initiative, which is a simple idea that the more people experience, connect with, and share their love for nature, the more support there will be for its conservation. The sourcebook is framed in a curricular approach with strategies drawn from #NatureForAll to (a) bring children into nature at an early age, (b) find and share the fun in nature, (c) use urban gateways (parks, museums, zoos) to nature, (d) embrace technology as a bridge to nature, (e) share cultural roots and ancestry in nature, (f) seek diverse partnerships, (g) empower a new generation of leaders, and (h) offer children and youth the tools they need to heal nature.

One approach to an environmental education ethos is to listen to indigenous leaders who are effective environmental leaders. This will help us relearn the ecological knowledge and sustainable principles we have lost [91] and enable us and our children to listen to the wisdom of elders. For example, Black Elk, a First Nation American leader, [12] said, "It is the story of all life that is holy and good to tell, and of us two-leggeds sharing in it with the four-leggeds and the wings of the air and all green things, for these are children of one mother and their father is one spirit." While Bepkororoti Paiakan, a Kayapo chief from Brazil put it this way: "We are trying to save the knowledge of the forest and this planet as alive–to give it back to you who have lost the understanding." [91] Humankind is place-centric. We learn first from our surroundings. So children raised in ecologically impoverished surroundings are deprived of the stimuli that nature provides. We shape our landscape preferences by what was familiar to us in our early years, which makes it even more important to connect with nature in those formative years. [82]

[cs] Accessed January 2017. http://iucnyouthvoices.org/ https://www.iucn.org/commissions/commission-education-and-communication/our-work/natureforall and http://natureforall.global/. [15; 19; 25]

It is important to learn from our elders (women and men) about nature and how it works, but this is not enough. We can put this into practice by upholding peoples' rights to land, knowledge, and resources as this requires awareness, understanding, and empowerment. It helps us rediscover the web of life as box 31 shows. Religions should emphasize the stewardship of creation for nature conservation. In its unique access to children through religious education and sponsorship of schools, the different religions can be powerful nature educators. Life and sacred nature are important for spiritual, cultural, and religious comfort and for ecological benefit.

> **Box 31: Mupo Foundation–An Example of Elders Teaching the Youth in South Africa** [69]
>
> The Mupo Foundation runs two educational awareness programs. First, elders pass knowledge to the youth on cultural diversity. Youth are taught to build traditional houses; carry out research on their culture; learn about important bush plants, foods, and medicines; and learn about sustainable use. Once they understand, they are amazed and proud of their roots. Second, they have a community ecological governance program. The elders discuss how they govern themselves in relation to nature. They identified sacred sites as a priority for their culture, where it is taboo to cut trees or kill animals. Such awareness and education aspects are simple to organize, effective and create local ownership. The challenge is to have them accepted and more widely available.

Rather than being told not to visit or touch, we should ask visitors to consider their actions. They are then more likely to respect cultures, conserve sacred sites, and learn from such experiences. This is why many sacred sites stay secret for fear of masses of visitors coming to take part in the power of the sacred. This happened to a Winnemem-Wintu sacred place in the United States. But a Winnemem healer Florence Jones led her community's fight to stop the construction of a new ski resort on their sacred Mount Shasta. "We take care of Nature. That is our religion." [73] The central law of the Nuu-Chah-Nulth, an indigenous First Nation people of Canada, is *tsawalk*, which means "we are one and we are connected." It is a worldview based on interrelationships between life-forms. As children, they listened to their grandmothers about the special songs to the earth, which emphasize the connection between human activities and natural phenomena. [93]

When we are aware and able to serve the cause of life, we can enhance the planetary community and sustain human relationships. Education is not just for self-promotion or self-interest or getting a good job for name and fame. Education is a journey of self-discovery and self-realization in the service of community and the planet Earth. [49] Indigenous peoples knew how to connect, relate to, and appreciate nature. Modern education creates humans who lack skills and confidence to be self-reliant. Rather it creates job seekers and employees. Even farmers hardly touch the soil, seeds, or harvest the crops or milk the cows with their hands. Machines now do all this. Education helps people become makers and creators by developing practical skills. [49]

Koreans are learning to appreciate nature. The Korean Forest Agency understands that children and the younger generation don't spend time in nature. Many of them think the forest is dirty or scary. If we do not change the mind-sets of children at a young age, it will be more difficult later. [113] When Korean children go for forest classes, they can't play with their normal electronic games. But playing in and exploring the forest is important to build interest and curiosity about nature. [113]

What is a nature teacher? Nature teaches that human beings can't control nature. There are forces bigger than humankind (e.g., the seasons and the nature of plant and human cycles), and about unpredictability and beauty. To be mindful of nature can heal the spirit and improve people's health and well-being. [80] Water can be our teacher and a source of life. We can learn from the way water flows, how to respect water, how water is sacred, and how we should use it with gratitude. So too, trees can be our teachers.

Good education connects intelligence with an emphasis on whole systems. [82] Nature and sacred groves provide such whole systems. Based on this, David Orr suggests six principles for education. [82] First, education is environmental. Second, subject matter is a tool to mastery of one's person. Third, knowledge carries with it responsibilities to use in the world.

Fourth, we cannot say we know something until we understand the effects of the knowledge on people and communities. Fifth, we must learn how important minute details are and the power of examples over words. And sixth, understanding how learning occurs is as important as the content of particular courses. As Aldo Leopold said, "Does a graduate know that he is only a cog in an ecological mechanism? If education does not teach us these things, then what is education for?" [55]

Our schools and education systems have to be enquiry-driven so that students are eager to learn and connect with nature. [21] We can ask, "What is this place we are living in? How does this place sustain life? What might we grow and nurture? Where might we see the clouds forming? What did we eat today, and where does our food come from?" We need to build such awareness about how important trees are and how schoolchildren and education can take responsibility for planting trees. Nelson Mandela reminds us "to value our children is to value our future." [70] This example from Germany also illustrates my point. Schoolchildren took initial steps to create awareness in schools in Germany because they wanted adults to stop talking and do something! [28] As a result, from small beginnings (2011), there are now more than ten thousand climate justice ambassadors—children from more than a

> **Box 32: Key Foundations for Mindfulness (and links to nature)**
>
> a) There is no need to judge. Just seeing is enough. Nature is. Sacred trees are just as they are.
> b) Things unfold in their own time, and the time scale of nature and especially of ancient sacred trees is different from ours.
> c) Beginner's mind is an attitude you are in the moment. Be present in the presence of sacred trees, groves, and nature.
> d) We need to trust our awareness and our heart. What do they tell us about nature and the spirituality of sacred nature?
> e) Not striving is related to the quality of the present moment. When we are in nature or in a sacred grove, we are present.
> f) Acceptance happens when we are in nature and in a sacred grove. We accept what is and maybe try to improve it.
> g) We should let things be and not cling to them. If we leave a sacred tree or grove as it is, that is letting be.

hundred countries who work with Plant for the Planet.^ct^ Since then, more than fifteen billion trees have been planted (as of 2017). This is one way to promote a tree culture. Trees enrich our lives, teach us, absorb greenhouse gasses, help regulate air temperature and quality, reduce soil erosion, and provide important wildlife habitat. [99] To promote a tree culture helps connect us with our spirituality. It is a rallying call for increasing a country's tree cover, and it is a means for education and health enhancement.

We can train ourselves to be mindful and bring our attention to current experiences. Meditation helps. It is personal and opens the door to greater awareness about how we relate with one another. [108] Mindfulness in turn makes us more compassionate to ourselves, others, and nature. [40] There are several attributes for mindfulness (see box 32 [40]), and the following questions might help you to mindfully explore nature: [13, 32, 100, 101]

➢ List some places that are special to you (e.g., a sacred grove or a long a river).
➢ What state are you in now, and what feelings does this place arouse in you?
➢ What do you feel like doing here?
➢ What did you notice? What did you think?
➢ Would you come here to do something in particular? What? Why?
➢ How would you sum up the quality of this place?
➢ What do you want to do before this tree and in this woodland?
➢ Which plants and trees make the strongest impression on you? Why?
➢ What is most special about this tree or grove? Why?
➢ Where in this grove would you find the quality you need?
➢ What parts of the natural world are you grateful for? Why?

Trees and Woods Are Good for Our Health

The positive effects of contact with nature do not stop with children but extend to adult health. Nature has positive effects on human health,

---

ct See https://www.plant-for-the-planet.org/en for more details.

specifically when it comes to stress-related illnesses. Forest therapies offer preventive treatment to relieve stress and can lower levels of cortisol, a stress hormone, blood pressure, and heart rate. A walk in the woods boosts the body's immune system by increasing anticancer proteins. [5] Trees are important healers as they bring healing energies, including peace, silence, stillness, and presence, which help treat various health conditions. A visit to the forest has us breathing essential oils from trees. This is natural aromatherapy in Japan where forest bathing trips have become popular. John Muir said, "Everybody needs beauty as well as bread, places to play in and pray in, where nature may heal and cheer and give strength to body and soul alike." [79] Contact with nature improves our psychological health by improving our moods and reducing fatigue. Nature also helps us get the exercise we need. So such contact with nature helps enhance the overall health of a nation. [5]

Nature is good for our health and our stress management, and it helps us concentrate. [86] We are happier in nature than in urban areas. There is much study about the links between nature and well-being, including assertions that nature [6, 65, 78] (a) affects the nervous system by reducing stress and improving attention; (b) has less noise and air pollution, which can cause sleep disturbance, hearing impairment, tinnitus, and increased stress, leading to high blood pressure, coronary heart disease, and strokes; [84] and (c) increases happiness with physically and mentally beneficial behaviors (e.g., exercise and recreation).

A recent article in the *Times* newspaper of England noted that more than seventy thousand children under eighteen are on antidepressant pills along with two thousand primary school children. Approximately one in six adults used antidepressants in 2017, an increase of half a million since 2015. In England, 7.3 million people took at least one antidepressant prescription in 2017. Prescriptions for antidepressants have doubled in a decade, costing the country £235 million. Three percent of children are thought to be depressed. Yet various walking therapies are often effective and recommended for therapy.[cu] Nature therapy could help reduce such depression and symptoms, and it's a free prescription!

Being in nature encourages us to be more active, less stressed, and calmer. Children are less hyperactive, concentrate better, and play more creatively and independently. Children need to play freely in streams and woods, [11] and not by doctrines of looking but not touching. Rachel Carson says, "The years of early childhood are the time to prepare the soil for later life." [18] Regular contact with nature promotes concentration and reduces stress, especially with direct experience (e.g., walking in a forest, sitting in a park, or gardening). Already there are health centers and hospitals that have green spaces or are close to a park or have access to gardens and allotments.

Forest bathing in Japan (called *Shinrinyoku*) entails visiting a forest. The Japanese enjoy the forest environment because of the quiet atmosphere, beautiful scenery, mild climate, and clean, fresh air. A forest bathing trip involves visiting a forest for relaxation and recreation while breathing in volatile substances called phytoncides (wood essential oils). Phytoncides are antimicrobial organic compounds derived from trees. [59] Forest bathing increases vigor and decreases anxiety, depression, and anger. If we walk in the woods, this boosts the body's immune system by increasing anticancer proteins (called human natural killer or NK cells). In Japan, doctors prescribe forest bathing or walking in woods to reduce stress, blood pressure, and heart rate. [4]

Natural forest environments enhance human NK cell activity. The phytoncides emitted help plants and trees protect themselves. Phytoncide exposure and decreased stress hormone levels contribute to increased NK activity, [58] which lasted more than thirty days after a forest-bathing trip, while a visit to the city did not. [57] NK cells kill tumor cells by releasing anticancer proteins. Forest bathing increases NK activity and levels of anticancer proteins, and it may have preventive effects on cancer. [57] Forest therapy shows how our health depends on the health of nature. The greater the stress levels, the greater the positive effects of forest bathing. Forests are

---

[cu] Accessed July 2018. https://www.thetimes. Countyuk/edition/news/over-70-000-children-put-on-pills-for-depression-kfc39l0xl

therapeutic landscapes, and forest bathing decreases risks of stress-related diseases. Even for children with attention deficit disorder, after twenty-minute walks in a city park, they experienced improved concentration compared to twenty-minute walks in downtown and residential settings.[cv]

In South Korea, there are three official healing forests with thirty-four more planned for, so most towns will have access to one. [113] Even the demilitarized zone between North and South Korea, which covers 1,068 square kilometers, could be a prime candidate as an international peace and healing park. The Korea Forest Service is remarkable amongst government forest agencies as it has a human welfare division. It plays a central role in improving ecosystem health and vitality by contributing to public safety and conservation. This highlights how forests' recreational and cultural functions can improve the quality of life and living environments in urban areas and mountain villages. The overall vision of the Korea Forest Service's fifth plan is "to realize a green nation with sustainable welfare and growth" by sustainably managing forests for strengthening the nation's economic development, land conservation, and improved quality of life.[cw]

The Forest Agency of Japan first proposed incorporating forest bathing into their lifestyles in 1982, and the practice is now well recognized for relaxation and stress management. Because forests occupy 67 percent of Japan, which includes most of the Shinto sacred groves, forest bathing is freely accessible. More than a quarter (or more than thirty million) of all Japanese people take part in forest bathing. Such forest bathing is possible throughout the world in rural areas or in urban woodlands. In addition, walking is one of the easiest forms of exercise as forests induce a quiet state of mind.

Green Care evolved in Europe to treat ailments, including dementia, stress-induced illnesses, and attention disorders. Doctors prescribe people to spend time on Green Care farms, do practical work, and be quiet in green surrounds. There are 1,935 Green Care farms that receive payments for taking in patients. [86] Most of these patients come from cities, further

---

[cv] Accessed June 2018. http://forest-therapy.net/healthbenefits.html.
[cw] Accessed June 2018. https://en.wikipedia.org/wiki/Korea_Forest_Service.

strengthening rural-urban ties. By 2006, there were five hundred Green Care farms in Norway, 430 in the Netherlands, 300 in Italy and Germany, 250 in Austria, 140 in Belgium, and 15 in Slovenia. The numbers are increasing too. As of 2015, there are 1,100 Green Care Farms in the Netherlands, one of the world's most densely populated countries. [86] These Green Care approaches can be extended to other countries and other aspects of nature (e.g., indigenous tree planting, walking in nature, and countryside management). This is an analogous approach to forest bathing in the woods in Japan.

In Finland, *Metsänpeitio* is about getting lost in nature, and it is also like forest bathing in Japan. Many Finnish health experts believe modern times call for a full if but occasional immersion in nature. [113] Even now the average Finn engages in nature-based recreation two to three times per week (with walking, skiing, or berry-picking). Research suggests that large urban (larger than five hectares) parks and woodlands have positive effects on the well-being of people. The more nature, the better you feel, and in Finland, nature is free for everyone everywhere. [113]

Who has not experienced the calming effects of time in the garden after a stressful phone call or a walk in the park? A 2007 report from Royal Society for the Protection of Birds showed that contact with nature had positive effects on anxiety and stress, on elderly people and those with dementia, on concentration levels in children and office workers, and on the reduction of crime and aggression. [2] Public health should act on such findings as such health benefits could have enormous implications, including reductions in health-care budgets. Nature contact may be used to (a) treat children with poor self-discipline, hyperactivity, and attention deficit disorder; (b) help people cope with anxiety and stress; (c) reduce crime and aggression; (d) help care for the elderly and treatment for dementia; (e) improve concentration levels in children and office workers; and (f) improve hospital environments, strengthen communities, and increase the overall sense of well-being and mental health. [10]

Sacred Trees and Sacred Groves—
Places for Peace-Building

Thich Hanh says, "If we are peaceful, if we are happy, we can blossom like a flower and everyone in our family, our entire society will benefit from our peace." [35] Yet war and militarization have a stronger hold on human affairs and actions than ever before. It is likely that violence will devour humanity. [82] But we as individuals, families, and communities, we can all be at peace. D. H. Lawrence bluntly says, "People always make war when they say they love peace."[cx] This is something we still hear at political levels—supporting the peace processes but arming the protagonists. George Bernard Shaw was more brutal when he said, "A nation armed and prepared for war can no more help going to war than a chicken can help laying an egg!" Yet peace is an inner sense of well-being. Religious orders encouraged their monks and nuns to live in nature, not just because of its sacredness but because living in nature was more conducive to a simple and peaceful life. With a vision to rely on experience and meditation as a path of knowing and understanding, it can transform the way we see ourselves in nature. [14] The well-being of humanity can express what nonviolence is about. But there can be no real peace while millions live in poverty and while nature is being degraded by the effects of economic growth. Sustainability, social justice, and fair governance are prerequisites for peace. [72]

People associate trees with peace because (a) we experience peace brought about by being in the presence of an important or sacred tree or grove, (b) people plant trees at the beginning of a new era or to be at peace, and (c) people use important trees to meet, discuss, negotiate, and make peace. [13] For example, many pastoralist societies use important and often sacred trees as the meeting place for resolving conflicts. So not making more effort to save and conserve our environment is an act of violence just like cutting rainforests. [106] If there is ecological ruin, there can be no freedom. We need to understand the links between the limits of human action and ecological health. [82] Sacred trees and groves can help us recreate harmony

---

[cx] D. H. Lawrence. www.brainyquote.com/authors/d_h_lawrence.

and the peace we need in our families and the world at large. We can live in peace and harmony, or we can live in conflict. It's our choice.

One of our challenges is the fact that we label ourselves. This divides us and creates disconnections and divisions. Yet we are nature, and we are members of this planetary community irrespective of who we are. Such a reverential ecology can foster peace, connections, and interdependencies. [52] This removes divisions, and then peace becomes the way. Pierre Rabhi explains we should teach children cooperation, not competition, and we should model for them a respect for nature and life. In doing so, we can stop manufacturing weapons and better enable humanity to survive as part of nature. Sacred trees and groves offer a strong focus, can show how important nature is for education and health, and help bring peace to our troubled world by reconnecting with nature. [53]

"A tree as great as a man's embrace springs from a small shoot; a terrace nine stories high begins with a pile of Earth; a journey of a thousand miles starts under one's foot." [110] This verse (64) of the Tao-Te-Ching refers to "out of little acorns, do mighty oak trees grow." From ideas great things can happen. But verse 76 says, "A tree (or plant) that is unbending is easily broken." If our leaders spend more time in nature, we would better understand how important flexibility and resilience are as attributes of peace. When humankind destroys nature, we destroy ourselves. Our world will be more peaceful if we live in harmony with nature. David Suzuki challenges us, "So we draw lines around our property, our counties, our cities, our states, our countries. And boy, do we act as if those lines are important. I mean, we go to war. We will kill and die to protect those boundaries. Nature couldn't give two hoots about our national boundaries." [cy] We have to revalue human life, [9] which is something Ms. Umra Omar, CNN Hero 2016, supports (see box 33).[cz] To do the opposite demeans life and results in violence.

[cy] www.azquotes.com/author/14336-David_Suzuki.
[cz] Accessed January 2018. https://www.forbes.com/sites/mikeharrison/2017/10/27/umra-omar-the-cnn-hero-on-why-she-works-in-a-danger-zone/5/#3601a5773cf6 (excerpt from interview with Mike Harrison). See also http://www.safaridoctors.org/.

If the ecology is fragile, peace is likely to be fragile. Examples of this include low-level conflicts in dry areas over critical resources (e.g., water and/or dry season forage). Where there is lawlessness, for example, in Somalia, more degradation occurs as there is a lack of respect for nature and people use trees for charcoal to fund conflict. In Colombia, conflict desecrated many sacred sites, groves, and springs. [92] Such low-level conflicts can—if not checked or mediated early—grow to become serious as happened in Somalia more than forty years ago. The elders still have the institutions for mediation, usually meetings under an important large tree, but this has to be used early in a conflict process. Now ecological stresses and conflicts over natural resources are exacerbated by global warming.

> **Box 33: Umra Omar of Safari Doctors—Lessons from Work in a Danger Zone**
>
> Ms Umra Omar leads Safari Doctors, an organization that provides health care in the Lamu area of Kenya, often in remote and hazardous parts, and also isolated communities along the coast close to the Somalia border. She emphasizes, "It is important for women to take a more active role in conservation so that young minds are better shaped to understand the importance of preserving their natural resources. By fueling passion and mentorship of the girl child, we stand a strong chance of better serving Mother Nature."
>
> In spite of being away from her family for long periods combined with the constant threat of militants and the harsh climate, Umra Omar is inspired and is working to "leave her children the Lamu that she knew many years ago, not one destroyed by unsustainable natural resource use and pollution. Marinating in comfort isn't an option. Fear is not an option. With a bit of faith, we can all be the change that our world screams for."
>
> This example sends a strong message on how important experiential education is for children, and it gives an impassioned call for peace in a risk-prone area of Kenya.

It's clear. Cutting ourselves off from nature makes us mentally and physically sick, but reconnecting makes us healthier. Illness, violence, and crime are expensive. Nature is free. There is an old saying from India that states, "Forests precede civilization. Deserts follow." [4] As Al Gore suggests, [33] "We need to mobilize our civilization with the urgency and resolve that have previously been only seen when nations mobilize for war." Being for peace and focusing on nature will help us make peace with the planet and ourselves. Otherwise, we will continue waging war on nature (climate change, pollution, overuse, misuse, degradation, conversion) and amongst humankind (wars, terrorism, violence). We need to be mindful to the wonders of life. But we are too busy to take time to be with nature, never mind looking at and being with the people we love. [35]

Pope Francis asks us to focus on nature to bring about peace in our troubled world, saying, "An integral ecology is also made up of simple daily gestures which break the logic of violence, exploitation and selfishness. In the end, a world of exacerbated consumption is a world which mistreats life in all its forms." [85] If we focus ourselves creatively as nature does, this will help us cope with the degradation and destruction that is happening. [104] So let us focus on the positive. Be for peace rather than just being against violence. Here, the fig tree and other trees are symbols of unity and peace across the globe. The fig tree is embedded in local culture and is where the elders go to settle disputes. [95]

Naomi Klein argues climate change is likely to change everything. [44] So how can sacred groves be one vehicle to combat climate change (in terms of adaptation and mitigation), or how much will sacred groves suffer because of climate change? Sacred groves can be one part of a larger approach to climate change. By their areas and numbers, sacred groves are carbon stores, and they adapt as nature adapts. This is an unrecognized mitigation approach. Sacred groves offer ways to better adapt to climate change, given their diversity, their connectivity, and the links to broader land use.

Nonviolence, local economies, human rights, and environmental well-being are our pathways to peace. We should tread that path. [37] Schumacher emphasized economic growth is good only to the point of sufficiency. Renewable resources are the basis for Buddhist economics. [94] Sufficiency and sustainability are key attributes to peace. Economic growth will not bring an end to poverty, destitution, and pollution. The economic paradigm tends to maximize profit and exploit nature. Infinite growth on a finite planet is unattainable. So we should move from a focus on economic growth to growth in well-being. [54] To achieve this, we need to reconnect with the land.

Scarcity of natural resources is an artifact of our system. A Chinese proverb says, "When you know enough is enough, you already have enough. But when you don't know enough is enough, you never have enough!" [26] Mahatma Gandhi said, "There is no way to peace. Peace is the way."[da] Life of elegant simplicity, local economy, decentralized politics, conservation of nature, compassion for animals, and respect for the rights of nature are part of nonviolence. [48] The most important teaching of Buddhism is Ahimisa or nonviolence to nature. Let us prepare for peace with nature at the helm.

About twenty-nine thousand children under five die per day from preventable causes, such as diarrhea, malaria, neonatal infection, or pneumonia,[db] which is 1.06 million children per year. Yet we have spent more $100 billion per annum on arms and equipment for war since 2010, though it is difficult to get exact estimates.[dc] Plus the total global military expenditure has risen from $1.14 trillion in 2001 to $1.74 trillion in 2017, a rise of 50 percent. It looks as though we are giving peace less and less of a chance. Nature has the ingredients for peace—the silence in nature, being in a sacred grove—and they do not cost much! Many societies discuss local disagreements and conflicts under the meeting tree, which is often a sacred tree. Can we not learn from such groups? Can we invest some of the billions of war dollars in nature for peace? Here a climate deal being truly implemented would be the greatest peace deal the world could have.[dd]

Much violence concerns scarcity or a lack of access to natural and other resources. This is linked to the economy of nature, people, and the market. There are three types of violence in unsustainable development—against

---

[da] Accessed September 2018. https://www.google.com/search?q=there+is+no+way+to+peace+peace+is+the+way+gandhi.
[db] Accessed September 2018. https://www.unicef.org/mdg/childmortality.html.
[dc] Accessed September 2018. https://www.amnesty.org/en/latest/news/2015/08/killer-facts-the-scale-of-the-global-arms-trade/ and https://www.sipri.org/databases/financial-value-global-arms-trade. Those figures do not include the unreported trade!
[dd] Accessed September 2018. https://www.sipri.org/publications/2016/climate-related-security-risks.

the earth (environmental degradation and destruction), against people (poverty, destitution, and displacement), and the violence of war and conflict where the more powerful try to take what is not theirs from others. [96] Humankind now looks at nature as something to exploit for economic growth and human benefit. We act as if we are on a mission to conquer nature. This is violence against the earth. Unless we learn to make peace with nature, we will not make peace with ourselves, or with humanity. [48] Ultimately, nature will let us destroy ourselves through ecological collapse. Will we be one of nature's most interesting failed experiments and go extinct? [20]

Earth has suffered violence over the past centuries. There has been massive forest destruction, ocean and and global warming, climate change, and the effects of pollutants. Sacred trees and groves have suffered as well because of human-induced degradation and destruction. Earth needs a good lawyer so that ecological damage is seen as a crime. The Rome Statue of the International Criminal Court recognizes four international crimes—the crime of genocide, crimes against humanity, war crimes, and crimes of aggression. [38] There was a fifth crime called ecocide, which was on the Rome Statute till 1996 when it was dropped. These five crimes contribute to the lack of peace we see. [31]

Ecocide results from a vicious cycle of resource depletion (e.g., loss of forests, water access, or economic assets), which in turn results in conflict that culminates in war. War results in damage and destruction on a large scale.[de] An international ecocide law can break this vicious cycle. Such a law will help better conserve nature and promote how important we are as trustees of nature by putting the rights of the earth first. We can experience this by taking a walk in the forest, knowing we are interconnected and interdependent. The world is moving from independence to interdependency with nature. The continued destruction of nature is not acceptable. We need to replace this and cocreate a world as a place of peace. We have a duty of care for future generations as the stewards and trustees of nature we have to be and treat the planet Earth

---

[de] Polly Higgins, TED Talk 2012. https://www.youtube.com/watch?v=8EuxYzQ65H4. Ecocide, 5th Crime Against Peace.

with reverence and attitudes of peace, not conflict.^{df} Land in an evolving ecological context would function with a greater sense of the inherent rights of nature. [7] This includes the right of all living beings to exist and not be abused or destroyed.

To cope with the abuses of the aristocracy in England (and reduce conflict), the Charter of the Forest (1217) reestablished people's rights of access to royal forests.^{dg} Many of its provisions were in force for centuries afterward, and these principles are the basis for respecting nature. Royal forests were the most important sources of fuel for cooking, heating, charcoal, and many other uses for ordinary people, who were increasingly alienated from these forests. The charter was almost unique in providing economic protection for the people who used the forest as it restored real rights, privileges, and protections. For many years this was an important component in England's constitutional history. Some clauses in the charter remained in force until the 1970s, and special courts still exist in the New Forest and the Forest of Dean. In this respect, the Forest Charter was the statute that has remained longest in force in England (1217–1971). The Wild Creatures and Forest Laws Act (1971) superseded it. To mark eight hundred years of the Charter of the Forest in 2017, the Woodland Trust and more than fifty organizations launched a Charter for Trees, Woods and People, reflecting modern relationships with trees and woods in the landscape for people in the United Kingdom. This charter has ten principles (see box 34).

Nonviolence is the path to peace, and the meek will be blessed and inherit the earth. [51] All the great enlightened people promote nonviolence. To be in nature, in a sacred grove, beside a river promotes peace, silence, and quiet. Let us work and be part of nature and be the peace we are. Silence comes naturally when you are present and mindful. To watch with silence creates an alertness and something that goes beyond words. [45]

---

^{df} Polly Higgins, TED Talk February 2013. https://www.youtube.com/watch?v=QPUmN88htCo. Dare to be great, Ted Talk May 2013. https://www.youtube.com/watch?v=zoYq7_x41D4 (Leadership and law of Ecocide).
^{dg} Accessed October 2018. https://en.wikipedia.org/wiki/Charter_of_the_Forest and https://treecharter.uk.

Democracy, environment, and peace are treated separately. For example, development, peace, and conservation are separate processes, and they are the responsibility of different government sectors. Yet they are intertwined and related. [71] Tree planting and care are a great way to bring such concepts together—to bring people together as a human right to plant and care for trees and transform landscapes. This increases biodiversity, and we learn about governance in terms of what it means to be at peace with oneself. For Wangari Mathai, good management of the environment is part of democratic governance and peace. But governance has to be part of education and government. Funding for education, development, and conservation is more important than spending funds on weapons and conflict. [71]

> **Box 34: The Ten Principles of the Charter for Trees, Woods, and People 2017**
>
> 1. Sustain landscapes rich in wildlife.
> 2. Plant for the future.
> 3. Celebrate the power of trees to inspire.
> 4. Recover health, hope, and well-being with the help of trees.
> 5. Protect irreplaceable trees and woods.
> 6. Grow forests of opportunity and innovation.
> 7. Plan green local landscapes.
> 8. Strengthen our landscapes with trees.
> 9. Make trees accessible to all.
> 10. Combat the threats to our habitats.

We desperately need mechanisms for peace, and nature can be one rallying call. Major security threats come from issues that do not relate just to power and weapons. They include climate change, water and natural resource scarcity, and the growing rich-poor gap. [27] Elworthy suggests we adopt three principles of dialogue, prevention, and valuing women. Nature—and in particular the sacredness of nature—is important as a locus to understand how important inner peace is. This creates positivity for dialogue and a vehicle for prevention. To build inner peace requires mutual respect irrespective of power and gender, which reduces the prospect of violence. Women tend to be more peace-focused because they are key stewards of nature and the home.

Nature and SNS (sacred trees, groves, wells, mountains, and rivers) form potent loci for peace-building and conflict resolution. This is so for low-level conflict (e.g., over water access or access to critical natural resources). If not addressed at this early stage, such conflicts can escalate. Thich Nhat Hanh suggests steps that can support successful conflict resolution [35] First, practice face-to-face sitting together mindfully. Second, practice remembering the history of the conflict. Third, avoid stubbornness so there is a willingness for reconciliation. Fourth, try to deescalate feelings of the concerned people, where a senior respected person can represent each side of the conflict. Fifth, all sides need to voluntarily reveal and be truthful about the different shortcomings, which creates an atmosphere that encourages and supports. Finally, reach decisions by consensus, and accept the verdict. These elements of peace-building were used by Buddhist monks and nuns in many countries for more than two thousand years. [35] We can learn and apply the lessons, and we can be that peace in our world.

Our wealth and weapons have made us cowards. Our fears condone injustices that underpin our consumptive ways of life and fuel the hostility that will destroy us. It is now time to heal our conflicts between nations and different ethnic groups. Neither can be solved by applying more of the thinking that created them. The connections between the two is humankind's addiction to violence. Likewise, neither can be solved without solving the other. [82]

For Nobel Laureate Wangari Maathai, trees were essential to her life and provided her with many lessons. "Trees are living symbols of peace and hope. A tree has roots in the soil yet reaches to the sky. It tells us that in order to aspire we need to be grounded and that no matter how high we go it is from our roots that we draw sustenance. It signifies that no matter how powerful we become in government or how many awards we receive, our power and strength and our ability to reach our goals depend on the people, those whose work remains unseen, who are the soil out of which we grow, the shoulders on which we stand." [64]

We need a new creativity–one that has as its primary concern the survival of Earth in its functional whole. Then humankind can adapt to be an integral part of this Earth community, not the lordly plunderer we have been for so long. [7] We can only understand the peace of the earth if we understand and respect the planet as a single community composed of many and varied parts. Berry recognizes that [7] (a) the earth is a single organic reality that must survive as an integral whole, (b) the peace of the earth is creative but has been disturbed by human plunderers and weapons of war, (c) the peace of earth increasingly depends on human decisions, many of which are happening in some nations, and (d) we must hold on to a hopeful optimism for the future.

Can we look at sacred trees and groves with a sense of reverence as our ancestors did? [43] To extend an olive branch is the emblem of peace and friendship. Look at a tree in its totality, not just above ground but below ground. Both parts are connected and interconnected by fungal mycelia. Then we will know trees are a real network that communicates, lives, and thrives as a community similar to those in the film *Avatar*. Paul Kingsnorth says, "These old stories, seeking us out, singing us the song of the tree, offer us a path and a warning. I think we can still hear them, if we climb up into the branches, shut our mouths, and listen." [43] If we do, we will be at peace with ourselves.

Nature Offers Us Ways to Enhance Education and Our Health and Be a Means for Peace

It is becoming clear from evidence what the benefits of being in nature are. [87] These restorative environments offer opportunities to receive nature's benefits in physical, mental, and spiritual terms. If we identify with nature, this helps us be part of the landscape and present for it, which reduces stress. We can make or gain access to our own piece of sacred nature in order to reconnect and bring peace and tranquility. Then we are able to go within, pause, and witness nature in silence. We may be lucky enough to have recognized sacred trees or groves to visit close by.

A walk in the park or forest is a spiritual and natural experience, and in that walk, we can reconnect in silence with the trees and nature around. We should not walk through nature deaf, blind, and senseless to its sounds and sights. Practice such walks in silence as a walking meditation. Try not to be disturbed. As you walk, tune in to nature, and use your breath to focus. Stay in a sacred grove or a woodland or in front of a tree, and be silent for at least twenty minutes without being disturbed. In this way, we can offer gratitude to the earth. Through trees we can achieve a stronger relationship with and connection to nature, but we have to do so with awareness. [101] Have you ever noticed when you walk in nature, you may be naturally pulled to a certain aspect such as a tree? Be open to such pulls, witness the tree, engage in silence, and see what you learn.

Be present for a tree in a sacred grove. Just be silent, and witness the tree. Use your senses, and see how the tree connects with the environment. What can you learn? [101] You can do the same in your garden, and you may even have a sacred corner of the garden where you can be still with trees, plants, and animals. You can have potted plants or trees in a corner of your home. You can use these plants to connect. [77] The nature you don't know is being replaced by the nature you do, and this creates a greater sense of peace and oneness. The more you connect with nature, the more you will want to live a life that supports nature. [101]

Education should focus more on experiential learning than conditioning children not to connect with nature. Through the work of Richard Louv and others, many schools bring students out to experience nature firsthand. While there are risks in learning and playing in nature, there are more serious risks of not doing so, including stress, attention deficit disorder, and diminishing mental health. Nature experience and therapy are growing in importance as we become more urbanized. Outdoor education should be an important part of education and health, and it should result in greater interest in nature and less on electronics. Schools can have a garden or trees to explore, or there may be a park nearby. You can also go to the countryside. Many schools are close to such green areas. Teachers can facilitate experiential learning rather than learning by rote. Access to nature needs to be part of schools, faith-based organizations, workspaces, neighborhoods, and cities. But this won't happen unless we acknowledge our need for nature. [113]

This lack of experience with nature is serious as the author George Monbiot points out in a poignant example.[dh] He spent two days with a group of ten-year-old children from a deprived London borough, exploring rock pools and roaming the woods in rural Wales. Many of them had never been to the countryside or the sea before. A staggering example of how city youth are not exposed to nature. In the woods, the children paddled in streams, rolled down a hill, ate blackberries, and tasted mushrooms. Most had not done these things, yet the exhilaration they showed in exploring nature seemed instinctive and natural. George Monbiot realized just how little contact they'd had with nature because not one of them had seen a nettle or knew what happens if you touched it! This summarizes how separate we are. These children become the next adults who are ignorant of nature and ecology.

The main ways to resolve disputes used to be the elders. It worked in the past. It still works in areas where traditional institutions are strong. But it is being replaced—often at great cost and maybe with less effect—by formal judicial systems. Maybe we should reinvigorate local customary conflict resolution at the community level with all religious and spiritual groups. We would then resolve most conflict well before it goes to violence and guns. This may seem naïve, but having devolved governance to the lowest accountable level would facilitate such local elders councils (or whatever we call them)—perhaps meeting under a sacred tree. A transformation to a nonviolent world requires courageous champions at all levels from family and community to the global level. But ordinary people will drive this as they realize how much we need to do things in smarter, more decent, negotiated, and peaceful ways. Somebody must begin this movement. [82]

The places you use to connect with do not have to be formal sacred sites or groves, but they can be sacred to you. We can imbue such sites with a sense of the sacred and communicate with them in silence. We can witness in silence the trees and plants around us, and we can be present and conscious to them. Take pleasure in noticing the world and the nature surrounding

---

[dh] http://www.monbiot.com/2013/10/07/rewild-the-child/ and http://www.wildernessfoundation.org.uk/wp-content/uploads/2013/01/TurnAround-2007-Executive-Summary-Stand-Alone-Document.pdf.

you. We can create our own (or our community's) rituals. Rituals are symbolic actions that can offer important messages. [41] They serve many purposes—community building, healing, peace, and exploring our own spirituality. Rituals may be simple (e.g., lighting a candle, sitting under a tree in a forest, witnessing a tree, walking in silence in a forest or along a river). [66] Offering kindness to ourselves, our communities, and nature is a simple but important act. Kindness is not just confined to humanity but for all our actions—being kind to animals, our farm, nature, and sacred nature. [9] We belong together, interdependent and interconnected. To be kind is invariably right, though being right is not always being kind!

We create our realities and how we perceive and relate to nature. Conscious choice creates that reality—whether we imbue a sacred tree with spirituality or cut and process it! Showing our interconnectedness with nature fosters peace with nature and the world at large. This is part of the common good that nature, sacred trees, and groves provide, and it is what Pope Francis says is the "sum of those conditions of social life which allow social groups and their members relatively thorough and ready access to their own fulfillment." [85] Thomas Berry agrees and says, "A degraded habitat will produce degraded humans. If there is to be any true progress, then the entire life community must progress." [7] While Wangari Mathai adds, "We are inextricably linked to nature, so we must take action, and stop the talk about the importance of nature." [64] Children need access to experience nature. [63] This is not a luxury, and it is at the heart of our and nature's well-being and on which the future of Earth depends.

When asked to sum up everything, Confucius said "reciprocity", which refers to bonding, giving, and receiving. [8] Earth and the universe are part of reciprocity. Everything on Earth is contingent on giving and receiving. Trees give us oxygen to breathe, and we give trees carbon dioxide. This is a simple example of reciprocity. Nature is about giving and receiving—teaching us, providing us with health, and being a locus for peace. In return, we must have the right attitude to and be at peace with nature. So too, trees teach us. We are their pupils, and we would be wise to learn from trees. [1]

Increased Practical Engagement for Religion, Spirituality, and Conservation in Nature for a Sustainable Future

CHAPTER 8

Be Praised, my Lord, through our Mother Earth, who feeds us and rules us, and produces various fruit with colored flowers and herbs.
—Saint Francis of Assisi, Canticle of the Creatures

We Simply Have to Learn from Nature and Our Past

Pope John Paul II said,

> Today the ecological crisis has assumed such proportions as to be the responsibility of everyone and cannot be left only to conservation organizations and groups. Its various aspects show the need for concerted efforts aimed at establishing the duties and obligations that belong to individuals, peoples, States and the international community. When the ecological crisis is set within the broader context of the search for peace within society, we can understand better the importance of giving attention to what the Earth and its atmosphere are telling us: namely that there is an order in the universe which must be respected, and that the human person, endowed with the capability of choice, really has a grave responsibility to

> preserve this order for the well-being of future generations. As such, the ecological crisis is a moral issue. [27]

Black Elk, the First Nation Lakota elder, spoke similar words in the United States.

> I learned their songs, but there are many songs out there. Like the fire, it has a song. That fire shapes and forms all life and each shape has a song. Even the Earth has a song. We call it Mother Earth. Then the water, it has a song. The water makes beautiful sounds. The water carries the universal sounds. This tree, every green has a song. They have a language of their own. There's life there. So, each green has a song, there are a lot of songs we don't know yet. One man could never get to know all of them. If you see a tree, it doesn't move. It doesn't talk or walk. You just see it. But the trees talk. They have a language of their own. So, all this green that you see, they communicate … What you know today, it's just a little bit—like the blink of an eye. So that power is immense. [3]

The final text of the Rio +20 declaration affirms Mother Earth and the rights of nature. Article 39 states, "We recognize that planet Earth and its ecosystems are our home and that Mother Earth is a common expression in a number of countries and regions, and we note that some countries recognize the rights of nature in the context of the promotion of sustainable development. We are convinced that in order to achieve a just balance among the economic, social and environmental needs of present and future generations, it is necessary to promote harmony with nature." [46]

The 1992 Rio Earth Summit stated, "Human beings are at the center of concerns for sustainable development." We must ask God for a positive outcome to such discussions for future generations, not to suffer the ill-advised delays of today. [26] The Sustainable Development Goals highlight some of these concerns, while Martin Luther King reminds us, "If we are to go forward, we must go back and rediscover those precious values—that all reality hinges on moral foundations and that all reality has spiritual control." [20] Unity with nature is the foundation of man's survival on Earth and of social relationships. Otherwise, our present civilization will decline, decay, [40] and go extinct. We need actions that entail the stewardship of the Earth systems—the biosphere, climate, and societies. [37]

It is a challenge for religious, spiritual, conservation, and land use groups to work together so that religion and spirituality become more meaningful to people and to the environment and exemplify how we live as part of, not separate from nature. The two groups share similarities that offer hope. Ecology without anthropology and sociology means ecology will fail. [26] Ecology underpins anthropology, sociology, and economics, which reflects the importance of conservation as an integral part of our livelihoods—more than the utilitarian use economists, planners, and people place on nature. We need to look again at how we perceive nature's bounty, trees, and forests.

How important sacred trees and groves are has to be part of that change. In this way, we can integrate sacred nature in our religious and spiritual beliefs, conservation, and land use. But this needs to be political without compromising our core values. In general, political leadership has failed humankind in terms of the climate crisis and degradation of nature. Sacred groves can be part of a more politicized change. Religious groups should be the consciousness of people, balancing the political and secular. Religious and faith-based groups may have a power at national and global levels not fully harnessed. But such change requires a new worldview that sees nature, other nations, and our own neighbors not as adversaries but as partners for mutual reinvention. [14] Ralph Waldo Emerson says, [6] "The problem of restoring to the world original and eternal beauty, is solved by redemption of the soul … The reason why the world lacks unity, and lies broken and in heaps is because man is disunited with himself. He cannot be a naturalist, until he satisfies all the demands of the spirit."

Humankind is part of nature just as forests, mountains and rivers are. [8] We ought to respect nature and sacred Earth as part of, not separate from humankind. Such positive attitudes will help us better steward Earth.

Only through reconnecting with nature, culture, spirituality, beauty, and art will we reduce our dependency on materialism and money. [16] Sacred trees and groves highlight the interlinking of knowledge, practice, and belief [45] in that (a) every life and type of place matter (diversity); (b) everything is connected (connectivity); (c) we are all related, including humankind, plants, and animals (kincentricity); (d) everything we use is a gift, but with the gift come obligations (accountability); (e) whatever we take, we need to give back (reciprocity); (f) we are not just physical beings as there are other dimensions tying us to the earth (spirituality); and (g) everything we do reflects on our ancestors and affects future generations (responsibility). [45] As the ecologist Pierre Rabhi says, "We are children of nature ... We are water, we are soil, we are air, we are Nature. It's the mind that created the separation between nature and us. That separation is not real, and that's why it's so important today to come back to the source—that is, back to Mother Earth herself." [18] This is one aim of this book—to help you connect and reconnect with nature by using the sacredness of nature.

Spirituality and science cannot stay separate. Yet materialism is taking over science as humanity strives for more is better. [42] It seems that we are increasingly seeking spirituality, but we cannot separate spirituality from science and materialism. If we do, we stay separated from planetary processes and the story of Earth. Yet most schools fulfill a role like initiation ceremonies—a rite of passage that perpetuates this separation. This is not real learning as it occurs without understanding the spiritual aspects of Mother Earth. In a similar way, theological curricula need to address the new senses of spirituality arising. We can no longer ignore Earth as it will no longer endure being despised, neglected, and mistreated. [24]

The Cree elders say our (Western) way of life is missing human spiritual fulfillment. The elders appreciate and accept the advantages and comforts of modern life. Mukash, a Cree elder says,

> We're here for a reason. But if that spiritual aspect, that spiritual element, is not part of your life, then you're breaking the law. And as an individual, you're off balance.

> All the problems that we have with regard to the economy, to the environment, all the problems of human conflict in the world—they all have to do with the absence of that balance that should be there. This is the knowledge that our elders are passing on to us. It's very difficult to understand but all these things that happen in the world, they're happening because there needs to be a balance. The parts of you have to be in balance: your physical, mental and spiritual health. They all three have to be functioning. If your spiritual side doesn't function, then you become greedy. This is a natural teaching; it's common to all nations. And that is what the problem is. We're way off balance.[38]

We need to relocalize economics and think about what we purchase, what we do, and how it is produced. Domestic and local has to be more important than global and national. [14] Our growth-based economics is in conflict with the planet's atmospheric limits. Our overall inaction on climate change is due to political apathy and weak climate policy, and as a result, we face changes that challenge the foundations of the expansionist logic at the heart of our economic systems. [14] With sacred nature, groves, and their custodians, both formal religious and spiritual traditions can be one part of the movement to unblock the legacy of market fundamentalism and the cultural narratives on which this is based. This will then enable life and Earth-saving climate action.

We can think differently about nature and the environment—positive and enabling, not negative and alienating. Terms such as privatization and cutting essential public services promote values of power, prestige, image, and status. It suppresses values of intimacy, kindness, self-acceptance, independent thought, and action. [22] The language we use to describe nature alienates. For example, the term reserve or park fosters detachment. Sites of special scientific interest, no-take zones, and ecosystem services all send negative messages. We need terms and approaches to embrace, evoke images, connect, and promote passion. Nature, living planet, and sacred nature are some such terms. [22] We need to be more positive. At present, we criticize, analyze, and dissect. But we offer little guidance on how to express gratitude—simply saying, "Thank you." Gratitude restores the cycle of giving and receiving on which Mother Earth depends. [24] Gratitude extends our awareness back in time to respect ancient obligations and forward to the future and to lives we need to honor and protect. Gratitude requires mindfulness, not just smartness, and it also requires perspective beyond self. [24]

Victoria Tauli-Corpuz, the UN special rapporteur on the Rights of Indigenous Peoples, supports these views and says "World leaders have a powerful solution on the table to save forests and protect the planet: recognize and support the world's indigenous peoples. We have stood as a proven solution to climate change for generations. Recognize our rights and we can continue to do so for generations to come."[di] Indigenous custodians manage most sacred groves though monastic and church forests are the responsibility of formal religions.

At present, the movement to sustain the habitability of the earth is doomed to fail. This is not due to lack of effort, data, or information. It is more to do with public and political attitudes. [24] We do not have an environmental crisis but rather a political one. We all want a decent and habitable world for our descendants. But we do science and publish books and articles. They do politics, take over the courts, control the media, and manipulate a changing society. [24] We need to be smarter and have a model of economy based on ecological economics to recognize how our economy is based on Earth's ecological life support systems. This recognizes that growth (increase in size or scale) and development (improvement and quality) are not always linked. Real development is improving sustainable well-being, not just growth in consumption. [5]

Marriages of different world views maybe called for—science, religion, and spirituality; environmentalism and economics; poets and politicians. [33] The examples of sacred trees and groves makes this clear and argues for developing approaches within religious, spiritual, conservation, and land use contexts to understand why nature is spiritually important and

---

[di] Accessed November 2018. https://www.corneredbypas.com/.

how this can influence improved stewardship. This calls us to work in partnership across sectoral divides.

We grew out of, depended on, and used to revere nature. We held nature sacred, including trees and groves, water sources and springs, mountains and other natural features. Much sacred nature predates formal religion and formal conservation. It was part of evolving spiritual traditions. We can learn from this wisdom and how important this knowledge is in our contemporary world and for the future of humanity. Their knowledge informs and complements other forms of knowledge as we tackle the challenges of climate change, degradation, conversion, urbanization, and our loss of connection with nature. As a Massongo oral tradition in Africa notes, "A man lives again through his children, the trees that he has planted, the words that he has uttered." [7]

We need to foster the spontaneity of nature. Nature had worked out the ecosystems that flourished when human civilization evolved a short time ago in geological time. So humankind is arrogant and destructive to intrude on this system without understanding why and how these ecosystems function the way they do. Then we can see how humans are best placed. Nature balances its forces, but at present, much of nature's assault on humankind is human in origin. [1]

Despite depending on nature and holding nature sacred, over the past fifty to a hundred years, our separation from nature has increased. We depend on nature, and for the foreseeable future, we always will; however, we no longer appreciate or respect the sources of our air, water, food, jobs, and homes. This results in increased abuse and destruction, stress-related illnesses, and a breakdown of peace. Yet there are encouraging signs. Sacred trees and groves survive despite great pressures. Many rural and traditional peoples have relationships with nature that are intimate and spiritual. Formal religions are starting to emphasize how important nature is. Formal conservation is starting to recognize the relevance of sacred nature as a key conservation asset. Based on these signs, a workshop at the World Parks Congress (Durban South Africa, 2003), the conclusions from the book on Asian sacred natural sites, and other sources, guidelines for managing SNS were suggested, [30; 47] and these inform this chapter.

Sacred Trees and Groves Are Older than Formal Religions and Formal Conservation

Wherever there is a tree on Earth, there is a sacred tree. Many of these trees and groves predate formal religion and conservation by hundreds or even thousands of years. They are examples of our respecting and rediscovering the sense of the sacred in nature and one another. Every culture has sacred trees and groves. Ancient and sacred trees such as the oak, fig, yew, and baobab are important keystone species.

In the interreligious ceremony (Basilica of St. Francis of Assisi, September 29, 1986), it was noted that "every major religion and tradition of the world is represented here. No one pretends that our respective beliefs are or can be held in common; but we do believe that religious concern for the conservation and ecological harmony of the natural world is our common heritage, our birthright and our duty." [49] We have to support greater religious responsibility for conservation in local and national action. Then we may see a return to the sacred loop of harmony, cooperation, and community. [31] We must be prudent in our use and act as guests not the exploiting proprietor. [35]

Increasingly, people integrate traditional wisdom into modern systems. Sacred grove plans can restore power to local communities. Awareness can help educate people about conservation, which can stimulate the revival of traditions. Western approaches to biodiversity now recognize the relevance of local knowledge and community forests, but many still ignore the conservation potential of sacred places because of culture-bound modernity and formal science. [36; 34]

Across the globe, individual trees—often ancient but not necessarily so—were and are revered. You may have a sacred tree in your neighborhood, but it does not stop you having your tree, which you hold sacred in your heart.

The examples of sacred trees in chapter 3 can be a guide. You may have planted a tree like my wife and I planted a tree when we married or when our children were born. Holding your own trees sacred and respecting other sacred trees will bring you peace, silence, and serenity.

There is a focus on expanding the global protected area network to achieve the goals of the Convention on Biological Diversity, the Sustainable Development Goals, and the Paris Climate Agreement on Climate Change. But we cannot do this through coercion or by taking land and forests from indigenous and local peoples. They must be a key part of the approach. [41] Such coercion and land sequestration are happening too frequently, which further exacerbates relationships between communities and conservation. We could better achieve such expansion by respecting, recognizing, and securing the rights and responsibilities of indigenous and local communities. In this way, huge areas can come under the flag of protected areas and conservation, under IUCN protected area categories V and VI. [41] The sheer number of sacred groves is a starting point for such a process.

Sacred groves do just that. Communities conserve, at little or no external cost, large areas of land across the globe. The areas may be small (one to five hectares), though some are large (more than four hundred hectares). Sacred groves are, in conservation terms, powerful examples of ICCAs. They contribute to conservation objectives, conserve important biodiversity, help create connectivity in the landscape, and are locally managed and owned. But people say they are too small and not formally recognized. Yet, a recent Rights and Resources Initiative report estimates communities contribute between $3.16 to $4.52 billion per year on ICCA management. This is approximately 16 to 23 percent of the total investment by the conservation community in protected areas. [41] Surely, ICCAs offer a more peaceful, positive, conservation-friendly means than forced eviction, hostility, and conflict.

To conserve sacred trees and groves through legal recognition that supports their management for sacred and conservation purposes is important, but we have to understand why and how this is so. How can we create greater awareness on the scale, scope, and extent of sacred groves and species for conservation agencies, religious and spiritual bodies, nations, and the world at large? I hope this book will be one small effort to help in answering these questions. But there is the challenge and the paradox. Many sacred trees and groves may be secret as their spiritual meaning may be diminished or threatened by having them known and listed. [9] There are trade-offs here—secrecy or risk loss ... or recognition and risk abuse of the spiritual. People can take precautions and not exert pressure on the community to compel them to disclose the secrecy of their groves. These choices belong to the custodians. Any listings, assessments, or improved, more secure management regimes should be implemented with the full understanding and agreement of the custodians and the communities who use them in terms of free and informed consent. This means building on customary rules and the institutions for the governance and management of these sites to give them legal recognition.

If sacred groves occur in protected areas or are recognized ICCAs, their recognition by government authorities can increase their overall protection. This instills pride and ownership for the local community of their sacred site and helps safeguard against desecration by those who may not know they are sacred. It will reduce friction between communities, conservation agencies, and government institutions. But official recognition can only be agreed to if the custodians are supportive. If a sacred natural site occurs outside protected areas, their official recognition as an ICCA can help increase its protection. For example, the Bhutanese government made an inventory of all *Nye* (sacred sites), and so far, there are eight volumes of books on the sacred sites in Bhutan. [50]

Sacred groves are more associated with Africa, Asia, and Latin America than with Europe and North America. Though there are still many sacred groves in Europe and North America, many were destroyed because of formal religion, growing dominance of scientific and reductionist approaches, and the need for wood and fuel for economies (e.g., shipbuilding and the industrial revolution). But we can do a lot as individuals, families, and communities by respecting and protecting existing sacred groves (e.g., the churchyard yews in Europe or giant redwoods in

California). We can treat sacred groves as important to us as a community like the Dai forests in China. Conservation groups could better understand and respect the relevance and potential for sacred groves, for conserving important and sometimes unique biodiversity, and for connectivity in the landscape.

Religions and Spiritual Groups Have Responsibilities for Conservation

Nature was a key aspect of religions in their formative years when everyone depended on nature. But religions may have lost many of these connections. Indigenous spiritual groups are still close to nature, yet other factors threaten their existence. Why do sacred trees and groves continue to be of spiritual and religious significance? What mechanisms can spiritual groups use to integrate these values at a practical level? Spirituality evolved in humans as early societies were an integral part of their environment. [29] Spirituality is similar across race, color, creed, and geography. Most societies have a creation story. They hold—or they held—nature in reverence, and they have sacred trees and groves and other SNS (springs, mountains, etc.). We need to link ecological, social, and spiritual aspects of nature more strongly so that they are mutually supportive, [29] and we must do so in the context of contemporary culture and the pressures that the planet Earth and people face.

Religions can integrate nature in their work as a number are now doing. But it is not enough to go to the church, mosque, or temple if you do not have a temple in your heart! The religions of the world should engage with and acknowledge the role of sacred trees and sacred groves in contemporary life in a practical manner at the local level. This is one avenue for the custodians as well as spiritual and religious leaders to support conservation as their governance arrangements add another management dimension. But this requires adjustments in our global heritage and conservation discourses about who has responsibility for what and how.

Traditional spiritual groups still have deep connections with nature—connections built over many years, maybe even thousands of years, where nature is a cornerstone of life and culture. Yet only in the past few decades are we understanding these connections, often through the lens of sacred trees and groves. We have much to learn from such groups about the sacredness and management of and respect for nature, sacred groves, and trees. Religions can also learn about (a) the spirituality that traditional communities have for nature, which we can build on and legitimate as sacred nature; b). how religions can learn from one another and cooperate better; (c) how religions can work for common environmental causes yet respect their differences, which also contributes to more harmonious interreligious relations; and (d) the fact that all religious texts contain strong references to nature. But for many years, we have not used those references in pastoral teaching often enough, though the Eastern religions are better. It is time to translate these great words into practical action on the ground by the different religions. Religions can take on their responsibilities for nature and for Mother Earth.

Conservation Has to Better Integrate and Respect Sacred Trees and Groves

Conservation has tools and approaches, which will help better secure sacred trees and groves from external pressures if used with respect and also empower local communities to be responsible stewards. The different protected area categories offer ways for protecting sacred sites, though this has to be done with the support of protected area managers and authorities. ICCAs are gaining respect and official recognition. We can recognize and document ICCAs so that they form part of the formal protected area movement. But this may need compromise by the custodians—recognition in return for greater respect and security. So how can we reinforce approaches to conserve such areas and species, where conservation is the responsibility of the group or community for whom such areas are sacred, especially in terms of various forms of ICCA? How can we better make the case for how important sacred trees, groves, and ICCAs are to enhance connectivity in the wider landscape?

Value-based management is popular in conserving our cultural heritage. This is a balance to formal or science-based management. They are not the same. Nor are they mutually exclusive. In fact, a merging might help us better address intangible values. [10] For example, policy and legal recognition of areas of land and natural resources can be important to people for cultural, religious, and spiritual reasons. There can be mechanisms to confer formal conservation value and acknowledge the institutions that manage such areas. For this to happen, communities and groups who own or have clear rights to sacred trees and groves ought to take on those rights, even if they are in nationally reserved areas. But there is still limited direct legal support for sacred groves. For example, only two countries in Africa have specific legal provisions.

There are opportunities for new arrangements through how social groups can secure sacred groves. This is occurring through, for example, community forests that have legal recognition. The majority of them were declared for a mix of social, economic, and environmental reasons. We should respect the fact that sacred trees and groves are important for cultural diversity and conservation. But we should not co-opt sacred trees and groves into dominant conservation paradigms because that can create enmity.

We can enhance sacred groves by establishing buffer zones. This could promote sustainable development where a buffer zone might contain woodlots or fodder banks or cash crops as in a UNESCO project in Ghana. Sacred groves can be indicators for natural vegetation and foster the restoration of degraded areas through the use of sacred places as reference sites and gene pools. Scientists and custodians can work together to understand culture-based conservation and develop practical guidelines for management. Natural scientists can make inventories of the plants and animals in sacred groves and show their importance in empirical terms. This means the interrelationships between people, the environment, and the spiritual powers in nature become central. [32]

How people manage sacred groves is based on long-term capacity and knowledge. Their complexity often calls for in-depth understanding of traditional management, special training, and capacity-building. This requires working with local communities and custodians. Protected area managers can compile and share experiences in managing sacred groves. Traditional custodians can benefit from training on modern management and conservation.

We can then move from centralized, state-owned protected areas to a model that is perhaps more complex and messier but is more embracing and brings local communities in as co-owners and custodians. This may well be more sustainable than centrally owned and managed protected areas that often alienate local people and expropriated lands from them. Partnerships are important so that we understand, recognize, and respect the rights and responsibilities of all parties. This will make for scenarios where (a) we respect sacred groves for what they are, (b) the custodians are recognized as the key stakeholders in management and ownership, (c) protected area managers view such custodians as true partners, and (d) protected area managers integrate the custodians into management. This will better achieve conservation goals, increase protected area coverage, and create greater connectivity in the landscape.

The very large number of sacred groves across the globe forces us to think and act locally. In this way local people will have the management rights and responsibilities at the local and wider landscape levels. It forces the protected area movement out of its ivory tower of state-owned and -managed areas. Thus, it becomes part of more complex and messier landscape management where conservation is one part of overall landscape mosaics. Sacred groves are important lands used for integrated landscape management. But this calls for greater recognition and respect for sacred trees and groves at all levels. At the national level, there has to be the enabling policy for recognizing sacred trees and groves and respecting their custodians and management regimes.

Stewardship Is the Glue for Joint Action and Partnerships

Stewardship is the glue to bring together these different sectors—even worldviews—that are or should be involved with sacred trees and groves. This includes religions, spiritual groups, conservation groups, different sectors, and those involved with landscape management and land use. Stewardship and conservation have similar values—use but don't overuse, recognize interdependence, and emphasis on the importance of future generations. There are four key virtues of stewardship—simplicity, moderation, frugality, and gratitude. Stewardship is embedded in all religions and spiritual groups and is a key underpinning for conservation, landscape, and land use planning and management. Pope Francis reiterated how important stewardship is for us all—individuals, communities, different religions, nations, spiritual traditions, and those responsible for managing nature. The term dominion as domination was firmly refuted through Pope Francis's encyclical!

Stewardship is finding its way into the scientific discourse on climate change. A recent article titled "Hothouse Earth" stated that we require collective human action to guide Earth from a potential threshold and tipping point to either a hothouse earth or one that stabilizes planet Earth. [37] Stewardship is the key, the authors suggested, for using the deep and integrated knowledge we have and carry out global to local actions to offset these risks (e.g., decarbonizing the global economy, enhancing carbon sinks, behavioral change, and improved governance). Humanity, the authors note, has to play an active stewardship role for us to maintain a livable planet. This requires deliberate, integrated, and adaptive steps for us to take. [37]

Gratitude, an important but hidden part of stewardship, restores the cycle of giving and receiving and requires us to be present for those we are being gracious to. We cannot legislate for gratitude. It comes from the heart, is embraced by compassion, and should be practiced. [23] We can be grateful for all nature provides us, be grateful for the sacred trees and groves found across the globe, be grateful for how we manage our sacred groves, and be grateful for our own pieces of sacred nature. This strengthens our connections with nature and our consciousness.

Sacred trees and groves help empower local economies and cultures. [17] They help us reconnect place with community (and family). To think globally and act locally should be the mantra. By acting locally, we can conserve sacred trees and groves as part of local culture and well-being. Thinking globally provides international recognition and support for the value of sacred trees and groves.

How we manage sacred groves has to apply to stakeholders through partnerships and respect for people's rights. We should consider the entire community for whom the sacred grove has value—the custodians, elders, men, women, and children. But the community of the wider area, who may not share the same beliefs as the sacred site community, ought to be consulted as conserving sacred groves can only be effective through voluntary participation. Indigenous peoples have first rights, and partners who wish to assist must respect those first rights. Many custodians have a wealth of knowledge about their environment and their roles in the management of sacred species and groves. A focus on traditional ecological knowledge with conservation science would be beneficial for all in the sustainable management of sacred groves. Integrated management requires us to use conservation science and traditional knowledge together.

As Earth is alive, we should take care of our land and recognize the inherent value of life. This is stewardship and the well-being of future generations. It is an approach coming from the heart, not the head. It is born of a deep wisdom based on the sacredness of life. If we take away the world that sustains us, soon we will perish. At present, our right to life is in danger because of climate change, greed, and destruction, yet we continue to ignore these signs. [11]

Vandana Shiva reflects our relationship with nature. It allows us to experience our humanity as nature stands out in her own right and imparts peace. We will not achieve the joy of living and peace by conquest and domination but by coexistence and cooperation. The forest shows us how to reconnect with nature and find sources of freedom. [28] There are two words which stand out in what Aldo Leopold said, "A thing is right when it tends to preserve the integrity, stability and beauty of the biotic community. It is wrong when it tends otherwise." [19] Biotic and community are the terms what makes this outlook so radical. [13]

One of our great challenges is to nurture sustainable communities to satisfy our aspirations without diminishing the chances of future generations. A community sustains the entire web of life on which we depend. This is designed so its ways of life, businesses, economies, physical structures, and technologies do not interfere with nature's ability to sustain life. [4] Our consciousness is shifting from individualism and independence to interdependence and kinship as the sense of a larger common good is emerging for the planet and its fragile biosphere. [43]

If we hold something in trust for future generations, we cannot abuse that trust. We can use but not overuse and also be good stewards. Traditional spiritual beliefs understand these values. We have much to learn from them about stewardship. So we have to recognize and respect contemporary values of spiritual systems to support being stewards of nature. At a local level, stewardship integrates people and nature. This strengthens the ethical core of our values for nature. We have to respect different cultural, social, religious, and spiritual traditions and beliefs through maintaining a strong sense of place.

Sacred Trees and Sacred Groves Are Key for Education, Health, and Peace

Sacred trees and groves are key for reconnecting with nature, enhancing experiential education, being a means for nature health, and serving as a locus for peace-building in our troubled times. Who has not felt a sense of calm, serenity, and peace when walking in a natural woodland or park, standing in front of an ancient tree, walking along a riverbank or the shoreline, or even contemplating a potted plant or tree in your living room? Do we ever really think why this is so?

Spirituality is a bridge between science and religion. Both need each other. Development embraces the earth and nature, not just economic growth. [15] This makes restraint explicit, so we should consume within sustainable limits and respect equity and governance. Linking development, religion and spirituality is one key. Another is cultural revival to build on the wisdom and institutions of the past, enhance conservation, and reduce environmental destruction in the present. [21] So our perceived science-based wisdom has to adapt to culture, traditional knowledge, and their institutions. To embrace science, culture, development, traditional knowledge, and conservation requires working together and across sectors. Rural people need to recapture the positive aspects of culture and integrate them with contemporary change. Science has to better respect and integrate traditional wisdom and culture. [21]

We used to have close relations with nature from dependency for sustenance and health, namely with agriculture and the organized production of food. Since the industrial revolution and over the past fifty years, we are increasingly separated from nature, whether spatially or socially as most of us are linked and maybe even addicted to technology (TV, computer, phone, PlayStation). Such separation results in various negative symptoms and disorders. It is related to education (nature deficit disorder) or our personal health (stress-related). As a result, we are more conflictual and less peaceful, more stressed and less calm, and unable to pay attention and less considerate.

Sacred groves are a tremendous opportunity for experiential education and awareness of biodiversity and landscapes, reconnecting with nature and the spirituality within nature. Increased awareness helps us understand the requirements for experiential education and how nature can help us reconnect for a more peaceful, less conflict-ridden world. We can connect to nature, learn from nature, allow nature to heal us, and return to nature. It requires effort and policy support to make this happen. Education can be more experiential as we see happening in places (e.g., the United States and Europe) where separation from nature is most acute. Some countries (e.g., Japan, Korea, China, and some of Europe) are prescribing forest health walks or working on a care farm to cure various stress-related ailments.

We can do a lot to create a greater awareness of sacred trees and groves in terms of the myths and stories that surround them and the reasons for their sacredness [51] but also in terms of their biodiversity importance. Then we can ensure our children can explore and understand why such sacred sites are important and essential for sustainability. Stewardship is one means for exposing children to nature. The importance of sacred trees and groves will gain added support if religions take on increased responsibility for environmental stewardship.

We need peace in our time. We have to reinvigorate traditional and local institutions for conflict resolution (e.g., consensus through discussion and negotiation under the sacred or ancient trees of the elders). Such mechanisms can again be part of our lives and be part of the legal systems. Resolving conflict when it is low level (as in disagreements over access to water or critical areas of vegetation), is easier than it would be if and when the situation escalates to violence.

We Can All Do Something and Be the Change We Want as Sacred Nature Really Does Matter

We have the responsibility to be the change we want—as individuals, communities, religious and spiritual groups, conservationists, and nations. We have responsibilities to be stewards and take care of nature for future generations. We have the responsibility to repair the damage done to Mother Earth. The lens of sacred trees and groves offers us ways to do so based on stewardship, conservation, restoration, and sustainable use. This needs to part of our spirituality. Our backgrounds may differ in terms of what we do and what religion or spiritual group we belong to, but our common cause for Mother Earth is clear. Let us use these differences to unite and not divide us in order to restore Mother Earth and be the stewards we must become. The earth is the larger sacred community we belong to. If we are separated from this community, we will be spiritually destitute in what makes us human. Then to damage this sacred community is to reduce the chances of humanity surviving. [1]

In our increasingly deforested and materially driven world, the healing concepts of restoration, repair, and rehabilitation have an emotional appeal not capitalized on. [9] These three Rs are more than planting trees or technical restoration. If we can imbue such activities with sacredness, we will help nature take care of herself through the active and spiritual involvement of humankind. While sustainable development, livelihood security, and poverty reduction are key goals, we must not forget our links with and dependency on nature. These are the goals to heal the earth, or else nature will take care of itself in ways that we may not like, including the increased ferocity of natural events (floods, droughts, tornadoes, hurricanes) that we now see. [37]

We are trustees of nature, her sacred trees, and her sacred groves. We hold nature in trust for future generations. Rachel Carson presented the deepest lesson that emerged from a lifetime of natural observation. *The world does not belong to us. We belong to the world.* [25] To become responsible stewards, we must transcend our differences, whether within or between different religious groups, between religion and conservation, or between conservation and development. This calls for greater tolerance for other people's views about trees and sacred sites. Sacred trees and groves are universal, and they transcend nationality, race, and religion.

It is clear conservation and religion need to promote the respect and importance of sacred trees and groves. We increasingly recognize the sacredness of nature and trees. There is greater awareness, and people are starting to take responsible action. But humankind needs to increase its resolve if we are to be responsible stewards and trustees of Earth's valuable natural heritage. In one form or other, nature will take care of itself. We need to pray humanity will take its responsibility as stewards.

Trees are at the core of the environmental narrative. They are critical to solving many of the challenges the world faces. Trees are important for ecological, social, economic, moral, and religious reasons. The future of humankind and of Mother Earth is linked with trees. [44] Trees have a seeming ageless spirituality. For us, trees and forests are places of peace, silence, and beauty—qualities that we so need in our increasingly stress-filled world. If all life on Earth is sacred, we must not give up on efforts to conserve such life. But we ought to recognize how much is at stake—the health of humanity and of future generations. [48] In doing so, we must express gratitude for all nature is and provides us with. The sacredness of nature is more than use. It is about all the sacred trees and groves we know of, and it is also about the trees we have made sacred. Gratitude comes from the heart. To acknowledge the gifts that nature and sacred trees offer is to acknowledge an obligation to the giver—nature and God in this case. We acknowledge that interdependence. [23]

Brian Swimme thinks one of the most exciting things we're learning is about how the world works and how it resembles pictures painted by indigenous peoples and ancient religions. [39] The empirical, scientific way of knowing how the universe works, as Brian Swimme puts it, "is simply a new way, one that is powerful and wonderful, but that corroborates much traditional understanding in often surprising ways." One example Brian Swimme cites is what he calls "the third great modern science: the realization that the Earth's system is itself self-organizing or self-regulating. And one easy way to capture this is to simply say the Earth is alive. But it's alive in the sense that it actually organizes itself so that the complexity of its life forms might continue." Ancient and traditional cultures long taught that Earth is alive. Brian Swimme goes on to say, "Intuitively, this was something understood by indigenous peoples for about the last 50,000 years. Four hundred years of science have enabled us to begin to approach this intuitive truth from an empirical way. We have the opportunity for a stronger understanding of the self-regulatory or living nature of Earth." Brian Swimme believes this fundamental change in how science views the world has far-reaching effects on culture. [39] He says, "We begin to see ourselves not just as individuals on planet Earth, but rather as sensing creatures that live within the organized life of Earth. We're part of a whole. And this perspective is, I think, very different from what we've been used to in modern industrial culture."

There are increasing numbers of people reconnecting with nature and rediscovering nature's spiritual energy. This is being encompassed by the modern spiritual movement. [51] Yet many sacred trees and groves still remain threatened because of (a) conversion for development and changed use, (b) degradation through negligence or excessive visitation (c) vandalism (e.g., cutting branches), and (d) road works and buildings. [51] Most countries lack strong legal support to conserve and protect sacred trees and groves. So conserving these sites is the responsibility of the people and communities who hold them sacred. But this may not be enough if people cannot defend their rights.

We need to overcome the nature-culture divide in institutions and policy to offer space for sacred groves to flourish. Conserving sacred groves can be a common goal for the custodians, religious leaders, and conservationists. It means we must work together as individuals, families, villages, and nations to care for Mother Earth. We need to be instruments of God in caring for our sacred earth. We all possess talents to redress the damage caused by the human abuse of God's creation. [26]

Custodians and local communities manage sacred trees and groves. They know the material and spiritual aspects of conservation. If their rights and responsibilities are better recognized and respected, they will become better conservationists who can defend their rights and responsibilities in a manner that respects human dignity. This supports how important spirituality is and how it contributes to conservation.

Our role is to deepen our consciousness so we resonate with Mother Earth and establish a civilization which is culturally diverse and locally vibrant so as to enable human life to flourish. [39] Sacred nature, sacred trees, and sacred groves are portals to a deeper awareness of our responsibility to Mother Earth, God, and ourselves. Will sacred nature help us better know who we are and agree on what we want to be? Sacred trees and groves illustrate sound advice from Wendell Berry. [2]

   a) Respect the way nature cares for the land. These ways were studied by early agricultural and land scientists and those working with indigenous forests.
   b) Learn from and build on traditional systems of land use, ecosystems, and forest management. They respected nature and embraced important natural processes.

c) Small is beautiful, and size depends on land. Small-scale land management is a precious attribute.
d) Learn from land users and farmers who still practice good land use, organic farming, landscape-based approaches and pastoralism.
e) Be more inclusive and respectful of some of these views and approaches in our local stewardship and respect for sacred nature.
f) Understand the importance of kindness, neighborliness, community, and love in our quest to conserve our land, sacred trees, and groves.

David Suzuki said, "I hope my grandchildren will never look at me and tell me Grandpa, you could have done more for us. If we adults fail to prioritize the environment, our children and their children will not have any hope of experiencing the abundance and diversity of life's creatures that existed when we were still young." [38] Many sacred trees and groves have existed for hundreds and thousands of years. Some ancient sacred trees and groves predate religious beliefs and the cultures of the people living in and around them. Most predate the formal the protected area movement. We can learn from these sentinels of bygone ages. Such areas contribute to our spiritual and material sustenance and development. They are an important source of biodiversity and can be a basis for restoration to promote connectivity. In addition, they can be an important means to convene for greater tolerance, conflict resolution, and peace. They offer us a locale and provide examples of how we can cope with nature deficit disorder in our education systems and urban landscapes. This is why we need to recognize and respect how important sacred trees and sacred groves are irrespective of our race, color, creed, or nationality. To conclude, I leave you with the poem Trees by Joyce Kilmer (1886–1918), [12] which summarizes much of the essence of the book (see box 35).

Box 35: Trees by Joyce Kilmer

I think that I shall never see
A poem lovely as a tree.
A tree whose hungry mouth is pressed
Against the Earth's sweet flowing breast;
A tree that looks at God all day,
And lifts her leafy arms to pray;
A tree that may in Summer wear
A nest of robins in her hair;
Upon whose bosom snow has lain;
Who intimately lives with rain.
Poems are made by fools like me,
But only God can make a tree.

Sources of Information and References by Chapter

Chapter 1

(1). Adams, C. (2012). Games People Play. Resurgence 273:34-35.
(2). Adams, M. (2014). *The Wisdom of Trees*. London: Head of Zeus Ltd.
(3). Aitkens, A. (2015). Only Connect: Joining the Dots for the Future We Want. *Resurgence & Ecologist* 289:30-33.
(4). Attenborough, D. (2018). Quotation. *Resurgence & Ecologist* 306:25.
(5). Barrow, E. (2010). Falling between the Cracks of Conservation and Religion: The Role of Stewardship for Sacred trees and Groves. In *Sacred Natural Sites: Conserving Nature and Culture*, edited by B. Verschuuren, R. Wild and J. McNeely. London: Earthscan.
(6). ———. (2015). The Importance of Trees and Forests for Faith Based Groups and Spiritual Traditions across the Globe. In *Proceedings of the Second International Forum of the Qur'anic Botanic Garden: Islamic Perspectives on Ecosystem Management*, edited by P. Wit, M. Hassona and F. Al-Khalaifi. Doha Qatar: Quar'anic Botanic Garden and IUCN Commission on Ecosystem Management.
(7). Bernbaum, E. (1997). *Sacred Mountains of the World*. Berkley, CA: University California Press.
(8). ———. (2010). Sacred Mountains and Global Changes: Impacts and Responses. In *Sacred Natural Sites - Conserving Nature and Culture*, edited by B. Verschuuren, R. Wild, J. McNeely and G. Oviedo. London: Earthscan.
(9). ———. (2016). Sacred Mountains in Asia: Themese and Implications for Protected Areas. In *Asian Sacred Natural Sites: Philosiphy and Practise in Protected Areas and Conservartion*, edited by B. Verschuuren and N. Furuta. London: Earthscan.
(10). Berry, T. (1988). *The Dream of the Earth*. San Francisco: Sierra Club Books.

(11).   ———. (2007). Interdependence. Resurgence 241:21.
(12).   ———. (2009). *The Sacred Universe: Earth, Spirituality, and Religion in the Twenty-first Century*. New York: Columbia University Press.
(13).   Berry, T., and T. Clarke. (1991). *Befriending the Earth: A Theology of Reconciliation between Human and the Earth*. Connecticut: Twenty-Third Publications.
(14).   Berry, W. (2015). *Our Only World - Ten Essays*. Berkeley: Counterpoint Press.
(15).   Bouchardon, P. (1998). *The Healing Energies of Trees*. London: Gaia Books.
(16).   Burch, W. Jr. (1999). Gods of the Forest - Myth and ritual in Community Forestry. In *Cultural and Spiritual Values of Biodiversity—A Complementary Contribution to the Global Biodiversity Assessment*, edited by D. Posey. London and Nairobi: Intermediate Technology and UNEP.
(17).   Calma, G. (2006). The Cultural and Natural Landscape of Uluru-Kata Tjuta National Park. In *Conserving Cultural and Biological Diversity: The Role of Sacred Natural Sites and Cultural Landscapes. Proc. Tokyo Symposium*, edited by T. Schaaf and C. Lee. Paris, France: UNESCO.
(18).   Capra, F. (1982). *The Turning Point: Science, Society, and the Rising Culture*. New York: Simon and Schuster.
(19).   ———. (1999). Reconnecting with the Web of Life: Deep Ecology, Ethics and Ecological Literacy. In *Cultural and Spiritual Values of Biodiversity - a Complementary Contribution to the Global Biodiversity Assessement*, edited by D. Posey. London and Nairobi: Intermediate Technology and UNEP.
(20).   ———. (2018). Science, Spirituality and Religion. Resurgence & Ecologist 310:22–25.
(21).   Capra, F., and P. Luisi. (2014). The Systems View of Life. Resurgence & Ecologist 284:56–57.
(22).   Chesterton, G. and A. Regis. (2012). *Saint Thomas Aquinas - the Dumb Ox*: Create Space Independent Publishing Platform.
(23).   Chief Seattle. (1854). Brother Eagle, Sister Sky (speech in 1854). London: Puffin.
(24).   Chopra, D. (2009). Quantum Entanglement. Resurgence 256:10–13.
(25).   Clarke, J. (1993). *Nature in Question - An Anthology of Ideas and Arguments*. London: Earthscan.
(26).   Collins. (1993). *Collins Concise English Dictionary*. Glasgow: Harper Collins.
(27).   Daly, H. (2014). Why We Need a Steady-State Economy. Resurgence and Ecologist 287:24–28.
(28).   Eisenstein, C. (2013). Latent Healing. *Rural Sociology*. (279):36–38.
(29).   El-Naggar, Z. (2015). Conservation of the Environment in Islam. In *Proceedings of the Second International Forum of the Qur'anic Botanic Garden: Islamic Perspectives on Ecosystem Management*. Edt. P. Wit, M. Hassona

(30). and F. Al-Khalaifi. Doha, Qatar: Quar'anic Botanic Garden, and IUCN Commission on Ecosystem Management.

(30). Erdelen, W. (2003). Preface. In *The Importance of Sacred Natural Sites for Biodiversity Conservation. Proc. Int. Workshop on the Importance of Sacred Natural Sites for Biodiversity conservation in Kunming and Xishuangbanna Biosphere Reserve, People's Republic of China*, edited by C. Lee and T. Schaaf. Paris: UNESCO.

(31). Evans, J. (2014). *God's Trees: Trees, Forests and Wood in the Bible*. Leominster, England: One Day Publications.

(32). Evans, S.(1999). Sherpa Protection of Mt. Everest Region in Nepal. In *Cultural and Spiritual Values of Biodiversity - A Complementary Contribution to the Global Biodiversity Assessment*, edited by D. Posey. London and Nairobi: Intermediate Technology and UNEP.

(33). FAO (1997). *State of the World's Forests 1997*. Rome, Italy: Food and Agriculture Organziation of the United Nations.

(34). Follmi, D. and O. Follmi (2003). *Buddhist Offerings 365 Days*. London: Thames and Hudson Ltd.

(35). Fox, M. (2007). Thomas Berry—A New Moses? Resurgence 244:52–53.

(36). Garfinkel, S. (2014). Stephen Grosz. Resurgence and Ecologist 282:18.

(37). Girardet, H. (1989). Forests on Fire. Resurgence 133:8–10.

(38). Golliher, J. (1999). Ethical, Moral and Religous Concerns. In *Cultural and Spiritual Values of Biodiversity - a Complementary Contribution to the Global Biodiversity Assesment*, edited by D. Posey. London and Nairobi: Intermediate Technology and UNEP.

(39). Goodland, R. (1990). Tropical Moist Forest Deforestation: Ethics and Solutions. In *Tropical Forests and the Conservation of Species*, edited by P. Scientiarum. Rome: Casina Pion IV, 00120 Citta del Vaticano.

(40). Griffiths, B. (1989). Christianity in the Light of the East. London: Hibbert Trust.

(41). Halifax, J., and M. Peale (1999). Interbeing: Precepts and Practices of an Applied Ecology. In *Cultural and Spiritual Values of Biodiversity—A Complementary Contribution to the Global Biodiversity Assesement*, edited by D.Posey. London and Nariobi: Intermediate Technology and UNEP.

(42). Hamilton, L. (1993). *Ethics, Religion and Biodiversity*. Cambridge, UK: White Horse Press.

(43). ———. (1998). Forest and Tree Conservation through Metaphysical Constraints. In *Natural Sacred Sites. Cultural Diversity and Biological Diversity. Proc. Int. Symp., Paris 1998*, edited by UNESCO. Paris: UNESCO.

(44). Harding, S. (2006). Animate Earth. Resurgence 236:55–57.

(45). ———. (2012). A Film for our time. Resurgence 270:66.

(46). Harmon, D., and A. Putney, eds. (2003). *The Full Value of Parks—From Economics to the Intangible.* New York: Rowman and Littlefield.
(47). Hennessy, V. (2015). Review of "The Wisdom of Trees" by Max Adams. *Resurgence and Ecologist* 289:64.
(48). Higgins, P. (2009). Restorative Justice. Resurgence 253:26–27.
(49). ———. (2012). What will our Legacy Be? Resurgence 270:30.
(50). Hosken, L. (2009). Potent Places. Resurgence 255:19–20.
(51). His Royal Highness The Prince of Wales. (2007). A Sense of Harmony. Resurgence 242:14–16.
(52). ———. (2011). Islam and the Environment. Resurgence 265:22–25.
(53). ———. (2013). Forword to T. Juniper's book "What has Nature ever Done for Us?". Resurgence and Ecologist 278:36–39.
(54). Jones, S., ed. (1999). *Simply Living: The Spirit of the Indigenous People.* California: New World Library.
(55). Juniper, T. (2004). Inspiring Change. 227:28–31.
(56). Kolmes, S. (1999). Mental Cartography in a Time of Environmental Crisis. In *All Creation is Groaning: An Interdisciplinary Vision for Life in a Sacred Universe*, edited by C. Dempsey and R. A. Butkus. Minnesota: Liturgical Press.
(57). Krishnamurti, J. (1991). *Nature and the Environment.* San Francisco: Harper.
(58). Kumar, S. (2005). Spiritual Imperative - Elegant Simplicity is the Way to Discover Spirituality. Resurgence 229:6–12.
(59). ———. (2007). Ecology and Economy. Resurgence 244:1.
(60). ———. (2009). Interview with Wangari Mathai: Trees are the Answer. Resurgence 257:30–31.
(61). ———. (2009). Nature Crunch. Resurgence 252:2–3.
(62). ———. (2009). Quantum Leap. Resurgence 256:3.
(63). ———. (2011). A New Paradigm. Resurgence 268:1.
(64). ———. (2014). Benevolent Universe. Resurgence and Ecologist 282:30–33.
(65). ———. (2014). New Year, New Philosophy. Resurgence and Ecologist 282:1.
(66). ———. (2016). Making Peace with the Planet. Resurgence and Ecologist 297:40–41.
(67). Lama-Karma, Venerable. (2012). Epilogue: Spirituality and Religion: Spiritualism and Ancient Wisdom from a Buddhist Perspective. In *Sacred Species and Sites: Advances in Biocultural Conservation*, edited by G. Pungetti, G. Oviedo and D. Hooke. Cambridge England: Cambridge University Press.
(68). Lovelock, J. (2005). At War with the Earth. Resurgence 228:6–7.
(69). Lovelock, J. (2005). *Gaia: Medicine for an Ailing Planet.* London: Gaia Books.
(70). ———. (2009). *The Vanishing Face of Gaia: A Final Warning.* London: Penguin Books.
(71). Mabey, R. (2006). Bioluxuriance. Resurgence 238:26–27.

(72). Maitreyabandhu. (2014). Poetry and Animism. Resurgence and Ecologist 282:52–53.
(73). Mallarach, J. M. (2009). The Eye of Reverence. Resurgence 255:30–31.
(74). ———. (2015). Management of Landscapes of Spiritual Importance for Different Faith Groups: Best Practises and Sources of Inspirtatio. In *Proceeedings of the Second International Forum of the Qur'anic Botanic Garden: Islamic Perspectives on Ecosystem Management*, edited by P. Wit, M. Hassona and F. Al-Khalaifi. Doha Qatar: The Qur'anic Botanic Garden and IUCN Commission on Ecosystem Management.
(75). Marshall, P. (1992). *Nature's Web: An Exploration of Ecological Thinking*. London: Simon and Schuster.
(76). Massingham, H. (2003). *The Tree of Life*. Oxfordshire: Jon Carpenter Publishing.
(77). Mathai, W. (2004). The Cracked Mirror. Resurgence 227:21–23.
(78). McDonagh, S. (1986). *To Care for the Earth - a Call to a New Theology*. London: Cassell Publishing.
(79). McIvor, A., and G. Pungetti. (2012). The Conservation Status of Sacred Species: a Preliminary Study. In *Sacred Species and Sites: Advances in Biocultural Conservation*, edited by G. Pungetti, G. Oviedo and D. Hooke. Cambridge England: Cambridge University Press.
(80). Musselman, L. (2015). Conservation Values and Ecologijcal Ethics in the Holy Bible. In *Proceedings of the Second International Forum of the Qur'anic Botanic Gardens: Islamic Perspectives on Ecosystem Management*, edited by P. Wit, M. Hassona and F. Al-Khalaifi. Doha, Qatar: Qur'anic Botanic Garden and IUCN Commission on Ecosystem Management.
(81). Nasr, S. (1998). The Spiritual and Relgous Dimensions of the Environmental Crisis. London: Temenos Academy.
(82). ———. (2000). The Spiritual and Relgous Dimensions of the Environmental Crisis. *The Ecologist* 30 (1):18–20.
(83). National Geographic Society. (2008). *Sacred Places of a Lifetime: 500 of the World's Most Peaceful and Powerful Destinations*. Washington DC: National Geographic Society.
(84). Naydler, J. (2013). Perennial Wisdom. *Rural Sociology*. (279):46–47.
(85). Ni, G. (1994). Hakka "Fenhshui Forests": Their Preservation and Value. *Forestry and Society Newsletter* 2 (2):6.
(86). Nyangila, J. (2012). Sacred Species of Kenyan Sacred Sites. In *Sacred Species and Sites: Advances in Biocultural Conservation*, edited by G. Pungetti, G. Oviedo and D. Hooke. Cambridge England: Cambridge University Press.
(87). O'Donoghue, J. (1998). *Eternal Echoes in Exploring our Hunger to Belong*. Great Britain: Bantam.

(88). Odum, E. (1963). *Ecology, Modern Biology Series*. New York: Holt, Rinehart and Winston.
(89). Oliver, J. (2005). Art of the Possible. Resurgence 228:20–21.
(90). Oreskes, N. (2015). Introduction. In *Encyclical on Climate Change: On Care for our Common Home*, Pope Francis. New York: Melville House Publishing
(91). Orr, D. (2011). *Hope Is an Imperative—The Essential David Orr*. Washington DC: Island Press.
(92). Oviedo, G. (2012). Spiritual Values and Conservation. In *Sacred Species and Sites: Advances in Biocultural Conservation*, edited by G. Pungetti, G. Oviedo and D. Hooke. Cambridge England: Cambridge University Press.
(93). ———. (2015). Reflections on Cultural and Spiritual Values, Traditions and Customs in Conservation. In *Proceedings of the Second International Forum of the Qur'anic Botanic Garden: Islamic Perspectives on Ecosystem Management*, edited by P. Wit, M. Hassona and F. Al-Khalaifi. Doha, Qatar: Qur'anic Botanic Garden and IUCN Commission on Ecosystem Management.
(94). Pandey, A., R. Kotru, and N. Pradhan. (2016). Kailash Sacred Landscape: Bridging Cultural Heritate, Conservation and Development through a Transboundary Landscape Approach. In *Asian Sacred Natural Sites: Philosophy and Practise in Protected Areas and Conservarion*, edited by B. Verschuuren and N. Furuta. London: Earthscan.
(95). Phillips, M. (2012). Silent Spring. Resurgence 270:28–29.
(96). Pope Francis. (2015). *Encyclical on Climate Change and Inequality: On Care for our Common Home*. New York: Melville House Publishing.
(97). Porritt, J. (2015). Climate - It Is a Moral Issue. Resurgence and Ecologist 291:24–27.
(98). Posey, D., ed. (1999). *Cultural and Spiritual Values of Biodiversity*. London: Intermediate Technology Publications and UNEP.
(99). Pretty, J. (2015). The Edge of Extinction: Stories from the Swamps. *Resurgence* 291:18–21.
(100). Pungetti, G. (2012). Sacred Species and Sites: Dichotomies, Concepts and New Directions in Biocultural Diversity Conservation. In *Sacred Species and Sites: Advance in Biocultural Conservation*, edited by G. Pungetti, G. Oviedo and D. Hooke. Cambridge England: Cambridge University Press.
(101). Pungetti, G., and F. Cinquepalmi. (2012). Sacred Sites, Sacred Landscapes and Biocultural Diversity: Applying the Principles. In *Sacred Species and Sites: Advances in Biocultural Conservation*, edited by G. Pungetti, G. Oviedo and D. Hooke. Cambridge England: Cambridge University Press.
(102). Reynolds, F. (2011). Rethinking Conservation. Resurgence 266:52–53.
(103). Rival, L. (2014). Review of book "The Falling Sky: Words of a Yanonami Shaman" by Davi Kopenawa and Bruce Albert. Resurgence and Ecologist 284:60.

(104). Robins, N. (2010). The Ecology of Growth. Resurgence 261:28–29.
(105). Rossi, V. (2000). Sacred Cosmology in the Christian Tradition. *The Ecologist* 30 (1):35–39.
(106). Roth, S. (2000). The Cosmic Vision of Hildegard of Bingen. *The Ecologist* 30 (1):40–42.
(107). Rowson, J. (2013). The Brains behind Spirituality. *J. Royal Society of Arts* Summer:40-43.
(108). ———. (2014). Spiritualize: Revitalizing Spirituality to Address 21st Century Challenges. London: RSA Action and Research Center.
(109). Rueckert, W. (1996). Literature and Ecology: An Experiment in Ecocriticism. In *The Ecocriticism Reader: Landmarks in Literary Ecology*, edited by Glotfelty and Fromm. Athens, Georgia: University Georgia Press.
(110). Schaaf, T. (2003). UNESCO's Experience with the Protection of Sacred Natural Sites for Biodiversity Conservation. In *The Importance of Sacred Natural Sites for Biodiversity Conservation. Proc. Int. Workshop on the Importance of Sacred Natural Sites for Biodiversity conservation in Kunming and Xishuangbanna Biosphere Reserve, People's Republic of China*, edited by C. Lee and T. Schaaf. Paris: UNESCO.
(111). Shengji, P. (2003). Opening Address. In *The Importance of Sacred Natural Sites for Biodiversity Conservation. Proc. Int. Workshop on the Importance of Sacred Natural Sites for Biodiversity conservation in Kunming and Xishuangbanna Biosphere Reserve, People's Republic of China*. Paris: UNESCO.
(112). Sheridan, M. (2008). The Dynamics of African Sacred Groves. In *African Sacred Groves: Ecological Dynamics and Social Change*, edited by M. Sheridan and C. Nyamweru. Oxford: James Currey.
(113). Singh, R., and P. Rana. (2016). Indian Sacred Natural Sites: Ancient Traditions of Reverence and Conservation Explained from a Hindu Perspective. In *Asian Sacred Natural Sites: Philisiphy and Practice in Protected Areas and Conservation*, edited by B. Verschuuren and N. Furuta. London: Routledge.
(114). Skelly, I. (2011). The Making of Harmony. *Resurgence* 264:26–29.
(115). Snyder, G. (2006). Writers and the War Against Nature. *Resurgence* 239:12–17.
(116). Spoon, J. (2010). Tourism meets the Sacred: Khumbu Sherpa Place-based Spiritul Values in Sagarmatha (Mount Everest) National Park and Buffer Zone, Nepal. In *Sacred Natural Sites: Conserving Nature and Culture*, edited by B. Verschuuren, R. Wild, J. McNeely and G. Oviedo. London: Earthscan.
(117). Stowe, J. (2003). *The Findhorn Book of Connecting with Nature*. Edinburgh: Findhorn Press.
(118). Suzuki, D., and H. Dressel. (1999). *From Naked Ape to Superspecies: A Personal Perspective on Humanity and the Global Eco-crisis*. Toronto: Stoddart.
(119). Swimme, B. and M. Tucker. (2011). *Journey of the Universe*. New Haven: Yale University Press.

(120). Teilhard de Chardin, P. (1969). *Human Energy*. New York: Helen and Kurt Wolff Books.
(121). Tickell, O. (2015). A Crisis this Big Changes Everything. *Resurgence and Ecologist* 288:16–19.
(122). Tolle, E. (2001). *The Power of Now*. London: Hodder and Stoughton.
(123). Tolle, E. (2005). *A New Earth: Awakening to Your Life's Purpose*. New York: Plume.
(124). Tudge, C. (2006). *The Secret Life of Trees: How They Live and Why They Matter*. London: Penguin Books.
(125). ———. (2008). Natural Religion - Where Science Meets Spirituality. Resurgence 251:10–13.
(126). Tzu, Lao. (2009). *Taoteching—Selected Commentary by Red Pine*. Translated by R. Pine. Washington: Copper Canyon Press.
(127). Verschuuren, B. (2012). Integrating Cultural Values in Nature Conservation: Perceptions of Culturally Significant Sites and Species in Adaptive Management. In *Sacred Species and Sites: Advances in Biocultural Conservation*, edited by G. Pungetti, G. Oviedo and D. Hooke. Cambridge England: Cambridge University Press.
(128). ———. (2016). Re-awakening the Power of Place: Ancient Philisophy and Practice with Relevance for Protected Areas and Conservation in Asia. In *Asian Sacred Natural Sites: Philosophy and Practice in Protected Areas and Conservation*, edited by B. Verschuuren and N. Furuta. London: Routledge.
(129). Verschuuren, B., R. Wild, J. McNeely, and G. Oviedo. (2010). Introduction: Sacred Natural Sites the Foundations for Conservation. In *Sacred Natural Sites - Conserving Nature and Culture*, edited by B. Verschuuren, R. Wild, J. McNeely and G. Oviedo. London: Earthscan.
(130). White, L. (1967). The Historical Roots of our Ecological Crisis. *Science* 155:1,203–7.
(131). Wild, R., and C. McLeod. (2008). Sacred Natural Sites: Guidelines for Protected Area Managers. In *Sacred Natural Sites: Guidelines for Protected Area Managers*, edited by R. Wild and C. McLeod. Gland, Switzerland: IUCN.
(132). Williams, F. (2017). *The Nature Fix: Why Nature Makes Us Happier, Healthier, and More Creative*. New York: W. W. Norton.
(133). Williams, R. (2004). Gift of God. Resurgence 227:6–10.
(134). Wilson, E. (1992). *The Diversity of Life*. London: Penguin Book.
(135). ———. (2006). *The Creation: An Appeal to Save Life on Earth*. New York: Norton and Co.
(136). ———. (2010). Sustaining Life. Resurgence 261:10–14.
(137). ———. (2014). *The Meaning of Human Existence*. London: W. W. Norton and Co. Ltd.

(138). Zucchelli, C. (2009). *Trees of Inspiration: Sacred Trees and Bushes of Ireland.* Cork Ireland: Collins Press.

Chapter 2

(1). Adams, M. (2014). The Wisdom of Trees. Head of Zeus Ltd., London.
(2). Airfield Trust, (2000) Airfield Tree Trail. Airfield Trust, Dublin, p. 12.
(3). Altman, N. (2000). Sacred Trees—Spirituality, Wisdom and Well-Being. Sterling Publishing Co., New York.
(4). Anderson, M. (2010). Food Rights and Wrongs. Resurgence 259, 25–27.
(5). Barrow, E., (2010). Falling between the Cracks of Conservation and Religion: The Role of Stewardship for Sacred trees and Groves, in: Verschuuren, B., Wild, R., McNeely, J. (Eds.), Sacred Natural Sites: Conserving Nature and Culture. Earthscan, London, pp. 42–52.
(6). Battersby, E., (2005). Holy and Magical, Irish Times, Dublin.
(7). Berry, T. (1988). The Dream of the Earth. Sierra Club Books, San Francisco.
(8). Berry, T., Clarke, T. (1991). Befriending the Earth: A Theology of Reconciliation between Human and the Earth. Twenty-Third Publications, Connecticut.
(9). Black-Elk, W., Lyon, W. (1991). Black Elk—The Sacred Ways of a Lakota. Harper, San Francisco.
(10). Bolton, B. (1975). The Secret Life of Plants. Sphere, London.
(11). Bouchardon, P. (1998). The Healing energies of Trees. Gaia Books, London.
(12). Byron, L., (1909). Manfred Vol XVIII, Act I, Scene I lines 11–13. Harvard Classics, New York.
(13). Cashford, J. (1989). The Tree of Life. Resurgence 133, 27–31.
(14). Clarke, J. (1993). Nature in Question - An Anthology of Ideas and Arguments. Earthscan, London.
(15). Cooke, R. (1974). The Tree of Life. Thames and Hudson, New York.
(16). Cooper, D. (2018). Mystery and the Way of the Garden. Resurgence and Ecologist 306, 20–24.
(17). Dalton, S., and J. Bailey (1986). The Secret Life of an Oakwood: A Photographic Journey. Century Hutchinson Ltd., London.
(18). di Sospiro, G. (2001). The Story of Yew. Findhorn Pres, Forres, Scotland.
(19). Evans, J. (2014). God's Trees: Trees, Forests and Wood in the Bible. One Day Publications, Leominster, England.
(20). Feehan, J., (2000). The Spirit of Trees—An Exploration of our Natural and Cultural Links with Trees from Pre-Celtic Times to our Present Day. Releafing Ireland, Millennium Supplement, Dublin, pp. 1–7.
(21). Fulwood, S. (1989). High Life. Resurgence 133, 22–23.

(22). Gadgil, M. (1987). Diversity: Cultural and Biological. Trends in Ecology and Evolution 2, 369–73.
(23). Giono, J. (1989). Tree Man. Resurgence 133, 24-25.
(24). Goldsmith, E. (2000). Religion at the Millennium. The Ecologist 30, 3–10.
(25). Greer, G. (2014.) Ecological Feminism. Resurgence and Ecologist 284, 40–43.
(26). Griffith, B. (2000). Return to the Center. The Ecologist 30, 9–10.
(27). Hamilton, L., (1998). Forest and Tree Conservation through Metaphysical Constraints, in: UNESCO (Ed.), Natural Sacred Sites. Cultural Diversity and Biological Diversity. Proc. Int. Symp., Paris 1998. UNESCO, Paris, p. 18.
(28). Hareuveni, N. (1980). Nature in our Biblical Heritage. Neot Kedumin, Kiryatone, Israel.
(29). Hulmes, D., (2009). Sacred Trees of Norway and Sweden, Henrik Ibsen: The Birth of "Friluftsliv" a 150 Year International Dialogue Conferences Jubilee Celebration. North Troendelag University College, Levanger, Norway, p. 35.
(30). Janick, J. (2007.) Fruits of the Bible. Hortcultural Science 42, 1,072–76.
(31). Kelly, F. (1999) .Trees in Early Ireland. J. Soc. Irish Foresters 56, 39–57.
(32). Khan, K., (1999). An Islamic Perspective on the Environment, in: Dempsey, C., Butkus, R. (eds.), All Creation is Groaning: An Interdisciplinary Vision for Life in a Sacred Universe. Liturgical Press, Minnesota, pp. 46-57.
(33). Kornevall, A. (2013). Trees in Schools. Resurgence and Ecologist 281, 26–27.
(34). Kumar, S. (2005). Spiritual Imperative—Elegant Simplicity is the Way to Discover Spirituality. Resurgence 229, 6–12.
(35). Lewington, A., and E. Parker (1999). Ancient Trees: Trees that Live for 1000 Years. Collins and Brown, London.
(36). Mac Coitir, N. (2003). Irish Trees—Myths, Legends and Folklore. The Collins Press, Cork.
(37). Matthiessen, P., and E. Porter (1972.) The Tree Where Man was Born, the African Experience. Collins, London.
(38). Morton, A. (2004). Tree Heritage of Britain and Ireland—A Guide to the Famous Trees of Britan and Ireland. Airlife Publishing, England.
(39). Mosse, K., (2011). Why the Yew Lives so Long, in: Chevalier, T., Prisser, S. (Eds.), Why Willows Weep—Contemporary Tales from the Woods. The Woodland Trust, England, pp. 117–21.
(40). Murray L., and C. Murray (1988). The Celtic Tree Oracle—A System of Divination. St. Martins Press, New York.
(41). Musselman, L. (2003). Trees in the Koran and the Bible. Unasylva 213, 45–52.
(42). Nasr, S. (1998). The Spiritual and Religous Dimensions of the Environmental Crisis. Temenos Academy, London.

(43). Nasr, S. (2000). The Spiritual and Religous Dimensions of the Environmental Crisis. The Ecologist 30, 18–20.

(44). Nelson, C., and W. Walsh (1993). Trees of Ireland: Native and Naturalized. Lilliput Press, Dublin.

(45). Norland, B. (2009). Apples. Resurgence 256, 50.

(46). Orr, D. (2011). Hope Is an Imperative—The Essential David Orr. Island Press, Washington DC.

(47). Pakenham, T. (2001). Meetings with Remarkable Trees. Cassell Paperbacks, London.

(48). Palmer, M. (2013). The Quiet Revolution. Resurgence and Ecologist 277, 44–45.

(49). Perth and Kinross Heritage Trust (2007). Fortingall—Kirk and Village. Perth and Kinross Heritage Trust, Scotland.

(50). Pope Francis (2015). Encyclical on Climate Change and Inequality: On Care for Our Common Home. Melville House Publishing, New York.

(51). Porteus, A. (1996). The Lore of the Forest: Myths and Legends. Senate, London.

(52). Rebbe, L., Schneeron, M., and T. Tauber (2004). The Human Tree: https://www.chabad.org/library/article_cdo/aid/2775/jewish/The-Human-Tree.htm.

(53). Roth, S. (2000). The Tree of Life. The Ecologist 30, 11.

(54). Ruthven, M. (2017). A Faith and the Power of Nature. Resurgence and Ecologist 305, 26–29.

(55). Schumacher, E, (1993). The Age of Plenty—A Christian View, in: Daly, H., Townsend, K. (eds.), Valuing the Earth—Economics, Ecology, Ethics. MIT Press, Massachusetts, pp. 159–72.

(56). Shanahan, M. (2016). Ladders to Heaven: How Fig Trees Shaped our History, Fed Our Imaginations, and Can Enrich Our Future. Unbound, London.

(57). Sheridan, M. (2008). The Dynamics of African Sacred Groves, in: Sheridan, M., Nyamweru, C. (eds.), African Sacred Groves: Ecological Dynamics and Social Change. James Currey, Oxford, pp. 9–41.

(58). Sholto Douglas, J., and R. Hart (1978) Forest Farming: Towards a Solution to Problems of World Hunger and Conservation. Rodale Press, USA.

(59). Smith, R., (2012). The Bear Cult among the Different Ethnic Groups of Russia (Sacred Russian Bear), in: Pungetti, G., Oviedo, G., Hooke, D. (dds.), Sacred Species and Sites: Advances in Biocultural Conservation. Cambridge University Press, Cambridge England, pp. 278–90.

(60). Snyder, G. (2006). Writers and the War Against Nature. Resurgence 239, 12–17.

(61). Tzu, L. (2009). Taoteching - Selected Commentary by Red Pine. Copper Canyon Press, Washington.

(62). Verschuuren, B., Wild. R., McNeely. J.,and G. Oviedo (2010). Introduction: Sacred Natural Sites the Foundations for Conservation, in: Verschuuren, B., Wild, R., McNeely, J., Oviedo, G. (Eds.), Sacred Natural Sites—Conserving Nature and Culture. Earthscan, London, pp. 1–13.

(63). Waisel, Y., and A. Alon, A. (1980). Trees of the Land of Israel. Division of Ecology, Tel Aviv.

(64). Watson, R. (2007). The African Baobab. Struik, Cape Town.

(65). Wood, P., (1990). The Tree—A Celebration of Our Living Skyline. David and Chalres, London, p. 128.

(66). Zucchelli, C. (2009). Trees of Inspiration: Sacred Trees and Bushes of Ireland. Collins Press, Cork Ireland.

Chapter 3

(1). Adams, M. (2014). The Wisdom of Trees. Head of Zeus Ltd., London.

(2). Batanouny, K. (1986). Plants in the Hadith of the Prophet. Directorate of Revival of Islamic Heritage, Qatar.

(3). Berry, T. (2007). Earth Community. Resurgence 244, 10–11.

(4). Bolton, B.L. (1975). The Secret Life of Plants. Sphere, London.

(5). Bouchardon, P. (1998). The Healing Energies of Trees. Gaia Books, London.

(6). Burbea, R. (2015). The Buddha and the Sacred Earth. Resurgence and Ecologist 288, 34–37.

(7). Butler, R. (2007). Review of Book "Unbowed" by Wangari Mathai. Resurgence 243, 58.

(8). Capra, F. (2017). We're All in This together. Resurgence and Ecologist 300, 32–35.

(9). Capra, F. (2018). Science, Spirituality and Religion. Resurgence and Ecologist 310, 22–25.

(10). Chiyate, H.C. (1993). Interview with Traditional Rules of Goba Tribe, Zambezi Valley, in: Lewis, D., Carter, N. (eds.), Voices from Africa—Local Perspectives on Conservation. WWF, Maryland, pp. 71–78.

(11). Chouin, G. (2008). Archaeological Perspectives on Sacred Groves in Ghana, in: Sheridan, M. J., Nyamweru, C. (eds.), African Sacred Groves: Ecological Dynamics and Social Change. James Currey, Oxford, pp. 178–94.

(12). Church of England Church Care, (2004). Provisional Guidance—Trees in Churchyards. Church of England, Canterbury, p. 8.

(13). Dafni, A., Levy, S., and E. Lev. (2005). The Ethnobotany of Christ's Thorn Jujube (*Ziziphus spina-christi*) in Israel. J. Ethnobiology and Ethnomedicine 1, 1–11.

(14). Dalglish, G. (2012).) Faith and Perseverance. Resurgence 273, 16–17.

(15). Das, P. (1997). Kailadevi Wildlife Sanctuary: Prospects for Joint Forest Management, in: Kothari, A., Vania, F., Das, P., Christopher, K., Jha, S. (eds.), Building Bridges for Conservation: Towards Joint Management of India's Protected Areas. Indian Institute of Public Adminstration, New Delhi.

(16). Encylopaedia Britannica (1997). International Version Encylopaedia Britannica CD 98. Encylopaedia Britannica Inc, Chicago.

(17). Evans, J. (2014). God's Trees: Trees, Forests and Wood in the Bible. One Day Publications, Leominster, England.

(18). Evans, S. (1999). Sherpa Protection of Mt. Everest Region in Nepal, in: Posey, D. (ed.), Cultural and Spiritual Values of Biodiversity—A Complementary Contribution to the Global Biodiversity Assessment. Intermediate Technology and UNEP, London and Nairobi, pp. 327–43.

(19). Felix and Friends (2011). Tree by Tree: Now We Children Save the World. Plant for the Planet, Germany.

(20). Franke, J. (1996). Faith in the Forest, New Internationalist, pp. 13–14.

(21). Fulwood, S. (1989). High Life. Resurgence 133, 22–23.

(22). Gadgil, M. (1987). Diversity: Cultural and Biological. Trends in Ecology and Evolution 2, 369–73.

(23). Ganjanapan, A. (2000). Local Control of Land and Forest: Cultural Dimensions of Resource Management in Northern Thailand. Regional Center for Social Science and Sustainable Development, Chiang Mai University, Chiang Mai, Thailand.

(24). Gottlieb, A. (2008). Loggers versus Spirits in the Beng Forest, Cote d'Ivoire: Competing Model, in: Sheridan, M., Nyamweru, C. (eds.), African Sacred Groves: Ecological Dynamics and Social Change. James Currey, Oxford, pp. 149–63.

(25). Hamilton, L. (1998). Forest and Tree Conservation through Metaphysical Constraints, in: UNESCO (ed.), Natural Sacred Sites. Cultural Diversity and Biological Diversity. Proc. Int. Symp., Paris 1998. UNESCO, Paris, p. 18.

(26). Hareuveni, N. (1980). Nature in our Biblical Heritage. Neot Kedumin, Kiryatone, Israel.

(27). Harmon, D., Putney, A. (2003). The Full Value of Parks—From Economics to the Intangible. Rowman and Littlefield, New York, p. 347.

(28). Hongmao, L., Zaifu, X., Youkai, X., and W. Jinxiu (2003). Conserving Plant Biodiversity through Traditional Beliefs in Xishuangbanna, Southwest China, in: Lee, C., Schaaf, T. (eds.), The Importance of Sacred Natural Sites for Biodiversity Conservation. Proc. Int. Workshop on the Importance of Sacred Natural Sites for Biodiversity conservation in Kunming and Xishuangbanna Biosphere Reserve, People's Republic of China. UNESCO, Paris, pp. 126–34.

(29). Hooke, D. (2012). The Sacred Tree in the Belief and Mythology of England, in: Pungetti, G., Oviedo, G., Hooke, D. (Eds.), Sacred Species and Sites:

Advances in Biocultural Conservation. Cambridge University Press, Cambridge England, pp. 307–21.

(30). Howarth, L. (2009). Book review "Beechcombings: The Narratives of Trees" by Richard Mabey. Resurgence 253, 70–71.

(31). His Royal Highness The Prince of Wales (2010). Facing the Future. Resurgence 258, 18–23.

(32). Huabin, H. (2003). Sacred Natural Sites in Xishuangbanna in South-Western China, in: Lee, C., Schaaf, T. (eds.), The Importance of Sacred Natural Sites for Biodiversity Conservation. Proc. Int. Workshop on the Importance of Sacred Natural Sites for Biodiversity conservation in Kunming and Xishuangbanna Biosphere Reserve, People's Republic of China. UNESCO, Paris, pp. 119–25.

(33). Hulmes, D. (2009). Sacred Trees of Norway and Sweden, Henrik Ibsen: The Birth of "Friluftsliv"—A 150 Year International Dialogue Conferences Jubilee Celebration. North Troendelag University College, Levanger, Norway, p. 35.

(34). Ingles, A. (1990). The Management of Religous Forests in Nepal, Department of Forestry. Australian National University, Canberra, Australia, p. 135.

(35). Ingles, A. (1995). Religious Beliefs and Rituals in Nepal - Their Influence on Forest Conservation, in: Halladay, P., Gilmour, D. (eds.), Conserving Biodiversity Outside Protected Areas: The Role of Traditional Agro-Ecosystems. IUCN, Gland, Switzerland and Cambridge, UK, pp. 205–24.

(36). Janick, J. (2007.) Fruits of the Bible. Hortcultural Science 42, 1,072–76.

(37). Kenya Wildlife Service, Forestry Department (1994). Kakemega Forest—The Official Guide. Kenya Indigenous Forest Conservation Program, Nairobi.

(38). Kumar, S. (2009). Economics of Place. Resurgence 253, 2–3.

(39). Kumar, S. (2013). Soil, Soul and Society. Resurgence and Ecologist 277, 38–41.

(40). Lewington, A., and E. Parker (1999). Ancient Trees: Trees that Live for 1000 Years. Collins and Brown, London.

(41). Maathai, W. (2006). Unbowed—A Memoir. William Heinemann, London.

(42). Majupuria, T. (1988). Religous and Useful Plants of Nepal and India. Botanical Survey and Herbarium, Katmandu.

(43). Mansberger, J. (1988). In Search of the Tree Spirit: Evolution of the Sacred Tree *Ficus religiosa*, in: Daragavel, J., Dixon, K., Semple, N. (eds.), Changing Tropical Forests. CRES, Australian National University, Canberra, pp. 399–411.

(44). Matthiessen, P., and E. Porter (1972). The Tree Where Man was Born, the African Experience. Collins, London.

(45). Morton, A. (2004). Tree Heritage of Britain and Ireland—A Guide to the Famous Trees of Britan and Ireland. Airlife Publishing, England.

(46). Musselman, L. (2003). Trees in the Koran and the Bible. Unasylva 213, 45–52.

(47). Natarajan, B. (1999). Traditional Knowledge, Culture and Resource Rights—The Case of Tulasi, in: Bodeker, G. (ed.), Valuing Biodiveristy for Human Health and Well-being: Traidtional Health Systems. In edit Posey D.: Cultural and Spiritual Values of Biodiversity. Intermediate Technology Publications and UNEP, London, pp. 268–70.

(48). National Geographic Society (2008). Sacred Places of a Lifetime: 500 of the World's Most Peaceful and Powerful Destinations. National Geographic Society, Washington, DC.

(49). Nyamweru, C., and M. Sheridan (2008). Introduction, in: Sheridan, M., Nyamweru, C. (eds.), African Sacred Groves: Ecological Dynamics and Social Change. James Currey, Oxford, pp. 1–8.

(50). Nyangila, J., (2012). Sacred Species of Kenyan Sacred Sites, in: Pungetti, G., Oviedo, G., Hooke, D. (eds.), Sacred Species and Sites: Advances in Biocultural Conservation. Cambridge University Press, Cambridge England, pp. 351–64.

(51). Okiria-Aketer, J. (1997). Use of Indigenous Knowledge in Tree Management among the Bagisu on Mt. Elgon. Makerere, Kampala.

(52). Pakenham, T. (2001). Meetings with Remarkable Trees. Cassell Paperbacks, London.

(53). Peng, L., Ning, W., Zhaoli, Y., P. Shengji (2003). Sacred Sites in Northwest Yunnan, China, in: Lee, C., Schaaf, T. (Eds.), The Importance of Sacred Natural Sites for Biodiversity Conservation. Proc. Int. Workshop on the Importance of Sacred Natural Sites for Biodiversity conservation in Kunming and Xishuangbanna Biosphere Reserve, People's Republic of China. UNESCO, Paris, pp. 139–50.

(54). Perrone, A. (2018). Italy, Save the Olives. New Internationalist September–October, 10–11.

(55). Pope Francis (2015). Encyclical on Climate Change and Inequality: On Care for our Common Home. Melville House Publishing, New York.

(56). Porteus, A. (1996). The Lore of the Forest: Myths and Legends. Senate, London.

(57). Pungetti, G., and S. Bhagwat (2012). Sacred Species and Biocultural Diversity: Applying the Principles, in: Pungetti, G., Oviedo, G., Hooke, D. (eds.), Sacred Species and Sites: Advances in Biocultural Conservation. Cambridge University Press, Cambridge England, pp. 367–406.

(58). Rackham, O. (1989). The Constant Spring. Resurgence 133, 11–13.

(59). Ramakrishnan, P. (1996). Conserving the Sacred: From Species to Landscapes. Nature and Resources 32, 11–19.

(60). Rebbe, L., Schneerson, M., and Y. Tauber (2004). The Human Tree: https://www.chabad.org/library/article_cdo/aid/2775/jewish/The-Human-Tree.htm.

(61). Ross, E. (2008). Palaver Trees Reconsidered in the Senegalese Landscape: Arboreal Monuments and Memorials, in: Sheridan, M., Nyamweru, C. (eds.), African Sacred Groves: Ecological Dynamics and Social Change. James Currey, Oxford, pp. 133–48.

(62). Sarvega, Gunavati (2008). Tulsi Devi, the Goddess of Devotion. Mata Amritanandamayi Trust, Kerala, India.

(63). Sene, E. (2003). Trees, Forests, Beliefs and Religions in Sahelian West Africa. Unasylva 213.

(64). Shanahan, M. (2016). Ladders to Heaven: How Fig Trees Shaped our History, Fed our imaginations, and Can Enrich our Future. Unbound, London.

(65). Sheridan, M. (2008). The Dynamics of African Sacred Groves, in: Sheridan, M., Nyamweru, C. (eds.), African Sacred Groves: Ecological Dynamics and Social Change. James Currey, Oxford, pp. 9–41.

(66). Shikibeta, C. (1993). Interview with Traditional Ruler of Luanga Valley, Zambia, in: Lewis, D., Carter, N. (eds.), Voices from Africa - Local Perspectives on Conservation. WWF, Maryland, pp. 71–78.

(67). Simbotwe, M. (1993). African Realities and Western Expectations, in: Lewis, D., Carter, N. (Eds.), Voices from Africa—Local Perspectives on Conservation. WWF, Maryland, pp. 15–21.

(68). Simon, B. (2012). Tales, Traditions and Folklore of Ireland's Trees. The Forest of Belfast, Belfast.

(69). Smith, R., (2012.) The Bear Cult among the Different Ethnic Groups of Russia (Sacred Russian Bear), in: Pungetti, G., Oviedo, G., Hooke, D. (eds.), Sacred Species and Sites: Advances in Biocultural Conservation. Cambridge University Press, Cambridge England, pp. 278–90.

(70). Solomar, M. (1999). Maori Cultural and Intellectual Property Claim Wai 262, in: Posey, D. (ed.), Cultural and Spiritual Values of Biodiversity—A Complementary Contribution to the Global Biodiversity Assessement. Intermediate Technology and UNEP, London and Nairobi, pp. 541–43.

(71). Stowe, J. (2003). The Findhorn Book of Connecting with Nature. Findhorn Press, Edinburgh.

(72). Tagore, R. (1975). Fireflies. Collier books, New York.

(73). Tont, S. (1999). Of Dancing Bears and Sacred Trees: Some Aspects of Turkish Attitudes towards Nature, and Their Possible Consequences for Biological Diversity, in: Posey, D. (ed.), Cultural and Spiritual Values of Biodiversity—A Complementary Contribution to the Global Biodiversity Assessement. Intermediate Technology, London and Nairobi, pp. 392–93.

(74). Tudge, C. (2006). The Secret Life of Trees: How They Live and Why They Matter. Penguin Books, London.

(75). Urtnasan, N. (2003). Mongolian Sacred Sites and Biodiversity Conservation, in: Lee, C., Schaaf, T. (eds.), The Importance of Sacred Natural Sites for Biodiversity Conservation. Proc. Int. Workshop on the Importance of Sacred Natural Sites for Biodiversity conservation in Kunming and Xishuangbanna Biosphere Reserve, People's Republic of China. UNESCO, Paris, pp. 83–97.

(76). Waisel, Y., and A. Alon (1980). Trees of the Land of Israel. Division of Ecology, Tel Aviv.

(77). Watson, R. (2007). The African Baobab. Struik, Cape Town.

(78). Wenjiang, L. (2003). Local Knowledge and Dryland Management in Xinjiang, Northwest China, in: Lee, C., Schaaf, T. (Eds.), The Importance of Sacred Natural Sites for Biodiversity Conservation. Proc. Int. Workshop on the Importance of Sacred Natural Sites for Biodiversity conservation in Kunming and Xishuangbanna Biosphere Reserve, People's Republic of China. UNESCO, Paris, pp. 135–38.

(79). Wit, P. (2015). Spiritual Values in Conservation—A Case Study from Mongolia, in: Wit, P. (ed.), Proceedings of the Second International Forum of the Qur'anic Botanic Garden: Islamic Perspectives on Ecoystems Management. Qur'anic Botanic Garden and IUCN Commission on Ecosystem Management, Doha Qatar, pp. 249–59.

(80). Wood, P. (1990). The Tree—A Celebration of Our Living Skyline. David and Chalres, London, p. 128.

(81). Zogib, L., Tashi, K., Gyalpo, T., Dendhup, S., Kuyakanon., Wangchuk, k., Tenzin, L., and N. Gyeltshen (2016). Sacred Mandala: Protecting Bhutan's Sacred Natural Site, in: Verschuuren, B., Furuta, N. (eds.), Asian Sacred Natural Sites: Philosophy and Practice in Protected Areas and Conservation. Routledge, London, pp. 57–68.

(82). Zucchelli, C. (2009). Trees of Inspiration: Sacred Trees and Bushes of Ireland. Collins Press, Cork Ireland.

Chapter 4

(1). Adimihardja, K. (1999). Cosmology and Biodiversity of the Kasepuhan Community in the Mt. Halimum Area of West Java, Indonesia, in: Posey, D. (ed.), Cultural and Spiritual Values of Biodiversity—A Complementary Contribution to the Global Biodiversity Assessment. Intermediate Technology and UNEP, London and Nairobi, pp. 223–27.

(2). Alden-Wily, L., and S. Mbaya. (2001). Land, People and Forests in Eastern and Southern Africa at the Beginning of the 21st Century. The Impact of Land Relations on the role of Communities in Forest Future. IUCN Eastern Africa Programme, Nairobi, Kenya.

(3). Barrow, E. (2010). Falling between the Cracks of Conservation and Religion: The Role of Stewardship for Sacred trees and Groves, in: Verschuuren, B., Wild, R., McNeely, J. (Eds.), Sacred Natural Sites: Conserving Nature and Culture. Earthscan, London, pp. 42–52.

(4). Berhane-Selassie, T. (2008). The Socio-Politics of Ethiopian Sacred Groves, in: Sheridan, M., Nyamweru, C. (eds.), African Sacred Groves: Ecological Dynamics and Social Change. James Currey, Oxford, pp. 103–16.

(5). Berry, W. (1998). The Selected Poems of Wendell Berry. Counterpoint, Berkeley, USA.

(6). Berry, W. (2015). Our Only World—Ten Essays. Counterpoint Press, Berkeley.

(7). Bhagwat, S. (2012). Sacred Groves and Biodiversity Conservation: A Case Study form the Western Ghats, India, in: Pungetti, G., Oviedo, G., Hooke, D. (eds.), Sacred Species and Sites: Advances in Biocultural Conservation. Cambridge University Press, Cambridge England, pp. 322–34.

(8). Bhagwat, S., C. Rutte. (2006). Sacred Groves: Potential for Biodiversity Management. Frontiers in Ecology and the Environment 4, 519–24.

(9). Bharucha, E. (1999). Cultural and Spiritual Values Related to the Conservation of Biodiversity in the Sacred Groves of the Western Ghats in Maharashtra, in: Posey, D. (Ed.), Cultural and Spiritual Values of Biodiversity—A Complementary Contribution to the Global Biodiversity Assessment. Intermediate Technology and UNEP, London and Nairobi, pp. 382–88.

(10). Brokensha, D., and A. Castro. (1987). Common Property Resources. Background Paper, Bangalore Expert Consultation on Forestry and Food Production/Security. FAO, Rome, p. 31.

(11). Byrne, D. (2010). Enchanted Earth: Numinous Sacred Sites, in: Verschuuren, B., Wild, R., McNeely, J., Oviedo, G. (Eds.), Sacred Natural Sites: Conserving Nature and Culture. Earthscan, London, pp. 53–61.

(12). Campbell, B., Grundy, I., and F. Matose. (1993). Tree and Woodland Resources—The Technical Practices of Small-Scale Farmers, in: Bradley, P. N., MacNamara, K. (eds.), Living with Trees: Trees for Forestry Management in Zimbabwe. World Bank, Washington DC., pp. 29–62.

(13). Chandrakanth, M., Gilless, J., Gowramma, V., and N. Nagaraja (1990). Temple Forests in India's Forest Development. Agroforestry Systems 11, 199–211.

(14). Chandrakanth, M., and J. Romm. (1991). Sacred Forests, Secular Forest Policies and People's Actions. Natural Resources Journal 31, 741–55.

(15). Chouin, G. (2008). Archaeological Perspectives on Sacred Groves in Ghana, in: Sheridan, M., Nyamweru, C. (eds.), African Sacred Groves: Ecological Dynamics and Social Change. James Currey, Oxford, pp. 178–94.

(16). Cinquepalmi, F., and G. Pungetti, G. (2012). Ancient Knowledge, the Sacred and Biocultural Diversity, in: Pungetti, G., Oviedo, G., Hooke, D. (eds.),

Sacred Species and Sites: Advances in Biocultural Conservation. Cambridge University Press, Cambridge England, pp. 46–62.
(17). Daneel, M. (1998). African Earthkeepers. UNISA press, University of South Africa.
(18). Daoud, A. (2003). Tree Formations around Places of Worship in the Near East. Unasylva 213, 47.
(19). Dudley, N., Higgins-Zogib, and S. Mansourian (2009). The Links Between Protected Areas, Faiths and Sacred Natural Sites. Conservation Biology 23, 568–77.
(20). Dwivedi, O. (1996). Satyagraha for Conservation: Awakening the Spirit of Hinduism, in: Gottlieb, R. (ed.), This Sacred Earth: Religion, Nature, Environment. Routledge, London, pp. 151–63.
(21). Evans, S. (1999). Sherpa Protection of Mt. Everest Region in Nepal, in: Posey, D. (ed.), Cultural and Spiritual Values of Biodiversity—A Complementary Contribution to the Global Biodiversity Assessment. Intermediate Technology and UNEP, London and Nairobi, pp. 327–43.
(22). Evers, Y. (1987). Subsistence Strategies and Wild Resource Utilizatin: Pugu Forest Reserve, Tanzania., Anthropology. University College, London.
(23). Fisher, R. (1997). If Rain Doesn't Come: An Anthropological Study of Drought and Human Ecology in Western Rajasthan. The Sydney Association for Studies in Society and Culture, Leichhardt, Australia.
(24). Fukamachi, K., and O. Rackham. (2012). Sacred Groves in Japanese Satoyama Landscapes: A Case Study and Prospects for Conservation, in: Pungetti, G., Oviedo, G., Hooke, D. (eds.), Sacred Species and Sites: Advances in Biocultural Conservation. Cambridge University Press, Cambridge England, pp. 419–20.
(25). Gadgil, M. (1987). Diversity: Cultural and Biological. Trends in Ecology and Evolution 2, 369–73.
(26). Ganjanapan, A. (2000). Local Control of Land and Forest: Cultural Dimensions of Resource Management in Northern Thailand. Regional Center for Social Science and Sustainable Development, Chiang Mai University, Chiang Mai, Thailand.
(27). Garg, A. (2013). A Typology of Sacred Groves and Their Discrimination from Sacred Sites. Current Science 104, 596–99.
(28). Githitho, A., (2003). The Sacred Mijikenda Kaya Forests of Coastal Kenya and Biodiversity Conservation, in: Lee, C., Schaaf, T. (eds.), The Importance of Sacred Natural Sites for Biodiversity Conservation. Proc. Int. Workshop on the Importance of Sacred Natural Sites for Biodiversity conservation in Kunming and Xishuangbanna Biosphere Reserve, People's Republic of China. UNESCO, Paris, pp. 19–27.

(29). Githitho, A. (2006). The Sacred Mijikenda *Kayas* of Coastal Kenya: Evolving Management Principles and Guidelines, in: Schaaf, T., Lee, C. (eds.), Conserving Cultural and Biological Diversity: The Role of Sacred Natural Sites and Cultural Landscapes. Proc. Tokyo Symposium. UNESCO, Paris, France, pp. 152–57.

(30). Glemet, R., Moore, P., Phommachanh, K., and M. Pholsena (2016). Customary Laws Governing the Sacred Natural Sites of the Xe Champhone Ramsar Site in Lao PDR, in: Verschuuren, B., Furuta, N. (eds.), Asian Sacred Natural Sites: Philosophy and Practice in Protected Areas and Conservation. Routledge, London, pp. 95–106.

(31). Golliher, J. (1999). Ethical, Moral and Religous Concerns, in: Posey, D. (ed.), Cultural and Spiritual Values of Biodiversity—A Complementary Contribution to the Global Biodiversity Assessement. Intermediate Technology and UNEP, London and Nairobi, pp. 435–502.

(32). Hamilton, L. (1998). Forest and Tree Conservation through Metaphysical Constraints, in: UNESCO (ed.), Natural Sacred Sites. Cultural Diversity and Biological Diversity. Proc. Int. Symp., Paris 1998. UNESCO, Paris, p. 18.

(33). Hamzah, A. (2016). The Asian Philosophy of Protect Areas: A Focus on Sacred Natural Sites, in: Verschuuren, B., Furuta, N. (eds.), Asian Sacred Natural Sites: Philosophy and Practice in Protected Areas and Conservation. Routledge, London, pp. 18–29.

(34). Harmon, D., and A. Putney. (2003). The Full Value of Parks—From Economics to the Intangible. Rowman and Littlefield, New York, p. 347.

(35). Hongmao, L., Zaifu, X., Youkai, X., and W. Jinxiu (2003). Conserving Plant Biodiversity through traditional Beliefs in Xishuangbanna, Southwest China, in: Lee, C., Schaaf, T. (eds.), The Importance of Sacred Natural Sites for Biodiversity Conservation. Proc. Int. Workshop on the Importance of Sacred Natural Sites for Biodiversity conservation in Kunming and Xishuangbanna Biosphere Reserve, People's Republic of China. UNESCO, Paris, pp. 126–34.

(36). Hosken, L. (2009). Potent Places. Resurgence 255, 19–20.

(37). His Royal Highness The Prince of Wales (2010). Facing the Future. Resurgence 258, 18–23.

(38). Huabin, H. (2003). Sacred Natural Sites in Xishuangbanna in South-Western China, in: Lee, C., Schaaf, T. (eds.), The Importance of Sacred Natural Sites for Biodiversity Conservation. Proc. Int. Workshop on the Importance of Sacred Natural Sites for Biodiversity conservation in Kunming and Xishuangbanna Biosphere Reserve, People's Republic of China. UNESCO, Paris, pp. 119–25.

(39). Hughes, J., and M. Chandran. (1998). Sacred Groves around the Earth: An Overview, in: Ramakrishnan, P., Chandrashekara, U., Saxena, K. (Eds.),

Conserving the Sacred for Biodiversity Management. Oxford and IBH Publishing, New Delhi, Kolkata, pp. 69–86.

(40). Ingles, A. (1990). The Management of Religous Forests in Nepal, Department of Forestry. Australian National University, Canberra, Australia, p. 135.

(41). Ingles, A. (1995). Religious Beliefs and Rituals in Nepal - Their Influence on Forest Conservation, in: Halladay, P., Gilmour, D. (Eds.), Conserving Biodiversity Outside Protected Areas: The Role of Traditional Agro-Ecosystems. IUCN, Gland, Switzerland and Cambridge, UK, pp. 205–24.

(42). Iwatsuki, K. (2006). Sacred Forests in Temples and Shrines of Japan, in: Schaaf, T., Lee, C. (eds.), Conserving Cultural and Biological Diversity: The Role of Sacred Natural Sites and Cultural Landscapes. Proc. Tokyo Symposium. UNESCO, Paris, France, pp. 90–92.

(43). Jeanrenaud, S. (2001). An International Initiative for the Protection and Sacred Natural Sites and Other Places of Indigenous and Traditional Peoples with Importance for Biodiveristy Conservation. A Concept Paper. WWF International—People and Conservation, Gland, Switzerland, p. 44.

(44). Kamanda, B., Angu, A., and J-C Nguinguiri (2003). The Social Value of the Nyangkpe Sacred Forest of South West Province, Cameroon, in: Harmon, D., Putney, A. (eds.), The Full Value of Parks: From Economics to the Intangible. Rowman and Littlefield, London, pp. 77–89.

(45). Khan, M., Khumbongmayum, A., and R. Tripathi (2008). The Sacred Groves and Their Significance in Conserving Biodiversity—An Overview. Int. J. of Ecology and Environmental Sciences 34, 277–91.

(46). Khiewtam, P., and P. Ramakrishnan. (1989). Socio-cultural Studies of the Sacred Groves at Cherrapunji and Adjoining Areas in Northeastern India. Man in India 69, 64–71.

(47). King, M. (2016). Nature on Holy Ground. Resurgence and Ecologist 198, 18–19.

(48). Knappert, J. (1987). East Africa: Kenya, Uganda and Tanzania. Vikas Publishing, New Delhi.

(49). Kothari, A., and P. Das. (1999). Local Community Knowledge and Practice in India, in: Posey, D. A. (ed.), Cultural and Spiritual Values of Biodiversity—A Complementary Contribution to the Global Biodiversity Assessment. Intermediate Technology and UNEP, London and Nairobi, pp. 185–92.

(50). Kumar, S. (2006). A Far Cry from Christmas. Resurgence 239, 3.

(51). Lebbie, A., and R. Guries. (2008). The Role of Sacred Groves in Biodiversity Conservatrion in Sierra Leone, in: Sheridan, M., Nyamweru, C. (Eds.), African Sacred Groves: Ecological Dynamics and Social Change. James Currey, Oxford, pp. 42–61.

(52). Lewington, A., and E. Parker. (1999). Ancient Trees: Trees that Live for 1000 Years. Collins and Brown, London.

(53). Loita Naimina Enkiyia Conservation Trust Company (1994). Forest of the Lost Child: Entim e Naimina Enkiyio—A Maasai Conservation Success Threatened by Greed, Nairobi, Kenya, p. 7.

(54). Loita Naimina Enkiyia Conservation Trust Company (1994). Statement by the Loita Naimina Enkiyia Conservation Trust to the Second Session on the Intergovernmental Committee on the Convention of Biodiversity. Forest, Trees and people Newsletter 25, 45.

(55). Luke, Q. (1996). The Coastal Forest Conservation Unit. In KWS, Forest Department MOU Secretariat, (Eds.), Proc. Workshop on Coastal Forested Ecosystems Management Taskforce Formation. KWS and Forest Department, pp. 36–40.

(56). Malhotra, K., Gokhala, Y., and S. Chatterjee. (2001). Cultural and Ecological Dimensions of Sacred Groves in India. Indian National Science Academy and New Delhi and Indira Ghandi Rashtriya Manav Sangrahalaya, New Delhi and Bhopal.

(57). Mallarach, J. M. (2012). Monastic Communities and Nature Conservation: An Overview of Positive Trends and Best Practices in Europe and the Middle East, in: Mallarach, J. M., Papayannis, T., Vaisanen, R. (eds.), The Diversity of Holy Lands in Europe. Proc. 3rd Workshop of the Delos Initiative—Inasi/Aanaar 2010. IUCN and Metsahallitus Natural Heritage Services Vantaa, Finland, Gland, Switzerland, pp. 157–73.

(58). Mallarach, J-M., Corco, J., and T. Papayannia (2016). Christian Monastic Lands as Protected Landscapes and Community Conserved Areas: An Overview. PARKS 22, 63–78.

(59). Mandela, N. (2006). Words of Wisdom. Mentor Books, Dublin.

(60). Marafa, L. (2003). Integrating Natural and Cultural Heritage: The Advantage of Feng Shui Landscape Resources. Int. J. of Heritage Studies 9, 307–23.

(61). Matose, F. (1992). Villagers as Woodland Managers., in: Piearce, G., Shaw, P. (eds.), Forestry Research in Zimbabwe. Forestry Commission, Harare.

(62). Meiggs, R. (1982). Trees and Timber in the Ancient Mediterranean World. Clarendon Press, Oxford, UK.

(63). Montealegre, K., and D. Victory. (2011). Costa Rica: For the Soul. Motmat Ediciones, San Jose.

(64). Muhumuza, M. (2012). Biocultural Diversity Conservation through Sacred Natural Sites in the Rwenzori Mountains National Park. Langscape 2, 40–43.

(65). Mwihomeke, S., Msangi, T., Mabula, C., Ylhäisi, J., and K. Mndeme (1998). Traditionally Protected Forests and Nature Conservation in the North Pare Mountains and Handeni District, Tanzania. J. East African Natural History 87, 279–90.

(66). National Geographic Society (2008). Sacred Places of a Lifetime: 500 of the World's Most Peaceful and Powerful Destinations. National Geographic Society, Washington, DC.

(67). Negussie, G. (1997). Use of Traditional Values in the Search for Conservation Goals: The Kaya Forests of the Kenyan Coast, in: Doolan, S. (Ed.), African Rainforests and the Conservation of Biodiversity. Proc. Limbe Conference, Limbe, Cameroon, pp. 160–62.

(68). Ngussie, G. (1997). Use of Traditional Values in the Search for Conservation Goals: The Kaya Forests of the Kenyan Coast, in: Dolan, S. (ed.), African Rainforests and the Conservation of Biodiversity. Proc. Limbe Conference, Limbe Botanic Gardens, Cameroon. Earthwatch, London, pp. 160–62.

(69). Nhira, C., and L. Fortmann. (1993). Local Woodland Management: Realities at the Grass Roots., in: Bradley, P. N., McNamara, K. (eds.), Living with Trees: Policies for Forestry Management in Zimbabwe. World Bank, Washington, DC.

(70). Ntiamoa-Baidu, Y. (1995). Indigenous v. Introduced Biodiversity Conservation Strategies: the Case of Protected Area Systems in Ghana. WWF-Biodiversity Support Program, Wahsington, p. 12.

(71). Nurse, M., and J. Kabamba. (1998). Defining Institutions for Collaborative Mangrove Management: A Case Study from Tanga, Tanzania, Workshop on Participatory Resource Management in Developing Countries, Mansfield College, Oxford, p. 25.

(72). Nyamweru, C., Kibet, S., Pakia, M., and J. Cooke (2008). The Kaya Forests of Coastal Kenya, in: Sheridan, M., Nyamweru, C. (eds.), African Sacred Groves: Ecological Dynamics and Social Change. James Currey, Oxford, pp. 62–86.

(73). Nyamweru, C., and M. Sheridan. (2008). Introduction, in: Sheridan, M., Nyamweru, C. (Eds.), African Sacred Groves: Ecological Dynamics and Social Change. James Currey, Oxford, pp. 1–8.

(74). Nyangila, J. (2012). Sacred Species of Kenyan Sacred Sites, in: Pungetti, G., Oviedo, G., Hooke, D. (Eds.), Sacred Species and Sites: Advances in Biocultural Conservation. Cambridge University Press, Cambridge England, pp. 351–64.

(75). Ono, T., Hongo, T., Yamamoto, K., and N. Furuta (2016). Mount Fuji's History as a Spiritual Realm and Means for its Preservation, in: Verschuuren, B., Furuta, N. (Eds.), Asian Sacred Natural Sites: Philosophy and Practice in Protected Area and Conservation. Routledge, London, pp. 159–70.

(76). Ormsby, A. (2012). Cultural and Conservation Values of Sacred Forests in Ghana, in: Pungetti, G., Oviedo, G., Hooke, D. (Eds.), Sacred Species and Sites: Advances in Biocultural Conservation. Cambridge University Press, Cambridge England, pp. 335–50.

(77). Ormsby, A., and S. Bhagwat. (2010). Sacred Forests of India: a Strong Tradition of Community-based Natural Resource Management. Environmental Conservation 37, 320–26.

(78). Orr, D. (2011). Hope Is an Imperative—The Essential David Orr. Island Press, Washington, DC.

(79). Ostberg, W. (1988). We Eat Trees: Tree Planting and Land Rehabilitation in West Pokot District, Kenya. A Baseline Study. Swedish University of Agricultural Sciences, International Rural Development Center, Uppsala.

(80). Palmer, M. (2008). Sites of Significance. Resurgence 250, 42–43.

(81). Parajuli, P. (1999). Peasant Cosmovisions and Biodiversity—Some Reflections from Southeast Asia, in: Posey, D. (ed.), Cultural and Spiritual Values of Biodiversity—A Complementary Contribution to the Global Biodiversity Assessment. Intermeditate Technology and UNEP, London and Nairobi, pp. 385–88.

(82). Peng, L., Ning, W., Zhaoli, Y., and P. Shengji (2003). Sacred Sites in Northwest Yunnan, China, in: Lee, C., Schaaf, T. (Eds.), The Importance of Sacred Natural Sites for Biodiversity Conservation. Proc. Int. Workshop on the Importance of Sacred Natural Sites for Biodiversity conservation in Kunming and Xishuangbanna Biosphere Reserve, People's Republic of China. UNESCO, Paris, pp. 139–50.

(83). Porteus, A. (1996). The Lore of the Forest: Myths and Legends. Senate, London.

(84). Pungetti, G., and S. Bhagwat. (2012). Sacred Species and Biocultural Diversity: Applying the Principles, in: Pungetti, G., Oviedo, G., Hooke, D. (eds.), Sacred Species and Sites: Advances in Biocultural Conservation. Cambridge University Press, Cambridge England, pp. 367–406.

(85). Rackham, O. (1989). The Constant Spring. Resurgence 133, 11–13.

(86). Rai, J., and S. Thing. (2016). A Biocultural Perspective on the Recognition and Support for Sacred Natural Sites in Nepal, in: Verschuuren, B., Furuta, N. (eds.), Asian Sacred Natural Sites: Philosophy and Practice in Protected Area and Conservation. Routledge, London, pp. 81–92.

(87). Ramakrishnan, P. (1993). Shifting Agriculture and Sustainable Development in North-Eastern India. Oxford University Press, New Delhi.

(88). Ramakrishnan, P. (1996). Conserving the Sacred: From Species to Landscapes. Nature and Resources 32, 11–19.

(89). Ramakrishnan, P. (2003). Biodiversity Conservation: Lessons from the Buddhist Demajong Landscape in Sikkim, India, in: Lee, C., Schaaf, T. (eds.), The Importance of Sacred Natural Sites for Biodiversity Conservation. Proc. Int. Workshop on the Importance of Sacred Natural Sites for Biodiversity conservation in Kunming and Xishuangbanna Biosphere Reserve, People's Republic of China. UNESCO, Paris, pp. 57–70.

(90). Ramakrishnan, P., Saxena, K., and U. Chandrashekara. (1998). Conserving the Sacred for Biodiversity Management. Science Publishing in Association with UNESCO, New Delhi and Oxford.

(91). Rathore, M., and N. Shekhawat. (2011). Ethnobotanical Importance of Orans—As a Means of Conserving Biodiversity. Int. J. of Agricultural Science, Research and Technology 1, 195–200.

(92). Reichel, E. (2012). The Landscape in the Cosmoscape, and Sacred Sites and Species among the Tanikuka and Yukuna Amerindian Tribes (North West Amazon), in: Pungetti, G., Oviedo, G., Hooke, D. (eds.), Sacred Specie and Sites: Advances in Biocultural Conservation. Cambridge University Press, Cambridge England, pp. 127–51.

(93). Robertson, S. (1987). Preliminary Floristic Survey of Kaya Forests of Coastal Kenya. A Report to the Director of Museums of Kenya. National Museums of Kenya, Nairobi, Kenya, p. 150.

(94). Rodgers, W. (1994). The Sacred Groves of Meghalaya. Man in India 74, 339–48.

(95). Samakov, A., and F. Berkes. (2016). Ysyk-Kol Lake, the Planet's Third Eye: Sacred Sites in Ysyk-Kol Biosphere Reserve, in: Verschuuren, B., Furuta, N. (eds.), Asian Sacred Natural Sites: Philosophy and Practice in Protected Areas and Conservation. Routledge, London, pp. 208–20.

(96). Sayer, J., Harcourt, C., and N. Collins (1992). The Conservation Atlas of Tropical Forests: Africa. IUCN, World Conservation Monitoring Center, Macmillan and BP, Cambridge, p. 288.

(97). Schaaf, T. (2003). UNESCO's Experience with the Protection of Sacred Natural Sites for Biodiversity Conservation, in: Lee, C., Schaaf, T. (eds.), The Importance of Sacred Natural Sites for Biodiversity Conservation. Proc. Int. Workshop on the Importance of Sacred Natural Sites for Biodiversity conservation in Kunming and Xishuangbanna Biosphere Reserve, People's Republic of China. UNESCO, Paris, pp. 5–12.

(98). School of Agriculture and Forest Science University of Wales, and the Institute of Biodiveristy Conservation and Research Addis Ababa (2001). Biodiversity Conservation in Ancient Church and Monastry Yards in Ethiopia—Addis Ababa. University of Wales and Institute of Biodiversity Conservation and Research, Bangor North Wales, and Addis Ababa Ethiopia, p. 25.

(99). Scott, P. (1996). Collaborative Management in Rwenzori Mountains National Park. IUCN, Kampala, p. 47.

(100). Shengji, P. (1999). The Holy Hills of the Dai, in: Posey, D. (Ed.), Cultural and Spiritual Values of Biodiversity—A Complementary Contribution to the Global Biodiversity Assessment. Intermediate Technology and UNEP, London and Nairobi, pp. 381–82.

(101). Shengji, P. (2003). The Role of Ethnobotany in the Conservation of Biodiversity, in: Lee, C., Schaaf, T. (eds.), The Importance of Sacred Natural Sites for Biodiversity Conservation. Proc. Int. Workshop on the Importance of Sacred Natural Sites for Biodiversity conservation in Kunming and Xishuangbanna Biosphere Reserve, People's Republic of China. UNESCO, Paris, pp. 111–18.

(102). Shengji, P. (2006). Biodiveristy in the Sacred Forests of Xishuangbanna Biosphere Reserve, China, in: Schaaf, T., Lee, C. (eds.), Conserving Cultural and Biological Diversity: The Role of Sacred Natural Sites and Cultural Landscapes. Proc. Tokyo Symposium. UNESCO, Paris, France, pp. 187–93.

(103). Shengji, P. (2010). The Road to the future? The Biocultural values of the Holly Hill Forests of Yunnan Province, China, in: Verschuuren, B., Wild, R., McNeely, J., Oviedo, G. (eds.), Sacred Natural Sites: Conserving Nature and Culture. Earthscan, London, pp. 98–106.

(104). Sheridan, M. (2008). The Dynamics of African Sacred Groves, in: Sheridan, M., Nyamweru, C. (eds.), African Sacred Groves: Ecological Dynamics and Social Change. James Currey, Oxford, pp. 9–41.

(105). Shiva, V. (2011). Forests and Freedom. Resurgence 266, 50–51.

(106). Simon, B. (2012). Tales, Traditions and Folklore of Ireland's Trees. The Forest of Belfast, Belfast.

(107). Smith, S., (1997). Aborigines, Land and National Parks in New South Wales. New South Wales Parliamentary Library, Sydney, p. 25.

(108). Soedjito, H., and Y. Purwanto. (2003). Sacred Sites of West Timor: Treasuries of Biodiversity and Cultural Heritage, in: Lee, C., Schaaf, T. (eds.), The Importance of Sacred Natural Sites for Biodiversity Conservation. Proc. Int. Workshop on the Importance of Sacred Natural Sites for Biodiversity conservation in Kunming and Xishuangbanna Biosphere Reserve, People's Republic of China. UNESCO, Paris, pp. 71–80.

(109). Stephenson, D. (1999). The Importance of the Convention on Biological Diversity to the Loita Maasai of Kenya, in: Posey, D. (ed.), Cultural and Spiritual Values of Biodiversity—A Complementary Contribution to the Global Biodiversity Assessment. Intermediate Technology and UNEP, London and Nairobi, pp. 531–33.

(110). Stoner, T., and C. Rapp (2008). Open Spaces, Sacred Places. TKF Foundation, Annapolis, USA.

(111). Sukhbaatar, H. (2017). Intoduction to Sacred Sites in Mongolia. The Alliance for Religion and Conservation.

(112). Tabarelli, M., and C. Gascon. (2012). Lessons from Fragmentation Research: Improving Management and Policy Guidelines for Biodiversity Conservation. Conservation Biology 19, 734–39.

(113). Telly, E. (2006). Sacred Groves, Rituals and Sustainable Community Development in Ghana, in: Schaaf, T., Lee, C. (Eds.), Conserving Cultural and Biological Diversity: The Role of Sacred Natural Sites and Cultural Landscapes. Proc. Tokyo Symposium. UNESCO, Paris, France, pp. 194–203.

(114). Thorley, A., and C. Gunn. (2008). Sacred Sites: An Overview. Report for the Gaia Foundation. The Gaia Foundation, London.

(115). UNEP-WCMC (2014). Global Statistics from the World Database on Protected Areas (WDPA), August 2014. UNEP-WCMC, Cambridge UK.

(116). UNEP-WCMC, and IUCN. (2014). The World Database on Protected Areas (WDPA). IUCN and UNEP-WCMC, Cambridge UK.

(117). Urtnasan, N. (2003). Mongolian Sacred Sites and Biodiversity Conservation, in: Lee, C., Schaaf, T. (Eds.), The Importance of Sacred Natural Sites for Biodiversity Conservation. Proc. Int. Workshop on the Importance of Sacred Natural Sites for Biodiversity conservation in Kunming and Xishuangbanna Biosphere Reserve, People's Republic of China. UNESCO, Paris, pp. 83–97.

(118). Verschuuren, B. (2016). Re-awakening the Power of Place: Ancient Philisophy and Practice with Relevance for Protected Areas and Conservation in Asia, in: Verschuuren, B., Furuta, N. (eds.), Asian Sacred Natural Sites: Philosophy and Practice in Protected Areas and Conservation. Routledge, London, pp. 1–14.

(119). von Hallermann, P. (2016). Tree Symbolism and Conservation in the South Pare Mountains, Tanzania. Conservation and Society 14, 368–79.

(120). Wickramasinghe, A. (2003). Adam's Peak Sacred Mountain Forest, in: Lee, C., Schaaf, T. (eds.), The Importance of Sacred Natural Sites for Biodiversity Conservation. Proc. Int. Workshop on the Importance of Sacred Natural Sites for Biodiversity conservation in Kunming and Xishuangbanna Biosphere Reserve, People's Republic of China. UNESCO, Paris, pp. 101–10.

(121). Wickramasinghe, A. (2006). Adam's Peak in the Cultural Landscape of Sri Lanka: Evidence for an Eco-cultural Basis for Conservation, in: Schaaf, T., Lee, C. (eds.), Conserving Cultural and Biological Diversity: The Role of Sacred Natural Sites and Cultural Landscapes. Proc. Tokyo Symposium. UNESCO, Paris, France, pp. 52–57.

(122). Wild, R., and C. McLeod. (2008.) Sacred Natural Sites: Guidelines for Protected Area Managers, in: Wild, R., McLeod, C. (eds.), Sacred Natural Sites: Guidelines for Protected Area Managers. IUCN, Gland, Switzerland.

(123). Wilson, K. (1987). Research on Trees in the Mazvihwa and Surrounding Areas. A Report prepared for ENDA. ENDA, Harare, Zimbabwe.

(124). Wolf, K., and E. Housley. (2016). The Sacred and Nearby Sacred in Cities. TKF Foundation, Annapolis, USA, p. 59.

(125). Ylhäisi, J. (2004). Indigenous Forests Fragmentation and the Significance of Ethnic Forests for Conservation in the North Pare, the Eastern Arc Mountains, Tanzania. Fennia 182, 109–32.

(126). Ylhäisi, J. (2006). Traditionally Protected Forests and Sacred Forests of Zigua and Gweno Ethnic Groups in Tanzania. Department of Geography, University of Finland Publication No. A139, Helsinki, Finland.

(127). Zeng, L., and G. Reuse. (2016). Holy Hills: Sanctuaries of Biodiveristy in Xishuangbanna, South West China, in: Verschuuren, B., Furuta, N. (eds.), Asian Sacred Natural Sites: Philosophy and Practice in Protected Areas and Conservation. Routledge, London, pp. 182–93.

(128). Zogib, L., Tashi, K., Gyalpo, T., Dendhup, S., Kuyakanon., Wangchuk, k., Tenzin, L., and N. Gyeltshen. (2016). Sacred Mandala: Protecting Bhutan's Sacred Natural Site, in: Verschuuren, B., Furuta, N. (Eds.), Asian Sacred Natural Sites: Philosophy and Practice in Protected Areas and Conservation. Routledge, London, pp. 57–68.

(129). Zucchelli, C. (2009). Trees of Inspiration: Sacred Trees and Bushes of Ireland. Collins Press, Cork Ireland.

Chapter 5

(1). Alden-Wily, L. (2008). Are Sacred Groves in Sub-Saharan Africa Safe? The Legal Status of Forests, in: Sheridan, M., Nyamweru, C. (eds.), African Sacred Groves: Ecological Dynamics and Social Change. James Currey, Oxford, pp. 207–20.

(2). Alderson, P. (2017). Cradles of Morality. Resurgence and Ecologist 302, 44–45.

(3). Anderson, D., R. Grove. (1987). The Scramble for Eden: Past, Present and Future in African Conservation, in: Anderson, D., Grove, R. (eds.), Conservation in Africa: Peoples, Policies and Practices. Cambridge University Press, Cambridge.

(4). Asmar, F., Hobeika, S., Khter, C., and G. Zouain (2006). The Qadisha, Lebanon: A Biological, Cultural, Historical and Religous Heritage, in: Schaaf, T., Lee, C. (eds.), Conserving Cultural and Biological Diversity: The Role of Sacred Natural Sites and Cultural Landscapes. Proc. Tokyo Symposium. UNESCO, Paris, France, pp. 233–39.

(5). Banana, A.Y., Bahati, J. Gombya-Ssembajjwe, W., and N. Vogt (2008). Legal Recognition of Customary Forests in Uganda: An Approach to Revitalizing Sacred Groves, in: Sheridan, M., Nyamweru, C. (eds.), African Sacred Groves: Ecological Dynamics and Social Change. James Currey, Oxford, pp. 195–206.

(6). Barrow, E., Clarke, J., Grundy, I., Kamugisha, J., and Y. Tessema (2002). Analysis of Stakeholder Power and Responsibilities in Community Involvement in Forest Management in Eastern and Southern Africa. IUCN—The World Conservation Union Eastern African Office, Nairobi.

(7). Barrow, E., and M. Murphree. (2001) Community Conservation from Concept to Practice, in: Hulme, D., Murphree, M. (eds.), African Wildlife and Livelihoods: The Promise and Practice of Community Conservation. James Currey, Oxford, pp. 24–37.

(8). Barrow, E. (1996). The Drylands of Africa: Local Participation in Tree Management. Initiatives Publishers, Nairobi.

(9). Barrow, E., Gichohi, H., and M. Infield (2000). Rhetoric or Reality? A Review of Community Conservation Policy and Practise in East Africa. IIED and IUCN, London.

(10). Barrow, E., and M. Murphree. (1998). Community Conservation from Concept to Practice—A Practical Framework. Institute for Development Policy and Management, University of Manchester, Manchester, p. 33.

(11). Beresford, M., and A. Philips. (2000). Protected Landscapes: A Conservation Model for the Twenty-First Century. George White Forum 17, 19.

(12). Berhane-Selassie, T. (2008). The Socio-Politics of Ethiopian Sacred Groves, in: Sheridan, M., Nyamweru, C. (eds.), African Sacred Groves: Ecological Dynamics and Social Change. James Currey, Oxford, pp. 103–16.

(13). Bhagwat, S., and C. Rutte. (2006). Sacred Groves: Potential for Biodiversity Management. Frontiers in Ecology and the Environment 4, 519–24.

(14). Borrini-Feyerabend, G. (2002). Editorial - Local Communities and Protected Areas—A Conservation at a Distance. PARKS 12.

(15). Borrini-Feyerabend, G., Dudley, N., Sandwith, T., Stevens, S., Kothari, A., Lassen, B., Berghofer, A., Balasinorwala, T., Budhatoki, P., and S. Bhatt (2008). Implementing the CBD Programme of work for Protected Areas: Governance a Key for Effective and Equitable Protected Area Systems. IUCN Commission on Environment, Economics and Social Policy, Gland, Switzerland, p. 16.

(16). Brown, J., Mitchell, N., and J. Tuxill (2003). Partnerships and Lived-in Landscape: An Evolving US System of Parks and Protected Areas. PARKS 12, 31–41.

(17). Capra, F. (2012.) Emerging Networks. Resurgence 273, 42–43.

(18). Chopra, D. (2006). Will God ever Leave Us Alone? Resurgence 239, 20–21.

(19). Cordeiro, A. (2008). Webs of Life. Resurgence 247, 22–23.

(20). Corrigan, C., Bingham, H., Pathak, N., Hay-Edie, T., Tabanao, G., and N. Kingston (2016) Documenting Local Contributions to Earth's Biodiversity Heritage: The Global Registry. PARKS 22, 55–68.

(21). Dasmann, R. (1985). The Relationship Between Protected Areas and Indigenous Peoples, in: McNeely, J. Miller, K. (Eds.), National Parks, Conservation and Development: the Role of Protected Areas in Sustaining Society. Smithsonian Press, Washington, DC.

(22). Dudley, N. (2008). Guidelines for Applying Protected area Management Categories. IUCN, Gland, p. x + 86.

(23). Dudley, N., and L. Higgins-Zogib. (2012). Protected Areas and Sacred Nature: a Convergence of Beliefs, in: Pungetti, G., Oviedo, G., Hooke, D. (eds.), Sacred Species and Sites: Advances in Biocultural Conservation. Cambridge University Press, Cambridge England, pp. 36–45.

(24). Dyer, W. (1997). Manifest Your Destiny: The Nine Spiritual Principles for Getting Everything You Want. Thorsons Audio.

(25). Gillingham, S. (1998). Giving Wildlife Value: A Case Study of Community Wildlife Management Around the Selous Game Reserve, Tanzania, Dept. Biological Anthropology. University of Cambridge, Cambridge, p. 290.

(26). Goldsmith, E. (1996). The Way: An Ecological World View. Green Books ltd, Dartington, Devon England.

(27). Hamzah, A. (2016). The Asian Philosophy of Protect Areas: A Focus on Sacred Natural Sites, in: Verschuuren, B., Furuta, N. (Eds.), Asian Sacred Natural Sites: Philosophy and Practice in Protected Areas and Conservation. Routledge, London, pp. 18–29.

(28). Harmon, D., and A. Putney. (2003). The Full Value of Parks - From Economics to the Intangible. Rowman and Littlefield, New York, p. 347.

(29). His Royal Highness The Prince of Wales (2007). A Sense of Harmony. Resurgence 242, 14–16.

(30). Huabin, H. (2003). Sacred Natural Sites in Xishuangbanna in South-Western China, in: Lee, C., Schaaf, T. (eds.), The Importance of Sacred Natural Sites for Biodiversity Conservation. Proc. Int. Workshop on the Importance of Sacred Natural Sites for Biodiversity conservation in Kunming and Xishuangbanna Biosphere Reserve, People's Republic of China. UNESCO, Paris, pp. 119–25.

(31). Hulme, D., and M. Murphree (2001). African Wildlife and Livelihoods: The Promise and Performance of Community Conservation. James Currey, Oxford, p. 336.

(32). IUCN, and UNEP (1986). Review of the Protected Areas system in the Afrotropical Realm. IUCN, Gland, Switzlerland.

(33). Jeanrenaud, S. (2001). An International Initiative for the Protection and Sacred Natural Sites and Other Places of Indigenous and Traditional Peoples with Importance for Biodiveristy Conservation. A Concept Paper. WWF International - People and Conservation, Gland, Switzerland, p. 44.

(34). Jonas, H., Lee, E., Jonas, H., Matallana-Tobon, C., Wright, K., Nelson, F., and E. Ennis (2017). Will "Other Effectively Areas-Based Conservation Measures" Increase Recognition and Support of ICCAs? PARKS 23, 63–78.

(35). Jones, B., and A. Mosimane (1999). Empowering Communities to Manage Natural Resources: Where Does the New Power Lie? Case Studies from Namibia., in: Shackelton, S. Campbell, B.(eds.), Empowering Communities to Manage Natural Resources. Case Studies from Southern Africa. SADC Wildlife Sector—Natural Resources Management Programme, Lilongwe, Malawi, pp. 69–101.

(36). Juniper, T. (2004). Inspiring Change. Resurgence 227, 28–31.

(37). Kadlec, S., and A. Rhodes. (2006). Tsunami—Beyond the Quick Fix. Resurgence 234, 22–24.

(38). Katz, B. (2018). Local Time. RSA Journal 1, 24–27.

(39). Kleymeyer, C. (1994). Cultural Traditions and Community-based Conservation, in: Western, D., Wright, R., Strum, S. (Eds.), Natural Connections: Perspectives in Community-based Conservation. Island Press, Washington, DC, pp. 323–46.

(40). Kothari, A. (2006). Community Conserved Areas: Towards Ecological and and Livelihood Security. PARKS 16, 3–13.

(41). Kothari, A., Corrigan, C., Jonas, H., Neumann, A., and H. Shrumm (2012). Recognizing and Supporting Territories and Areas Conserved by Indigenous Peoples and Local Communities: Overview and National Case Studies. Secretariat of the Convention on Biological Diversity, ICCA Consortium, Kalpavriksh, and Natural Justice, Montreal Canada.

(42). Kothari, A., and N. Pathak (2008). Defenders of Diversity. Resurgence 250, 36–37.

(43). Kumar, S. (2006). From Ownership to Relationship. Resurgence 235, 6–7.

(44). Lamprey, H. (1990). Challenges facing protected area management in sub-Saharan Africa. PARKS 1, 27–31.

(45). Lee, C., and T. Schaaf. (2003). The Importance of Sacred Natural Sites for Biodiversity Conservation. Proc. Int. Workshop on the Importance of Sacred Natural Sites for Biodiversity Conservation in Kunming and Xishuangbanna Biosphere Reserve, People's Republic of China. UNESCO, Paris, p. 167.

(46). Lovelock, J. (2006). Making Peace with Gaia. Resurgence 238, 59–61.

(47). Mallarach, J. M., Corco, J., and T. Papayannis (2016). Christian Monastic Lands as Protected Landscapes and Community Conserved Areas: An Overview. PARKS 22, 63–78.

(48). Mansberger, J. (1988). In Search of the Tree Spirit: Evolution of the Sacred Tree *Ficus religiosa*, in: Daragavel, J., Dixon, K., Semple, N. (eds.), Changing Tropical Forests. CRES, Australian National University, Canberra, pp. 399–411.

(49). Martin, R. (1986). Wildlife Human Interaction, in: Bell, R., McShane-Caluzi, E. (eds.), Conservation and Wildlife Management in Africa. US Peace Corps, Washington.

(50). McCay, B. (2000). Post-modernism and the Management of Natural and Common Resources. Int. Assoc. for the Study of Common Property 54, 1–9.

(51). McNeely, J. (1984). Introduction: Protected Areas Are Adapting to New Realities, in: McNeely, J., Miller, K. (eds.), National Parks, Conservation and Development: the Role of Protected Areas in Sustaining Society. Smithsonian Press, Washington, DC.

(52). McNeely, J. A., and D. Pitt. (1985). Culture: The Missing Element in Conservation and Development, in: McNeely, J.A., Pitt, D. (eds.), Culture and Conservation: The Human Dimension in Environmental Planning. Croom Helm, London.

(53). Millennium Ecosystem Assessment (2005). Ecosystems and Wellbeing: Synthesis. Island Press, Washington, DC.

(54). Moukala, E, (2003). Integrating People and Culture within Environmental Strategies, in: Lee, C., Schaaf, T. (eds.), The Importance of Sacred Natural Sites for Biodiversity Conservation. Proc. Int. Workshop on the Importance of Sacred Natural Sites for Biodiversity Conservation in Kunming and Xishuangbanna Biosphere Reserve, People's Republic of China. UNESCO, Paris, pp. 98–100.

(55). Murphree, M. (1996). "Ex Africa Semper Aliquid Novi?" Considerations in Linking Environmental Scholarship, Policy and Practice, Pan African Symposium on the Sustainable Use of Natural Resources and Community Participation, Harare, Zimbabwe, p. 11.

(56). Murphree, M. (2000). Community Based Conservation: Old Ways, New Myths and Enduring Challenges, in: College of African Wildlife Management (ed.), African Wildlife Management in the New Millenium, Mweka, Tanzania, p. 18.

(57). Murphree, M. (1991). Communities as Institutions for Resource Management, National Conference on Environment and Development, Maputo, Mozambique.

(58). Murphree, M. (1996). Approaches to Community Participation, in: Overseas Development Administration (ed.), African Policy Wildlife Policy Consultation. Final Report of the Consultation. Overseas Development Administration, London, pp. 153–88.

(59). Nair, N., and C. Mohanan (1981). On the Rediscovery of Four Threatened Species from Sacred Groves in Kerala. Economic Taxonomy and Botany 2, 233–34.

(60). National Geographic Society (2008). Sacred Places of a Lifetime: 500 of the World's Most Peaceful and Powerful Destinations. National Geographic Society, Washington, DC.

(61). Nyamweru, C., Kibet, S., Pakia, M., and J. Cooke (2008). The Kaya Forests of Coastal Kenya, in: Sheridan, M., Nyamweru, C. (eds.), African Sacred Groves: Ecological Dynamics and Social Change. James Currey, Oxford, pp. 62–86.

(62). Nyamweru, C., and M. Sheridan (2008). Introduction, in: Sheridan, M., Nyamweru, C. (eds.), African Sacred Groves: Ecological Dynamics and Social Change. James Currey, Oxford, pp. 1–8.

(63). Oakerson, R. (1992). Analyzing the Commons: A Framework, in: Bromley, D. (ed.), Making the Commons Work: Theory, Practise and Policy. ICS Press, San Francisco, pp. 41–59.

(64). Orr, D. (2011). Hope Is an Imperative—The Essential David Orr. Island Press, Washington, DC.

(65). Philips, A. (2003). Turning Ideas on Their Head—The New Paradigm for Protected Areas. George Wright Forum 20, 8–20.

(66). Pope Francis (2015). Encyclical on Climate Change and Inequality: On Care for our Common Home. Melville House Publishing, New York.

(67). Ramakrishnan, P. (2003). Biodiversity Conservation: Lessons from the Buddhist Demajong Landscape in Sikkim, India, in: Lee, C., Schaaf, T. (eds.), The Importance of Sacred Natural Sites for Biodiversity Conservation. Proc. Int. Workshop on the Importance of Sacred Natural Sites for Biodiversity Conservation in Kunming and Xishuangbanna Biosphere Reserve, People's Republic of China. UNESCO, Paris, pp. 57–70.

(68). Republic of Ecuador (2008). Constitution of the Republic of Ecuador. Government of Ecuador, Quito, p. 190.

(69). Robertson, S., and Q. Luke (1993). Kenya Coastal Forests: The Report of the NMK/WWF Coast Forest Survey. WWF Project 3256, Coastal Forest Status, Conservation and Management. WWF, Kenya.

(70). Roe, D. (2001). Community Based Wildlife Management: Improved Livelihoods and Wildlife Conservation. IIED, Londond, p. 4.

(71). Schreckenberg, K., Franks, P., Martin, A., and B. Lang (2016). Unpacking Equity for Protected Area Conservation. PARKS 22, 11–26.

(72). Shaw, M. (2016). Listening to the Spirit of Place. Resurgence and Ecologist 298, 28–29.

(73). Shepherd, G. (2007). The Ecosystem Approach: Five Steps to Implementation. IUCN, Gland, Switzerland, x + 30 pp.

(74). Sheridan, M. (2008). The Dynamics of African Sacred Groves, in: Sheridan, M., Nyamweru, C. (Eds.), African Sacred Groves: Ecological Dynamics and Social Change. James Currey, Oxford, pp. 9–41.

(75). Shiva, V. (2012). Choosing Simplicity. Resurgence 273, 50–51.

(76). Siebert, U. (2008). Are Sacred Groves in Northern Benin "Traditional Conservarion Areas"?—Examples from the Bassila Region, in: Sheridan, M.,

Nyamweru, C. (eds.), African Sacred Groves: Ecological Dynamics and Social Change. James Currey, Oxford, pp. 164–77.

(77). Soedjito, H., and Y. Purwanto (2003). Sacred Sites of West Timor: Treasuries of Biodiversity and Cultural Heritage, in: Lee, C., Schaaf, T. (eds.), The Importance of Sacred Natural Sites for Biodiversity Conservation. Proc. Int. Workshop on the Importance of Sacred Natural Sites for Biodiversity Conservation in Kunming and Xishuangbanna Biosphere Reserve, People's Republic of China. UNESCO, Paris, pp. 71–80.

(78). Studley, J., and W. Bleisch (2018). Juristic Personhood of Sacred Nature Sites: A Potential Means for Protecting Nature. PARKS 24, 81–96.

(79). Tauli-Corpuz, V., Alcorn, J., and A. Molnar (2018). Cornered by Protected Areas: Replacing Fortress Conservation with Rights-based Approaches Helps Bring Justice for Indigenous Peoples and Local Communities, Reduces Conflict, and Enables Cost-Effective Conservation and Climate Action. Rights and Resources Initiative, Washington, DC, p. 14.

(80). UNESCO, World Heritage Convention (2002). Operational Guidelines for the Implementation of the World Heritage Convention. UNESCO, Paris, p. 54.

(81). Uphoff, N. (1992). Local Institutions and Participation for Sustainable Development. IIED, London, p. 16.

(82). Verschuuren, B. (2012). Integrating Cultural Values in Nature Conservation: Perceptions of Culturally Significant Sites and Species in Adaptive Management, in: Pungetti, G., Oviedo, G., Hooke, D. (eds.), Sacred Species and Sites: Advances in Biocultural Conservation. Cambridge University Press, Cambridge England, pp. 231–46.

(83). Verschuuren, B., Wild, R., McNeely, J., and G. Oviedo (2010). Introduction: Sacred Natural Sites the Foundations for Conservation, in: Verschuuren, B., Wild, R., McNeely, J., Oviedo, G. (eds.), Sacred Natural Sites—Conserving Nature and Culture. Earthscan, London, pp. 1–13.

(84). Weymouth, A. (2009). Where Spirit Lies. Resurgence 253, 36–37.

(85). Wild, R., and C. McLeod (2008). Sacred Natural Sites: Guidelines for Protected Area Managers, in: Wild, R., McLeod, C. (eds.), Sacred Natural Sites: Guidelines for Protected Area Managers. IUCN, Gland, Switzerland.

(86). Wilson, E. (1998). Consilience: The Unity of Knowledge. Vintage Books, New York.

(87). Zogib, L., Tashi, K., Gyalpo, T., Dendhup, S., Kuyakanon., Wangchuk, K., Tenzin, L., and N. Gyeltshen (2016). Sacred Mandala: Protecting Bhutan's Sacred Natural Site, in: Verschuuren, B., Furuta, N. (eds.), Asian Sacred Natural Sites: Philosophy and Practice in Protected Areas and Conservation. Routledge, London, pp. 57–68.

Chapter 6

(1). Ackling, R. (2016). The Artist who Drew in the Sun. Resurgence and Ecologist 297, 56–57.
(2). Adams, C. (2012). Games People Play. Resurgence 273, 34–35.
(3). Anantananda, S. (2004). Learning Session 14: Questions and Answers—Living Siddha Yoga Wisdom, A Practical Application of Siddha Yoga Philosophy. SYDA Foundation, South Fallsberg, New York, p. 16.
(4). Anielski, M. (2011). Genuine Wealth. Resurgence 269, 26–27.
(5). Baasten, M. (1999). Christian Values, Technology and the Environmental Crisis, in: Dempsey, C., Butkus, R. (Eds.), All Creation is Groaning: An Interdisciplinary Vision for Life in a Sacred Universe. Liturgical Press, Minnesota, pp. 58–76.
(6). Bernbaum, E. (1997). Sacred Mountains of the World. University California Press, Berkley, USA.
(7). Berry, T. (1988). The Dream of the Earth. Sierra Club Books, San Francisco.
(8). Bhagwat, S. (2012). Sacred Groves and Biodiversity Conservation: A Case Study form the Western Ghats, India, in: Pungetti, G., Oviedo, G., Hooke, D. (eds.), Sacred Species and Sites: Advances in Biocultural Conservation. Cambridge University Press, Cambridge England, pp. 322–34.
(9). Bhagwat, S., Kushalappa, C., Williams, P., and N. Brown (2005). A Landscape Approach to Biodiversity Conservation of Sacred Groves in the Western Ghats of India. Conservation Biology 19, 1853-1862.
(10). Bookless, D. (2011). Inspiring Leadership. Resurgence 264, 18-19.
(11). Borrini-Feyerabend, G. (2002). Editorial: Local Communities and Protected Areas—A Conservation at a Distance. PARKS 12.
(12). Brown, J. (1998). Stewardship: An International Perspective. Environments: A Journal of Interdisciplinary Studies 26, 3–7.
(13). Capra, F. (2014). Pedagogy of Sustainability. Resurgence and Ecologist 283, 28.
(14). Capra, F. (2018). Science, Spirituality and Religion. Resurgence and Ecologist 310, 22–25.
(15). Carson, R. (1956). A Sense of Wonder. Harper and Row, New York.
(16). Carson, R. (2002). Silent Spring (first published 1962). Mariner Books, New York.
(17). Chidvilasananda, G. (1990). The Dawn is a Tray of Gold - Reflection on Nature. Darshan, Syda Foundation 36, 76–87.
(18). Clarke, J. (1993). Nature in Question—An Anthology of Ideas and Arguments. Earthscan, London.
(19). Cowan, F. (2001). Francis—A Saint's Way. Hodder and Stoughton, London.

(20). Cullinan, C. (2002). Wild Law. Siber Ink in Association with the Gaia Foundation, Capetown.
(21). Dahl, A., (2017). Why Should the UN and in Particular UN Environment Engage More with Faith-Based Organizations. UN Environment Perspectives, Nairobi, p. 7.
(22). Dempsey, C., and R. Butkus (1999). All Creation is Groaning: An Interdisciplinary Vision for Life in a Sacred Universe. Liturgical Press, Minnesota.
(23). Eaton, H. (2005). Book Review: "Worldly Wonder: Religions enter their Ecological Phase" by Mary Evelyn Tucker. Resurgence 228, 67.
(24). El-Naggar, Z. (2015). Conservation of the Environment in Islam, in: Wit, P., Hassona, M., Al-Khalaifi, F. (Eds.), Proceedings of the Second International Forum of the Qur'anic Botanic Garden: Islamic Perspectives on Ecosystem Management Quar'anic Botanic Garden, and IUCN Commission on Ecosystem Management, Doha, Qatar, pp. 9–23.
(25). Evans, J. (2014). God's Trees: Trees, Forests and Wood in the Bible. One Day Publications, Leominster, England.
(26). Fjeld, F. (1986). The Mother Earth vs Western Man: The American Confrontation Between Two Opposing Value Systems. San Francisco State University, San Francisco.
(27). Fox, W. (2014). Beautiful Days. Resurgence and Ecologist 286, 42–44.
(28). Francescato, G., and D. Talamo (2012). The Roman Goddess Care: A Therapy for the Planet, in: Pungetti, G., Oviedo, G., Hooke, D. (eds.), Sacred Species and Sites: Advances in Biocultural Conservation. Cambridge University Press, Cambridge England, pp. 178–91.
(29). Gari, L. (2006.) A Hisotry of the *Hima* Conservation System. Environment and History 12, 213–28.
(30). Girardet, H. (2018). A Call for Regeneration. Resurgence and Ecologist 306, 26–28.
(31). Goodland, R. (1990). Tropical Moist Forest Deforestation: Ethics and Solutions, in: Scientiarum, P. A. (ed.), Tropical Forests and the Conservation of Species. Casina Pion IV, 00120 Citta del Vaticano, Rome, p. 53.
(32). Hamilton, L. (1998.) Forest and Tree Conservation through Metaphysical Constraints, in: UNESCO (ed.), Natural Sacred Sites. Cultural Diversity and Biological Diversity. Proc. Int. Symp., Paris 1998. UNESCO, Paris, p. 18.
(33). Harding, S. (2013). Book Review "Thinking like a Plant: A Living Science for Life" by Craig Holdrege. Resurgence and Ecologist 281, 65.
(34). Harmon, D., and A. Putney (2003). The Full Value of Parks—From Economics to the Intangible. Rowman and Littlefield, New York, p. 347.
(35). Harris, P. (2000). Under the Bright Wings. Regent College Publishing, Vancouver.

(36). Hill, M., and A. Press (1994). Kakadu National Park: An Australian Experience in Comanagement, in: Western, D., Wright, R., Strum, S. (eds.), Natural Connections: Perspectives in Community-Based Conservation. Island Press, Washington, DC, pp. 135–57.
(37). Holder, R. (2001). Karl Barth and the Legitimacy of Natural Theology. Themelios 26, 22–37.
(38). Horning, N. (2008). Behind Sacredness in Madagascar: Rules, Local Interests and Forest Conservation in Bara Country, in: Sheridan, M., Nyamweru, C. (eds.), African Sacred Groves: Ecological Dynamics and Social Change. James Currey, Oxford, pp. 117–32.
(39). Hosken, L. (2017). Learning from Nature's Laws and Lore. Resurgence and Ecologist 304, 21-23.
(40). Howarth, L. (2012). Book Review: "The Global Forest - 40 ways Trees Can Save Us" by Diana Kruger. Resurgence 270, 63.
(41). His Royal Highness The Prince of Wales (2011). Islam and the Environment. Resurgence 265, 22–25.
(42). Hutchins, G. (2013). Business Harmony. Resurgence and Ecologist 278, 64.
(43). Jeanrenaud, S., (2001). An International Initiative for the Protection and Sacred Natural Sites and Other Places of Indigenous and Traditional Peoples with Importance for Biodiveristy Conservation. A Concept Paper. WWF International - People and Conservation, Gland, Switzerland, p. 44.
(44). Kallistos, Bishop of Diokleia (1995). Through the Creation to the Creator. Fifth Marcus Pallis Memorial Lecture of Friends of the Center/REEP. Royal Institution of Great Britain, London.
(45). Katz, B. (2018). Local Time. RSA Journal 1, 24–27.
(46). Khan, K. (1999). An Islamic Perspective on the Environment, in: Dempsey, C., Butkus, R. (eds.), All Creation Is Groaning: An Interdisciplinary Vision for Life in a Sacred Universe. Liturgical Press, Minnesota, pp. 46–57.
(47). Kilani, H., Serhal, A., and O. Othmn. (2007). *Al Hima*: A Way of Life. IUCN West Asia Regional Office, Amman, Jordan.
(48). Klein, N. (2014). This Changes Everything. Penguin - Random House, London.
(49). Kleymeyer, C. (1994). Cultural Traditions and Community-Based Conservation, in: Western, D., Wright, R., Strum, S. (Eds.), Natural Connections: Perspectives in Community-Based Conservation. Island Press, Washington, DC, pp. 323–46.
(50). Kothari, A., and N. Pathak. (2008). Defenders of Biodiversity. Resurgence 250, 36–37.
(51). Kumar, S. (2004). Development and Religion. Resurgence 227, 16–20.
(52). Kumar, S. (2005). Spiritual Imperative—Elegant Simplicity is the Way to Discover Spirituality. Resurgence 229, 6–12.

(53). Kumar, S. (2005). Spirituality and Politics. Resurgence 229, 3.
(54). Kumar, S. (2006). If We Live Well, All Shall be Well. Resurgence 237, 3.
(55). Kumar, S. (2009). Pilgrims or Tourists. Resurgence 255, 3.
(56). Kumar, S. (2011). The Stort of Schumacher. Resurgence 267, 1.
(57). Kumar, S. (2013). The Ecozoic Era. Resurgence and Ecologist 279, 1.
(58). Kumar, S. (2013). Reaching out - Time has Come to Spread the Word. Resurgence and Ecologist 277, 1–2.
(59). Kumar, S. (2015). Unconditional Empathy. Resurgence and Ecologist 289, 38–39.
(60). Leach, M., Mearns, R., and I. Scoones (1997). Environmental Entitlements: A Framework for Understanding the Institutional Dynamics of Environmental Change. IDS Discussion Paper, 30.
(61). Leach, M., Mearns, R., and I. Scoones (1999). Environmental Entitlements: Dynamics and Institutions in Community Based Natural Resource Management. World Development 27, 225–47.
(62). Lent, J. (2018). If We Want to Prosper, Even Survive, We Need New Meaning in Life. Resurgence and Ecologist 309, 26–28.
(63). Leopold, A. (1970). A Sand County Almanac—And Sketches Here and There. Oxford University Press, London.
(64). Lovelock, J. (2005). At War with the Earth. Resurgence 228, 6–7.
(65). Lovelock, J. (2005). Gaia: Medicine for an Ailing Planet. Gaia Books, London.
(66). Lovelock, J. (2009). The Vanishing Face of Gaia: A Final Warning. Penguin Books, London.
(67). Mandela, N. (2006). Words of Wisdom. Mentor Books, Dublin.
(68). Mason, I. (2008). Earth Jurisprudence. Resurgence 247, 26–27.
(69). McDonagh, S. (1986). To Care for the Earth - a Call to a New Theology. Cassell Publishing, London.
(70). Merton, T. (1969). The Way of Chuang Tzu. New Direction Publications, New York.
(71). Mitchell, B., and J. Brown (1998). Stewardship: A Working Definition. A Journal of Interdisciplinary Studies 26, 8–17.
(72). Mitchell, B., and J. Brown (2003). Stewardship and Protected Areas in a Global Context: Coping with Change and Fostering Civil Society, in: Minteer, B., Manning, R. (eds.), Reconstructing Conservation—Finding Common Ground. Island Press, Washington, pp. 297–311.
(73). Mosse, K. (2011). Why the Yew Lives so Long, in: Chevalier, T., Prisser, S. (eds.), Why Willows Weep—Contemporary Tales from the Woods. The Woodland Trust, England, pp. 117–21.
(74). Nasr, S. (1998). The Spiritual and Religous Dimensions of the Environmental Crisis. Temenos Academy, London.

(75). Nasr, S. (2000). The Spiritual and Religous Dimensions of the Environmental Crisis. The Ecologist 30, 18–20.
(76). Oliver, J. (2005). Art of the Possible. Resurgence 228, 20–21.
(77). Oreskes, N. (2015). Introduction, in: Pope Francis, Encyclical on Clinate Change: On Care for Our Common Home. Melville House Publishing New York, pp. vii–xxiv.
(78). Orr, D. (2011). Hope Is an Imperative—The Essential David Orr. Island Press, Washington, DC.
(79). Osland, J. (1999). The Stewardship of Natural and Human Resources, in: Dempsey, C., Butkus, R. (eds.), All Creation Is Groaning: An Interdisciplinary Vision for Life in a Sacred Universe. Liturgical press, Minnesota, pp. 168–92.
(80). Ostrom, E. (1990.) Governing the Commons: The Evolution of Instituions for Collective Action. Cambridge University Press.
(81). Oviedo, G. (2012). Spiritual Values and Conservation, in: Pungetti, G., Oviedo, G., Hooke, D. (eds.), Sacred Species and Sites: Advances in Biocultural Conservation. Cambridge University Press, Cambridge England, pp. 28–35.
(82). Oviedo, G. (2015). Reflections on Cultural and Spiritual Values, Traditions and Customs in Conservation, in: Wit, P., Hassona, M., Al-Khalaifi, F. (eds.), Proceedings of the Second International Forum of the Qur'anic Botanic Garden: Islamic Perspectives on Ecosystem Management. Qur'anic Botanic Garden and IUCN Commission on Ecosystem Management, Doha, Qatar, pp. 87–101.
(83). Parry, G. (2016). Think of Time as Nature Thinks. Resurgence and Ecologist 294, 21–24.
(84). Pigem, J. (2005.) The Greening of Religions—A Reverence for Life. Resurgence 229, 53.
(85). Pope Francis (2015). Encyclical on Climate Change and Inequality: On Care for Our Common Home. Melville House Publishing, New York.
(86). Prsewozny, B., Savini, C., and O. Todisco (1987). Elements of a Catholic Doctrine of Humankind's Relation to the Environment. Ecologia Francescana, Quaderni Francescani 13, 223–55.
(87). Pungetti, G., Oviedo, G., and D. Hooke (2012). Sacred Species and Sites: Advances in Biocultural Conservation. Cambridge University Press, Cambridge, p. 472.
(88). Putney, A., and T. Schaaf (2003). Guidelines for the Management of Sacrfed Natural Sites—First Draft Version, in: Putney, A. (Ed.), A Report on the Contribution to the World Parks Congress of the World Commission on Protected Areas, Task Force on Cultural and Spiritual Values. IUCN—The World Conservation Union, Durban.
(89). Rai, J., and S. Thing (2016). A Biocultural Perspective on the Recognition and Support for Sacred Natural Sites in Nepal, in: Verschuuren, B., Furuta,

N. (eds.), Asian Sacred Natural Sites: Philosophy and Practice in Protected Area and Conservation. Routledge, London, pp. 81–92.
(90). Robinsion, E. (2018). Forward Thinking. RSA Journal 1, 11–15.
(91). Sainsbury, J. (2012.) The New Moral Compass. Resurgence 270, 13.
(92). Sayer, J., Maginnis, S., Laurie, M., and D. Sengupta (2004). Changing Realities: Ecosystem Approaches and Sustainable Forest Management—Arborvitae Special. Arborvitae October 2004, 12.
(93). Schettler, T. (2010). Ecological Health. Resurgence 261, 15–16.
(94). Schumacher, E., (1993). The Age of Plenty—A Christian View, in: Daly, H., Townsend, K. (eds.), Valuing the Earth—Economics, Ecology, Ethics. MIT Press, Massachusetts, pp. 159–72.
(95). Sen, A. (1981). Poverty and Famines: An Essay on Entitlement and Deprivation. Oxford University Press, Oxford.
(96). Shepherd, G. (2007). The Ecosystem Approach: Five Steps to Implementation. IUCN, Gland, Switzerland, x + 30 pp.
(97). Sheridan, M. (2008). The Dynamics of African Sacred Groves, in: Sheridan, M., Nyamweru, C. (eds.), African Sacred Groves: Ecological Dynamics and Social Change. James Currey, Oxford, pp. 9–41.
(98). Shrumm, H., and S. Booker (2012). Protecting the Sacred: The Role of Community Protocols Play in the Protection of Sacred Natural Sites. Langscape 2, 34–39.
(99). Sponsel, L., and P. Ndadecha-Sponsel (2003). Buddhist Views of Nature and the Enironment, in Selin S. (ed.), Nature Across Cultures: Views of Nature and the Environment in Non-Western Cultures. Springer, Netherlands, pp. 351–72.
(100). Stiglitz, J. (2009). Progress What Progress? OECD Observer 272, 6.
(101). Stowe, J. (2003). The Findhorn Book of Connecting with Nature. Findhorn Press, Edinburgh.
(102). Suzuki, D., and H. Dressel (1999). From Naked Ape to Superspecies: A Personal Perspective on Humanity and the Global Eco-crisis. Stoddart, Toronto.
(103). Tolle, E. (2005). A New Earth: Awakening to Your Life's Purpose. Plume, New York.
(104). Turnbull, S. (2011). Gentle Stewardship. Resurgence 264, 12–13.
(105). Tuxill, J. (2000). The Landscape of Conservation Stewardshiop. The Report of the Stewardship Initiative Feasibility Study. Marshall-Billings-Rockefeller National Heritage Park Conservation Study Institute, Vermont, p. 77.
(106). Tzu, L. (2011). Leadership. Resurgence 264, 11.
(107). Union of Concerned Scientists (1992). World Scientists Warning to Humanity. Union of Concerned Scientists, Cambridge, USA.

(108). Van Zyl, M. (2007). Karl Barth's Theology of Nature: Safeguard against the Natural Theologians of Fundamentalism and Secularism. Stellenbosch Theological Journal 48.
(109). Verschuuren, B. (2012). Integrating Cultural Values in Nature Conservation: Perceptions of Culturally Significant Sites and Species in Adaptive Management, in: Pungetti, G., Oviedo, G., Hooke, D. (eds.), Sacred Species and Sites: Advances in Biocultural Conservation. Cambridge University Press, Cambridge England, pp. 231–46.
(110). Verschuuren, B., and N. Furuta (2016). Asian Sacred Natural Sites: Philosophy and Practice in Protected Areas and Conservation. Routledge, London, p. 318.
(111). Verschuuren, B., Wild, R., McNeely, J., and G. Oviedo (2010). Sacred Natural Sites: Conserving Nature and Culture. Earthscan, London, p. 310.
(112). Williams, R. (2004). Gift of God. Resurgence 227, 6–10.
(113). Wilson, E. (1992). The Diversity of Life. Penguin Book, London.
(114). Wit, P., Harrona, M., and F. Al-Khalaifi (2015). Proceedings of the Second Forum of the Qur'anic Botanic Garden: Islamic Perspectivs on Ecosystem Management. Qur'anic Botanic Garden and IUCN, Doha, Qatar, p. 354.
(115). Zogib, L., Tashi, K., Gyalpo, T., Dendhup, S., Kuyakanon., Wangchuk, k., Tenzin, L., and N. Gyeltshen (2016). Sacred Mandala: Protecting Bhutan's Sacred Natural Site, in: Verschuuren, B., Furuta, N. (eds.), Asian Sacred Natural Sites: Philosophy and Practice in Protected Areas and Conservation. Routledge, London, pp. 57–68.

Chapter 7

(1). Adams, M. (2014). The Wisdom of Trees. Head of Zeus Ltd., London.
(2). Aitkens, A. (2015). Only Connect: Joining the Dots for the Future We Want. Resurgence and Ecologist 289, 30–33.
(3). Armstrong, K. (2006). Compassion Is the Key. Resurgence 235, 33–34.
(4). Atwood, M. (2011). New Frontiers. Resurgence 268, 8–12.
(5). Barton, J., Hine, R., and J. Pretty (2009). The Health Benefits of Walking in Greenspaces of High Natural and Heritage Value. J. of Integrative Environmental Sciences 6, 261–78.
(6). Barton, J., and J. Pretty (2010). Urban Ecology and Human Health and Wellbeing, in: Gaston, J. (ed.), Urban Ecology. Cambridge University Press, Cambridge, pp. 202–29.
(7). Berry, T. (1988.) The Dream of the Earth. Sierra Club Books, San Francisco.
(8). Berry, T., and T. Clarke (1991). Befriending the Earth: A Theology of Reconciliation between Human and the Earth. Twenty-Third Publications, Connecticut.
(9). Berry, W. (2015). Our Only World—Ten Essays. Counterpoint Press, Berkeley.

(10). Bird, W. (2007). Natural Thinking: Investigating the Links Between the Natural Environment, Biodiversity and Mental Health. Royal Society of the Protection of Birds, London, p. 116.
(11). Bird, W. (2010). NHS—A Natural Health Service. Resurgence 258, 10–12.
(12). Black-Elk, W., and W. Lyon (1991). Black Elk—The Sacred Ways of a Lakota. Harper, San Francisco.
(13). Bouchardon, P. (1998). The Healing Energies of Trees. Gaia Books, London.
(14). Burbea, R. (2015). The Buddha and the Sacred Eart. Resurgence and Ecologist 288, 34–37.
(15). Canadian Parks Council, #NatureForAll, and IUCN (2016). The #NatureForAll Playbook: An Action Guide for Inspiring Love of Nature. Canadian Parks Council, Peterborough, Canada.
(16). Capra, F., (2011). Foreword to book "Hope is an Imperative: the Essential David Orr, in: Orr, D. (Ed.), Hope is an Imperative: the Essential David Orr. Island Press, Washington, DC, pp. xi–xiii.
(17). Capra, F. (2012). Ecological Literacy. Resurgence 272, 42–43.
(18). Carson, R. (1956). A Sense of Wonder. Harper and Row, New York.
(19). Charles, C., Keenleyside, K., Chapple, R., Kilburn, B., van der Leest, P., Allen, D., Richardson, M., Giusti, M., Franklin, L., Harbrow, M., Wilson, R., Moss, A., Metcalf, L., and L. Camargo (2018). Home to Us All: How Connecting with Nature Helps Us Care for Ourselves and the Earth. IUCN, Children and Nature Network, Gland, Switzerland.
(20). Chopra, D. (2007). Evolution of Wisdom. Resurgence 243, 12–15.
(21). Clarke, P. (2015). A Beetle's View of the Cosmos Might Suit our Schools. Resurgence and Ecologist 293, 34–35.
(22). Dahl, A., (2017). Why Should the UN and in Particular UN Environment Engage More with Faith-Based Organizations. UN Environment Perspectives, Nairobi, p. 7.
(23). Davies, K. (2009). A Learning Society. Resurgence 257, 42–43.
(24). Dolesh, R. (2014). A Walk in the Park. Resurgence and Ecologist 284, 16–17.
(25). East-West-Center (2017) .Youth Voices Curriculum Sourcebook. IUCN, Gland, Switzerland.
(26). Eisenstein, C. (2014). A Beautiful World of Abundance. Resurgence and Ecologist 286, 34–37.
(27). Elworthy, S. (2017). Working for a World without War. Resurgence and Ecologist 302, 34-36.
(28). Felix and Friends (2011). Tree by Tree: Now We Children Save the World. Plant for the Planet, Germany.
(29). Follmi, D., and O. Follmi (2005). African Wisdom 365 Days. Thames and Hudson Ltd., London.

(30). Freire, P. (1968). Pedagogy of the Oppressed. Continuum International Publishing Group, New York.

(31). Gauger, A., Rabatel-Fernel, M., Kulbicki, L., Short, D., and P. Higgins (2012). The Ecocide Project: Ecocide Is the Missing 5th Crime Against Peace. Human Rights Commission, London, England, p. 13.

(32). Giracca, A. (2016). Into the Field. https://orionmagazine.org/article/into-the-field/ accessed 2016, 7.

(33). Gore, A. (2008). Peace with the Planet. Resurgence 248, 14–15.

(34). Hallen, P. (2014). Walking in Kimberley. Resurgence and Ecologist 284, 34–35.

(35). Hanh, T. (1987). Being Peace. Rider Ltd., London.

(36). Hosken, L. (2009). Potent Places. Resurgence 255, 19–20.

(37). Howarth, L. (2004). Welcome—A Local Economy Is One that Cannot Afford Weapons of Mass Destruction. Resurgence 222, 3.

(38). International Criminal Court (2011). Rome Statute of the International Criminal Court. International Criminal Court, Hague, the Netherlands, p. 81.

(39). Jucker, R. (2004). Review of book by C. Bowers titled "Mindful Conservatism." Resurgence 227, 74–75.

(40). Kabat-Zinn, J. (2012). Mindfulness for Beginners: Reclaiming the Present Moment—And Your Life. Sounds True, Boulder USA.

(41). Kelly, S. (2016). Rites to Touch the Sacred. Book Review: "Re-enchanting the Forest: Meaningful Ritual in a Secular World" by William Ayot. Resurgence and Ecologist 296, 64.

(42). Kingsnorth, P. (2016). The Man who Saw Fire in the Eye of the Wolf. Resurgence and Ecologist 294, 33–34.

(43). Kingsnorth, P. (2017). The Axis and the Sycamore. Orion Magazine https://orionmagazine.org/article/the-axis-and-the-sycamore/ accessed 2017, 6.

(44). Klein, N. (2014). This Changes Everything. Penguin—Random House, London.

(45). Krishnamurti, J. (1991). Nature and the Environment. Harper, San Francisco.

(46). Kumar, S. (2005). Nature Knows Us—Do We Know Nature? Resurgence 232, 3.

(47). Kumar, S. (2005). Welcome. Resurgence 230, 3.

(48). Kumar, S. (2014). The Power of Nonviolence. Resurgence and Ecologist 286, 38–40.

(49). Kumar, S. (2016). Knowledge Requires Life Experience, Not Just Facts. Resurgence and Ecologist 298, 38–39.

(50). Kumar, S. (2016). One Earth, One Humanity, One Future. Resurgence and Ecologist 294, 44–45.

(51). Kumar, S. (2016). War is Hell—We Must Stop it. Resurgence and Ecologist 296, 42–43.

(52). Kumar, S. (2017). A Deeper Appreciation of Nature. Resurgence and Ecologist 305, 40–41.
(53). Kumar, S. (2017). Storyteller of the Life that Could Be. Resurgence and Ecologist 303, 40–41.
(54). Kumar, S. (2018). The True Meaning of Economy. Resurgence and Ecologist 307, 38–39.
(55). Leopold, A. (1953). Round River. Oxford University Press (1987), New York.
(56). Leopold, A. (1970). A Sand County Almanac—And Sketches Here and There. Oxford University Press, London.
(57). Li, Q. (2010). Effect of Forest Bathing Trips on Human Immune Function. J. Environmental Health and Preventative Medicine, 9–17.
(58). Li, Q., Kobayashi, M., Wakayama, Y., Inagaki, H., Katsumata, M., Hirata, K., Hirata, K., Shimizu, T., Kawada, T., Park, J., Ohira, T., Kagawa, T., and Y. Miyazaki (2009). Effect of Phytoncides from Trees on Human Natural Killer Cell Function. Int. J. of Immunopathology and Pharmacology 22, 951–59.
(59). Li, Q., Kobayashi, M., Inagaki, H., Katsumata, M., Hirata, K., Hirata, K., Susuki, H., Li, Y., Wakayama, Y., Kawada, T., Park, J., Ohira, T., Matsuf, N., Kagawa, T., Miyazaki, Y., and A. Krensk (2008). Visiting a Forest, but not a City, Increases Human Natural Killer Activity and Expressions of Anti-Cancer Proteins. Int. J. of Immunopathology and Pharmacology 21, 117–27.
(60). Louv, R. (2008). Last Child in the Woods: Saving Our Children from Nature-Deficit Disorder. Workman Publishing, New York.
(61). Louv, R. (2009). Nature-Deficit Disorder. Resurgence 254, 14–15.
(62). Louv, R. (2010). Nature Deficit Disorder. Resurgence 260, 16–17.
(63). Louv, R. (2017). Leave No Child Inside. Orion Magazine https://orionmagazine.org/article/leave-no-child-inside/ 6.
(64). Maathai, W. (2006). Unbowed—A Memoir. William Heinemann, London.
(65). MacKeeron, G., and S. Mourato (2013). Happiness is Greater in Natural Environments. Global Environmnental Change, 1–23.
(66). MacNamee, J. (2016). Walking Back to Happiness. Resurgence and Ecologist 295, 26–28.
(67). Maira, S. (2009). A Master Key. Resurgence 253, 40–42.
(68). Maira, S. (2010). Eternal Beauty. Resurgence 261, 24–27.
(69). Makaulule, M., and H. Swanby (2008). Wisdom—African Spirit. Resurgence 247, 28–29.
(70). Mandela, N. (2006). Words of Wisdom. Mentor Books, Dublin.
(71). Mathai, W. (2005). Learning from Trees. Resurgence 233, 24–25.
(72). Mathai, W. (2007). Poverty and Empowerment. Resurgence 245, 27–29.
(73). McCloud, C. (2009). The Kiss of Earth. Resurgence 255, 28–29.
(74). McKibben, B. (2005). Enoughness. Resurgence 229, 23.

(75). Melville, H. (1852). Pierre, or the Ambiguities (Book XIV Ch. 1). Harper and Brothers, New York.
(76). Montealegre, K., and D. Victory (2011). Costa Rica: For the Soul. Motmat Ediciones, San Jose.
(77). Moore, T. (2008). Pray to Gaia. Resurgence 247, 47.
(78). Morris, N. (2003). Health, Wellbeing, and Open Space Literature Review, Edinburgh Openspace.
(79). Muir, J. (2012). The Yosemite. The Century Company and https://vault.sierraclub.org/john_muir_exhibit/writings/the_yosemite/ New York.
(80). Neuberger, J. (2013). My Green Life—Environmental Issues are Moral Issues. Resurgence and Ecologist 277, 32.
(81). Nyerere, J. (1967). Èducation for Self-Reliance. Government Printer, Dar-es-Salaam.
(82). Orr, D. (2011). Hope Is an Imperative—The Essential David Orr. Island Press, Washington, DC.
(83). Palmer, M. (2013). The Quiet Revolution. Resurgence and Ecologist 277, 44–45.
(84). Passchier-Vermeer, W., and W. Passchier (2000). Noise Exposure and Public Health. Environmental Health Perspectives 108, 123–31.
(85). Pope Francis (2015). Encyclical on Climate Change and Inequality: On Care for our Common Home. Melville House Publishing, New York.
(86). Pretty, J. (2006). Green Care—Working the Land Is Good for Your Health. Resurgence 234, 9.
(87). Priest, P. (2006). Walking Testimonies. Resurgence 234, 26–27.
(88). Randall, B. (2007). Kanyini—The Four Dimensions of Aboriginal Life. Resurgence 243, 26–27.
(89). Reid, K. (2013). From Fragmentation to Wholeness. Resurgence and Ecologist 279, 32–35.
(90). Reynolds, F. (2011). Rethinking Conservation. Resurgence 266, 52–53.
(91). Rivah, L. (2008). Sacred Creation. Resurgence 250, 16–17.
(92). Rodriguez-Navarro, G., (2012). Sacred Natural Sites in Zones of Armed Conflicts: the Sierra Nevada de Santa Marta in Colombia, in: Pungetti, G., Oviedo, G., Hooke, D. (Eds.), Sacred Species and Sites: Advances in Biocultural Conservation. Cambridge University Press, Cambridge England, pp. 152–64.
(93). Samuel, K. (2015). Building for Belonging: Making our Cities Feel Like Home. Resurgence and Ecologist 290, 30–32.
(94). Schumacher, E. (2011). Buddhist Economics. Resurgence 267, 2–33.
(95). Shanahan, M. (2016). Ladders to Heaven: How Fig Trees Shaped our History, Fed Our Imaginations, and Can Enrich Our Future. Unbound, London.
(96). Shiva, V. (2007). How Wealth Creates Poverty. Resurgence 240, 14–15.

(97). Siddons, E. (2018). Kids at Work. New Internationalist 509, 18–21.
(98). Sigman, A. (2009). Videophilia. Resurgence 254, 16–17.
(99). Simon, B. (2012). Tales, Traditions and Folklore of Ireland's Trees. The Forest of Belfast, Belfast.
(100). Sobel, D. (2012). Look, Don't Touch. Orion Magazine https://orionmagazine.org/article/look-dont-touch1/, 8.
(101). Stowe, J.R. (2003). The Findhorn Book of Connecting with Nature. Findhorn Press, Edinburgh.
(102). Strife, S., and L. Downey (2009) Childhood Development and Access to Nature: a New Direction for Environmental Inequality Research. Organization and Environment 22, 99–122.
(103). Suzuki, D., and I. Hanington (2012). Everything Under the Sun: Toward a Brighter Future on a Small Blue Planet. Greystone Books, Vancouver, Canada.
(104). Swimme, B., and M.Tucker (2011). Journey of the Universe. Yale University Press, New Haven.
(105). Thinley, J. (2010). Exploring How Bhutan Might Now Implement Its Unique Concept of Gross National Happiness into Its Education Systems. Resurgence 260, 20–23.
(106). Thorpe, A. (2005). A Thin Veil of Anger. Resurgence 232, 9–11.
(107). Tolle, E. (2005). A New Earth: Awakening to Your Life's Purpose. Plume, New York.
(108). Toomey, C. (2015). On Course for Compassion. Resurgence and Ecologist 293, 36–38.
(109). Turner, A. (2004). Healing the Air. Resurgence 224, 10–11.
(110). Tzu, L. (2009). Taoteching - Selected Commentary by Red Pine. Copper Canyon Press, Washington.
(111). Waine, P. (2012). Making Life Worth Living. Resurgence and Ecologist 274, 50–51.
(112). Warwick, H. (2017). Lines of Hope in the Land. Resurgence and Ecologist 303, 10–12.
(113). Williams, F. (2017). The Nature Fix: Why Nature Makes Us Happier, Healthier, and More Creatie. W. W. Norton, New York.
(114). Wilson, E. (2006). The Creation: An Appeal to Save Life on Earth. Norton and Co., New York.

Chapter 8

(1). Berry, T. (1988). The Dream of the Earth. San Francisco: Sierra Club Books.
(2). Berry, W. (2015). *Our Only World—Ten Essays*. Berkeley: Counterpoint Press.

(3). Black-Elk, W., and W. Lyon. (1991). *Black Elk—The Sacred Ways of a Lakota*. San Francisco: Harper.

(4). Capra, F. (2014). Pedagogy of Sustainability. Resurgence and Ecologist 283, 28.

(5). Constanza, R. (2013). Sustainable Wellbeing. Resurgence and Ecologist 279, 39–41.

(6). Emerson, R. W. (2009). *Nature and Other Essays (originally published 1836)*. New York: Dover Publications.

(7). Follmi, D., and O. Follmi. (2005). *African Wisdom 365 Days*. London: Thames and Hudson Ltd.

(8). Gomez, S., and N. Ortiz. (2009). Laws of Origin. *Resurgence* 255 (July/August), 26–27.

(9). Hamilton, L. (1998). Forest and Tree Conservation through Metaphysical Constraints. In *Natural Sacred Sites. Cultural Diversity and Biological Diversity. Proc. Int. Symp., Paris 1998*, edited by UNESCO. Paris: UNESCO.

(10). Harmon, D., and A. Putney, eds. (2003). *The Full Value of Parks—From Economics to the Intangible*. New York: Rowman and Littlefield.

(11). Higgins, P. (2012). What will our Legacy Be? *Resurgence* 270, 30.

(12). Kilmer, J. (1913). Trees. *Poetry, a Magazine of Verse* II (5), 160.

(13). Kingsnorth, P. (2016). The Man who Saw Fire in the Eye of the Wolf. Resurgence and Ecologist 294, 33–34.

(14). Klein, N. (2014). *This Changes Everything*. London: Penguin - Random House.

(15). Kumar, S. (2004). Development and Religion. Resurgence 227 (November/December), 16–20.

(16). ———. (2009). Art for Earth's Sake. *Resurgence* 257 (November/December), 46–48.

(17). ———. (2017). From Nationalism to Glocalism. Resurgence and Ecologist 302 (May/June), 40–41.

(18). ———. (2017). Storyteller of the Life that Could Be. Resurgence and Ecologist 303 (July–August), 40–41.

(19). Leopold, A. (1970). *A Sand County Almanac—And Sketches Here and There*. London: Oxford University Press.

(20). Luther-King, M. (2004). *Quotations of Martin Luther King Jr*. Washington, DC: Applewood Books.

(21). Mathai, W. (2004). The Cracked Mirror. *Resurgence* 227 (November/December), 21–23.

(22). Monbiot, G. (2014). An Ounce of Hope Is Worth a Ton of Dispair. Resurgence and Ecologist 287, 14–15.

(23). Orr, D. (2008). The Rythm of Gratitude. Resurgence 247, 10–11.

(24). ———. (2011). *Hope Is an Imperative—The Essential David Orr*. Washington, DC: Island Press.
(25). Phillips, M. (2012). Silent Spring. *Resurgence* 270, 28–29.
(26). Pope Francis. (2015). *Encyclical on Climate Change and Inequality: On Care for our Common Home*. New York: Melville House Publishing.
(27). Pope John Paul II. (1990). Message of His Holiness Pope John Paul II for the Celebration of the World Day of Peace. Vatican.
(28). Porritt, J. (2011). Challenging the Greens. Resurgence 268, 26–27.
(29). Pungetti, G., G. Oviedo, and D. Hooke. (2012). Conclusions: the Journey to Biocultural Conservation. In *Sacred Species and Sites: Advances in Biocultural Conservation*, edited by G. Pungetti, G. Oviedo and D. Hooke. Cambridge England: Cambridge University Press.
(30). Putney, A. and T. Schaaf. (2003). Guidelines for the Management of Sacrfed Natural Sites—First Draft Version. Paper read at A Report on the Contribution to the World Parks Congress of the World Commission on Protected Areas, Task Force on Cultural and Spiritual Values, at Durban.
(31). Rueckert, W. (1996). Literature and Ecology: An Experiment in Ecocriticism. In *The Ecocriticism Reader: Landmarks in Literary Ecology*, edited by Glotfelty and Fromm. Athens, Georgia: University Georgia Press.
(32). Schaaf, T. (2003). UNESCO's Experience with the Protection of Sacred Natural Sites for Biodiversity Conservation. In *The Importance of Sacred Natural Sites for Biodiversity Conservation. Proc. Int. Workshop on the Importance of Sacred Natural Sites for Biodiversity Conservation in Kunming and Xishuangbanna Biosphere Reserve, People's Republic of China*, edited by C. Lee and T. Schaaf. Paris: UNESCO.
(33). Shanahan, M. (2016). *Ladders to Heaven: How Fig Trees Shaped our History, Fed Our Imaginations, and Can Enrich Our Future*. London: Unbound.
(34). Shengji, P. (2003). The Role of Ethnobotany in the Conservation of Biodiversity. In *The Importance of Sacred Natural Sites for Biodiversity Conservation. Proc. Int. Workshop on the Importance of Sacred Natural Sites for Biodiversity Conservation in Kunming and Xishuangbanna Biosphere Reserve, People's Republic of China*, edited by C. Lee and T. Schaaf. Paris: UNESCO.
(35). Shiva, V. (1999). Homeless in the Global Village. In *Cultural and Spiritual Values of Biodiversity—A Complementary Contribution to the Global Biodiversity Assessment*, edited by D. Posey. London and Nairobi: Intermediate Technology and UNEP.
(36). Sponsel, L., P. Natadecha-Sponsel, N. Ruttanadakul, and S. Juntadach. (1998). Sacred and/or Secular Approaches to Biodiversity Conservation in Thailand. *World Views - Environment, Culture and Religion* 2, 155–67.
(37). Steffen, W., J. Rockstrom, K. Richardson, T. Lention, C. Folke, D. Liverman, C. Summerhayes, A. Barnosky, S. Cornell, M. Crucifix, J. Donges, I. Fetzer, S.

Lade, M. Scheffer, R. Winkelmann, and H. Schellnhuber. (2018). Trajectories of the Earth System in the Anthropocene - Perspectives. *PNAS* 115 (33), 8,252–259.

(38). Suzuki, D., and H. Dressel. (1999). *From Naked Ape to Superspecies: A Personal Perspective on Humanity and the Global Eco-crisis.* Toronto: Stoddart.

(39). Swimme, B., and M. Tucker. (2011). *Journey of the Universe.* New Haven: Yale University Press.

(40). Szekely, E. (2000). Quotation from Edmond Bordeaux Szekely. *Ecologist* 30 (1):30.

(41). Tauli-Corpuz, V., J. Alcorn, and A. Molnar. (2018). Cornered by Protected Areas: Replacing Fortress Conservation with Rights-based Approaches Helps Bring Justice for Indigenous Peoples and Local Communities, Reduces Conflict, and Enables Cost-Effective Conservation and Climate Action. Washington, DC: Rights and Resources Initiative.

(42). Tickell, O. (2018). Living Well in the Non-Materialist World. Resurgence and Ecologist 306, 14–16.

(43). Tucker, M. (2014). Our Place in the Universe. Resurgence and Ecologist 283, 52–54.

(44). Tudge, C. (2006). *The Secret Life of Trees: How They Live and Why They Matter.* London: Penguin Books.

(45). Turner, N. (2008). Lessons of the Birch. Resurgence 250, 46–48.

(46). United Nations. (2012). Resolution Adopted by the General Assembly on 27th July 2012. New York: United Nations.

(47). Verschuuren, B., and N. Furuta, eds. (2016). *Asian Sacred Natural Sites: Philosophy and Practice in Protected Areas and Conservation.* London: Routledge.

(48). Wilson, E. (2010). Sustaining Life. Resurgence 261, 10–14.

(49). WWF. (1986). Religion and Nature - Interfaith Ceremony. Gland, Switzerland: WWF.

(50). Zogib, L., K. Tashi, T. Gyalpo, S. Dendhup, R. Kuyakanon, K. Wangchuk, L. Tenzin, and N. Gyeltshen. (2016). Sacred Mandala: Protecting Bhutan's Sacred Natural Site. In *Asian Sacred Natural Sites: Philosophy and Practice in Protected Areas and Conservation*, edited by B. Verschuuren and N. Furuta. London: Routledge.

(51). Zucchelli, C. (2009). *Trees of Inspiration: Sacred Trees and Bushes of Ireland.* Cork Ireland: Collins Press.

Index

A

Aboriginal 26, 31, 131, 182, 188, 327
Administrative 38, 157, 159–160, 169
African Myths 44, 54
Aichi Targets 193
Albert Einstein 14
Alder tree 51
Aldo Leopold 1, 14, 201, 222, 227, 235, 239, 275
Al Gore 247
Allah 27, 49, 183
Alliance of Religion and Conservation 203
Ancient trees 14, 44, 53, 64, 85, 88, 112, 116, 277, 292, 296, 303
Anthropocentric 6, 20–21, 178, 228
Anthropology 261, 301, 312
Apple tree 51, 57, 66
Arbor Tree 75–76
Assisi 12, 24, 112, 124, 178, 180–181, 206, 223, 259, 266
Attention Deficit Disorder, ADD 96, 142, 226, 228–229, 243–244, 255, 269
Australia 26, 31, 56, 79, 93, 182, 192, 296, 301, 303

B

Baha'i 24
Banyan tree 78
Baobab tree 68
Bauxite in Orissa 107
Benefits 20, 84, 123, 141–143, 145, 149, 152, 156–157, 163, 165, 174, 180, 185–186, 190, 197, 210, 213, 230, 244, 254, 323
Bengal Quince tree 107
Bhagavad-Gita 7
Bhutan 5, 81, 115, 195, 197, 233, 268, 299, 310, 316, 323, 328, 331
Bible xi, 7, 22, 44, 47, 49–50, 52, 58, 67, 70, 72–73, 85–86, 90, 122–123, 183, 285, 287, 291–292, 295–297, 318
Biocentric 6, 21, 178, 203
Biodiversity ix, 6, 10, 12, 29, 35–36, 64, 66, 72, 90, 94–95, 98, 100, 103, 106, 108–110, 112, 119–122, 124, 128–130, 133–134, 137–139, 142–143, 148, 150, 154–158, 173, 178, 180, 185, 193, 195–197, 207–208, 210, 213, 252, 266–267, 269, 276–277, 281, 284–285,

288–289, 295–309, 311–317, 319, 324, 330
Birch tree 75
Bishnoi(s) 119–120
Black Elk (Lakota) 59, 236, 260, 291, 324, 329
Bodhi, Bo tree 56
Botswana 86
Brahma 81, 83
Brazil 236
Brehon Law 51
Brian Swimme 279
Brundtland Commission 195
Buddha, Buddhism 6, 24, 30, 35, 47, 53, 56, 66, 72–73, 78, 81, 84, 91, 105, 110–111, 123, 125–126, 178, 209, 232, 249, 294, 324
Burial Grounds 79, 94, 97–98, 122

C

Cameroon 101, 303, 305
Canada 26, 89, 117, 132, 237, 313, 324, 328
Canelo tree 89
Capacity Building 100, 185
Carob tree 50
Categories 6, 96–98, 145–146, 149–151, 153–154, 156, 158–159, 167, 178, 206, 208, 267, 270, 312
Cedar(s) of Lebanon 52, 69–70, 89, 161
Celts 45–46, 51, 54, 75, 80
Children, Youth 39, 69, 74, 76, 79, 83, 90, 112, 119, 130, 182, 188, 199, 205, 218–221, 223–244, 246–247, 249, 255–257, 262, 265, 267, 274, 277, 281, 295, 324, 326
Chile 89
China 31, 36, 68, 81, 84, 88, 94, 108–109, 127–128, 143, 151, 154, 178, 269, 276, 285, 289, 295–297, 299, 301–302, 306–310, 312–316, 330
Christianity xi, 6–7, 24, 29, 45, 48, 50, 53–54, 57, 59, 75, 87–88, 90–91, 117, 123, 126, 130, 161, 178, 181, 205, 285
Climate change 6–7, 23, 86, 96, 179, 189–190, 192–193, 195, 219, 248, 250, 252, 263–265, 267, 273–274, 288, 293, 297, 315, 321, 327, 330
Collaborative Management 102, 145–148, 307
Commercial 16, 69, 96, 100–101, 130, 171
Common Property 105, 113, 167, 174, 202, 300, 314
Community Based Conservation 314
Community Conservation 124, 131, 135, 137–140, 142–143, 145–149, 152–153, 162–163, 165–166, 200, 203, 210, 311–312
Community-Conserved Areas 11, 38, 155
Community Forests 78, 110–111, 154–155, 167, 266, 271
Community Institutions 157, 163–164, 174
Compassion 8–9, 86, 222, 249, 273, 323, 328
Conflict 65, 151, 157, 162–163, 167–168, 172, 180, 187, 192, 221, 229, 246–247, 250–253, 256, 263, 267, 276–277, 281, 316, 331
Conflict resolution 163, 229, 252–253, 256, 277, 281
Connectivity, connecting xii, 34, 57, 64–65, 95, 119, 127–128, 130–131, 133, 137–138, 144, 151, 154, 156, 159, 171–173,

181, 196–198, 208–210, 212, 218–219, 224, 248, 262, 267, 269, 271–272, 281, 289, 298, 322, 324, 328
Consciousness 21, 23–25, 45–46, 55, 159, 178–179, 186, 205, 212, 218, 231–232, 261, 274–275, 280
Conservation x, xii–xiii, 2, 9, 11–12, 19, 22, 24, 27, 33–34, 36–39, 45, 49, 53, 58–60, 63–64, 66, 72, 84, 86, 90, 93, 95–98, 100, 103, 105–106, 108–114, 116, 119–120, 122–125, 128–133, 135, 137–153, 155–166, 171–173, 175, 177–187, 190–191, 193–204, 206–214, 221–223, 230, 233–234, 236–237, 243, 247, 249, 252, 259, 261, 264–274, 276–278, 280, 283–323, 327, 329–331
Conservation Science 9, 144, 209, 274
Conservation Stewardship 185, 197–199, 207, 213
Consilience 153–155, 316
Convention on Biological Diversity 12, 185–186, 196, 213, 267, 308, 313
Cornelian Cherry tree 75
Cultural Landscape 88, 116, 161, 309
Culture, cultural, cultural values 4–5, 9–10, 12, 14, 18, 22, 26–27, 31–33, 37, 43–46, 55, 63–64, 67–68, 70–72, 78, 83–84, 86, 88, 94, 96–97, 99, 102–103, 105, 108–110, 112–114, 116–118, 123, 126–130, 133, 137, 140, 142, 144, 147–161, 164, 168, 172, 179–180, 182–184, 186–188, 191–193, 196–199, 206, 208, 211–212, 214, 221, 229, 236–237, 240, 243, 248, 262–263, 266, 269–271, 274–276, 279–280, 283–285, 288–292, 294–295, 297–310, 313–314, 316, 318–319, 321, 323, 329–330
Custodians 26, 32, 38, 46, 99, 124, 132, 139, 141–143, 148–150, 155, 157–158, 161–162, 164–166, 168–172, 175, 191–192, 196, 201, 206–207, 210–211, 213, 263–264, 268–272, 274, 280
Customary 71, 89, 94, 98–99, 117, 130, 138, 141, 145–146, 148, 151, 155–156, 159, 161–163, 165, 168, 171–172, 174, 197, 200, 206–207, 213, 256, 268, 302, 310
Cypress tree 81

D

Dai People 109
Dalai Lama 33
Date Palm 47, 49, 54, 85, 91
David Attenborough 5
David Orr 60, 219, 222, 238, 288, 293, 306, 315, 321, 324, 327, 330
David Suzuki 2, 15, 29, 173, 224, 231, 246, 281
Decentralization 161, 171–172
Decision Making 9, 142, 156, 168
Deep Ecology 20–21, 65, 179, 284
Deforestation 12, 100, 118, 140, 285, 318
Degradation 29, 31, 61, 96, 99, 109, 115, 118, 134, 140, 170, 234, 247–248, 250, 261, 265, 280
Democracy 97, 154, 164, 171, 252
Democratic Governance 252

Development ix–x, xiv, 11, 15–16, 18, 22, 36, 46, 100, 107, 113–114, 127, 130, 140, 145, 163, 169, 184, 188, 190–193, 195, 197–198, 201–202, 220–221, 228, 233, 235, 243, 249, 252, 260, 264, 267, 271, 276, 278–279, 281, 288, 295, 300–301, 306, 309, 311–312, 314, 316, 319–320, 328–329
Devolution 153, 159
Dhup Tree 107
Dialogue 181, 196, 206, 219, 252, 292, 296
Dipterocarpus tree 108
Disconnected from nature 14
Domination 17, 28–29, 61, 182–183, 189–190, 194–195, 273–274
Dominion 17, 28–29, 34, 59, 183, 189–190, 273
Dragon Tree 102
Druids 36, 45–47, 50–51

E

Earth Community 18, 253, 294
Eastern Religions 6, 45, 47, 123, 178, 270
Eckhart Tolle 3, 25, 204, 211
Ecocentric 6, 23, 178, 203, 228
Ecocide 250–251, 325
Ecological Literacy, Ecoliteracy 24, 184, 222, 235, 284, 324
Ecology ix, 2, 4–6, 15–16, 18–21, 24, 26, 59, 65, 112, 144, 158, 160, 174, 178–180, 188, 194, 199, 202–203, 207, 211, 218, 221–224, 246–248, 256, 261, 284–286, 288–289, 292–295, 299–301, 303, 311, 322–323, 330
Economy, economics 3, 5–6, 9, 15, 18–21, 37, 45, 109, 130, 134, 152, 154, 164–165, 173–174, 182, 188, 191–192, 202, 211, 248–249, 261, 263–264, 273, 284, 286, 293, 295–296, 302–303, 311–312, 318, 322, 325–327, 329
Ecosystem Approach 172, 184–185, 196, 315, 322
Ecosystems 3, 5, 7, 9–10, 14, 19–20, 27, 31, 64, 98, 117, 119, 129, 132, 139, 142, 155–157, 164, 178–179, 184–186, 204, 260, 265, 280, 296, 303–304, 314
Ecosystem Services 131, 149, 185, 263
Ecozoic 211, 320
Ecuador 138–139, 315
Education 2, 5, 17, 22, 31, 34, 40, 59, 94, 100, 116, 130, 133, 141, 158, 164, 170, 180, 183, 185, 193, 206–207, 212–213, 217–223, 226–231, 233–240, 246–247, 252, 254–255, 275–276, 281, 328
Edward Goldsmith 144
Edward Wilson 5, 10, 15–16, 19, 153, 188, 224, 227, 234
Emily Dickinson 58
Encyclical 6–7, 11, 27, 187, 189, 202, 273, 288, 293, 297, 315, 321, 327, 330
Encyclical on Climate Change 6–7, 189, 288, 293, 297, 315, 321, 327, 330
Endowments 200
England 52, 75–77, 80, 85, 87, 205, 241, 251, 285–288, 290–298, 300–301, 305–307, 312, 316–318, 320–321, 323, 325, 327, 330
Entitlement 200, 322
Environment 3, 5–6, 10–12, 14, 18, 20, 23–24, 27–29, 31–32, 35,

43–44, 49, 84, 88, 94, 107–108, 123, 131, 133, 137, 139, 141–143, 162, 165, 173, 178–179, 183–184, 186, 190, 194–195, 197, 202–203, 206, 213, 220, 222–223, 225, 230, 232, 242, 245, 252, 255, 261, 263, 269, 271, 274, 281, 284, 286, 292, 300–301, 311, 314, 318–319, 321–322, 324–325, 328, 330

Eritrea 68, 121
Ernst Schumacher 180
Ethics 6, 8, 151, 154, 171, 199, 203, 209, 224, 284–285, 287, 293, 318, 322
Ethiopia 121–122, 143, 163, 307
Ethnic, Ethnicity 109–112, 115, 126, 151, 167, 228, 253, 293, 298, 310
Europe 4, 13, 29, 45–49, 53, 59, 85, 87, 93–94, 115, 123–124, 129, 170, 218, 243, 268, 276, 304
Experiential 34, 133, 183, 219–220, 222, 224–226, 228–229, 231–233, 235, 247, 255, 275–276
Exploitation 16, 29, 96, 98, 114–116, 139, 152, 163–164, 171, 180, 234, 248
Exposure to Nature 226–227

F

Fairy Trees 69
Feng Shui 36, 127–128, 304
Fig tree 35, 53, 56–57, 65, 67–68, 72–74, 102, 248
Findhorn 64, 289, 291, 298, 322, 328
Finland 244, 304, 310
First Nations Peoples 237
Fir tree 115
Florence Jones 237
Food Webs 164
Forest Bathing 241–244, 326

Forest Goddess of Venezuela 115
Forest Health walking 276
Forest Management 105, 140, 154, 184, 201, 280, 295, 311, 322
Forest Monks 203
Frameworks for Community Conservation 165
France 85, 89, 124, 284, 302–303, 308–310
Francis of Assisi 112, 124, 180–181, 259, 266
Frankincense tree 82
Fritjof Capra 15, 20, 191
Fundamentalism 221, 263, 323

G

Gaia 18, 20, 25, 179, 219, 284, 286, 291, 294, 309, 313, 318, 320, 324, 327
Gambia 89
Ganges 29–30, 32, 73, 154, 165
Garden of Gethsemane 52, 86, 96, 128, 154
Generosity 28, 205
George Bernard Shaw 245
George Monbiot 256
Germany 25, 235, 239, 244, 295, 324
Germplasm 95
Ghana 68, 74, 94, 97–100, 127, 130–131, 145, 147–148, 152, 154, 162, 166, 170, 211, 271, 294, 300, 305, 309
Giant Redwood trees 129
Glastonbury Thorn tree 87
Governance 39, 95, 105, 132–133, 141, 149, 159–160, 165, 172, 193, 200, 205, 207, 213, 233, 237, 245, 252, 256, 268–269, 273, 276, 311
Gratitude 57, 111, 182, 186, 194, 238, 255, 264, 273, 279, 329

Greeks 25, 46–47, 67, 73, 85–86
Green Care 243–244, 327
Green Man 87
Gross Domestic Product 5, 194–195
Gross National Happiness 195, 233, 328
Gurumayi Chidvilasananda xi, 177, 179–180

H

Harim 202
Harmony with Nature 13, 180, 182, 189, 206, 233, 246, 260
Hassein Nasr 204
Hawthorn tree 77
Hazel tree 51
Herman Daly 14, 19, 164, 191
Herman Melville 221
Hildegard of Bingen 23, 289
Hima 202–203, 318–319
Hinduism 6–7, 24, 30, 95, 105, 119, 130, 178, 301
His Royal Highness The Prince of Wales 11, 28, 286, 296, 302, 312, 319
Holly 47, 50–51, 85, 112, 308
Holy Hill Forests 84, 108–109, 144
Holy wells 45, 69
Honey tree 107
Humankind 4–7, 9, 11, 13–16, 18–19, 21–23, 26–29, 34, 39, 46, 49, 53, 58–59, 66, 72, 94, 109, 137, 179, 182–184, 189, 191, 194–195, 204, 228, 232, 236, 238, 246, 248, 250, 253, 261–262, 265, 278, 321
Humility xii, 59, 181, 205–206, 209, 219

I

ICCA's xiii, 124, 133, 138, 140, 151, 154, 156–157, 267–268, 270, 313
Incentives 139, 162, 174, 185
India x, xiii, 28, 31–32, 44, 47, 67–69, 72–73, 78–79, 81, 83–84, 89, 91, 93–95, 97, 106–108, 118–119, 129–130, 138, 147, 152, 154, 171, 178, 200, 203, 209, 230, 247, 295–296, 298, 300, 303–304, 306–307, 315, 317
Indigenous and Community-Conserved Areas, ICCAs 38, 155
Indigenous, First Nations ix–x, xii–xiii, 4, 6, 10–11, 21–22, 25–27, 31, 38, 59, 73, 98, 107–111, 117, 120, 122–123, 132, 137, 147, 150–151, 155–157, 162, 178, 182, 185, 189, 209–212, 222, 224, 228, 234, 236–238, 244, 264, 267, 269, 274, 279–280, 286, 296–297, 303, 305, 310, 312–313, 316, 319, 331
Indonesia 94, 115, 118, 299
Industrial Revolution 13, 15, 22, 66, 268, 276
Inequities 166, 214, 231
Institutional Systems 160, 187
Institutions 34, 59, 91, 101, 103, 113, 117, 119, 131–134, 141, 146, 149–151, 157–158, 160–165, 168–175, 202, 206, 208, 213, 247, 256, 268, 271, 276–277, 280, 305, 314, 316, 320
Intangible 4, 11, 14, 22, 35, 37, 65, 89, 137, 173, 179, 184, 192, 271, 286, 295, 302–303, 312, 318, 329
Integral Ecology 202, 248
Interconnected, interconnectedness, interconnections 5–6, 12, 14, 19, 21, 23, 26, 65, 95, 134, 144,

178–180, 191, 200, 202, 209, 224, 228–229, 250, 254, 257
Interdependence 12, 19, 21, 57, 65, 189, 192, 211, 232, 273, 275, 279, 284
Ireland 1, 22, 45–48, 50–51, 56, 65, 68–69, 75, 77, 80, 85, 88–89, 115, 128, 220, 225, 235, 291–294, 296, 298–299, 308, 310, 328, 331
Islam xi, 6–7, 24, 27–28, 49, 54, 57, 90–91, 117, 178, 180, 183–184, 190, 202, 204, 284, 286, 318–319
Isle of Man 68, 77
IUCN, International Union for Conservation of Nature xiii, 11, 100, 149–151, 153–154, 156, 158, 206, 208, 236, 267, 283, 285, 287–288, 290, 296, 299, 303–304, 307, 309, 311–312, 315–316, 318–319, 321–324
Ivory Coast 167

J

Jainism, Jains 24, 30
Japan 116, 126–127, 241–244, 276, 303
Jean Giono 43
John Muir 227, 231, 234, 241
Jordan 202, 319
Joseph Stiglitz 194
Joyce Kilmer 281
Judaism xi, 6, 24, 57, 69, 91, 178
Judas Tree 50
Judy Dench 80
Julian Evans 4
Julius Nyerere 220
Juniper tree 203

K

Kabbalah 56
Kailash 30–31, 165, 207, 288
Kapok tree 81
Kaya 86, 112–114, 131, 138, 143, 147, 149, 154, 162, 166, 170, 201, 301, 305, 307, 315
Kenya xi, xiii, 9, 32, 65, 67–68, 74, 79–80, 86, 89, 101–102, 112–113, 130–131, 143, 147, 150, 154, 162, 166, 170, 201, 211, 219, 225, 235, 247, 296, 299, 301–308, 315
Keystone species 65–66, 86, 143, 204, 266
Kipumbwi Tanzania 102
Korea, Korean 55, 238, 243, 276
Krishnamurti 8, 286, 325
Kyrgyzstan 116

L

Landscape 17, 30–32, 36, 64, 66, 70, 80, 89, 94, 96, 100, 112, 116, 118, 124–125, 130, 133, 138, 144, 147, 154, 160–161, 168, 171–173, 177–178, 180, 196–199, 208–210, 236, 251, 254, 267, 269, 271–273, 281, 284, 288, 298, 304, 306–307, 309, 311, 315, 317, 322
Landscape Management 160, 172–173, 177, 209, 272–273
Land use 2, 13, 60, 133, 138, 142, 144, 147–148, 150, 152, 158–159, 161, 177, 179, 182, 187, 192, 196–197, 200, 207, 209–210, 248, 261, 264, 273, 280–281
Lao PDR 117, 302
Lao Tzu 25, 28, 190, 201
Learning by doing 219

Learn, Learning xii, 2, 10, 12, 16, 21, 24, 32, 58–59, 90, 119, 121, 123–124, 129–130, 133, 141, 182, 189, 196–197, 204, 217–220, 224–226, 228–229, 231–239, 249–250, 252–253, 255, 257, 259, 262, 265, 270, 275–276, 279–281, 317, 319, 324, 326
Lebanon 52, 69–70, 89, 154, 161, 203, 310
Legal Protection 131
Lesotho 131
Lithuania 85
Local Communities ix, 100, 106, 111, 114, 126, 130–131, 139, 141, 145, 148, 150–152, 156–157, 185, 195, 209, 266–267, 270, 272, 280, 311, 313, 316–317, 331
Local Governance 39, 141, 200
Loita 102, 304, 308
Lynne and Del Sherrod 197

M

Madagascar 68, 80, 144–145, 319
Magnolia tree 84
Mahatma Gandhi 3, 141, 187, 249
Maidenhair tree 12, 84
Malaysia 79
Maori 298
Maple 89
Mapping 200, 213
Margaret Mead 187
Maria Montessori 218
Mariano Lopez 188
Martin Luther King 260, 329
Mary Evelyn Tucker 194, 318
Mass Trees 85
Mayan 234
Mbeere 101
Mechanistic 21, 212

Meditation 66, 134, 223, 240, 245, 254
Millennium Ecosystem Assessment 141, 314
Mindfulness, mindful xii, 3, 8, 21–22, 93, 129, 134, 204, 209, 223, 232–233, 238–240, 248, 251, 264, 325
Miyakazuki 225
Mohammad (Peace Be Upon Him) 47, 49, 73, 85, 202
Monastic, monastery 51, 65, 77–78, 84, 120–124, 127, 143, 146, 154, 161, 163, 170, 210, 264, 304, 313
Mongolia 75, 116–117, 299, 308
Monkey Puzzle Tree 89
Morocco 128
Mother Earth 3, 7, 13–14, 16, 21, 34, 44, 59, 61, 98, 138, 141, 175, 181–182, 188, 195, 205, 224, 259–260, 262, 264, 270, 277–278, 280, 318
Mountain Ash tree 51
Mount Everest 32, 289
Mount Fuji 116, 305
Mount Kenya 32
Mozambique 131, 167, 314
Mukash (Cree) 13, 26, 117, 262
Mulberry tree 50
Muslim 80, 89, 103, 128, 223
Myristica tree 108
Myrrh tree 82

N

Naomi Klein 248
National Flags 89
National Monuments 86, 89–90, 113, 131, 154, 162, 170
National Park(s) 32, 100, 102, 116, 124, 127, 131, 145–147, 152,

154, 162, 166, 170, 284, 289, 304, 307, 319
Natural Killer Cells 242
Nature ix–xiii, 1–7, 9–25, 27–30, 32–40, 43–46, 54–55, 57–61, 63–64, 66–67, 74, 78, 83–86, 97–98, 100, 104–106, 108–110, 112, 115, 123–124, 126–127, 129, 132–134, 137–142, 144–151, 153–157, 159, 162, 164–165, 168, 173–175, 177–184, 186–197, 199, 201–207, 209–214, 217–242, 244–252, 254–257, 259–266, 269–271, 273–281, 283–284, 286–287, 289–295, 297–298, 300–301, 303–304, 306, 308, 312, 316–317, 319, 321–326, 328–329, 331
Nature based solutions 16, 29
Nature Deficit Disorder 39, 219, 224–226, 228, 276, 281, 326
Nelson Mandela 93, 177, 217, 221, 239
Nepal 31–32, 66, 70, 79, 94, 104–105, 125, 138, 141, 285, 289, 295–296, 301, 303, 306, 321
Networks 64, 119, 153–154, 164, 171, 191, 210, 213, 311
New Zealand 70–71, 116, 132
Niger 67
Nigeria 101
Nile Tulip tree 68
Norman Meyers 20
North America 59, 79, 93, 268
Norway 88, 244, 292, 296

O

Oak tree 46, 67, 85
Olive tree 52, 57
Ownership, tenure 102, 119, 121, 123, 127, 131, 138, 141, 146–149, 153, 164–168, 200, 213, 237, 268, 272, 313

P

Palaver trees, talking trees 50, 81, 298
Palm Sunday 48
Participatory, Participation 12, 110, 139, 153–154, 164, 166, 169, 220, 274, 305, 311, 314, 316
Paulo Freire 219
Peace xii, 1–2, 9, 11–12, 22–25, 28–29, 34–36, 39–40, 43–44, 47, 49, 52, 59, 73, 83, 85–86, 88–89, 97, 112, 124, 127, 134, 151, 175, 180, 196, 199, 202–204, 217–218, 220–223, 226, 231–233, 241, 243, 245–255, 257, 259, 265, 267, 274–275, 277–278, 281, 286, 313–314, 325, 330
Peace Parks 221
Peepal tree 72
Peter Marshall 24
Pierre Rabhi 218, 246, 262
Pilgrim 126, 130, 194, 203
Plant for the Planet 74, 231, 240, 295, 324
Podocarpus, yellow wood tree 70, 80, 122
Pomegranate tree 56
Pope Francis 2–3, 6–7, 11, 17–18, 20, 27–28, 59, 165, 175, 187, 189, 202, 229, 234, 248, 257, 273, 288, 293, 297, 315, 321, 327, 330
Pope John Paul II 11, 259, 330
Poverty 18, 67, 141, 175, 200, 221, 245, 248, 250, 278, 322, 326–327
Power ix, 3, 16, 23–24, 35, 47, 53–55, 59, 61, 67, 70, 97, 99, 103, 116, 128, 130, 153, 157, 160,

162–163, 168–172, 175, 183, 200, 203–204, 237, 239, 252–253, 260–261, 263, 266, 290, 293, 309, 311, 313, 325
Preservationist 210
Prosopis tree 119
Protected Area Authorities 132, 139, 147, 150, 158, 213
Protected Area Categories 150–151, 154, 158, 206, 208, 267, 270
Protected Area Managers 101, 270, 272, 290, 309, 316
Protected Area Outreach 145, 147

Q

Qadisha Valley 161
Qur-ān iv, 7, 27–28, 46–47, 49, 52, 72, 85–86, 90, 183–184, 189

R

Rachel Carson 15–16, 199, 207, 227, 230, 234, 242, 278
Ralph Waldo Emerson 217, 261
Reciprocity 107, 257, 262
Recognition 78, 98, 111, 113, 131, 138, 140, 142, 147–149, 153, 156–161, 165–166, 169, 171–174, 196, 208, 213, 267–268, 270–272, 274, 306, 310, 313, 321
Reconnect 1, 10, 17, 40, 60, 85, 141, 185, 195, 199, 204–205, 212–213, 217–221, 231, 233, 236, 249, 254, 262, 274–276
Reconnect with nature 10, 40, 85, 195, 199, 205, 218–219, 221, 262, 275
Redesign 211
Reductionist 15, 17, 144, 268
Redwood Groves, Sequoias 64, 117
Rekindle 212
Religious Education 17, 237
Representation 72, 166

Resilience 34, 44–45, 64, 96–97, 129, 132, 199, 208, 246
Restoration, restorative, regenerative 66, 95, 98, 100, 111, 116, 119, 123–124, 129–130, 133–134, 139–140, 142, 153, 195–196, 203, 210–211, 213, 224, 254, 271, 277–278, 281, 286
Restraint 107, 205, 276
Reverence, Reverent 7, 14, 22, 35, 45–48, 66, 83, 89, 96, 129, 161–162, 180, 194, 205, 251, 254, 269, 287, 289, 321
Rhododendron tree 70
Richard Louv 219, 225, 227–228, 230, 255
Rights and Responsibilities 146, 155–157, 162, 165–172, 174, 178, 197, 200, 267, 272, 280
Rights of Nature 138–139, 249, 251, 260
Rio +20 Declaration 260
Rowan tree 69
Rowan Williams 19
Russia 26, 77, 115, 127, 147, 293, 298
Rwenzori 304, 307

S

Sacred Groves x, xii, 2, 9, 12, 18, 29–30, 32–33, 35–36, 38–40, 44, 51, 54–55, 58–59, 72, 85, 93–101, 103–108, 110–120, 122–127, 129–134, 137–138, 140–141, 143–161, 163–175, 177–179, 184–185, 192–193, 195–197, 199–201, 204–205, 207–213, 217, 222, 238, 243, 245, 248, 261, 264, 267–276, 278, 280–281, 289, 293–295, 297–298, 300–305, 307–311, 314–317, 319, 322

Sacred Landscapes 29, 37–38, 81, 116–117, 155, 178, 288
Sacred Natural Sites, SNS xiii, 4, 11, 18, 21–22, 32, 44, 123, 131–132, 139–140, 142–143, 147, 150, 156, 159, 165, 206, 214, 252, 266, 269, 283–285, 288–291, 294–297, 299–310, 312–316, 319, 321–323, 327, 330–331
Sacred spring, well 118
Sacred Texts 23, 43, 45, 90, 178–179, 204
Sacred Trees xii, 1–2, 4–5, 11–12, 18, 21, 26, 29, 33–40, 44–45, 47, 50–51, 53–54, 63–68, 71, 73, 81, 88–91, 96, 102–104, 116, 119, 123, 125, 129, 131–132, 137–138, 140–144, 147–152, 156–157, 159–162, 169, 171, 177–178, 181, 184–185, 187, 191–193, 195–197, 200, 203–204, 206, 208–210, 212–213, 217–221, 239, 245–246, 250, 252, 254, 257, 261–262, 264–275, 277–281, 283, 291–292, 294, 296, 298–300, 310, 331
Safari Doctors 247
Sagarmatha 32, 289
Saint Francis 112, 180, 259
Sal Tree 72
Satish Kumar 5–6, 194, 201, 223, 232
Saudi Arabia 202
Sausage Tree 79
Scientific 5, 13, 15–16, 23, 27, 36, 44, 59, 63–64, 72, 137, 150, 153, 159, 171, 173, 179, 185, 194, 199, 201, 212–213, 220–221, 263, 268, 273, 279
Scotland xii, 48, 69, 75, 77, 291, 293
Senegal 80–81, 86, 89, 208

Shallow ecology 20–21
Shaman 26, 154, 288
Sherpa 32, 70, 125, 285, 289, 295, 301
Shinto Shrines 116, 126–127
Shiva 30–31, 60, 66, 81, 83, 97, 126, 200, 274, 308, 315, 327, 330
Shrines 55, 68, 70–71, 85–86, 102, 114, 116, 125–128, 303
Sierra Leone 116, 303
Sikhism 24, 30
Silence xii, 1, 25, 29–30, 34, 36, 47, 63, 66, 129, 134, 151, 211, 218, 221, 232–233, 241, 249, 251, 254–257, 267, 278
Silent Spring 16, 207, 288, 317, 330
Small is Beautiful 281
Sobonfu Somé 233
Sociology 188, 261, 284, 287
Somalia 247
South Africa 11, 58, 79, 86, 167, 237, 265, 301
Species Diversity 118, 121, 143–144
Spirituality ix, xii, 1–3, 6–9, 11–12, 16–17, 33–35, 37–38, 40, 44–46, 51, 53, 58, 60, 65, 93, 116, 120, 125, 127, 132–133, 139, 141, 173, 177, 179–181, 184, 186–188, 193–194, 198, 201, 204–207, 209, 212, 218, 239–240, 257, 259, 261–262, 264, 269–270, 276–278, 280, 284, 286, 289–292, 294, 317, 319–320
Spiritual landscape 36
Spiritual Traditions 7, 9, 20, 22, 27, 36, 38, 43–44, 46, 59, 72, 133, 137, 140, 150, 155, 175, 180, 184, 187, 189, 199, 205, 263, 265, 273, 275, 283
Sri Lanka 73, 125–126, 309
Sri Pada Peak 125

Stewardship x, 14, 17, 28–29, 34, 38, 59–61, 135, 138, 141, 152, 157–158, 168, 177, 179–202, 204–205, 207, 209, 213–214, 225, 234, 237, 261, 265, 273–275, 277, 281, 283, 291, 300, 317, 320–322
Struggles 31, 78, 170–171
Sudan 56, 86, 89
Sustainability, sustainable 2, 11–12, 14–16, 24, 37, 64, 70, 84, 97, 113, 123–124, 131, 142, 146, 148, 151, 154–156, 163, 165, 169, 171–173, 175, 177, 184, 187, 189–193, 195–198, 201–202, 211–212, 222, 233–234, 236–237, 243, 245, 248, 259–260, 264, 267, 271–272, 274–278, 295, 301, 306, 309, 314, 316–317, 322, 329
Sustainable Development Goals 192–193, 195, 260, 267
Sustainable Forest Management 184, 322
Sweden 88, 292, 296
Sycamore tree 73, 79, 122, 325

T

Tagore 63, 97, 298
Tamarind tree 68
Tamarisk tree 75
Tanzania 102–103, 117, 131, 162, 167, 301, 303–305, 309–310, 312, 314
Taoism, Tao-Te-Ching 6, 25, 44, 178, 246
Tatora Tree 70
Teilhard de Chardin 25, 186, 290
Thailand 78, 110–111, 121, 154, 203, 295, 301, 330
Thich Nhat Hanh 253

Thinley, Prime Minister of Bhutan 233, 328
Thomas Aquinas 22, 284
Thomas Berry 13, 17, 20, 22, 211, 257, 285
Thomas Merton 320
Toothbrush Tree 85
Totara tree 71
Tourist 9
Tradition 11, 39, 50–51, 59, 65, 67, 81, 84, 87–88, 91, 106, 108, 122, 126, 132, 149, 183, 207, 265–266, 289, 306
Traditional authorities 99, 170
Traditional beliefs 72, 93, 99–100, 103, 109, 117, 140, 295, 302
Tree Culture 240
Tree of Enlightenment 53
Tree of Knowledge, Life 2–8, 10–13, 16, 18–27, 30, 33–34, 37–38, 46, 48, 50–59, 64–67, 69, 72–74, 80, 83–84, 86–88, 97, 101, 104–105, 107, 115, 117, 119–123, 125, 127–128, 139, 158, 164, 178–180, 182, 184, 186–188, 190–192, 194–195, 198–199, 201, 204–205, 209, 211–212, 219–220, 222, 224–225, 227, 230–239, 242–243, 245–246, 248–249, 253, 255, 257, 260, 262–264, 269–270, 274–275, 279–281, 284, 286–287, 290–295, 298, 311, 317–323, 325–329, 331
Tree ordination 65
Trees adorned 75
Trees and Heraldry 89
Trees of Liberty 89
Tree Worship 52, 55, 105
Trustees of Nature 250, 278
Tsawalk (we are one) 18, 189, 237

Tulip tree 68
Tulsi (Holy Basil) tree 83
Turkana xi, 65, 89, 219
Turkey 79

U

Uganda 68, 102, 146, 149, 162, 164, 167, 303, 310
Uluru Kata Tjuta 131
Umra Omar 246–247
UN Environment 223, 318, 324
UNESCO xiii, 99, 112, 271, 284–285, 289, 292, 295–297, 299, 301–303, 306–310, 312–316, 318, 329–330
Urban, urbanization 13, 15, 64, 67, 100, 128–130, 140, 218, 220, 226, 230, 235–236, 241, 243–244, 265, 281, 323
USA 26, 219, 293, 300, 308–309, 317, 322, 325
US Parks Service 151
Utilitarian Values 63

V

Vandana Shiva 60, 200, 274
Vedic 10, 56, 72, 83, 95, 106
Venezuela 115
Vietnam 68, 127
Vishnu 81, 83, 203

W

Wales 11, 28, 88, 256, 286, 296, 302, 307–308, 312, 319
Wangari Maathai 63–64, 67, 74–75, 253
Wayne Dyer 137
White Birch tree 115
Whitethorn tree 68
Wild loquat tree 104
William Berry 93
William Blake 1, 30
William Bryant 93
William Wordsworth 231
Willow tree 70
win more - lose less 171
Wishing Tree 75
Wood-apple tree 66
World Bank 36, 194, 300, 305
World Heritage 31–32, 101–102, 112–113, 116, 131, 159, 161, 316
World population 13, 29, 53
World Tree 38, 53, 56–57, 73
Worldview ix, 5, 7, 21, 23, 29, 63, 138, 188, 191, 205, 228, 235, 237, 261

Y

Yew tree 48, 65, 88
Yunnan China 81, 108, 308

Z

Zimbabwe 68, 103, 300, 304–305, 309, 314
Ziziphus tree 58

Lightning Source UK Ltd.
Milton Keynes UK
UKHW011845240920
370458UK00001B/80